J. Banks

The Idylls of Theocritus, Bion, and Moschus

And the War-Songs of Tyrtæus

J. Banks

The Idylls of Theocritus, Bion, and Moschus
And the War-Songs of Tyrtæus

ISBN/EAN: 9783337191016

Printed in Europe, USA, Canada, Australia, Japan

Cover: Foto ©ninafisch / pixelio.de

More available books at **www.hansebooks.com**

THE IDYLLS

OF

THEOCRITUS, BION, AND MOSCHUS,

AND THE

WAR-SONGS OF TYRTÆUS.

Literally translated into English Prose,

BY

THE REV. J. BANKS, M.A.

WITH

METRICAL VERSIONS

BY

J. M. CHAPMAN, M.A.

LONDON: GEORGE BELL AND SONS, YORK STREET,
COVENT GARDEN.

1878

CONTENTS.

	PAGE
PREFACE	v
BIOGRAPHICAL NOTICE OF THEOCRITUS	vii
——————————— BION	xviii
——————————— MOSCHUS	xx
——————————— TYRTÆUS	xxi

Idylls of Theocritus.

IDYLL		PROSE	VERSE
I.	THYRSIS THE SHEPHERD, AND THE GOATHERD	1	205
II.	THE SORCERESS	9	209
III.	THE GOATHERD, OR AMARYLLIS, OR THE SERENADER	18	215
IV.	THE HERDSMEN; OR BATTUS AND CORYDON	21	217
V.	THE WAYFARERS, OR COMPOSERS OF PASTORALS	25	219
VI.	THE SINGERS OF PASTORALS	34	225
VII.	THE THALYSIA	37	226
VIII.	THE SINGERS OF PASTORALS	45	231
IX.	THE PASTOR, OR THE HERDSMEN	50	234
X.	THE WORKMEN, OR REAPERS	53	235
XI.	THE CYCLOPS	57	238
XII.	AITES	62	240
XIII.	HYLAS	65	241
XIV.	THE LOVE OF CYNISCA, OR THYONICHUS	70	244
XV.	THE SYRACUSAN WOMEN; OR, ADONIAZUSÆ	74	247
XVI.	THE GRACES; OR, HIERO	83	253
XVII.	THE PRAISE OF PTOLEMY	90	256
XVIII.	THE EPITHALAMIUM OF HELEN	97	260
XIX.	THE STEALER OF HONEY-COMBS	102	262
XX.	THE HERDSMAN	103	263
XXI.	THE FISHERMEN	106	264
XXII.	THE DIOSCURI	110	266
XXIII.	THE LOVER; OR, LOVE-SICK	122	273
XXIV.	THE LITTLE HERCULES	125	275
XXV.	HERCULES THE LION-SLAYER, OR, THE WEALTH OF AUGEAS	132	279
XXVI.	THE BACCHANALS	144	287
XXVII.	THE FOND DISCOURSE OF DAPHNIS AND THE DAMSEL	146	288

IDYLL		PROSE.	VERSE.
XXVIII.	THE DISTAFF	150	292
XXIX.	LOVES	151	293
XXX.	THE DEATH OF ADONIS.	153	294
	A FRAGMENT FROM THE BERENICE	155	295
	EPIGRAMS	156	*ib.*

Idylls of Bion.

		PROSE.	VERSE.
I.	THE EPITAPH OF ADONIS.	166	301
II.	EROS AND THE FOWLER	170	304
III.	THE TEACHER TAUGHT	171	*ib.*
IV.	THE POWER OF LOVE	172	305
V.	LIFE TO BE ENJOYED	173	*ib.*
VI.	CLEODAMUS AND MYRSON	174	306
VII.	ON HYACINTHUS	175	307
VIII.	FRIENDSHIP	*ib.*	*ib.*
IX.-XIV.	FRAGMENTS	176	*ib.*
XV.	THE EPITHALAMIUM OF ACHILLES AND DEIDAMIA	177	308
XVI.	TO THE EVENING STAR	179	309
XVII.	LOVE RESISTLESS	*ib.*	310

Idylls of Moschus.

		PROSE.	VERSE.
I.	LOVE A RUNAWAY	180	310
II.	EUROPA	181	311
III.	THE EPITAPH OF BION, A LOVING HERDSMAN	188	316
IV.	MEGARA, THE WIFE OF HERCULES	194	319
V.	THE CHOICE	199	323
VI.	"LOVE THEM THAT LOVE YOU"	*ib.*	*ib.*
VII.	ALPHEUS	200	*ib.*
	AN EPIGRAM	*ib.*	324
	FRAGMENT	201	*ib.*

	THE WAR-SONGS OF TYRTÆUS.	325	337

PREFACE

In the following translation of Theocritus, Bion, and Moschus, the text of Kiessling has been mainly adopted. But where a passage appeared obscure or corrupt, the translator has used his own judgment in deciding between the readings suggested by Heindorf, in 1810, Briggs, in 1821, and Wordsworth, in 1844; and has either recorded in notes, or admitted into the body of the translation, whichever he deemed preferable. He has also had recourse to the Poetæ Græci Minores, of Gaisford; to "Theocritus Sacram Scripturam illustrans," by Chr. Porschberger, Lipsiæ, 1744; and to the several metrical translations of Theocritus, &c., by Creech, Fawkes, Polwhele, and Chapman, the latter of which is appended to this volume. And he has given, in the form of notes, much information derived from these, and from scattered criticisms in the Classical Museum and elsewhere, including Smith's Dictionaries of Greek and Roman Antiquities, and Biography. This labour has been undertaken and completed in the hope that it may be useful to those who have not leisure to search for themselves, and yet would fain refresh their memory with the sweet strains of the Doric minstrelsy, as well as to those who require assistance towards mastering these confessedly difficult poets.

Whatever the labour, the translator is aware that the credit attaching to a prose translation is by no means large. Yet he believes that, properly applied, such a work may be of great advantage: and though a resolute opponent of the indiscriminate use of a "crib," he is not the less persuaded that there are many hard-working tyros, as well as advanced students, to whom it may be a great boon, and whose progress in classical knowledge it will assist rather than impede. He has taken up the work "con amore;" inasmuch as the taste for the Bucolic Poets, which he imbibed under one who had a keen appreciation of their beauties,—and who, in his too brief tenure of the head-mastership of one of our principal schools, manifested singular felicity in inspiring his pupils with a zest for their song,—has grown into an ardent desire to do somewhat towards their more extended study. He rejoices to hear that there is hope of a fresh edition of the Greek Bucolic Poets from the University of Cambridge, the promise of which is not likely to be imperfectly fulfilled, considering the hand from which it is to come. Meanwhile, if through this unpretending translation, which, without being servile in its literality, is, the translator hopes, sufficiently close, a score more men within the next two years shall be induced to place Theocritus on their list for the public examinations at Oxford, he will not regret the labour bestowed upon rendering into bare prose a bard whose lays are so full of poetry.

J. B.

Grammar School of King Edward VI.,
  Ludlow.

BIOGRAPHICAL NOTICE

OF

THEOCRITUS.

B. C. 284—280.

For the biography of the foremost of Bucolic minstrels, the pastoral poet Theocritus, unfortunately few materials exist. Indeed the little which is known is inferred either from the actual poems of Theocritus himself, or from such as have been published under his name. Of the latter class is the 22nd epigram, from which we gather his parentage and birth-place, and which is generally held to have been the work of Artemidorus the grammarian. Evidently written with a view to distinguishing between our poet and his Chian namesake, an orator and sophist, it fixes for his native place Syracuse, and for his parents Praxagoras and Philinna. With this account Suidas substantially agrees, though he adds that some make Theocritus the son of Simichus, or Simichidas, and holds that, being originally a native of Cos, he had become a metœch or foreign settler at Syracuse. Now if we compare this notion with the Scholia on the 7th Idyll, vs. 21, (where it is suggested by some that the name is an assumed one, derived from σίμος, flat-nosed,) as well as with the Θεοκρίτου γένος, it seems that a confusion has arisen with regard to the identity of Theocritus with Simichidas, into whose mouth the 7th Idyll is put. It does not seem to have occurred to those who make Simichus the father of the Syracusan poet, that bards are wont to shadow forth their own words, thoughts, and acts, under fictitious names and unreal characters, and that Theocritus might really have described what happened to himself in the "Thalysia," and yet not have used the name of Simichidas, otherwise than Virgil uses that of Tityrus.—Nor is there any reason to suppose that the claims of Cos to the honour of his birth and early training rest on stronger grounds than that he studied under Philetus of Cos, whom he mentions in Idyll vii. 40, whether at Cos itself or in Alexandria is not clear. Of Philetus, and Asclepiades, of whom he speaks as τὸν ἐσθλὸν Σικελίδαν τὸν ἐκ Σάμω, (Idyll vii. 40,) it is known that they were distinguished poets of the Alexandrian school, whom Theocritus professedly admired, and of the former of whom he was probably a pupil.

There is internal evidence in the Idylls of the poet, that he resided for some space at Alexandria, and afterwards at Syracuse, whilst the 7th Idyll shows such a knowledge of the localities of Cos, as could hardly, one should think, have been obtained without a personal acquaintance with the island. Here may have arisen his intimacy with Nicias of Miletus, the physician to whom he dedicated the 11th and 13th Idylls, and to whose wife, Theugenis, he wrote a pleasing ditty, (28th,) with a silver distaff. But this is mere conjecture, arising probably out of the nearness of Cos to Miletus. To Alexandria Theocritus was no doubt attracted by the fame of its library, founded by Ptolemy Soter, and raised to its highest point of eminence by his son Philadelphus, under whose care it became the resort of the most distinguished literati of the day, Zenodotus, Callimachus, Hegesias, Euclid, Aratus. To the last of these, the astronomer and poet, who was the author of the Phænomena, he addressed his 6th Idyll, and his name occurs again in the Idyll following. Association with such a man would not be without its advantages, and we here and there discover traces of his having imbibed from his friend some acquaintance with astronomical matters. But it was probably at Alexandria, too, that he found access to the pages of the Septuagint, itself a lasting monument of the Egyptian monarch's zeal in the collection of literary treasures. No one can read the 16th, 18th, 20th, and 23rd Idylls without being struck by the similarity of thought and expression of passages in each, to portions of the Psalms of David, the Book of Job, the Song of Solomon, and the Prophecies of Isaiah. The parallels have been pointed out in the notes to the present translation: but the strength of internal evidence to the supposition that Theocritus availed himself of the access, which he might undoubtedly have had, to the Septuagint, receives additional force in the comparison of the whole scene of altercation between Pollux and Amycus with the historical record of the encounter between David and Goliath in the First Book of Samuel. It can hardly be doubted that Theocritus composed the 14th, 15th, and 17th Idylls at Alexandria: he could not have enjoyed even the passing favour and brief notice of Ptolemy Philadelphus, without becoming interested in the law and records of that strange race, the Jews of many wanderings; one hundred and twenty thousand of whom had been liberated by that monarch from the slavery in which Ptolemy Soter had bound them. Josephus (Antiq. xii. 2) writes at length respecting the interest shown by Ptolemy Philadelphus in obtaining for his vast library an accurate translation of the Books of the Old Testament. We find from him how the monarch strove to purchase the good will of the nation by sending splendid gifts to the God of Israel: how he valued the translators and their translations: and how he conversed with his librarian, Demetrius Phalereus, on the deep meaning and superior wisdom of the Jewish law. And we know enough of the tide of fashion, especially if it is royal taste that lifts the floodgate, which carries onward successful literature of any class, to feel sure that a scholar could hardly have tarried even for a brief space at Alexandria without inspecting that volume, which even to heathens was a work of wonder, fostered by reflecting credit upon one of the foremost of the then rulers of the world. A poet likewise, imbued, as was Theocritus, with a sense of the charm of natural simplicity, and having withal, as some of his poems show, no mean appreciation of the glorious epic, could never have been content with a transient glance at a collection of such infinite graces, simplicity, grandeur, natural colouring, and noble imagery, as the translation of the Seventy elders, inferior though it be in diction to the original. No! like others, he dipped often into that well of wisdom, albeit he knew not the spell which renders it sweeter to the taste than all other waters. Hovering around those sacred pages, he caught the scent of flowers of poesy, which he has transferred into his Idylls, and we have the gratification of an involuntary testimony from a heathen poet to the charms of composition and material, with which the sacred volume is so richly fraught.

Our taste will be wilfully dull, if it acknowledge not the extreme probability that the Syracusan saw the Septuagint, and there need be no stumbling-block in the argument that he no where mentions the Jews. He dived for pearls of poesy, leaving unexplored the buried treasures of history and religion. Without satisfactory data for any certain conclusion, we can at least give the benefit of probabilities in favour of our poet's acquaintance with the Septuagint. From this we pass on to other matter.

Theocritus, while at Alexandria, was allowed, we presume, to dedicate his 17th Idyll to Ptolemy Philadelphus; and we have reason to suppose that the 14th and 15th were composed there also. But it is clear that he did not find the monarch and his capital such kindly fosterers of his Muse as he might have expected: for very soon we find him hymning at Syracuse the praises (considerably qualified by doubts of his open-handedness) of King Hiero the Second. That monarch had ascended the throne B. C. 270: and the Idyll to which reference has been made, appears to have been written during the 1st Punic War, if we may judge from the allusion which he makes to the failing Carthaginians, and Hiero's alliance with their implacable foe. This would fix the date of the Idyll as 263 B. C.; when a treaty between Hiero and the Romans was concluded. But the rays of courtly favour must have been here also any thing but warm, the atmosphere chilly, when a poet was to be cherished, or creative genius to be saved from starvation and blight. Hiero's munificence was bestowed rather on kingdoms and potentates, than on minstrels and their songs. Perhaps Theocritus discovered at this point the mistake of trusting in princes for the advancement of poetic excellence: at any rate, the greater portion of his Idylls show him to have sought in the calm tranquillity of country life and pastoral scenery, that independent self-reliance, which, after all, is the safest nurse of the lovely rhyme. Though when he rises to heroics, as in the encomiums on Ptolemy and Hiero, and in the 22nd, 24th, and 25th Idylls, he fully sustains his reputation, and no where falls into poverty of language, or mediocrity of conception; yet it is on the first eleven Idylls, the 14th, 15th, and 21st, that his title to the fame, which has been universally accorded to him, is most really and justly based. Bion and

Moschus are pretty conceit-weavers: they sometimes delight us with passages unrivalled for warmth of colouring and tenderness of pathos:—but for simple rural life, accurately and tastefully depicted, for the thorough appreciation of nature, and reliance thereupon for the staple of his song, Theocritus ranks immeasurably above them. He stands alone, with a crowd of imitators at a wide interval of merit. Virgil's Eclogues have no inherent stamp of reality about them. We lack the shepherd's account of his own life among his sheep. There is more of polish than of nature. We have the courtier drawing smooth pictures from fancy; not the passionate lover of the country deriving his materials from the real landscapes on which he is actually looking out. To borrow an apt expression, Virgil's Eclogues are pictures of a polished mind playing at shepherd.

And as to our own pastoral writers, Spenser, Pope, Gay, Lyttleton, and Shenstone, none reach to half the height of Bucolic minstrelsy, to which their great model undeniably attained. Spenser's dialect and metre are unfavourable to his subject; and he can lay no claim to be a true bard of nature; while it is matter of fact that beneath his rural images there is an under-current of allusion to matters of religion. Who can enjoy with true zest the pastoral, where the shepherd Roffin symbolizes a bishop of Rochester, and the watch-dog Lowder, one of his chaplains? (See Shepherd's Calendar, Ecl. ix.) And as for Pope, whose pretensions rank next, his pastorals deserve credit only because they were written by a boy of sixteen; it were an insult to compare them with the mature productions of Theocritus. For smoothness of versification, they have indeed won praise from Macaulay and the Earl of Carlisle; but these two most capable judges assign to them no higher meed. Indeed, had Pope's pastorals alone survived their author, we may well question whether his name would have even been remembered. As for the rest, they claim still less right to tread the same ground, to rank in the same order with Theocritus, in that portion of the temple of fame which good taste will always assign to the Pastoral or Bucolic poets.

Coarse though the Syracusan bard be here and there, he is indeed, as Quinctilian calls him, "admirabilis in suo genere," nor is it any detraction from his well-won laurels that the same critic goes on to say, "sed musa illa rustica et pastoralis non forum modo, verum ipsam etiam urbem reformidat." (Inst. Orator. x. 1.) It must be borne in mind, when we stumble on grave objections against the poems of Theocritus, that his idea of simplicity is not a transcendental, but a natural one. He has no model Arcadia in view : his eye is all the while upon the woods and vales and river pastures of his native Sicily ; taking his shepherds as he found them there, making them speak what they did speak, not what they ought to have spoken. There are blemishes to his Idylls, which certainly render an expurgated edition of them a desideratum : but these affect more or less all the chief writers of antiquity. The question however which is just now dividing the educational world of France, seems to us to admit of but one solution. What is true of most of the Greek and Latin Classics, is of course true of Theocritus, as one of them. We cannot forego the charms of the whole, because our delicacy is offended, our purity shocked, by one or two Idylls, which, while they illustrate the darkest traits in the life of a heathen, only make us the more thankful that Christianity has at least gone far to banish one of the worst forms of human guilt and degradation. But upon the whole, the poems of Theocritus, without aiming at any deep moral lesson, are eminently calculated to nourish in us a growth of that keen taste for rural scenery, which is one of the purest and finest of earthly yearnings : whilst in liveliness, variety, and rhythm they certainly surpass anything of their kind, ancient or modern. And this must have arisen from the familiarity in which, we infer, Theocritus passed his latter years with rural scenes and characters.

It is seldom that we have no notice, at any rate no tradition, respecting the death of the poets of the ancient world. Of Hesiod, Simonides, Æschylus, Sophocles, Callimachus, Apollonius, Rhodius, (and these are but a few names taken haphazard,) we find some story at least, vague though it be, of their death or their burial-place. But Theocritus seems to have vanished from before the eyes of men, after he had lamented at Syracuse the small account in which bards of his day were held of tyrants. May he not have ended his days unnoticed in some quiet spot, to rise long after into fame by his depiction of it, while his bones lay sepulchred on one of the headlands which he puts before us so vividly ? Did he not fall.

asleep afar from the din of cities, bewept, like his fabled Daphnis, by universal nature? Ovid, we can hardly doubt, was in his Ibis confusing the poet with his Chian namesake, where he says,

> Utque Syracosio præstrictâ fauce poetæ
> Sic animæ laqueo sit via clausa tibi. Lib. in Ibim, 554.

In a note upon this passage in the Delphin edition, it is observed, that the old interpreters understood this to mean that Theocritus was hung by the son of Hiero, king of Sicily, on account of his invectives against him. But this only proves the fear of him, who wrote the epigram before alluded to, as distinguishing the name-sakes of Syracuse and Chios, to have been a well-grounded fear. Ovid, if, by the Syracusan poet, he means Theocritus, seems to have stumbled on the rock of which that epigram might have warned him. The fate of the Chian seems to have been transferred in his mind to the Syracusan, as will be seen by the following extract from Macrobius, Saturnalia, lib. vii. c. 3.

"King Antigonus put to death the Chian Theocritus, although he was bound by an oath to spare him, on account of an unfortunate joke of that individual at his expense. For when he was being dragged before Antigonus as if to receive punishment, and his friends were comforting him, and affording hopes 'that he would experience the royal clemency, when once he had come before the *eyes* of the king; Then,' observed he, 'the hope you hold out of safety is a vain one.' For the king had lost one eye. So the ill-timed witticism cost the prisoner his life."

Now if we thus clear away this very apparent confusion between the two, we have no account of the death of the pastoral poet; no, nor the vaguest allusion to it. But the works which survive him are evidence that he has not all died: while taste survives, he must hold undisputed supremacy in his own branch of the poetic art.

Of the origin and nature of that species of poetry which dates its ascendency from Theocritus, there is little which has not been said again and again. The student who desires to arrive at the results of older lucubrations on this subject, must wade through subtle distinctions and learned disquisitions respecting pastoral and heroic poetry. He will find that the birth-place of the former is contended by some to have been Sicily, by others Arcadia. And while one and another ascribe its first authorship to various poets of more or less historical periods, some have been fain to date it from the golden age. Now, when we gain experience of the difficulties which arise in reconciling so many and diverse statements, and find that the more effort we make, the further we drift into a sea of troubles, our natural inclination coincides with some sort of likelihood, which is in favour of that last opinion. The truth may be that some kind of pastoral was the first form of poetry. What more natural, when we reflect that the eldest of the human race reckoned their superiority by their flocks and herds. Men were all shepherds: and so little of shame was there connected with an occupation now so lowly, that no higher or more expressive title for a mighty ruler was sought than that of "shepherd of his peoples." Of course, under these circumstances, the pastoral was likely to be an early form of poetry, and withal one not likely to be despised. Indeed, among those who practised it at an early date were Moses and Miriam, Deborah and Barak, as well as the sweet Psalmist of Israel.

When therefore we discuss the age of its invention, we can but say that it was of every age. The first up-rising of it was, we may conclude, in that primæval condition of men, when the system of concentration into towns and fenced cities had not yet begun: but when men led a nomad life, and whiled their hours afield by alternate strains, whilst they were pasturing their flocks. It was the song of nature, little polished perhaps, but still not without its inspiration, because it flowed directly from the shrines of her, whom he that worships most is ever the truest and most accepted poet. The rustling of the trees, the vocal pine, the murmurings of rivulets, the very notes of birds, were so many of nature's hints to man to create for himself a harmony more excellent in proportion as the gift of speech excels all inarticulate sounds. And when we add to this the influence of a sunny sky, a genial atmosphere, a mind unruffled with the cares and sins which harass and pollute the life of crowded cities, the wonder would be if song had not arisen; and that song, in common gratitude, of such a kind as should depict and hold up to imitation the life which was so singularly blessed. Gratitude, too, led them no doubt to celebrate the festivals of their gods, the tutelar deities of light and shade, of cattle and of fruits—Apollo, Diana, Pan, and Ceres. Prizes offered for such strains at these holy seasons would kindle a rivalry promotive of advancement, and render easier the steps by which they should pass into an art. This is probably the key to the mythical ascription of pastoral poetry to Apollo Nomius, the herdsman whilome in the halls of Admetus. Diomus, Daphnis, and Stesichorus, all of them Sicilian, may have been its first promoters upon Dorian soil; and as Theocritus seems to have been the first who applied a highly cultivated mind to the task of infusing into Amœbœan strains the grace and beauty which he has wrought into his Idylls, his country Sicily stands justly foremost as the birth-place of Bucolic minstrelsy. The Dorian character, too, was apter than that of other races to this kind of poetry: mimetic art had its eminent representative in the Sicilian Sophron: and among them mimetic and comic dialogue, as well as pastoral, arose in some measure out of the unstudied repartees of the Lydiastæ and Bucolistæ, or of some such performers. These gave a basis, whereon the more studied Idyll might take its stand, and the great master of whom we are treating, was not slow to apply all his varied knowledge of nature and of art to this lively form of poetry, so calculated to keep the interest from flagging, the hearer or reader from becoming wearied. He first moulded these rude strains into grace and beauty. He smoothed the ruggednesses of verse. He inspired the picture with novel life; and, whilst he preserved the guise of nature throughout, evinced that master power which is most teeming with the perfection of art, when its creations look likest nature.

It remains that we should attempt a classification of the various poems of Theocritus which have come down to us. The arguments to each of these have been prefixed in the body of the translation. Of the thirty Idylls extant, ten are properly Bucolics, the 1st, the 3rd, and all up to the 12th. The 2nd Idyll can scarcely come under this head, though the wider term εἴδη, or εἰδύλλια, pictures, that is, of common everyday life, may embrace that as well as the 14th, 15th, the 21st, and perhaps some others. Some, however, claim the 2nd and 15th for a separate class under the head of mimetic Idylls. The 12th, 18th, 19th, 20th, 23rd, 27th, and 29th, are erotic: the 16th and 17th, encomiastic: the 22nd, 24th, 25th, and 26th, belong to the epic class; whilst the 28th is epistolary, and the 30th Anacreontic. Of those classed as erotic, the manner and form is various, as the reader will observe. The genuineness of all the Idylls after the 18th has been much questioned: this however is not a matter either likely to repay great research, or calculated to interest the general reader. They are for the most part in hexameter verse: the thirty-two epigrams are some of them elegiac, some epodic.

It is difficult to fix upon one beauty beyond another in these matchless pastorals, by singling out which one may send the uninitiated reader with a whetted appetite to the whole volume. A thousand charms of poesy press forward, each claiming foremost commemoration. In the first Idyll we linger long over the sorrows of Daphnis, which Virgil has transfused into his Eclogues, over the immortal lines (66—69) which have lost none of their pristine sweetness, when, having passed the ordeal of transplantation, they bloom anew in the Lycidas of Milton, (Lycidas, l. 50,)

"Where were ye, nymphs, when the remorseless deep," &c.;

or yet again in the same Idyll, over that (to the translator's taste at least) most enviable epitaph, (140, 141,)

χὼ Δάφνις ἔβα ῥόον· ἔκλυσε δίνα
τὸν Μώσαις φίλον ἄνδρα, τὸν οὐ Νυμφαισιν ἀπεχθῆ.

In the second Idyll, we view the fierceness of disappointed love, in the raging passion of Simætha: in the sixth, a more rustic and clownish, yet not less touching, hopelessness, attributed to the Cyclops in the song of Damætas. Or if pretty picturings of scenery are more the object of our search, what translation can do justice to the 13th Idyll, the Hylas, the charming rural scene in the end of the 7th, or the 25th Idyll from the 34th to the 50th line? There are passages in the Hylas unsurpassed by any poet of whatever age or clime; as, for instance, from the 35th to the 60th line, where the capture of the youth by the enamoured Naiads is depicted. The Gossips of Theocritus are such a life-like picture, so capitally drawn, that it were a work of supererogation to point it out, or to commend it. It is nature itself, not as it was seen in Sicily, or in Alexandria, but as it ever has been throughout the world. The Epithalamium of Helen (18th) and the Infant Hercules (24th) are excellent in their kinds; and the Honey-stealer (19th) won the notice and translating hand of the poet Moore, by its Anacreontic savour. And by no means must any reader pass by the fishermen of the 21st Idyll. Their wattled cabin is an old favourite of every lover of Theocritus: and there is untold humour in Asphalion's dream, and his sage comrade's advice thereupon. But it is invidious to mention these. The beauties uncommemorated may with ease be proved to eclipse the few which we have instanced. The touch of Theocritus left no subject without some impress of native grace and liveliness. "Nihil, quod tetigit, non ornavit."

Of the Epigrams, the 6th, "on the loss of the kid," the 14th, an epitaph on Eurymedon, and the 15th, another on the same, are very beautiful. The Epigram on the Bank of Caicus, (23rd,) might fitly stand translated over the doors of the safest establishments of a like nature in modern days; whilst, on the principle of keeping the best till last, we are bound to set before all, as praise the noblest in the aim, the most glorious in the acquisition, the conclusion of the Epigram on the Sicilian Epicharmus (Epigr. xvii.):

πολλὰ γὰρ πότ' τὰν ζόαν τοῖς παισὶν εἶπε χρήσιμα.
  Μεγάλα χάρις αὐτῷ·
    Full many a rule of life he drew,
    Still pointing to the fair, the true,
  The youthful mind: High favour crowns the bard. (Polwhele.)

BIOGRAPHICAL NOTICE

OF

BION.

If materials are scanty for a Life of Theocritus, they are much more so for those of his first imitators, Bion and Moschus. An Elegy of the latter is the only faint glimmer of light, by which we can guess at, we cannot say discern, aught of history of the former. Yet it would interest us if we could know how far Bion professedly reverenced Theocritus, what value he set upon simplicity in Pastorals, whether he aimed at a new school of that branch of the poetic art, and whether he would account as an improvement that over-refined sentimentality which robs his Muse of all claim to be a child of nature.

But, except the 3rd Idyll of Moschus, no data for his life exist—unless we take upon the authority of Suidas that he was born beside that river, which by tradition is reputed to have reared on its banks the greatest of poets, the immortal Homer, the river Meles, at Phlossa in the neighbourhood of Smyrna.

From the Elegy above referred to, we assume that Bion left his native country for Sicily, and spent at least his latter days in cultivating the Bucolic minstrelsy, so thoroughly identified with that pastoral isle. It seems hardly safe however to lay it down, with some, on the faith of the words in Moschus, (Id. iii. 17, &c.,) that Bion visited Thrace and Macedonia; because the sense of the passage does not necessarily imply more than that Strymonian swans and Æagrian nymphs might well mourn and weep afresh, since a Dorian, equal to their native Orpheus, had ceased to breathe forth his lovely lays. One fact, however, stands out distinctly, namely, that the poet came to an untimely death by poison, which was administered to him by more than one individual, and that the murderers, whosoever they were, paid the penalty of their crime. The age of Bion can be determined only by the statement of Moschus, (iii. 100—105,) that he was one of his disciples, and that Theocritus mourned his loss. Granting this, we must take his date as 280 B. C.

As has been before observed in the Life of Theocritus, the poems of Bion which have come down to us are vastly inferior in pastoral beauty, in natural simplicity, and inherent truthfulness, to the works of the Syracusan master. But here and there we chance upon a passage of eminent loveliness. Every where the Asiatic softness seems to add luxurious grace to his tuneful songs; though this is but a poor substitute for the vigorous and healthy freshness of the Father of Pastorals. Bion standing alone would soon fade from our memories. He is fortunate in being preserved with his pupil and elegiast to complete the volume of Greek Pastoral Poets, which is, alas! our sole legacy in this kind from the Alexandrian school. His versification is very elegant; his language, Doric, with some few Ionicisms and Atticisms.

BIOGRAPHICAL NOTICE

OF

MOSCHUS.

THE poet Moschus seems to have found no kindred spirit to embalm his memory in harmonious numbers: or if he had that fortune, it has not survived the oblivion which so remorselessly overwhelms the rest of his personal history. We reckon him a Syracusan, whose day was about the close of the third century before Christ. And he must have been contemporaneous with Bion, probably in age somewhat younger. He does not reach the excellence of his friend and teacher, far less that of Theocritus. Indeed there lies over all his pieces a clothing of affectation, and study of ornament, which makes them read as forced and unnatural compositions. Still many passages might be quoted which are highly poetic, none more so perhaps than that exquisite passage in the third Idyll, (105—114,) where, in a lament over the briefness of this mortal life, the mighty of the earth are contrasted with the flowers of the field in such an earnest tone of pathos, as shows the enlightened heathen dissatisfied with prevailing religions, whilst it teaches our own higher privileges, to us who have held out and within our grasp, "the sure and certain hope of the resurrection to eternal life."

BIOGRAPHICAL NOTICE

OF

TYRTÆUS.

B. C. 660 ?

THE elegiac poet, Tyrtæus, whose remains, in an English garb, close the present volume, follows immediately in his branch of the poetic art, the founder of Greek elegy, Callinus. An elegy, according to the Greek notion, is a poem composed of a combination of hexameters and pentameters. It seems often to have been of the nature of a dirge or lament, and the word ἔλεγος has no distinct reference to metrical form, though ἐλεγεία has. Its origin was undoubtedly Asiatic. Crossing the Ægean, it found one of its most eminent cultivators in Tyrtæus, the poet whom tradition has handed down to us as the Athenian present to their hereditary enemies the Spartans, when they had been directed by the Delphic oracle to seek a leader from Athens for the second Messenian war. The story runs, that Athens, never hearty towards Sparta, save in her hatred, sent her the worst selection that, according to appearances, could be made,—a lame schoolmaster and composer of verses, who dwelt at Aphidnæ, a village of Attica : and that this Ionian inspired the Dorian warriors who adopted him, with such spirit through his fiery strains, that victory crowned their prowess. The second Messenian war is placed by Pausanias between Ol. 23, 4 and 28, 1, that is, between B. C. 685 and 668 : but this date is considered by the latest authorities too high, and indeed, as Callinus probably flourished about B. C. 660, and we are led to believe that Tyrtæus was but a few years junior to him, this would seem to be the more probable date.

The main features of the popular tradition, however pleasing to our school-day notions of history, must of course be taken only as containing the germ of certain truths, and not as being themselves broad historical truths. Castor and Pollux, according to old legends, had been adopted by Aphidnus, the hero from whom Aphidnæ was named: and as the Dioscuri were Spartan, the Aphidnæans may have been moved by some feelings or ties of kindred, and not by the will of Athens, to send Tyrtæus to the aid of Laconia. This would crush the fable of intentional insult on the part of Athens. And then as to the origin of Tyrtæus, it cannot be doubted that he was of Ionian stock, (whether a native of Attica, or a settler in it from one of her Asiatic colonies, as Suidas states, it matters not, for the inventions of the colonies would soon find their way to their polished metropolis:) because we know that the branch of poetry in which he excelled was peculiarly Ionian; and not such as can claim any early vigour or native success among the Dorians. Whether he came from Miletus to Aphidnæ, or was born at the latter place, we need not inquire; there is no ground at any rate for the supposition that he was a Lacedæmonian by birth, as Strabo and Athenæus have stated on the authority of Philochorus and Callisthenes. Surely his elegiac strains disprove this. With regard to his lameness, and his supposed office of village schoolmaster at Aphidnæ, the truth to be evolved from these statements is probably that he wrote uneven couplets, and, like other early poets, taught the art, of which he was so skilful a master. If he was either by birth or by sojourn an Aphidnæan, there is no wonder in his interest for Sparta, nor, on the other hand, any difficulty in understanding why, coming from Attica, he yet became a favourite with the Lacedæmonians. And, certain it is, that whatever may have been his bodily defects, whatever his inexperience in generalship, his martial strains and wise counsels achieved much, in which a skilful general might have failed without them. As a bard, he was no mean leader of his adopted countrymen: for ages afterwards, their evening meal on their campaigns closed with the recitation of his spirit-stirring war-songs: and when the foe was vanquish-

THEOCRITUS.

IDYLL I.

ARGUMENT.

The Poet, proposing to celebrate the end of Daphnis, the hero of Sicilian shepherds, finds an opening of his subject in a dialogue between a goatherd and a shepherd named Thyrsis. The latter begs the former to sing with the accompaniment of his pipe. This he declines, for fear of awakening Pan, and strives to prevail upon Thyrsis, by the offer of a goat and a most highly wrought drinking-cup, to sing of the death of Daphnis. Thyrsis accordingly begins by invoking the Nymphs: describes the grief of the brute creation at the sorrows of Daphnis: the sympathy of Pan and Mercury, as well as the shepherds their worshippers: the bitterness of Daphnis towards Venus, who had caused his sorrows, but is now inclined to relent. The song concludes with the farewell of Daphnis to all the objects of his former joys. After which performance, the goatherd presents Thyrsis with the meed of his song.

THYRSIS THE SHEPHERD, AND THE GOATHERD.

Thyrsis. [1] OF a sweet nature, goatherd, is the murmuring of yon pine, which tunefully rustles by the fountains: and sweetly too do you play on the pipe: next to Pan you shall carry off the second *prize.* If he shall have taken the horned he-goat, you shall receive the she-goat: and if he

---

[1] Compare Pope, Past. iv. 80,
  In some still evening when the whispering breeze
  Pants on the leaves, and dies among the trees.
And again in the same Pastoral,
  Thyrsis, the music of that murmuring spring,
  Is not so mournful as the strains you sing.
Add to these Virg. Ecl. viii. 22. τὸ ψιθύρισμα καὶ ἁ πίτυς, is an instance of the figure *hendiadys*, so common in Greek and Latin poets. The "Pateris libamus et auro," of Virgil, for "pateris libamus auratis," will serve for an illustration. So Bion, Fragm. xii. 2, ψαμαθόν καὶ ἠϊόνα for ψαμαθὸν ἠϊόνος.

shall have received as a gift of honour the she-goat, ²the yearling falls to your share: and the flesh of the yearling-kid is good, until you shall have milked it.

Goatherd. ³ Sweeter, good shepherd, is thy melody, than yon resounding water pours down from the rock above. If the Muses bear-off for themselves the sheep as a gift, you shall receive as your prize the ⁴young lamb: but should it please them to receive the lamb, then you shall afterwards bear away the sheep.

Thyrs. Are you willing, I ask you by the Nymphs, are you willing, goatherd, to take your seat here at this sloping mound, ⁵where the tamarisks are, *and* to play upon your pipe? And I meanwhile will tend your she-goats.

Goath. It is not right, good shepherd, it is not right for us to pipe at mid-day: ⁶we are afraid of Pan; for in truth *it is* then he reposes wearied from the chase: and he is crabbed, and sharp anger ever rests upon his nostril. But (since you in fact, Thyrsis, have seen the sorrows of Daphnis, and have arrived at the summit of Bucolic minstrelsy) come, let us sit under the elm, opposite to *the statue of* Priapus, and the fountain-nymphs, even where that pastoral seat is, and the oaks. And if you shall have sung, as of old you sang, *when* contending against Chromis from Libya, I will

---

² The yearling falls, &c.] Compare Horat. i. Od. xxviii. 28, Tibi defluat æquo ab Jove, &c. Compare also Bion, i. 55.

³ Virgil, Ecl. v. 45—47,
   Tale tuum carmen nobis, divine Poeta,
   Quale sopor fessis, &c.
And ibid. 83, 84, Nec percussa juvant fluctu tam littora, nec quæ
   Saxosas inter decurrunt flumina valles.
Pope, Past. iv., Nor rivers winding through the vales below,
   So sweetly warble, or so sweetly flow.

⁴ The young lamb.] σακίταν. Literally, stall-fed: hence young and tender.

⁵ Virg. Ecl. iv. 2, Non omnes arbusta juvant, humilesque myricæ.

⁶ This habit of the gods sleeping in the mid-day heat, is introduced by Virgil, Georg. iv. 401,
   Ipsa ego te, medios cum Sol accenderit æstus,
   In secreta ducam senis, quò fessus ab undis
   Se recipit.
Warton quotes 1 Kings xviii. 27, "And it came to pass at noon, that Elijah mocked them, and said, Cry aloud: for he *is* a god; either he is talking, or he is pursuing, or he is in a journey, *or* peradventure he sleepeth, and must be awaked."

give you both a she-goat, [7] that suckles twins, to milk thrice a day, which though it has two kids will give milk to fill two pails, and a deep drinking-cup of ivy wood, rubbed with sweet wax, with two handles, fresh made, still smacking of the graving tool: around whose lips ivy twines on [8] high, ivy interspersed with marigold ; and the helix winds round about it rejoicing in the yellow fruit. But on the inner surface, a woman, a cunning kind of work of divine art, has been wrought, decked out in a flowing robe, and [9] a coif of-net-work, and, beside her, men with-beautifully-long-hair are contending with words, alternately, one from one side, another from another: yet the *words* are not reaching her heart: but one while she is glancing with a smile towards that man, and at another time she is again casting her thoughts on this: whilst they by reason of love straining their eyes for a long time, are labouring to no purpose. And [10] besides these, an old fisherman and a rugged rock have been wrought, over which the old man is busily dragging a huge net for a cast, [11] like a man toiling with all his might. You would say that he was fishing with the whole strength of his limbs, to such a degree are the sinews swelling every where about his neck, even though he is grey-headed: Yet his powers are worthy of youth. [12] And at a little distance from the sea-worn old man, a vineyard is beautifully laden with ripe clusters: which a little boy is watching, as he sits at the hedge-rows: and around him two foxes, [13] one

[7] Virg. Ecl. iii. 30, Bis venit ad mulctram, binos alit ubere fœtus. ἐς δύο πέλλας, i. e. two pails full.
[8] Compare Pope's Past. i. 25,
    And I this bowl where wanton ivy twines,
    And swelling clusters bend the curling vines.
And Virg. Ecl. iii. 38—45.
[9] ἄμπυξ, reticulum, a head-band or snood, for binding up women's front hair. Just above, for ἔντοσθεν, compare Virg. Ecl. iii. 40, In medio duo signa.
[10] Besides these.] For this use of μέτα with a dative, compare Idyll xvii. 84 and xxv. 129.
[11] The full expression here would be κατὰ τόσον σθένος, ὅσον γυίων ἐστὶν, or rather, perhaps, τοσοῦτον ὅσον ἐστὶ γυίων σθένος, omnibus membrorum viribus.
[12] τυτθὸν δ' ὅσσον, "non procul." Schol. τοσοῦτον διάστημα ὅσον ὀλίγον. Virg. Ecl. vi. 16, (Heyne,) Serta *procul tantum* capiti sublapsa jacebant.
[13] Compare Canticles or Song of Solomon ii. 15, "Take us the

is roaming up and down the rows, spoiling the ripe grapes, while the other, preparing all his subtlety for *the boy's* wallet, is vowing he will not leave the lad, before that [14]he shall have brought him to beggary, *as being* without his breakfast. But he in sooth is weaving a fine locust-trap with asphodel stalks, fitting them on rushes: and neither is he at all concerned for his wallet, nor for the fruits, so much as he is delighting about his platting. But all about the cup clusters the moist [15]bear's-foot, a kind of Æolian sight: the marvêl would astonish your senses. As the price of it, I gave to the Calydonian boatman, a goat and a large cheese cake of white milk, nor has it at all anywise reached [16]my lip, but it still lies untouched. With this I would right willingly gratify you, if you would sing me, friend, that lovely hymn. And I do not envy you at all. Come, good sir! for by no means shall [17]you ever hoard your song, at any rate for Hades that bringeth forgetfulness.

Thyrs. [18]Begin, dear Muses, begin the pastoral strain.

Here am I, Thyrsis from Ætna, and this is the voice of Thyrsis. [19]Wherever, I wonder, wherever were ye, Nymphs,

foxes, the little foxes, that spoil the vines; for our vines have tender grapes."

[14] ἐπὶ ξηροῖς καθίζειν τινα. To run one aground; bring to a nonplus; ruin utterly. Wordsworth shows that καθίζειν often has the sense of reducing to a certain state, and leaving in it (redigendi et destituendi). Xenoph. Sympos. iii. 11. Plat. Theæt. p. 146, a. Thuc. i. 109. So Ovid. Fast. iii. 52, In siccâ pueri *destituuntur* humo. For ἀνάριστον, breakfast-less, Wordsworth proposes πράτιστον, i. q. πρᾶτον.

[15] Moist bear's foot.] Virg. Ecl. iii. 45, Et molli circum est ansas amplexus acantho. Virg. Georg. iv. 123, Flexi vimen acanthi. Plin. Ep. v. 6, 16, Acanthus in plano mollis, et pœne dixerim *lubricus*.

[16] Virg. Ecl. iii. 43, Necdum illis labra admovi sed condita servo.

[17] Hom. Il. ii. 600. Moschus Epitaph. Bion, 21, Ἀλλὰ παρὰ Πλουτῆι μέλος λαθαῖον ἀείδει. Above τὸν ἐφίμερον ὕμνον ἀείσῃς. So Psalm xlv. is called, "a song of the Loves."

[18] Compare this with Virg. Ecl. viii. Incipe Mænalios mecum, mea tibia, versus. Pope, Pastoral iii.,

    Resound, ye hills, resound my mournful strains.

[19] Virg. Ecl. x. 9—12,

    Quæ nemora aut qui vos saltus habuere, puellæ
    Naiades, indigno cum Gallus amore periret?
    Nam neque Parnassi vobis juga, nam neque Pindi
    Ulla moram fecere, nec Aonia Aganippe.

Compare too the lines of Milton's Lycidas, beginning,

when Daphnis pined away? were ye along the fair vales of the [20] Peneus, or along those of Pindus? for ye were not occupying, I ween, the broad stream of Anapus at any rate, nor the height of Ætna, nor the sacred wave of Acis.

Begin, dear Muses, begin the pastoral strain.

Him indeed the panthers, him the wolves bewailed. For him, when dead, even the lion from the thicket wept aloud.

Begin, dear Muses, begin the pastoral strain.

At his feet many cows, ay and many bulls, and again many young heifers and steers lamented.

Begin, dear Muses, begin the pastoral strain.

Foremost came Hermes from the mountain, and said, 'Daphnis, who wastes thee away? of whom, my good friend, art thou so enamoured?'

Begin, dear Muses, begin the pastoral strain.

[21] The herdsmen came, the shepherds, the goatherds came. All kept asking, what harm had befallen him. Priapus came and said, 'Wretched Daphnis, why pinest thou? And the maiden too is ———— afoot past all the fountains along all the groves—'

Begin, dear Muses, begin the pastoral strain.

[22] 'Seeking— Surely thou art *of* a very lovesick *nature*, and

   Where were ye, Nymphs, when the remorseless deep, &c.

Pope and ———— have imitated this passage.

[20] Pene———, a mountain and river, of Thessaly. Anapus a———— Sicily. Anapus is mentioned, Id. vii. 151, and Acis by ————,

   Qui———— Acis petit æquora fines
   Et d———— Nereida perluit undâ.

For the 72nd v——— compare Virg. Ecl. v. 27,

   Daphni tuum Pænos etiam ingemuisse leones
   Interitum montesque feri silvæque loquuntur.

[21] Virg. Ecl. x. 19,

   Venit et upilio, tardi venere bubulci.
   Omnes, unde amor iste, rogant tibi. Venit Apollo.
   Galle quid insanis inquit? tua cura Lycoris
   Perque nives alium, perque horrida castra secuta est.

Pope Past. iii. 81,

   Pan came and ask'd, what magic caused my smart,
   And what ill eyes malignant glances dart?

[22] Respecting this line there is endless difficulty; for ζατεῦσ' there are various emendations, of which Hermann's ζάτευ' ("quin quære eam," "nay, but seek her") seems the best. Bindemann is at a loss to see

beyond-help. Thou wast called indeed a herdsman, but now art thou like a [23] goat-feeder'......

Begin, dear Muses, begin the pastoral strain.

'And thou too, when thou beholdest the maidens, how they smile, wastest away in thine eyes, because thou dancest not with them.' But to these the herdsman answered nothing; but kept going-on-with his own bitter love, and kept going-on-with it to the end of destiny.

Begin, dear Muses, begin the pastoral strain.

Ay and there came indeed sweetly, even Venus smiling, [24] smiling indeed secretly—but cherishing severe anger; and said she, 'Thou indeed, Daphnis, didst boast that thou [25] wouldst bend Love! Hast not thou, in thine own person, been bent by grievous love?'

Begin, dear Muses, begin the pastoral strain.

And Daphnis, I wot, answered her thus, 'Harsh Venus, Venus to be dreaded, Venus hateful to mortals:—for at length all things declare that my sun is setting: [26] Daphnis even in the shades will be a bitter grief of Love.'

Begin, dear Muses, begin the pastoral strain.

[27] 'As to Venus, is not—the herdsman said—Away to

why Daphnis should pine away, if she whom he loved was at such pains to find him out. From Virgil's imitation, (Ecl. x. 20, 21,) one would imagine she was following another. If so, we may perhaps explain the present reading, by supposing Priapus to see that the subject is distasteful, and so to break off at the word ζατεῦσ'—ἁ δυσερώς, &c.

[23] Ὠπόλος—ἔγεντο, two lines sensu obscœno. Caprarias quando videt capras, ut inscenduntur, tabescit oculis quod non hı̃rcus ipse natus est. Chapman renders them,

   The goatherd, when he sees his goats at play,
   Envies their wanton sport, and pines away.

For line 91, compare Horat. Epod. v. 39,

   Cum semel fixæ cibo
   Intabuissent pupulæ.

[24] λάθρια μὲν. Wordsworth reconciles the difficulties of this passage, by reading ἀθρῆν for ἀθρεῖν, smiling to look upon, which certainly suits the sense better.

[25] λυγιξῆν, ἐλυγίχθης. A term taken from wrestling, which here means, to master or overthrow.

[26] i. e. "But, even should I, Daphnis, die, my very shade shall sorely trouble the god of love." Compare Bion, Idyll viii. 10, Οἰνώνᾳ κακὸν ἄλγος.

[27] This is an instance of aposiopesis, a figure common in Greek and Latin poets. Compare Virg. Ecl. iii. 8, Novimus et qui te, transversa tuentibus hircis, et quo—sed faciles nymphæ risere—sacello. Also see

Ida. Go to Anchises. There (*in Ida*) are *sheltering* oaks, here *only* marsh plants. Here bees buzz sweetly at the hives.'

Begin, dear Muses, begin the pastoral strain.

[28] 'Adonis too in the prime of youth, since he too tends sheep, both strikes down hares, and hunts all wild beasts.'

Begin, dear Muses, begin the pastoral strain.

[29] 'See thou go take thy stand again in close combat with Diomed, and say, I conquer the herdsman Daphnis, come contend with me.'

Begin, dear Muses, begin the pastoral strain.

'Ye wolves, ye lynxes, ye bears lurking-in-dens along the mountains, farewell! For you no more is the herdsman Daphnis along the wood: no more up and down the oak-coppices or the groves. Farewell, Arethusa ; and ye rivers, that pour beautiful water down [30] Thymbris.'

Begin, dear Muses, begin the pastoral strain.

'Here am I, that Daphnis, who tend heifers hereabouts : [31] Daphnis, who lead the bulls and calves to water in these parts.'

Begin, dear Muses, begin the pastoral strain.

'O Pan, Pan, if thou art on the long mountain *ranges* of Lycæus, or if thou art engaged on [32] great Mænalus, come thou to the Sicilian isle, and leave the foreland [33] of Helice,

---

Æn. i. 135, Quos ego—sed motos præstat componere fluctus. Æn. ii. 100; v. 195; and a similar instance in the Book of Exodus, xxxii. 32. It is an abrupt breaking off in the midst of a sentence. Here Venus is taunted with her intrigue with Anchises. Compare Homer Hymn to Venus, 53.

[28] Virg. Ecl. x. 10, Et formosus oves ad flumina pavit Adonis. The poet is making Daphnis defend a pastoral life.

[29] Compare Homer Iliad v. 336, for this encounter, and understand in construction ὅρα before ὅπως. See Æsch. Prom. v. 68, ὅπως μὴ σαυτὸν οἰκτιεῖς ποτέ.

[30] Thymbris, a mountain of Sicily, according to Toup and Valkenaer. Servius, at Virgil Æn. iii. 500, says, that about Syracuse there was a dyke called Thybris, mentioned by Theocritus. He seems to allude to this passage.

[31] See Virg. Ecl. v. 41, Daphnis ego in silvis hinc usque ad sidera notus, &c.

[32] Compare Virg. Georg. i. 16, Tua si tibi Mænala curæ. Georg. iii. 314, Summa Lycæi.

[33] ῥίον seems to mean any promontory, headland, foreland. See Idyll xxv. 228. Helice was a city of Achaia, but from the connexion

and that lofty tomb of the son of Lycaon, which is admirable even to the blest *immortals*.'

[34] Cease, Muses, come cease the pastoral strain.

'Come, O king, and bear off this beautiful pipe sweetly smelling from the well-fastened wax, curved about the mouth-piece; for in truth I am by Love dragged to Hades at last.'

Cease, Muses, come cease the pastoral strain.

'Now may ye brambles bear violets, and may ye thorns bear them; and may [35] the beautiful narcissus flower on the junipers: and may all things become changed, and the pine bear pears, since Daphnis dies: and may the stag trail the dogs, and the owls from the mountains contend-in-song with nightingales.'

Cease, Muses, come cease the pastoral strain.

And he indeed having said thus much, made an end: and Aphrodite was willing to raise him up: but all the threads, I ween, had been exhausted by the Fates: and Daphnis crossed the [36] stream. The eddy washed away the man

of the name here with the son of Lycaon it would seem that we must rather take it for an Arcadian city, Lycaon and his son being connected with that country. Tombs are held as great land-marks among the Pastoral poets. Virg. Ecl. ix. 60, Namque sepulchrum Incipit adparere Bianoris.

[34] Desine Mænalios jam desine tibia versus. Virg. Ecl. viii. 61.

[35] Virg. Ecl. v. 38,
   Pro molli violâ, pro purpureo narcisso
   Carduus, et spinis surgit paliurus acutis.
And for an elegant imitation of this passage compare Ecl. viii. 27, 28, and 52, &c.,
   Jungentur jam gryphes equis, ævoque sequenti
   Cum canibus timidi venient ad pocula damæ.
   *   *   *   *   *   *   *
   Nunc et oves ultro fugiat lupus: aurea duræ
   Mala ferant quercus: narcisso floreat alnus:
   *   *   *   *   *   *   *
   Certent et cycnis ululæ.
Virgil, however, in his Georgics, ii. 71, declares art to have achieved what seemed to Theocrit. i. 134, an impossibility: Ornusque incanuit albo Flore pyri. πάντα δ' ἔναλλα. Ovid. Met., Omnia naturæ contraria legibus ibunt. Virg. Ecl. iii. 58, Omnia vel medium fiant mare. Elmsley thinks that Virgil here, having the passage of Theocritus in view, translated it, as if the reading were ἔναλα.

Pope Past. iii., Let opening roses knotted oaks adorn,
   And liquid amber drop from every thorn.

[36] ἐκ μοιρᾶν. Virg. Æn. x. 814, Extremaque Lauso Parcæ fila legunt. ῥοόν, the stream, that is, of Acheron.

who was dear to the Muses, who was not odious to the Nymphs.

Cease, Muses, come cease the pastoral strain.

And give thou me the she-goat and the cup, that I may milk her, and offer a libation to the Muses: O hail, hail oftentimes, ye Muses: and I to you will also at a future time sing more sweetly.

Goatherd. May thy lovely mouth, Thyrsis, be full of honey, ay full of honey-combs, [37] and mayest thou eat sweet dried-figs from Ægilus, since thou, for thy part, singest better than a cicala. Lo! here is the cup for thee: observe, my friend, how beautifully it smells. You will think that it has been washed in [38] the fountains of the Hours. Come hither, Cimætha: and do you milk her. And, ye she-goats, skip not, lest the he-goat mount you.

IDYLL II.

THE SORCERESS.

ARGUMENT.

Simætha, a maid of Syracuse, of middle rank, (70—74,) seeing herself slighted by Delphis, of whom she is enamoured, becomes suspicious and jealous, and strives to regain his love by charms and philters. At night, by the light of the moon, she holds a magic rite, to which chosen attendants are admitted. The object of these is, that the person on whom the charm is designed to work, may suffer the same as the inanimate objects used in the ceremonial. The rite being over, and Thestylis gone, Simætha details the rise and progress of her love, and her suspicions of the faithlessness of Delphis, addressing herself to the Moon, as presiding over the solemnity. Lastly, she threatens

---

[37] The goatherd wishes Thyrsis, besides other good things, Attic dried figs from the canton (δῆμος) Ægilus; from which the best fruit of this kind came. Valkenaer and Warton think ἀπ' Αἰγίλω ἰσχάδα is the same as Αἰγιλίδα ἰσχάδα.

[38] This line is a periphrasis for a very beautiful cup. It is a constant usage with Theocritus, Bion, and Moschus, to introduce the Hours adding grace and elegance to every thing which comes beneath their influence. Compare Theocr. Idyll. xv. 105, which see, and Mosch. ii. 160, καὶ οἱ λέχος ἔντυνον ὧραι.

heavy doom to the faithless youth, if he return not to his love for her. This Idyll with others, the 15th and 28th, treat of town, not country life. Virgil, in the 8th Eclogue, has borrowed from it largely.

Where, prythee, are my laurels? Bring them, Thestylis. And where the love-charms? Crown the pail [1] with choicest purple wool! that I may [2] overpower *by magic* the lover who is cruel to me, for, wretch that he is, [3] 'tis twelve days since he has ever been to see me: neither knows he whether I am dead or [4] alive, nor has he knocked-furiously at the doors, being untoward: surely Eros has gone off with his fickle heart elsewhere, and Aphroditè. I will go to-morrow to the palæstra of Timagetus, that I may see him, and reproach him for the way in which he treats me. But now I will compel him *to love* by magic rites. However, [5] O Moon, shine brightly, for to thee will I sing softly, O goddess, and to infernal Hecate, at whom even whelps tremble, as she goeth along the tombs and the dark gore of the corpses. Hail! [6] frightful Hecate, and be thou with me to the end, making

---

[1] ἀώτῳ, the flower, the best of its kind. Cf. Idyll xiii. 27, and consult Butmann's Lexilogus on the word. Il. xiii. 599.

[2] Virg. Ecl. viii. 64—66,
Effer aquam, et molli cinge hæc altaria vittâ:
Verbenasque adole pingues et mascula thura:
Conjugis ut magicis sanos avertere sacris
Experiar sensus.

[3] Δωδεκαταῖος. This form of speech for δῶδεκα ἡμέραι εἰσί occurs also at vs. 157. Compare Matthiæ, Gr. Gr. § 446, 8, respecting adjectives in αιος chiefly derived from ordinal numerals.

[4] See Matth. Gr. Gr. § 436, 4, a. here also on the use of the plur. masc. by a woman speaking of herself.

[5] The Moon and Hecate are special goddesses invoked by witches. So Ben Jonson, (quoted by Chapman,) "Sad shepherd."

When our dame Hecatè
Made it her gaing night over the kirk-yard,
With all the barking parish-tikes set at her,
While I sat whirling of my brazen spindle.

See Tibullus, i. 2, 52,
Sola tenere malas Medeæ dicitur herbas,
Sola feros Hecatæ perdomuisse canes.

Virg. Ecl. viii. 69, Carmina vel cœlo possunt deducere Lunam.
So our own Shakspeare introduces Hecate in the witch-scene of Macbeth.

[6] Horace, Epod. v. 51, Nox et Diana quæ silentium regis

these potions nowise inferior either to those of [7]Circè, or of Medea, or the yellow-haired Perimedè.

[8] Wheel, draw thou that man to my house.

[9] Meal, look you, is first consumed in the fire: nay, sprinkle it over, Thestylis; wretched girl, whither hast thou flown in wits? Is it really so then, that I have become, you loathsome creature, an object of malignant joy even to you? Sprinkle, and say these words withal, I sprinkle the bones of Delphis.

Wheel, draw thou that man to my house.

[10] Delphis has grieved me: and I burn the laurel over Delphis: and as it cracks loudly, when it has caught fire, and is suddenly in a blaze, and not even its ashes do we see; even so may Delphis too waste in flame as to his flesh.

Wheel, draw thou that man to my house!

[11] As I melt this wax by the help of the goddess, so may Myndian Delphis be presently wasted by love: and as this brazen wheel is whirled round, so may that man be whirled about by the influence of Aphroditè at my doors.

Wheel, draw thou that man to my house!

Now will I sacrifice the bran, and thou, O Artemis, might-

> Arcana cùm fiunt sacra,
> Nunc num adeste.

[7] Tibull. i. 2, 51, above quoted, and Propertius, ii. 4, 7,
> Non hic herba valet, non hic nocturna Cytæis,
> Non Perimedeâ gramina cocta manu.

The scholiast says Perimedè is the witch whom Homer calls Agamede.

[8] ἴυγξ, first the 'wry-neck,' so called from its cry. It came to signify the wheel to which wizards and witches bound this bird, believing that they drew along with it men's souls as by a charm. See Liddell and Scott, Greek Lex. at the word.

For the intercalary verse, see Virg. Ecl. viii.,
> Ducite ab urbe domum, mea carmina, ducite Daphnim.

[9] Sparge molam, &c. Virg. Ecl. viii. 83.

[10] Virg. Ecl. viii. 82, 83,
> Fragiles incende bitumine lauros,
> Daphnis me malus urit: ego hanc in Daphnide laurum.

Compare Propert. ii. 28, 35. Lucret. vi. 153.

[11] Virg. Ecl. viii. 80,
> Limus ut hic durescit et hæc ut cera liquescit,
> Uno eodemque igni, sic nostro Daphnis amore.

See Ovid. Met. iii. 487, Sed ut intabescere flavæ
> Igne levi ceræ, matutinæve pruinæ
> Sole tepente solent, sic attenuatus amore
> Liquitur.

est move the Adamantine *god* in Hades, and even whatever else is stedfast-in-purpose. Thestylis, the bitches are howling for us up and down the city. [12]The goddess is in the cross-roads: sound the brass with all speed.

Wheel, draw thou that man to my house.

[13] Behold, the sea is still, and the breezes are still, yet my grief is not still within my bosom: but I am all on fire for him, who has made wretched me to be base and unmaidenly, instead of a wife.

Wheel, draw thou that man to my house.

[14] Thrice I offer a libation, and thrice say I these words, O venerable goddess! 'Whether woman lies beside him, or even man, may as much of oblivion hold him, as, they say, *held* Theseus of yore, *when* in [15] Dia he forgot Ariadne of the beauteous locks.'

Wheel, draw thou that man to my house.

[16] Hippomanes is a plant among the Arcadians: after it all the colts and fleet mares along the mountains are mad. So may I see Delphis also arrive even at this house, like unto a madman, from out the glowing palæstra.

Wheel, draw thou that man to my house.

[17]Delphis lost this border from his mantle, which I now, tearing in pieces, throw down on the raging fire. Alas, alas,

---

[12] ἀνὰ πτόλιν. Virg. Æn. vi., Visæque canes ululare per urbem
        Adventante Deâ.
Compare Statius Theb. iv. 429. Of Diana Trivia, see Ovid Trist. iv. 4, 73.

[13] The poets loved to represent the winds, waves, and all nature calm and placid at the approach of Deity. See Virg. Ecl. ix. 57,

    Et nunc omne tibi stratum silet æquor, et omnes,
    Aspice, ventosi ceciderunt murmuris auræ.

See also the description (Æn. iv. 522, &c.) of Nature hushed in sleep, but Dido still awake through cares.

[14] Virg. Ecl. viii. 73, Terque hæc altaria circum effigiem duco, &c.

[15] Naxos, where Theseus left Ariadne, was anciently called Dia. See Catull. Nupt. Pelei el Thel. lxiii. 122.

[16] Hippomanes.] See Virg. Georg. iii. 280, who disagrees with Theocritus in the nature of this ingredient in charms. Virg., in Æn. iv. 515, calls it "Nascentis equi de fronte revulsus Et matri præreptus amor."

[17] Virg. Ecl. viii. 91,
    Has olim exuvias mihi perfidus ille reliquit
    Pignora cara sui.

See also Æn. iv. 495.

grievous Eros, why hast thou drunk out all the dark blood from my flesh, clinging like a leech from the marsh?[18]

Wheel, draw thou that man to my house.

[19] For thee, *Delphis*, having bruised a lizard, to-morrow I will bring a baneful potion. But now, Thestylis, take you these drugs and smear them above that man's door-post, to which, ay even now, I am bound in affection, (yet he takes no account of me!) and [20] say as you spit upon it, I smear the bones of Delphis.

Wheel, draw thou that man to my house.

Now then, being alone, from what source shall I bewail my love? Whence shall I begin? Who brought this evil upon me? Anaxo, the daughter of Eubulus, came to me, [21] bearing a basket to the grove of Artemis: and for her in truth then many other wild beasts were going in procession round about, and among them a lioness.

[22] Observe my love, whence it arose, O Lady Moon!

And Theucharila, the Thracian nurse of blessed memory, dwelling near my doors, begged and prayed me *to go and* view the procession, and I, all wretched as I am, followed her, [23] trailing a fair tunic of fine-linen, [24] and having clad myself in the fine robe-and-train of Clearista.

Observe my love, whence it arose, O Lady Moon!

[18] Horace, Ars Poetica, 476,
   Non missura cutem nisi plena cruoris hirudo.
[19] A favourite ingredient for hell-broths. See Macbeth, act iv. sc. 1,
   Lizard's leg, and owlet's wing,
   For a charm of powerful trouble,
   Like a hell-broth boil and bubble.
[20] Tibull. Ter cane, ter dictis despue carminibus. I. ii. 56.
[21] καναφόρος. The basket-bearer, a maiden at Athens, who carried on her head a basket at the festivals of Demeter, Bacchus, and Athena. See Liddell and Scott, Gr. Lex. ad voc. Dict. Gr. and Rom. Antiq. (Smith) p. 193. Cf. Idyll xxvi. 7. Callimach. Hymn to Ceres, vs. 1. The festival of Diana, the goddess of chastity, was the great time of match-making, when maidens about to marry deprecated the wrath of the goddess, carrying torches, baskets of flowers, and pans of incense, and leading animals in procession.
[22] πότνα, generally supposed to be the feminine of πόσις, "Lord," as δέσποινα of δεσπότης.
[23] βύσσοιο. See article "Byssus," in Dict. Gr. and Rom. Antiq. p. 169.
[24] Having clad myself,] i. e. having borrowed it for the occasion. The poorer classes used to hire fine dresses for festivals. Juvenal, vi. 364, Ut spectet ludos, conducit Ogulnia vestem. Cf. Eurip. Electr. 190.

²⁵ And when I was now about the middle of the road, where Lycon's *house* is, I beheld Daphnis and Eudamippus walking together: and their beards were yellower indeed than the marigold ²⁶ while their breasts shone far more than thou, O Moon, since they had but just left the noble toil of the palæstra.

Observe my love, whence it arose, O Lady Moon!

²⁷ And as I looked, how I maddened, how my heart, wretched woman *that I am*, was smitten through: my beauty too wasted away, and neither did I at all regard that procession, nor did I know how I returned home: but a disorder of a burning nature exhausted me; and I lay on my couch ten days and ten nights.

Observe my love, whence it arose, O Lady Moon!

And my skin indeed became like oftentimes to ²⁸ box-wood: and all my hair fell from my head: and only skin and bones were left any longer: and to whose house did I not go? Or the home of what old woman, that used incantations, did I ²⁹ miss? But there was no relief: and time kept passing fleetly.

Observe my love, whence it arose, O Lady Moon!

And so I told my slave the true statement. 'Come now, Thestylis, devise me some remedy for sore disorder. The Myndian possesses me wholly, wretched woman that I am. Go then, and watch at the palæstra of Timagetus, for thither he resorts, and there it is pleasant to him to sit.'

Observe my love, whence it arose, O Lady Moon!

'And whensoever you shall have learnt that he is alone, beckon quietly, and say that Simætha bids thee, and lead him hither.' Thus spoke I. And she went and brought to

---

²⁵ Virg. Ecl. ix. 59, Hinc adeo nobis media est via.

²⁶ See Theocr. Idyll. xviii. 26, and Tibull. iii. 4, 29, Candor erat, qualem præfert Latonia Luna.

²⁷ Ecl. viii. 41, Ut vidi, ut perii, ut me malus abstulit error. See Hom. Il. xiv. 294. Theocr. iii. 42.

²⁸ θάψῳ. According to the Scholiast, this was a plant brought from the island of Thapsus, of a yellowish colour, used for dyeing wool, and the hair. Hor. Od. x. 14, Book iii. Tinctus violâ pallor amantium. Ovid. Met. iv. 134, Oraque buxo Pallidiora gerens exhorruit. Hers, says Chapman, was a green and yellow melancholy.

²⁹ ἔλιπον—λείπειν often signifies prætermittere, as "relinquere" is sometimes used in Latin. Virg. Æn. vi. 509, Nihil, O, tibi amice relictum. Cicero, Verr. iii. 44, Prætereo et relinquo. Eurip. Androm. 299, τίν' οὐκ ἐπῆλθε; ποῖον οὐκ ἐλίσσετο Δαμογερόντων.

my house the sleek-skinned Delphis. But, when I beheld him just crossing with light foot the threshold of the door;
  Observe my love, whence it arose, O Lady Moon;
[30] I became more chilled than snow all over, and from my brow perspiration began to stream down, like the southern dews. Neither was I able to say any thing, not even as much as children in sleep murmur forth, calling to their dear mother; but I became stiff in my fair body, all over, like a plaster [31] doll.
  Observe my love, whence it arose, O Lady Moon!
  And when he had looked on me, the cruel man, having fixed his eyes on the ground, sate upon the couch, and as he sate spake thus! 'Surely, Simætha, thou hast [32] been as much beforehand with me, inasmuch as thou invitedst me to thy house before that I arrived there, as I in sooth some time ago was beforehand with graceful Philinus in the race.'
  Observe my love, whence it arose, O Lady Moon!
  'For I too would have come, yea, by sweet Eros I would have come, with [33] two or three friends immediately at nightfall, keeping in my bosom the apples [34] indeed of Bacchus, and having on my head a wreath of poplar, sacred shoot of [35] Hercules, twined all round with purple ribbons.'
  Observe my love, whence it arose, O Lady Moon!
  'And if indeed ye should have received me, this would

---

[30] Æn. iii. 308, Diriguit visu in medio: calor ossa reliquit. Compare Sappho, Od. ix. Propert. ii. 18, 12. Apollon. Rhod. iii. 954, &c., the meeting of Medea and Jason.

[31] δαγύς, a wax doll, used in magic rites; a puppet, called by Callimach. in Cerer. 91, πλαγγών, from πλάσσω, and by the Attics, (see Schol. at this place,) κόρα. Briggs suggests that one of the meanings of δαγύς is "coral."

[32] The construction is ἔφθασας καλέσασα, ἢ μεπαρεῖναι, τόσον ὅσον ἔφθασα. There is no need to understand πριν; the force of which is contained in ἔφθασας.

[33] τρίτος ηε τέταρτος ἰὼν φίλος—"Cum duobus aut tribus aliis amatoribus," i. e. I would have come myself the third or fourth. A common phrase in Greek poets and prose writers. Cf. Hom. Odyss. xx. 185.— αὐτικὰ νυκτός, (understand γενομένης,) "Simul ac nox appetisset."

[34] Apples, as lovers' presents, are mentioned, iii. 10; xi. 10. Some say the apples of Bacchus mean pomegranates.

[35] Virg. Ecl. vii. 61, Populus Alcidæ gratissima. Georg. ii. 66, Herculeæque arbos umbrosa coronæ. Æn. viii. 286, Populeis adsunt evincti tempora ramis.

have been agreeable, for I am called active and beautiful among all the youths. And I should have been [36] at rest, if only I had kissed thy beauteous mouth. But if ye repelled me to some other quarter, and the door was held by a bar, by all means then axes [37] and torches should have come against you.'

Observe my love, whence it arose, O Lady Moon!

'But now I declare that I owe thanks indeed to Venus first, and after Venus, thou in the second place hast plucked me, maiden, from the fire, by having invited me to this thine house, when I was absolutely half consumed. For Eros in sooth ofttimes kindles a hotter blaze than even Liparæan Vulcan.'

Observe my love, whence it arose, O Lady Moon!

'And, by the aid of baneful phrensy, he is wont to hurry away both the virgin from her woman's chamber, and the wedded wife having just deserted the warm bed of her husband.[38]' Thus he indeed spoke. But I, too-credulous woman, having seized his hand, made him recline on the soft couch.

And quickly body was warmed by body, and our faces grew hotter than before: and we were whispering sweetly. And that I may not prate to thee too long, dear Moon, greatest things took place, and we both reached the object of our desire. And neither at all did that man find fault with me up to yesterday, nor I on the other hand with him: but there came to me to-day [39] the mother of Philista, her, I mean, who is my flute-player, and of Melixo, *to-day*, even when the

---

[36] See Sophocl. Fragm. 563. Εὐδούσῃ φρενί, a mind at rest, listless. Tibullus uses "securus" in the same sense, I. i. 48. So "dormire." Horat. Sat. ii. 1, 6, Peream male si non
    Optimum erat, verum nequeo *dormire*.
Juvenal i. 77, Quem patitur *dormire* nurus corruptor avaræ.

[37] Tibull. i. 1, 73,
    Nunc levis est tractanda Venus, dum frangere postes
    Non pudet et rixas inseruisse juvat.
Horat. i. Od. 25, Parciùs junctas quatiunt fenestras,
    Ictibus crebris juvenes protervi.
Compare Horat. Od. iii. 26, 7.

[38] Supply *no wonder then if he overcomes you.*

[39] The mother of Philista and Melixo, the former a flute-player, the latter probably a dancer, (for the flute-player and dancer were usual accompaniments of Greek feasts,) was present with her daughters at a banquet, where she learned the faithlessness of Delphis.

steeds were coursing up to heaven, bearing the rosy-armed dawn from the ocean. And she told me much else, indeed, and that in sooth Delphis is in love: but whether again love for a woman possesses him, or for a man, she said that she knows not accurately: but only thus much, that he [40] was pouring forth of unmixed wine to Eros, and at last went hurriedly [41] away: and she said that he was going to cover that house *of his love* with wreaths. These things my friend has told me: and she is truthful. For certainly at other times he was wont to resort to me thrice and four times *a day:* and often would leave with me the Dorian oil-flask: but now 'tis even twelve days since I have ever seen him. Has he not then some other delight, and *has he not* forgotten me? Now indeed I will compel him by love-charms; and if he should still vex me also, by the Fates *I swear* he shall knock at the gate of Hades. Such baneful drugs I affirm that I am keeping [42] for him in a box, having learned them, O Queen, from an Assyrian stranger. But fare thou well, and turn thy steeds, *dread* Lady, toward ocean. And I will bear my trouble, even as I have undertaken. Farewell, bright complexioned [43] Moon, and farewell, ye other stars, attendants on the chariot of stilly night.

[40] See xiv. 18. To drink of unmixed wine as a toast to any one. ἐπιχεῖσθαι. οὕνεκα is for ὅθουνεκα or ὅτι—ἀκράτου depends on τι understood, and ἔρωτος is another genitive case of the person pledged. See Aristoph. Eq. 106, σπονδὴν λαβὲ δή, καὶ σπεῖσον, ἀγαθοῦ δαίμονος. Callimach. Epig. xxxi. ἔγχει καὶ πάλιν εἰπέ, Διοκλέος. Meleag. Ep. 98, ἔγ- 'ει καὶ πάλιν εἰπέ πάλιν, πάλιν, Ἡλιοδώρας.
Wordsworth seems to prefer to make ἀκράτω agree with ἔρωτος. In f debat de liquore meraco Amoris. As he observes, " Amore ebrius," is frequent idea of Theocritus and other poets. Catullus, xlv. 11, speaks o' '" ebrios ocellos," with reference to a lover.
Lucret. iv. 1171,
At lacrumans exclusus amator limina sæpe
Floribus et sertis operit, posteisque superbos
Unguit amaracino, et foribus miser oscula figit.
[42] See Virg. Ecl. viii. 95,
Has herbas atque hæc Ponto mihi lecta venena
Ipse dedit Mœris, nascuntur plurima Ponto.
Tibull. i. v. 15, Ipse ego velatus filo, tunicâque recenti
Vota novem Triviæ nocto silente dedi.
[43] Tibull. ii. 1, 87,
Jam nox jungit equos, currumque sequuntur
Matris lascivo sidera fulva choro.

c

IDYLL III.

THE GOATHERD, OR AMARYLLIS, OR THE SERENADER.

ARGUMENT.

A goatherd, the care of his flock having been intrusted to the shepherd Tityrus, goes to the cave of his sweet-heart Amaryllis; and there, after many complaints of her estranged affections, endeavours by gifts, entreaties, rage, and threats, to re-awaken her former love for him. Then, in hopes she may come nearer, and in order to fix her heart and eyes on himself, he sings a sweet melody and recounts the men of old, whose love Venus has favoured. At last, seeing that she is deaf ever to this, he gives way to despair. The Scholiast thinks the scene is laid in the country about Croto; and that Theocritus introduces himself under the character of the Goatherd. But there seem no sufficient grounds for the assumption.

[1] I GO a-serenading to Amaryllis; whilst my goats brows on the mountain, and Tityrus drives them. Tityrus, belove by me in the highest degree, feed my she-goats; and lea them to the fountain, Tityrus; and mind that tawny Libya he-goat, lest he butt thee.

O graceful Amaryllis, why do you not any longer pee forth at this cave, and call me, your sweet-heart? Do yo really hate me? Or is it that, forsooth, when near, I appe to thee, O nymph, to be flat-nosed and long-chinned? [2] Y will make me hang myself. [3] Lo, I bring thee ten apple and I plucked them from that *tree*, from which you ba me pluck them: and to-morrow I will bring thee mo Regard, I pray you, my heart-grieving pain. [4] I would could become your buzzing bee, and *so* enter into your ca penetrating the ivy and the fern, with which you are cove

---

[1] See how closely Virgil has borrowed this, Eclog. ix. 21—25,
   Vel quæ sublegi tacitus tibi carmina nuper,
   Cum te ad delicias ferras Amaryllida nostras.
   Tityre, dum redeo, brevis est via, pasce capellas
   Et potum pastas age, Tityre, et inter agendum
   Occursare capro, cornu ferit ille, caveto.
Comp. Ecl. v. 24. Tibull. II. iii. 15.
   [2] Virg. Ecl. ii. 7, Mori me denique coges.
   [3] Ecl. iii. 70, Aurea mala decem misi : cras altera mittam.
   [4] Compare Psalm lv. 6, "Oh that I had wings like a dove! for would I fly away, and be at rest," &c.

in. ⁵ Now know I Eros! cruel god! Surely he sucked the teat of a lioness, and in a thicket his mother reared him. *For it is he* who is consuming me, and wounding me even to the bone. O you that look all-beautifully, *and yet* are altogether stone, ⁶ O dark-browed nymph, embrace me, your goatherd, that *so* I may kiss you. There is sweet delight even in empty kisses.' You will make me immediately pluck into small pieces the wreath which I am keeping for you, dear Amaryllis, of ivy *leaves*, having interwoven it with ⁷ rosebuds and sweet-scented parsley. O woe is me! what will become of me? What ⁸ of me, lost man that I am! Do you not hear me? Throwing off my coat of ⁹ skins, I will leap into the waves yonder, where Olpis the fisherman is watching for the tunnies. And even if I shall not have perished, thy pleasure at all events has been done. I learned *my fate* but lately, when upon my bethinking me whether you loved me, ¹⁰ not even did the poppy leaf coming in contact make a sound, but withered away just so upon my soft arm. Agræo too, the prophetess of the sieve, who was lately going beside the reapers, and sheaving up the corn, told me the true tale, that I indeed am wholly devoted to you; but you take no

⁵ Ecl. viii. 43, Nunc scio quid sit Amor. Comp. Æn. iv. 365—367, and Pope Past. iii. 88,

      I know thee, Love; on foreign mountains bred,
      Wolves gave thee suck, and savage tigers bred.

Catull. l. and lxiii. 154.
⁶ Chapman here quotes Spenser,

      A thousand graces on her eyelids sate,
      Under the shadow of her even brows.

⁷ Virg. Ecl. viii. 43, Floribus atque apio crines ornatus amaro.
⁸ Ecl. ii. 58, Heu heu quid volui misero mihi.
⁹ Pope Past. iii. 95, One leap from yonder cliff shall end my pains. Virg. Ecl. viii. 59, 60,

      Præceps aerii speculâ de montis in undas,
      Deferar: extremum hoc morientis munus habeto.

This was Sappho's remedy for love. See Wordsworth's note on this passage. The tunny fishing is fully described by Oppian, Halieut. iii. 637, and Herodotus, bk. i. chap. 62.

¹⁰ Lovers were wont to guess by the poppy leaf, or anemonè, placed between forefinger and thumb of the left hand, and then struck by the right, whether their love was reciprocated. ποτιμαξάμενον, in a middle sense; mordicùs adhærens. Wordsworth. The other mode of divination was common in this country in the days of witchcraft. See Ben Jonson's Alchymist, "Seeking for things lost through a sieve and shears."

account of me. In truth I am keeping [11] for you a white she-goat with two kids, which also the dark-skinned Erithacis, daughter of Mermnon, has been begging of me: and I will give it to her, since you play the coquet with me. [12] My right eye throbs! I wonder whether I shall see her? I will sing, having reclined here beside the pine. And haply she may regard me, since she is not made of adamant. [13] Hippomenes, when in truth he was desirous to wed the maiden, took apples in his hands and accomplished the race: and when Atalanta beheld him, how she maddened, how she leapt into the depths of love! [14] The prophet Melampus too drove the herd from Othrys to Pylos: but she, the graceful mother of sensible Alphesibæa, reclined in the arms of Bias. And did not Adonis, tending his sheep on the mountains, drive the lovely Venus to such an excess of phrensy, that not even when he is dead, does she deprive him of her bosom? Enviable indeed to me is [15] Endymion, who enjoys his change-

[11] Virg. Ecl. ii. 40—44,
Præterea duo, nec tutâ mihi valle reperti,
Capreoli, sparsis etiam nunc pellibus albo;
Bina die siccant ovis ubera, quos tibi servo.
Jampridem a me illos abducere Thestylis orat
Et faciet: quoniam sordent tibi munera nostra.

[12] ἄλλεται, κ. τ. λ. This the Greeks and Egyptians deemed a good omen. The goatherd hopes from it that he shall see his love. Casaubon quotes here Plautus, Pseudol. I. i. 105,
 Ca. At id futurum unde? Ps. Unde? unde dicam? Nescio
 Nisi, quià futurum sit! ita supercilium salit.

[13] Hippomenes, son of Megareus, by aid of the golden apples given to him by Venus, won the race against Atalanta, daughter of Jasus and Clymene. Vid. Ovid. Met. x. 560—700. And Virg. Ecl. vi. 61, Tum canit Hesperidum miratam mala puellam, &c.

[14] Pero, the mother of Alphesibæa, was so beautiful, that her father Neleus promised her to him alone who should steal the bulls from Iphiclus. Melampus, to win the bride for his brother Bias, ran the risk, and was captured in the attempt by the herdsmen of Iphiclus. He was freed from prison through his art of Divination, and having received the oxen and delivered them to Neleus, he gained Pero in marriage for his brother. Propert. ii. 3, 51, Turpia perpessus vates est vincla Melampus,
 Cognitus Iphicli surripuisse boves.
 Quem non lucra, magis Pero formosa coegit,
 Mox Amithaoniâ nupta futura domo.
Comp. Hom. Odyss. xvi. 226.

[15] Upon Endymion, the lover of Luna, Jove sent eternal sleep, because Juno had been smitten with love of him. Ap. Rhod. iv. 57. Theocr. Id xx. 37.

less sleep: and I count happy, dear maiden, [16] Jasion, who obtained so many favours, as ye, that are uninitiated, shall not hear. My head is in pain. But you do not care. No more do I sing; but I will fall and lie low, and here the wolves shall eat me: that this may be *as* sweet honey down your throat.

IDYLL IV.

THE HERDSMEN; OR, BATTUS AND CORYDON.

ARGUMENT.

This Idyll is wholly of a Bucolic and mimic character. Two hireling herdsmen chat together without any fixed subject of conversation. The one, Corydon, is tending the herds of Ægon, who has become a wrestler and gone with Milo to the Olympic games. The other, Battus, is a man of a sarcastic turn, and keeps annoying his fellow with various sharp sayings; above all, predicting death to the ill-tended herds of Ægon. Corydon, being easy and good-tempered, answers him mildly. While they are chatting, the calves bark the straying olive branches, and Battus, driving them off, is pricked by a thorn. While Corydon is tending his wound, they spy the old father of Ægon, and get into a smart talk about his wanton way of living. This Idyll abounds in pictures of pastoral life and manners. Its scene is laid in the country, at the foot of an olive-clad hill. Virgil imitates it in his third Eclogue, together with the next Idyll.

Battus. [1] TELL me, Corydon, whose are these heifers? Are they *the property* of Philondas?

Corydon. No! but of Ægon! and he gave them to me to tend.

---

[16] Ceres came to Jasion while he slept. She became the mother of Pluto by him. Her mysteries were withheld from the common herd of men. Ovid Amor. III. x. 25,

    Viderat Iasium Cretæa Diva sub Idâ
      Figentem certâ terga ferina manu,
    Viderat: ut teneræ flammam rapuere medullæ
      (Hinc pudor, ex aliâ parte trahebat amor)
    Victus amore pudor.

Virg. Ecl. iii. 1, 2,
    Dic mihi, Damæta, cujum pecus? An Melibœi?
    Non, verum Ægonis; nuper mihi tradidit Ægon.

Batt. ² Do you happen any where to milk them all by stealth at even ?

Coryd. Nay, the old man puts the calves to their dams *to suck*, and watches me.

Batt. And to what quarter has the cowherd himself disappeared ?

Coryd. Have you not heard ? Milo has gone off with him to the ³ Alpheus.

Batt. ⁴ Why, when has that fellow seen oil with his eyes ?

Coryd. They say that in strength and force he vies with Hercules.

Batt. And *so* my mother said that I was better than Pollux.

Coryd. ⁵ And he is gone off with a hoe, and twenty sheep from hence.

Batt. ⁶ Milo, methinks, would persuade the wolves too to rave straightway.

Coryd. ⁷ But the young heifers here show their loss of him, *by* lowing.

Batt. ⁸ Ay, wretched are they ! How bad a cowherd they have found !

Coryd. ⁹ Why yes, in very truth *they are* wretched: and they no longer care to feed.

² ψε here is Doric for σφε, or σφεας, as ψιν for σφιν elsewhere. For the idea compare Virg. Ecl. iii. 6, Et succus pecori, et lac subducitur agnis.

³ The Alpheus was the chief river of the Peloponnese, in Elis. It flowed past Olympia, where the games were held, into the Ionian Sea. Milo is represented to have taken Ægon with him to the games.

⁴ A homely phrase, significative of the herdsman's wonder at an unexperienced and untrained man like his master, aspiring to the Olympic crown.

⁵ A hoe.] This was used by athletes for exercise, for thirty days previous. The "twenty sheep," show that Ægon was up to the mark of ancient wrestlers, at least in his powers of stomach.

⁶ Various readings have been suggested to make sense of this line, which, as it stands, lacks point. Eichstadt for αὐτίκα would read ἀμνίδα, and for καὶ τὼς λύκος, κάτ' τῶ λύκω. Another reading is λαγὸς (i. e. λαγοὺς) for λυκὸς. Dahl thinks the common reading will stand if we take τὼς for ὡς, and construe "τὼς λυκὸς like wolves, 'luporum instar.'" It will then be, "Milo would persuade him (Ægon) to be rabid like a wolf;" in allusion to his going off with twenty sheep. Battus seems to mean that Milo has no hard task to persuade one so wolf-like as Ægon, to a savage occupation.

⁷ Virg. Ecl. i. 36, Tityrus hinc aberat, &c.

⁸ Virg. Ecl. iii. 3, Infelix, O semper oves pecus.

⁹ Not unlike this is Pope's Past. iv. 37,

Batt. [10] Now of yon calf look you there is nothing but the bones left. Does she [11] feed on dew-drops, like the cicada?

Coryd. No! by earth. Sometimes I put her to graze near the [12] Æsarus, and give her a nice wisp of soft grass; and at other times she frolics in the neighbourhood of shady Latymnus.

Batt. Lean too is yon red bull? I would the members of the [13] Lamprian deme, look you, might light on such an one, when they sacrifice to Juno: for the deme is [14] in bad case.

Coryd. [15] And yet he is driven to the salt-water lake, and to the ground about Physcus, and to the *river* Neæthus, where all beautiful plants grow, cammock, and [16] flea-bane, and sweet-smelling baulm.

Batt. Fie, fie! these heifers also, O wretched Ægon, will go to Hades, since you too have become enamoured of an evil victory; and the pans-pipe, which you formerly put together, is besprinkled with mould.

Coryd. [17] Nay, not it! no, by the Nymphs: since as he was going off for Pisa, he left it to me for a gift: and I am [18] somewhat of a minstrel. And well indeed do I play the prelude

> For her the flocks refuse their verdant food;
> The thirsty heifers shun the gliding flood.

Add to these, Mosch. Idyll iii. 7 and 23.

[10] Ecl. iii. 102, Vix ossibus hærent.

[11] Ecl. v. 77, Dum rore cicadæ. Compare Plin. N. H. ii. 26, Habent in pectore fistuloso quiddam aculeatum—eo rorem lambunt, &c.

[12] Æsarus a river, and Latymnus a mountain, in that part of Italy called Magna Græcia, near to Croton. Livy xxiv. 3.

[13] Lampra was a deme at Athens. The Sicilians were fond of quizzing the Athenians, ob tenuem victum. Battus wishes evil to his enemies: a lean bull to a poor deme. For the line above, see Virg. Ecl. iii. 100, Eheu quàm pingui macer est mihi taurus in ervo.

[14] For κακοχράσμων some read κακοφράσμων, "of evil counsel."

[15] στομάλιμνον. Salt-water lake. According to Casaubon on a passage of Strabo, locum prope mare, qui ipsum mare suo ostio ingrediatur. D. Heinsius thought a certain spot in the district of Croto, the scene of the Idyll, was meant.

Physcus was a mountain near Croto. Neæthus, a river to the north of Croto. Ovid Met. xv. 51, Salentinumque Neæthum.

[16] κνύζᾳ, i. q. κόνυζα, flea-bane, cf. vii. 68. μελίτεια, i. q. μελισσο βότανον, apiastrum, baulm.

[17] Virg. Æn. ix. 208, Equidem de te nil tale verebar: nec fas; non.

[18] τίς, aliquis insignis, no mean minstrel. Compare Idyll xi. 79.

to the songs of [19] Glauca, and well to those of Pyrrhus. I celebrate Croton also: and a fair city is Zacynthus too: and *I celebrate* [20] Lacinium which looks eastward, where the boxer Ægon devoured, all alone, eighty cheese-cakes: and there he seized by the hoof and brought from the mountain the bull, and gave it to Amaryllis: and the women cried out loudly, whilst the herdsman laughed aloud.

Batt. O graceful Amaryllis, of thee alone, not even though thou art dead, shall we be forgetful: [21] dear as are my goats to me, so *wast thou dear who* hast died. Alas, alas for the exceeding hard fate which has possessed itself of me!

Coryd. One ought to take heart, friend Battus: perchance 'twill be better to-morrow. [22] Hopes *are* among the living: and the dead are beyond hope. And Jove is one while indeed fair, whilst at another time he rains.

Batt. I take heart. [23] Drive down yon calves: for the wretched creatures are nibbling the young shoots of the olive. St! away, you white-skin!

Coryd. Away, Cymætha, to the hillock. Don't you hear me? I will come, yes, by Pan, and soon make a bad end to you, if you do not get away from that! See, she is stealing back again thither. I would I had my crooked staff, that I might strike thee.

Batt. Look at me, Corydon, I pray you [24] by Jove. For

---

[19] Glauca—Pyrrhus.] The former was a Chian musician, in the time of Ptolemy Philadelphus. The latter, a composer of melodies, and native of Erythra or Lesbos.

[20] Lacinium, a promontory of the Bruttii, now Capo della Colonne. Zacynthus, a city of the island so called, near to Ætolia, mentioned by Livy, xxvi. 24, now called Zante. Croton, now Cotrone.

[21] The full construction would be, ὅσον αἱ αἶγες ἐμοὶ φίλαι εἰσί, τοσοῦτο σὺ φίλη εἶς, ἤ ἀπέσβης, i. e. ἀπέθανες. ὅσος—ὅσος and τόσος—τόσος stand promiscuously for tantus—quantus in the Pastoral Poets. Propertius in a like vein says,

    Tam multa illa meo divisa est millia lecto
    Quantum Hypanis Veneto dissidet Eridano. I. xii. 3.

[22] Tibullus, ii. 7, 1, 2,
    Credula vitam
    Spes fovet, et fore cras semper ait melius.
Comp. Eurip. Troad. 628,
    οὐ ταὐτὸν ὦ παῖ τῷ βλέπειν τὸ κατθανεῖν,
    τὸ μὲν γὰρ οὐδέν, τῷ δ' ἔνεισιν ἐλπίδες.

[23] Drive down,] i. e. by throwing his crook among them. Cf. Hom. Il xxiii. 845. Virg. Ecl. iii. 96, Tityre pascentes a flumina reice capellas.

[24] By Jove.] Compare Idyll v. 74; xv. 70.

the thorn has [25] just struck me here under the ancle : and how deep these [26] thistles are. A plague upon the heifer. I was wounded *in* gaping after her. Pray do you see it?

Coryd. Yes, yes, and I have it in my nails : and here it is.

Batt. How slight is the wound! and how great a man it brings low!

Coryd. When you go to the mountain, come not unshod, Battus : for on the mountain flourish both [27] prickly shrubs and white thorns.

Batt. Come tell me, Corydon, does the little old man still court that dark-eyebrowed love of his, with whom he was formerly smitten?

Coryd. Ay to the full, O wretch. Only lately at any rate I myself, having come upon him, surprised him by the fold when he was at work.

Batt. Well done, lecher! thy race in sooth closely rivals either the Satyrs or the thin-shanked Pans.

IDYLL V.

THE WAYFARERS, OR COMPOSERS OF PASTORALS.

ARGUMENT.

Two hirelings, one of Eumaras, a goatherd of Sybaris, the other of a shepherd of Thurium, meeting each other with their flocks, mutually provoke a conflict of words. At last, after many recriminations, the one challenges the other to a contest in singing : and when they have disputed much about the prize for the victor, and the spot for the trial, they fetch one Morson, a woodcutter, for umpire. They engage in an

---

[25] ἁρμοῖ, a Syracusan or Doric word : which is explained to be the same as ἀρτίως or νεωστί.

[26] ἀτρακτυλλίς. Carthamus lanatus. Linnæus.

[27] Aspalathus, the rose of Jerusalem, a very prickly shrub. Rhamnus, a kind of thorny shrub, perhaps " gorse ? "
 Calpurnius Siculus had this psssage in view, when he wrote Ecl. iii. 4,
  Duris ego perdita ruscis
  Jamdudum, et nullis dubitabam crura rubetis
   Scindere.

Amæbæan or alternate strain, in which, with no fixt subject, they wander through various topics, supplied either by the condition of the singers, the nature of the country and spot, the memory of the past, or by their very anger and inclination. At last Morson adjudges the prize to Comatas; who, on receiving it, brags of it proudly, and promises to offer a victim to the Nymphs. Much of this Idyll, though not to the taste of our more refined age, is yet eminent for its poetic power and lively colouring of rustic manners. Its scene is a glade near Sybaris in Lower Italy. Virgil has gathered from the Idyll many of the verses, as well as the plan, of his third Eclogue.

COMATAS AND LACON.

Comatas. My she-goats, shun yon shepherd of [1] Sybartas, Lacon: yesterday he stole my goat-skin.

Lacon. [2] St! Won't you be off from the fountain, my lambkins? Do you not spy Comatas, that lately stole my pipe?

Com. What sort of pipe, *pray?* Why, when did you, slave of Sybartas, get possession of a pipe? [3] And why are you no longer content to have a pipe of straw, and to hiss on it, with Corydon?

Lac. 'Tis one which Lycon gave me, [4] my gentleman! but what sort of goat-skin in the world have I, Lacon, stolen from you and gone off with? Tell me, Comatas: for not even had your master Eumaras *one* to sleep on.

Com. That which Crocylus gave me, the spotted one, when he had sacrificed the she-goat to the Nymphs: [5] but you, rascal, were even then wasting yourself away with envy, [6] and now at last you have stripped me of it.

[1] We seem obliged, for sense, to adopt Hermann's reading, τόνδε Συβάρτα, sc. δοῦλον. For we gather from vss. 72—74, that Comatas, the goatherd, was slave to Eumaras of Sybaris, and Lacon, a shepherd, slave to Sybartas of Thurium. Both these cities were of Magna Græcia, in the south of Italy.

[2] οὐκ ἀπό. See verse 102. Aristoph. Acharn. 864, οἱ σφῆκες οὐκ ἀπὸ τῶν θυρῶν.

[3] Virg. Ecl. iii. 25, Non tu in triviis, indocte, solebas
     Stridenti miserum stipulâ disperdere carmen.
Whence in Milton's Lycidas—
    Their lean and flashy songs,
  Grate on their scrannel pipes of wretched straw.

[4] ὦ ἐλεύθερε seems to be spoken ironically, a retort called forth by Comatas, who had called Lacon δῶλε.

[5] Virg. Ecl. iii. 14, Et cum vidisti puero donata dolebas.

[6] βασκαίνων, envying, (from βάσκω or βάζω,) the verb signifies—

Lac. Nay, in truth, nay, by Pan who frequents the shore, I, Lacon, the son of [7]Calœthis, have not robbed you, at any rate of your goat-skin: or else, my man, may I leap down yon rock madly into the Crathis.[8]

Com. No, in truth, no, by these Nymphs of the marsh, my good sir : and may they be both propitious and benevolent to me ! I, Comatas, did not secretly steal your pipe.

Lac. Could I believe you, I would undertake the sorrows of Daphnis. But however, if you choose to stake a kid, [9](for 'tis nothing wonderful !) why then I will go on contending with you in song, until you shall have cried "enough."

Com. [10] The sow strove a strife with Minerva ! See, there lies the kid : [11] but come, do you match *against it* the well-fed lamb.

Lac. And pray how, thou shameface ; will *these terms* be fair between us ? Whoever sheared for himself hair instead of wool ? and who, when a goat that has borne her first young is at hand, [12] prefers to milk a filthy bitch ?

Com. Whosoever is confident, as you are, that he shall surpass his neighbour, a buzzing wasp against a cicala. But however the kid is no equal stake to thee : do you contend ; *for* lo, here is the he-goat.

Lac. Be in no hurry : [13] for you are not scorched by fire :

1st, to slander ; 2nd, to bewitch, fascinare, in which sense it is used at Theocr. vi. 39, and at St. Paul's Ep. to Galat. iii. 1 ; and, 3rd, to envy.

[7] ὁ Καλαίθιδος. This naming of his mother instead of his father, seems to mark the low rank of this slave.

[8] Κρᾶθιν, a river of Magna Græcia, flowing near Sybaris, and having a temple of Pan near its banks. Æschyl. (Pers. 454, Blomf.) shows that Pan was wont to haunt the shores.

[9] Est quidem nihil magnum cantu te vincere. A proverb arising, so says the Scholiast, from Hercules's scorn at finding worship paid to Adonis at Dium of Macedonia. "A cat may look at a king," is something similar.

[10] A proverb significative of a contest between the wise and foolish. Such comparisons occur at Idyll i. 136 ; v. 136. Virg. Ecl. ix. 36, Argutos inter strepere anser olores. Cf. Ecl. viii. 55.

[11] ἔρειδε, the regular Greek word, for staking any prize, which the Latins call "deponere." See Virg. Ecl. iii. 31 ; ix. 62, Hic hædos depone.

[12] δῆλεται, a Doric form for βούλεται. Δήλεσθαι, θέλειν, βούλεσθαι. Hesychius. Two lines above we have adopted Wordsworth's reading, ὦ κίναδος σύ—

[13] A proverb dissuasive of hurry ; for the next verse, compare Virg Ecl. x. 42, 43,

you will sing more sweetly, when you have taken your seat here under the wild olive and these groves: there cool water flows down: here springs herbage, and here is a bed of grass, and the locusts chirp here.[14]

Com. Nay, I do not hurry at all! but I am greatly annoyed, since you, whom once, when you were yet a boy, I used to teach, dare now to look me [15] straight in the face. See to what the favour comes! Rear even wolf's [16] whelps, rear dogs, that they may eat you.

Lac. And when do I remember to have learned or even heard from you aught good, O you envious and absolutely disgraceful mannikin?

Com. [17] * * * * * * * * *
* * * * * * * *
Lac. * * * * * *
But however come, come hither, and you shall sing pastorals for the last time?

Com. [18] I will not approach thither! here are oaks: here *is* 'galingale:' [19] here bees buzz sweetly at their hives. Here

    Hic gelidi fontes, hic mollia prata, Lycori,
    Hic nemus.
Compare Calpurnius, Ecl. i. 8, &c.,
    Hoc potius, frater Corydon, nemus, ista petamus
    Antra patris Fauni, graciles ubi pinea densat
    Silva comas.
For καὶ τἄλσεα, Wordsworth reads neatly κἀπ' ἄνθεα, under the flowering shrubs.

[14] ἀκριδες, the locusts, whatever they were, are constantly mentioned by Theocritus in terms of praise for their song.

[15] Cf. Horat. i. 3, 18, Qui siccis oculis monstra natantia, &c.

[16] For a most graphic illustration of this sentiment, compare Æsch. Agamemnon, 717—734, Dindorf. Compare too St. Matth. vii. 6, "Neither cast ye your pearls before swine, lest they trample them under their feet, and turn again and rend you."

[17] Sensu obscœno.
    Com. Quum prædicabam te tuque dolebas—capellæ autem
    Istæ balabant; et caper eas terebrabat.
    Lac. Ne profundius illâ pædicatione, O gibbose, sepeliaris.

[18] κύπειρος, a sweet-smelling marsh plant, probably 'galingal.' Hom. Hymn to Merc. 107.

[19] Virg. Eclog. vii. 13, Eque sacra resonant examina quercu.
Chapman has enriched his notes to his admirable translation with many gems of English poetry; and in no place more so than on this passage, upon which he quotes Ben Jonson's Faithful Shepherdess; and Shak-

are two fountains of cool water, and the birds on the trees are chirping: and the shade is nowise like that with you: but the pine also showers down cones from above.

Lac. [20] In good truth here you shall tread upon lamb-skins and wool, if you shall have come, softer than slumber: whereas the goat-skins that are beside you smell stronger than even you smell: [21] and I will set up a great bowl of white milk in honour of the Nymphs: and I will set also another of sweet oil.

Com. But if you shall come, too, here you shall tread soft fern, and flowering [22] penny-royal: and underneath shall be skins of kids, four times as soft as your lambs. And I will set up to Pan eight pails of milk, and eight bowls of honey having full combs.

Lac. Contend with me there: and there sing your pastoral. Treading your own ground keep to the oaks. [23] But who, who shall judge us? Would that by hap the herdsman Lycopas would come hither.

Com. I want nothing of him. But if you will, we will call in the oak-cutter who is gathering the heather there beside you. And it is Morson.

Lac. Let us shout.

Com. Call you him.

Lac. Come, friend, come hither and listen a little, for we are contending which is the better pastoral minstrel. But do not you, good Morson, either decide on me by favour, nor on the other hand, help this man as far as you are concerned.

Com. Yes, by the Nymphs, dear Morson, neither assign the advantage to Comatas: nor do you for your part favour this man here. This, look you, is the flock of Sybartas of Thu-

---

speare's Midsummer Night's Dream; and the Merchant of Venice, act v. sc. 1. These will requite a reference.

[20] Compare Idyll xv. 125, πορφύρεοιδε τάπητες ἄνω, μαλακώτεροι ὕπνω. Virg. Ecl. vii. 45, Somno mollior herba. Pope, seemingly borrowing from Antipater, has the line,

"The sleepy eye that told the melting soul."

[21] Compare Virg. Ecl. v. 67, Craterasque duo statuam tibi pinguis olivi.

[22] γλάχων, pulegium, 'penny-royal.' Polwhele translates it the horned-poppy.

[23] Virg. Ecl. iii. 50, Audiat hæc tantum vel qui venit, ecce Palæmon. And ibid. 53, Tantum, vicine Palæmon,
Sensibus hæc imis, res est non parva, reponas.

rium, and you see, friend, the goats of Eumaras, the Sybarite.

Lac. Did any one ask you, by Jove, whether 'tis the flock of Sybartas or my own, most worthless fellow? how babbling you are!

Com. My most worthy sir, I indeed am declaring the whole truth, and am not bragging at all: but you are too fond of jeering.

Lac. [24]Come, say on, if you have aught to say! and let the stranger off [25]again with his life to the city. O Pæan, surely thou wert a talkative fellow, Comatas!

Com. [26]The Muses love me far more than the minstrel Daphnis: and I sacrificed to them two kids but very lately.

Lac. Well! Apollo loves me greatly: and I am feeding a fine ram for him. But the [27]Carneian festival is even now coming on.

Com. I am milking the rest of the she-goats with twins except two: and the damsel beholding me says, Wretched man, do you milk by yourself?

[24] λέγειν here signifies "canere," as "dicere" often among the Latin poets. Dicite, quandoquidem in molli consedimus herbâ, Virg. Ecl. iii. 55. For the like form of speech, see Virg. Ecl. iii. 52, Quin age, si-quid habes.

[25] ζῶντ' ἄφες, a proverb relating to garrulous persons. Plautus. Miles gloriosus, iv. 2, 29, Jamjam sat, amabo, est, sinite abeam, si possum viva a vobis.

[26] "Of these Amæbæic songs as existing a century before Theocritus, Livy has left a remarkable notice, in which he shows that they were produced extemporaneously by the respective candidates, the art being evidently of Tuscan origin. Liv. vii. 401, Imitari deinde eos juventus simul inconditis inter se jocularia fundentes versibus cœpere. Incompositum temerè ac rudem alternis jaciebant." E. Pococke on Gr. Pastoral Poetry, in the Encyclopædia Metropolit. All nations seem to have known this custom; something of a very similar nature forms, I believe, a portion of the Welsh Eisteddvods.

[27] Virg. Ecl. iii. 62,
  Et me Phœbus amat: Phœbo sua semper apud me
  Munera sunt.

The Carneian festival was observed by the Spartans and Doric race in early winter, on the 7th day of the month, (thence called Carneian,) in honour of Apollo, whose priest Carnus was slain by Aletas, one of the Heraclids. Vid. Callimach. H. in Apollinem, 71, 78, 85.

  Ἦ ῥ' ἐχάρη, μέγα Φοῖβος, ὅτε ζωστῆρες Ἐνυοῦς
  Ἀνέρες ὠρχήσαντο μετὰ ξανθῆσι Λιβυσσῆς
  Τέθμιαι εὖτέ σφιν Καρνειάδες ἤλυθον ὧραι.

See Spanheim, at that passage.

Lac. Alas, alas, Lacon fills, look you, nearly twenty baskets with cheese: and caresses the beardless boy amid the flowers.

Com. [28] Clearista too pelts the goatherd with apples, as he drives his goats past: and cries 'hist' after a sweet fashion.

Lac. Why me too the shepherd, smooth Cratidas, maddens, as he meets me: [29] and about his neck waves glossy hair.

Com. But [30] sweet brier and anemone are not to be compared with roses, beds of which grow beside the hedge-rows.

Lac. Why no, nor are wild-apples with acorns. The latter indeed have a thin soft bark from the holm-oak; but the former are sweet as honey.

Com. And I indeed will give presently to the maiden a ring-dove, having taken it from the juniper—for there it broods.

Lac. [31] But I will present to Cratidas, myself, a soft-fleece for a cloak, whensoever I shall have shorn the dusky sheep.

Com. St! Off from yon wild olive, ye bleating ones: feed here, at this sloping hillock, where the tamarisks are.

Lac. Won't you be off there from the oak, you, Comarus! and you, Cynætha? Ye shall feed here to the east, as Phalarus does.

Com. But I have a pail of cypress-wood, and I have a goblet, the work of Praxiteles: and I am keeping these for my maiden.

Lac. And I have a dog fond of the flock, which throttles the wolves: and I am keeping him for the lad, to chase all wild beasts.

Com. Ye locusts, that overleap my fence, do not spoil my vines, [32] for they are young.

---

[28] Apples were sacred to Venus, Idyll iii. 40. Virg. copies this passage, Ecl. iii. 64, Malo me Galatea petit, lasciva puella.

[29] Horat. III. xx. 14, Sparsum odoratis humerum capillis. In the preceding line, Wordsworth suggests ἀμός for λεῖος, comparing Virg. Ecl. i. 56.

[30] κυνόσβατος, dog-thorn, rubus caninus, L. and S.

[31] Virg. Ecl. iii. 68, 69,
Parta meæ Veneri sunt munera: namque notavi,
Ipse locum, aeriæ quo congessere palumbes.
Shenstone,—I have found out a gift for my fair,
I have found where the wood-pigeons breed.

[32] ἄβαι, h. e. ἡβῶσαι καὶ ἀκμάζουσαι. Virg. Georg. iii. 126, Pubentes herbæ. Wordsw. would read ὤμαι, unripe. Cf. Theocr xi. 21, ὄμφακος ὠμᾶς.

Lac. Ye cicalas, see how I vex the goatherd! So ye too, in truth, vex the reapers.

Com. I hate the bush-tailed foxes, which are ever going and [33] gathering the grapes of Micon at evening.

Lac. And so do I hate the may-bugs, which devour the figs of Philondas, and are borne off with the wind.

Com. Don't you remember when I beat you, and you, showing your teeth, [34] wriggled famously, and clung to yon oak?

Lac. This indeed I do not recollect! When however once upon a time Eumaras bound you here, and [35] dusted your jacket, that at all events I know very well.

Com. At length, Morson, some one is growing angry: Have you not slightly perceived it? Go and pluck old squills forthwith from the tomb.

Lac. I too, Morson, am vexing some one! ay, and you perceive it. Go then to [36] the Hales, and dig up the sow-bread.

Com. May the [37] Himera flow with milk instead of water! and mayest thou too, Crathis, grow purple with wine! [38] and may the yellow-water cresses, look you, bear fruit!

Lac. And for my sake may the fountain of Sybaris flow

---

[33] ῥαγίσδονται, gather grapes, from ῥάξ, a grape. In the following verses, the one seems to hint at the other's thievish propensities.

[34] εὖ ποτεκιγκλίσδευ, Dor. for προσεκιγκλίζου, from προσκιγκλίζω, to move to and fro, and wag the tail at, from κίγκλος, a wagtail.

[35] ἐκάθηρε, "purgavit te," a metaphor to which Plautus, Menæchm. 915, has a parallel, i. e. Pecte pugnis, "dress 'em well with your fists." Cf. Terent. Heaut. v. i. 78, depexum. Plaut. Capt. 823, Fusti pectito. Pænul. 227, Ne tu hunc pugnis pectas. Rud. 564, Leno pugnis pectitur—πλύνειν, νίπτειν, σμήχειν, λέπειν, are similar euphemisms for giving a man a beating.

[36] Hales, a river of Lucania in Italy. κυκλάμινος, cyclamen or sow-bread, a tuberous-rooted plant with a fragrant flower used in garlands. (Liddell and Scott.) It appears to have been used to cure madness.

[37] Ἱμέρα, a river in the west of Sicily (now Fiume di Termini). Crathis, a river of Lucania, flowing into the Gulf of Tarentum, near the town of Sybaris. Compare Eurip. Bacch. 142, ῥεῖ δέ γάλακτι πέδον Add Ovid. Met. I. iii.,

    Flumina jam lactis, jam flumina nectaris ibant,
    Flavaque de viridi stillabant ilice mella.

And Numbers xvi. 13, "A land flowing with milk and honey."

ῥείτω γάλα. Several intransitive verbs are used by poets as transitive, with an accusative of the object. Math. Gr. Gr. § 423. Eurip. Hec. 531

[38] Virg. Ecl. iii. 89, Mella fluant illi, ferat et rubus asper amomum.

with honey! and, towards dawn, may the maiden in her pitcher ³⁹ draw combs instead of water!

Com. My goats indeed eat hadder and ægilus, and tread on mastich-twigs, and lie among arbute-trees!

Lac. But my sheep have at hand baulm to browse, and the wild eglantine, too, blooms in abundance, like roses.

Com. I love not Alcippe, for but lately she did not kiss me, having caught me ⁴⁰ by the ears; what time I gave her the ring-dove.

Lac. But I love Eumedes vastly: for when I held out the pipe to him, he kissed me in a very sweet manner.

Com. 'Tis not right, Lacon, that jays should contend with a nightingale, or ⁴¹ hoopoos with the swans: but you, wretched man, are prone to strife.

Morson. I bid the shepherd cease! And to thee, Comatas, Morson presents the lamb: and *so* do you sacrifice to the Nymphs, and presently send a fine *portion of* meat to Morson.

Com. I will send it, yes, by Pan. Wanton now, all my herd of he-goats! For see how great is the laugh that I also shall raise against this Lacon the shepherd, ⁴² because at last I have gained the lamb: I will leap for you to heaven. Be of good cheer, my horned she-goats: ⁴³ to-morrow I will wash you all in the fountain of Sybaris. You, sir, the white goat, ⁴⁴ that butt-with-the-horn, if you molest any of the she goats, I will beat you, yes, before I sacrifice the ewe-lamb to the

---

³⁹ βάψαι, "to dip," here used for "to draw," ἀρύσασθαι. Eurip. Hipp. 121, βαπτὰν παγάν. Eurip. Hecub. 605, βάψασ' ἔνεγκέ δεῦρο ποντίας ἁλός. Four lines below this Wordsw. would read for ὡς ῥόδα κίστος, κ. τ. λ., πολλὸς δὲ βάτων ῥόδα κισσὸς ἐπανθεῖ. Hedera corymbos fundit super ruborum rosas.

⁴⁰ A kiss, which Suidas calls χύτρον, (the pot,) when the person was taken by both ears, is meant in this verse. It was afterwards called the Florentine. Tibullus mentions it, ii. 5, 92,

Gnatusque parenti
Oscula comprensis auribus eripiet.

So Plaut. Pœnul., Sine te exorem, sine te prendam auriculis, sine dem suavium

⁴¹ Virg. Ecl. viii. 55, Certent et cycnis ululæ

⁴² ἀνυσάμαν τὸν ἀμνόν, mihi confeci, lucratus sum. Idyll xviii. 17, ὡς ἀνύσαιο, ut (nuptias) consequerere. Cf. Aristoph. Plut. 196. Add. Propert. I. viii. 43, Nunc mihi summa licet contingere sidera plantis.

⁴³ Virg. Ecl. iii., Ipse, ubi tempus erit, omnes in fonte lavabo.

⁴⁴ ὁ κορύπτιλος, cornupeta. Ecl. ix. 25, Cornu ferit ille.

Nymphs. Yet he is at it again. Well, may I become [45] Melanthius, instead of Comatas, if I don't beat you.

IDYLL VI.

THE SINGERS OF PASTORALS.

ARGUMENT.

Damætas and Daphnis, having driven their herds to water, while away the time in Amæbœan strains. The youths picture Polyphemus seated on a rock overlooking the sea; and Galatea, his love, on the other hand, sporting in the waves at no great distance from the shore. Daphnis begins, directing his song to the Cyclops: and Damætas responds under the character of Polyphemus. The performance is ended by mutual presents between the swains. The Idyll is commended by the manner in which the character and temper of the Cyclops is shadowed forth. Its subject is the same as that of Idyll xi. Compare also Moschus, Idyll iii. 59—63.

DAMÆTAS and Daphnis, the herdsman, once drove the herd to one spot, [1] O Aratus: now one of them was reddish *in beard*, and the other had but half a one: and both of them, taking their seats at a certain fountain, in summer-time at mid-day, began to sing as follows. And Daphnis struck up first, since he too was first to challenge.

Daphnis. [2] Galatea, O Polyphemus, pelts your flock with apples, calling you the goat-herd inaccessible-to-love: and you do not regard her, wretched, wretched man, but sit playing sweetly on your pipe. See again, she is pelting the bitch,

---

[45] Melanthius, a suitor of Penelope, whose punishment by order of Ulysses is recorded by Homer, Odyss. xxii. 474—477.

[1] Aratus. This was the author of the Phænomena, a friend of our poet, and a native of Cilicia. He is the poet whom St. Paul quotes, Acts xvii. 28, Τοῦ γὰρ καὶ γένος ἐσμέν. He is again mentioned Idyll vii. 98, 102, 122. See Virg. Ecl. vii. 2, Compulerantque greges Corydon et Thyrsis in unum. Also Ecl. vii. 47.

Pope Past. ii. 84, 85,
 But see the shepherds shun the noon-day heat,
 The lowing herds to murmuring brooks retreat.

[2] Malo me Galatea petit, lasciva puella. Virg. Ecl. iii. 64.

which follows you as sheep-watch: but it is barking, looking toward the sea; and the fair waves, as they gently plash, [3] show it running on the shore. Take care, lest it rush against the legs of the damsel, as she comes forth from the brine, and tear her beauteous flesh. Yet she, even on the spur of the moment, coquets, like the dried down from a thistle, when the fine summer parches: and [4] she flies you, if you love her, and if you love her not, pursues you; and [5] moves the stone from the line: for surely, Polyphemus, ofttimes to love what is not fair, seems fair.

And after him Damætas struck up to sing sweetly.

Damætas. I saw her, yes, by Pan, when she was pelting my flock, and she escaped not my notice, no, by my one sweet eye, with which I look till the end *of my days;* [6] but may the prophet, Telemus, declaring hostile things, [7] carry off to his home what is hostile, that he may lay it up for his children. However, I myself too, *attempting* to vex her, do not regard her in turn; but say, that some other woman possesses me: and she, when she hears it, is jealous of me, O Pæan, and pines away: [8] and she runs wild, peering forth from the sea toward

---

[3] καχλάσδοντα. Compare Hippol. Eurip. 1210, περὶξ ἀφρὸν πολὺν καχλάζον. καχλάζειν, according to the Scholiast, is the same as ψοφεῖν, to plash against the pebbles of the beach.

[4] Terence has a similar notion of the coquettishness of woman-kind. Eunuch. iv. 7, 43, Nolunt ubi velis: ubi nolis, cupiunt ultrò. Compare B. Jonson, "Follow a shadow, it still flies ye," as quoted by Chapman.

[5] γραμμή, was a mid-line on a board, like our draught-board, also called ἡ ἱερά. Hence the proverb τὸν ἀπὸ γραμμῆς κινεῖν λίθον, to move one's man from this line, "to try one's last chance." (Liddell and Scott, Lex.) The meaning is, "She confounds the law of love, that it be reciprocated." ἡ γὰρ ἔρωτι. So Horat. Serm. I. iii. 38,

Illuc præwertamur, amatorem quod amicæ
Turpia decipiunt cæcum vitia, aut etiam ipsa hæc
Delectant.

[6] Telemus, son of Eurymus, had predicted to Polyphemus, whose character Damætas here sustains, that Ulysses would rob him of his single eye. Compare Odyss. ix. 509. Ov. Met. xiii. 772, 773,

Telemus Eurymides quem nulla fefellerat ales
Terribilem Polyphemon adit: lumenque, quod unum
Fronte geris mediâ, rapiet tibi, dixit, Ulysses.

[7] Similar imprecations occur Hom. Od. ii. 178. Virg. Æn. xi. 399, Capiti cane talia, demens, Dardanio rebusque tuis. Hom. Il. i. 106—108. 2 Chron. xviii. 7.

[8] She runs wild.] οἰστρεῖ. Maddened as by a gad-fly. Comp. Eur

my caves, and toward my flocks. And I bade my dog bark at her: for when I was enamoured of her, it used to whine, keeping its nose to her hips. Now perhaps when she sees me doing this frequently, she will send a messenger. But I shall shut my doors, until she shall have sworn that she will herself strew for me a beautiful couch [9] on this island. For [10] in truth neither have I so ugly a form as they say *I have*. For surely *but* lately I was looking into the sea (and it was a calm): and beautiful indeed my beard, and beautiful my solitary eyeball, (as it has been determined by my judgment,) appeared; [11] and it reflected a brightness of teeth, whiter than Parian marble. And that I might not be bewitched, [12] I spat thrice upon my breast: for thus the old woman [13] Cotyttaris instructed me *to do*, who of late used to sing to the reapers in the fields of Hippocoon.

Having sung thus much, Damœtas kissed Daphnis; and the latter gave the former a pipe, and he a beautiful flute to the latter. Damœtas was playing the flute, and the herdsman Daphnis the pipes. Forthwith the calves were leaping on soft herbage. However neither one conquered, but they were unsurpassed.

Iph. Aul. 77, Ὁ δὲ καθ' Ἑλλάδ' οἰστρήσας. In the next line, for σῖγα we may adopt with Briggs and Wordsworth εἶπα.

[9] This island, i. e. Sicily.

[10] Virg. Ecl. ii. 25,

    Nec sum adeò informis, nuper me in littore vidi
    Cum placidum ventis staret mare: non ego Daphnim
    Judice te metuam, si nunquam fallit imago.

Compare Ov. Met. xiii. 840,

    Jam, Galatea, veni nec munera despice nostra,
    Certe ego me novi, liquidæque in imagine vidi—
    Nuper aquæ: placuitque mihi mea forma videnti.

[11] Horat. i. 19, 5, Urit me Glyceræ nitor

    Splendentis Pario marmore puriùs.

[12] I spat thrice.] Compare with this, Idyll ii. 43—62; vii. 127. Tibull. I. ii. 100, Despuit in molles et sibi quisque sinus. Add Idyll xx. 12.

[13] Some suppose Cotyttaris to be the old woman's name, whilst others refer it to the orgies of the goddess Cotytto, and the witches connected therewith. See Hor. Epod. xvii. 56,

    Inultus ut tu riseris Cotyttia
    Vulgata, sacrum liberi cupidinis.

[14] οὐ δ' ἄλλος, here the same with οὐδ' ἕτερος. τὸν ἄλλον for τὸν ἕτερον, occurs in Idyll xxiv. 61. For a parallel to the verse see Virgil, Ecl. iii. 108. Non nostrum est tantas componere lites

    Et vitulâ tu dignus, et hic.

IDYLL VII.

THE THALYSIA.

ARGUMENT.

In this Idyll, one Simichidas is represented describing a celebration of the festival in honour of Demeter after harvest, in which he himself and some friends had been engaged at the house of Phrasidamus and Antigenes, on the banks of the Hales. The former part of the Idyll is a narration of the journey to the feast; the latter, a description of the feast itself. On their road, Simichidas and his friends fall in with a goatherd, Lycidas, of great poetic talent, whom they invite to while the length of the way by his song. He accordingly sings his love for the boy Ageanax. After which, Simichidas in turn celebrates the passion of Aratus for the lad Philinus. The songs being ended, Lycidas presents Simichidas with a crook, and turns off on another route. The rest go forward to their proposed destination, where beside the murmuring fountain, in a most delightful spot, they indulge in wine and good cheer. The scene, according to the Scholiast, is laid in Cos; though Heinsius maintains that Sicily is represented. Theocritus is known to have stayed some time at Cos to hear Philetas, which makes for the Scholiast's view. It has been supposed that the poet describes himself under the character of Simichidas, and a Cydonian poet of his own day under the name of Lycidas. Virgil has planned his ninth Eclogue somewhat on the model of this Idyll.

[1] IT was the time when I and Eucritus were sauntering from the city to the Hales, and with us a third, Amyntas. For to Ceres both Thrasidamus and Antigenes, two sons of Lycopeus, were preparing the Thalysia; *worthy men,* if aught is worthy *that springs* from the good men of old, being descended both from [2] Clytia and Chalcon himself; [3] *he* who by his foot raised the fountain Burinna, having planted strongly his knee against

---

[1] The festival to which our travellers were going, was one to Ceres, or Demeter, held in autumn after harvest, to thank her for her benefits to man. Compare Callimach. Hymn to Demeter, 20. Hom. Il. ix. 529.
The scene lies in Cos. Hales was a river of the island; and the city mentioned, vs. 2, was the chief city of the island, also named Cos.

[2] Clytia and Chalcon.] Clytia was the daughter of Merops, wife of Eurypylus, (who is mentioned by Homer, Iliad ii. 677,) king of Cos, and the mother of Chalcon. Scholiast. For εἴ τί περ ἐσθλὸν, see Ovid. Amor. iii. El. xv. Si quid id est, usque a proavis vetus ordinis hæres.

[3] Genu fortiter in rupem innixus pedis ictu fontem excitavit. Valkenaer. ἐκ ποδὸς, ictu pedis, cf. Bion. iv. 2.

the rock: and beside it, [4] the poplars and elms were yielding a grove of shade, [5] overhanging, as they waved, with green foliage.

[6] Nor yet had we finished half our way, nor did the tomb of Brasilas *yet* come in sight to us, when we fell in with a wayfarer, [7] a favourite with the Muses, a man of Cydon, whose name was Lycidas; he was a goatherd, nor could any one that looked upon him have mistaken him, for he was exceedingly like a goatherd. For on his shoulders he wore a [8] tawny skin of a shaggy thick-haired goat, smelling of new rennet: an old cloak was fastened by a broad belt about his breast; whilst in his right hand he held a crooked club of wild-olive: and grinning, he said to me softly with a smiling eye (and laughter played upon his lip): [9] 'Simichidas, where, prythee, art thou dragging thy steps at mid-day? when in sooth even [10] the green lizard sleeps on the fences, and the crested larks roam not abroad? Art invited and hastening

[4] Horat. i. 21, 5, Vos lætam fluviis, et nemorum comâ, &c.
[5] Æn. i. 164,   Silvis scena coruscis
    Desuper, horrentique atrum nemus imminet umbrâ.
Ecl. ix. 41, Hic candida populus antro
    Imminet, et lentæ texunt umbracula vites.
[6] Compare Virg. Ecl. ix. 59,
    Hinc adeo nobis media est via; namque sepulchrum
    Incipit apparere Bianoris.
And see Theocr. Idyll i. 125, 126.
[7] σὺν Μοίσαισι ἐσθλὸν. Beneficio Musarum bonum. Compare Idyll ii. 28, σὺν δαίμονι. A Cydonian. Cydon was a city of Crete, whence Lycidas is supposed to have come.
[8] Virgil in his "Moretum," vs. 22, has "Cinctus villosæ tergore capræ." Ovid. Met. ii. 680,
    Illud erat tempus, quo te pastorea pellis
    Texit, onusque fuit dextræ silvestris oliva.
[9] Simichidas.] A patronymic which seems to have been used without any change for father and son alike. Theocritus is said to have been the son of Simichus or Simichidas, and to have called himself Simichidas patronymically. Amyntas and Amyntichus, in this Idyll, stand for one and the same person, and there is clearly some ground for supposing the patronymic was used by both father and son. But the obscurity may be solved by supposing, as we may safely do, that Simichidas is a feigned name, like Virgil's Tityrus.
[10] σαῦρος. Vid. Idyll ii. 58. Comp. Virg. Ecl. ii. 9, Nunc virides etiam occultant spineta lacertos. Nemesian. iv. 38,
    Toto non squamea tractu
    Signat humum serpens.

to a banquet? or art for storming the wine-vats of some city? since as thou footest it along, every stone rings, as it strikes against [11] thy half-boots.' Then I answered him, 'Friend Lycidas, all say you are a piper greatly distinguished both among herdsmen and among reapers: which in truth vastly delights my mind; yet in my fancy, I hope to rival you. Now this is our way to the [12] Thalysia: for our friends in sooth are making a feast to Demeter of the beautiful robe, offering the first-fruits of their abundance: since for them, in very bounteous measure, the goddess hath piled the threshing-floor [13] with barley. But come now, (for our road is in common, and the day is alike ours,) let us sing pastorals; perhaps the one will gratify the other. For I [14] too am a clear voice of the Muses, and all men call me an excellent minstrel; but I am one not of easy persuasion. No! by earth! for not yet, to my own fancy, do I surpass in singing either the good [15] Sicelidas from Samos, or Philetas, but strive *with them*, like a frog among locusts.'

So spake I, on purpose: but the goatherd smiling pleasantly, 'I give you this [16] club,' quoth he, 'because you are a scion of Jove, fashioned altogether for sincerity. [17] For as the architect is odious to me, who attempts to build a house

[11] ἀρβυλίς, a half-boot used by hunters and rustics. Æschyl. Ag. 944, ὑπαί τις ἀρβύλας λύοι. Euripides calls it Mycenæan.

[12] Compare Hom. Il. ix. 529,

καὶ γὰρ, τοῖσι κακὸν χρυσόθρονος Ἄρτεμις ὦρσε
χωσαμένη, ὅτ᾽ οἱ οὔτι θαλύσια γουνῷ ἀλωῆς
Οἰνεὺς ῥέξ᾽, ἄλλοι δὲ θέοι δαίνυνθ᾽ ἑκατόμβας.

[13] The construction is ἁ δαίμων ἀνεπλήρωσεν ἀλωάν (ὥστε εἶναι,) εὐκρίθου, (so that it should be,) full of barley. Cf. Virg. Georg. i. 49, Illius immensæ ruperunt horrea messes. In the next line ἀὼς is used for ἡμέρα, as in Bion. vi. 18. J. Wordsworth quotes at this passage the Excursion, Book iii. p. 109,

With hearts at ease, and knowledge in our hearts,
That all the day and all the grove was ours.

[14] Virg. Ecl. ix. 32—36, Et me fecere poetam
Pierides: sunt et mihi carmina: me quoque vatem
Dicunt pastores, sed ego non credulus illis.
Nam neque adhuc Varo videor, nec dicere Cinnâ
Digna, sed argutos inter strepere anser olores.

[15] Sicelidas, or Asclepiades, a poet of Samos. Philetas, an Elegiac poet of Cos, under whom Theocritus studied. His date is about 290 B.C.

[16] Virg. Ecl. v. 88, At tu sume pedum. Such meeds of song and extemporized gifts are common among pastoral poets and their swains.

[17] See an opposite idea, Idyll xv. 49, ἐξ ἀπατᾶς κεκροτημένοι ἄνδρες.

equal to the top of Mount [18]Oromedon, so are birds of the Muses, as many as, crowing against the Chian minstrel, toil to no purpose. But come, let us commence at once the pastoral strain, Simichidas: as I will—see now, friend, if this ditty, which I erst finished off on the mountain, suits your taste.'

'Ageanax shall have a fair voyage to Mitylene, when the south wind chases the moist waves [19]in the season of the Kids at-their-setting, and when [20] Orion rests his feet on the ocean, if haply he shall have rescued Lycidas scorched by Aphrodite: for ardent love of him consumes me. And halcyons shall [21] smooth the waves, and the sea, and the south-west wind, and the south-east, which stirs the remotest seaweeds: halcyons, which have been beloved most of birds, whose prey is on the sea, by the green Nereids. May all things be seasonable to Ageanax, seeking a fair wind for Mitylene: and may he reach the harbour after a favourable voyage. [22] And I, on that day, crowning my head with a chaplet of dill, or of roses, or even of white [23]violets, will drain from the bowl the [24]Pteleatic wine, as I recline beside the fire: and one shall roast

[18] Oromedon, a mountain in Cos. Hermann says a giant. Cf. Propert. iii. 9, 48. The verses (45—48) mean nothing less than "I hate quacks." Theocritus compares vain boasters to architects trying to overtop the mountains, and poets (μοισᾶν ὄρνιχες) labouring to equal Homer. ὡς in line 45 is "nam." καὶ τέκτων—καὶ ὄρνιχες are the same as ὡς τέκτων οὕτως ὄρνιχες.

[19] The Kids.] The time indicated was probably December. Virg. Æn. ix. 668, Quantus ab occasu veniens pluvialibus hædis
   Verberat imber humum.

[20] Orion, a constellation whose setting was attended with violent storms at the end of autumn, the time of the equinoctial gales. Hbrat. Od. i. 28, 21, Devexi rapidus comes Orionis. Comp. Virg. Æn. i. 535; iii. 517; iv. 52.

[21] Virg. Ecl. ix. 57, Et nunc tibi stratum silet æquor. According to the Scholiast, the sea is calm in winter fourteen days: seven before the halcyon produces her eggs, and seven more while she sits on them, floating in the nest on the surface of the sea.

[22] εὔπλοος (Græf. Schæf. Kiessl.) seems far preferable to εὔπλοον, since the word refers rather to the sailor than to the port to which he sails.

[23] Virg. Ecl. ii. 47, Pallentes violas.

[24] Pteleatic wine.] So called from Ptelea, a place in Cos. Virgil imitates this passage, Ecl. v. 69,
   Et multo imprimis hilarans convivia Baccho
   Ante focum, si frigus erit, si messis, in umbrâ
   Vina novum fundam calathis Ariusia nectar.

me a bean in the flame, and the bed of leaves shall be covered thickly elbow-deep with flea-bane, and asphodel and curling parsley. ²⁵ Then freely will I drink, in memory of Ageanax, pressing my lip to the very cup even to the dregs. ²⁶ And there shall pipe for me two shepherds, one an Acharnian, and one from Lycope: and near them Tityrus shall sing, how once the herdsman Daphnis loved the foreign maid, and how he traversed the mountain, and how the oaks bewailed him which grow beside the banks of the river ²⁷ Himeras: when he wasted away, as any snow on lofty Hæmus, or Athos, or Rhodope, or remotest Caucasus: he shall sing too how once a wide chest received the goatherd yet living, ²⁸ through the baneful violence of his master; and how the flat-nosed bees coming from the meadows to the sweet cedar, were wont to feed him on soft flowers, because the Muses had poured down his throat pleasant nectar. O fortunate Comatas, thou in sooth hast experienced these delights, and thou hast been enclosed in a chest, and thou, being fed on the combs of bees, ²⁹ hast completed the spring of the year. ³⁰ Would that in my day thou hadst been numbered among the living, since I would

---

²⁵ μαλακῶς, carelessly, easily. Scholiast.

²⁶ Virg. Ecl. v. 72, Cantabunt mihi Damætas et Lyctius Ægon.

'Αχαρνεύς. Attic, from the deme so called. Λυκωπίτας. Ætolian, from a city named Lycope.

²⁷ Himeras. Compare Idyll v. 124. Hæmus, Athos, Rhodope, mountains of Thrace. Caucasus, the eastern barrier of Asia Minor. For the sentiment, see Callimach. H. to Ceres, 92. Ὡς δὲ Μίμαντι χιών, &c. And Job xxiv. 19, "Drought and heat consume the snow waters: so doth the grave those that have sinned." Ovid. Ep. ex Pont. I. i. 67,

Nil igitur mirum, si mens mihi tabida facta
De nive manantis more liquescit aquæ.

²⁸ The Scholiast explains this of a goatherd named Comatas or Menalcas, who, while engaged in tending his master's herds, was wont to sacrifice to the Muses. To try whether they would preserve him, his master caused him to be shut up in a chest, which, after some months, he found, upon opening it, full of honey-combs, and his prisoner alive.

²⁹ ἔτος ὥριον, 'trimestre tempus exegisti.' Steph. Totum annum exegisti. Crispinus. The Scholiast seems to consider the words to designate "the spring." The three months of spring in which the flowers, &c., mentioned just before, would bloom chiefly. ὥρα signifies specially τὸ ἔαρ, which Homer calls commonly ὥρη εἰαρινή. See Lex. Doric. Æ. Porti, at the word ὥριος.

³⁰ Comp. Virg. Ecl. x. 35,

Atque utinam ex vobis unus, vestrique fuissem
Aut custos gregis, aut maturæ vinitor uvæ, &c.

then have tended for thee thy beautiful she-goats, along the mountains, while listening to thy voice : and thou, divine Comatas, shouldst have reclined under the oaks or under the pines, sweetly singing.'

And Lycidas having sung thus much, made an end : but to him in turn I also spoke as follows: 'Many other good things, friend Lycidas, have the Nymphs taught me too, as I tend my herd along the mountains: *things* which [31] haply fame hath carried even to the throne of Jove. But this at any rate is far pre-eminent beyond all, with which I will proceed to favour you. Hearken then, since you are a friend to the Muses.'

[32] 'On Simichidas indeed the Loves have sneezed: for of a truth the luckless *wight* is as much in love with Myrto, as the she-goats love spring. But Aratus, who is in the highest degree beloved by that man, cherishes at heart a yearning for a lad. [33] Aristis, a worthy man, and highly excellent, (whose singing with *the accompaniment of* the lyre not even Phœbus himself beside his tripods would refuse,) knows that by a lad Aratus is consumed to the very bone with love. Him I pray thee, O Pan, who hast obtained for thy portion the lovely surface of [34] Homole, mayest thou place unbidden in the dear hands of that man, whether it is in sooth the tender Philinus, or some other. And if indeed thou shouldst do thus, O dear Pan, *then* may [35] Arcadian boys in no wise

---

[31] Virg. Ecl. iii. 73, Partem aliquam, venti, divom referatis ad aures. Ecl. v. 73, Hinc usque ad sidera notus.

[32] One of the various omens which the Greeks drew from themselves was the πταρμός, or sneezing, referred to here, and Xenoph. Exped. Cyr. iii. 2, 9. Propert. Eleg. ii. 3, 23,
    Num tibi nascenti primis, mea vita, diebus
    Aureus argutum sternuit omen amor ?
Catull. xlv. 9, Amor sinistram ut ante,
    Dextram sternuit approbationem.
Compare also Idyll xviii. 16.

[33] Ἄριστις—μέγ' ἄριστος, a play on words, which cannot be rendered faithfully. Theocritus affects it ; see Idyll xv. 26, πένθημα καὶ οὐ Πενθῆα. Shaksp. Of Hotspur, cold-spur. This is Rome and room enough. Not on thy sole, but on thy soul, harsh Jew, thou makest thy knife keen. For μέγα used adverbially see Monk, Alcest. 758, Hom. Il. ii. 32.

[34] Homole, a mountain of Thessaly. It is mentioned by Euripides, Herc. Fur. 371, σύγχορτοί θ' Ὁμόλας ἔναυλοι.
    Virg. Æn. vii. 675,   Homolen Othrynque nivalem
            Linquentes rapido cursu.

[35] σκίλλαισιν, comp. Idyll v. 121. The poet alludes to a feast of Pan,

scourge thee with squills on ribs and shoulders, at such times as scanty feasts are provided: but shouldst thou have decided otherwise, mayest thou be scratched all over thy flesh by the nails, and mayest thou sleep among nettles: and in mid-winter mayest thou be on the [36] mountains of the Edonians, beside the river Hebrus, facing towards and nigh to the north; and in summer mayest thou tend herds among the extremest Æthiopians, [37] under the rock of the Blemyes, whence the Nile is no longer to be seen. But do ye, having left the sweet water of [38] Hyetis and Byblis, and dwelling in the lofty [39] seat of golden-haired Dione, [40] O Loves like unto ruddy apples, strike, I pray you, with your arrows, the lovely Philinus: strike, for the wretched *youth* pities not my guest. And yet he is more over-ripe than a pear, and the women say, Alas, alas, Philinus, thy beauty's bloom wastes away. No longer, look you, Aratus, let us keep watch at the vestibules, nor wear out our feet, but let the early cock consign [41] another, as he crows,

in Arcadia, where it was the custom to scourge his image, if the Choragi had offered a mean sacrifice. Scholiast.

[36] Edones, a nation of Thrace. Hebrus, a river of the same. Virg. Ecl. x. 63, Nec si frigoribus mediis Hebramque bibamus. Some commentators have wondered that Theocr. places the Edones and the river Hebrus near each other. But Wordsworth shows that Greek and Latin poets, (as Lucan, Ovid, Horace,) were ignorant of the geography of Macedon, Thrace, and Northern Greece, which they deemed Barbarian. This passage supports, as Wordsworth shows, Bentley's emendation, "Edonis," for "ex somnis," at Horat. Od. iii. 25, 9,

> Non secus in jugis,
> Edonis stupet Evias
> Hebrum prospiciens, et nive candidam
> Lustratam Rhodopen.

[37] Blemyes, a nation of Æthiopia.

[38] Hyetis and Biblis, mountains and springs of Miletus. See Ovid. Met. ix. 445—665.

[39] ἕδος αἰπὺ Διώνης, h. e. Cyprus, the abode of Venus, who often is called by her mother's name, Dione.

[40] Tibull. III. iv. 34,

> Candor erat qualem præfert Latonia Luna
> Et color in niveo corpore purpureus.
> Ut juveni primum virgo deducta marito
> Inficitur teneras ore rubente genas;
> Ut cum contexunt amaranthis alba puellæ
> Lilia, ut Autumno candida mala rubent.

Comp. Idyll xxvi. 1.

[41] Propert. I. xvi. 23, 24,

to *this* painful numbness: and let Molon alone, my best of friends, be harassed in this sharp exercise: and to us let both quietness be a care, and an old woman be at hand, who, [42] by spitting, may keep afar off what is not good.'

Thus much I spoke: and he, having smiled sweetly, as before, presented me with his crook to be a friendly gift [43] *arising* out of our songs. And he indeed, having turned off to the left, proceeded on his way to Pyxa: but I and Eucritus, having bent our steps to the house of Phrasidamus, with the beautiful [44] Amyntichus, reclined *there*, both on deep low-couches of the sweet mastich-tree, and on fresh-cut vine-twigs, rejoicingly. And, from above, down upon our heads were waving to and fro many poplars and elms; and the sacred stream hard by kept murmuring, as it flowed down from the cave of the Nymphs. And the fire-coloured cicalas on the shady branches were toiling at chirping; while, from afar off, in the thick thorn-bushes the thrush was warbling. Tufted larks and [45] gold-finches were singing; the turtle-dove was cooing; [46] tawny bees were humming round about the fountains: all things were breathing-the-incense of very plenteous summer, and breathing-the-incense of fruit-time. [47] Pears indeed at our feet, and by our sides apples, were rolling for us in abundance; and the boughs hung-in-profusion, weighed down to the ground, with damsons. [48] Moreover the pitch of

> Me mediæ noctes, me sidera prona jacentem
> Frigidaque Œoo me videt aura gelu.

Horat. Sat. ii. 6, 45, Matutina parum cautos jam frigora cædunt.

[42] ἐπιφθύσδοισα, Idyll ii. 62. Tibull. I. ii. 53, Ter cane, ter dictis despue carminibus.

[43] ἐκ μοισᾶν. Compare vii. 102, ἐκ παιδός, 55, ἐξ Ἀφροδίτας.

[44] Ἀμύντιχος, i. q. Ἀμύντας, vs. 2; comp. not. ad vs. 21. And see Wordsworth at this passage, who quotes Lucret. ii. 132,

> Prostrati gramine molli
> 'Propter aquæ rivum sub ramis arboris altæ
> Non magnis opibus jucundè corpora curant,
> Præcipuè cum tempestas arridet, et anni
> Tempora conspergunt viridantes floribus herbas.

[45] Ἀκανθίδες, the Acalanthis of Virg. Georg. iii. 338, Littoraque Alcyonem resonant, acalanthida dumi. Cf. Song of Solomon ii. 12.

[46] Compare Hippol. Eurip. 76, 77: ἀλλ' ἀκήρατον
μέλισσα λειμῶν, ἠρινὸν διέρχεται.

For περί and ἀμφί thus connected, see Hom. Il. ii. 305. Odyss. xi. 608

[47] Virg. Ecl. vii. 54, Strata jacent passim sua quæque sub arbore poma.

[48] Hor. Od. III. viii. 9,

four years' date was loosened from the mouth of the wine jars.

Ye Castalian Nymphs, inhabiting the height of Parnassus, I wonder whether [49] at all in the rocky cave of Pholus, aged Chiron set up for Hercules a goblet such as this! I wonder if haply 'twas nectar like *this*, which induced that shepherd by the Anapus, the strong Polyphemus, who [50] used to hurl crags on the mountain-ranges, to dance about in the sheep-pens? *Such nectar I mean*, as, O Nymphs, ye then broached, beside the altar of Demeter presiding over the threshing-floor: on the heap of which may I again fasten a great winnowing shovel, and may she smile, holding in both hands [51] wheat sheaves and poppies.

IDYLL VIII.

THE SINGERS OF PASTORALS.

ARGUMENT.

In this Idyll two pastors are represented as contending, Daphnis and Menalcas, both skilled in music and in Amæbæan song. A challenge is given, and a prize set up, and a goatherd called in as umpire. They begin the song, so as to answer one another first with four, afterwards with eight verses each. At last the goatherd adjudges the prize to Daphnis—and the poet represents this victory as laying the foundation

---

Hic dies, anno redeunte, festus
Corticem adstrictum pice dimovebit, &c.
Amphoræ—
Cf. Hor. Od. I. ix. 6. Terent. Heaut. III. i. 51, Relevi dolia omnia, omnes serias.

[49] A poetic digression, touching the cave of the centaur Pholus, and Chiron, who was the instructor of Hercules in astronomy and Apollo in music. Cf. Orph. Argonaut. 419. Juvenal, Sat. xii. 44, Urnæ cratera capacem Et dignum sitiente Pholo.

[50] Compare Hom. Odyss. ix. 481. There is no ground for the reading νᾶας here, with Heinsius and Brunck.

[51] Δράγματα. Cf. Callimach. Hymn to Delos, 284, and the note of Th. Græv. at the passage.—A sheaf, as much as a gleaner can bind up together is meant. Tibul. I. x. ad fin., At nobis, pax alma, veni spicamque teneto. Demeter's symbols are spikes of corn and poppies.

of all the future fame of Daphnis, in pastoral poetry. The scene is laid in Sicily. Virgil has copied this Idyll much in Eclogues iii and vii.

DAPHNIS. MENALCAS. A GOATHERD.

MENALCAS, [1] as they say, whilst tending his sheep along the high mountains, fell in with the graceful Daphnis a-driving his herd. [2] Now both of them were [3] red-haired, both lads: each skilled in playing on the pipes, each in singing. And first then Menalcas, gazing at Daphnis, addressed him.

Menalcas. Daphnis, watcher of the lowing oxen, wilt thou sing with me? I maintain that I will beat you at singing, to my heart's content.

And him, I ween, Daphnis answered in speech like the following.

Daphnis. Shepherd of woolly sheep, piper Menalcas, you at all events shall never beat me in singing, no, not if you should die for it.

Men. [4] Are you desirous then to see into it? Are you desirous to stake a prize?

Daph. I do desire to see into this. I am desirous to stake a prize.

Men. Well what shall we stake, that would be *of* sufficient *value* for us?

Daph. I will stake a calf: and do you stake on your part [5] a lamb like its mother.

Men. [6] I will never stake a lamb, for both my father is strict, and my mother, and they count all the sheep at evening.

---

[1] Pierson reads Διόφαντε for ὡς φαντί: taking the idea from the commencement of Idyll xxi., which Theocritus dedicates to Diophantus.

[2] Virg. Ecl. vii. 4,
   Ambo florentes ætatibus, Arcades ambo
   Et cantare pares, et respondere parati.

[3] πυρρότριχω. Polwhele, in his version, finds here the original of Collins's expression, "the fiery-tressed Dane."

[4] Virg. Ecl. iii. 28,
   Vis ergo inter nos quid possit uterque vicissim
   Experiamur, ego hanc vitulam, ne forte recuses,
   Depono: tu dic mecum quo pignore certes.
   Virg. Æn. ix. 628,
   Et statuam ante aras auratâ fronte juvencum
   Candentem, pariterque caput cum matre gerentem.

[6] Virg. Ecl. iii. 32,

Daph. Well then, what will you stake? And what shall be the advantage the winner shall have?

Men. [7] A shepherd's-pipe, which I made beautiful with nine notes, *and* having white wax *about it,* equal below, equal above. This I would stake: but my father's property I will not stake.

Daph. In truth I too, look you, have a pipe with nine notes, having white wax *about* it, equal below, equal above. I lately fastened it together. Even still I have a pain in this finger, since the reed, i'fegs, split and cut me. But who shall try us? Who shall be our listener?

Men. How if we should call hither yon goatherd, whose dog [8] with-the-white-spot, is barking near the kids.

And the youths indeed shouted *to him,* and the goatherd came, having heard them. And the youths on their part began to sing, and the goatherd was willing to be umpire. So then first the [9] piper Menalcas proceeded to sing, having obtained *precedence* by lot. And then Daphnis took up the alternate pastoral strain. And thus began Menalcas first.

Men. Ye dells and rivers, [10] a divine progeny, if haply ever the piper Menalcas has sung a pleasant melody, may ye feed my lambkins [11] to my heart's content: and should Daphnis ever chance to have come with his calves, may he find nothing less.

De grege non ausim quicquam deponere tecum,
Est mihi namque domi pater, est injusta noverca,
Bisque die numerant ambo pecus, alter et hædos.

[7] Ecl. ii. 37, 38, Est mihi disparibus septem compacta cicutis
    Fistula.
Ibid. 32,   Pan primus calamos cerâ conjungere plures
    Instituit.
Wordsworth refers, for the modern use of this pipe by Greek shepherds, to G. M. Leake's Northern Greece, i. p. 290.

[8] φαλαρὸς, ' white spot,' a name given to a ram, in Idyll v. 104.

[9] ἰυκτὰ, i. e. ὁ συρικτής, ὁ λιγύφθογγους. The termination a was Æolic. Homer has Θυέστα. μητίετα—νεφεληγερέτα, εὐρυόπα. ἱππότα. Hence the Latin Cometa ' planeta' poeta, from κόμήτης πλανητης, &c., and the Latins generally turned the Greek names in ας into a. The Greeks did just the reverse, adding s to Latin names in ' a.' See Matt. Gr. Gr. § 68, 8. (Edit. 1832.) For the order of singing, see Virg. Ecl. vii. 18.

[10] θεῖον γένος, because every river with the Greeks, and every fountain, was a god or goddess. Denique cœlesti sumus omnes semine nati. Lucret.

[11] ἐκ ψυχᾶς, exanimi mei sententiâ. Though Grœfius understands ψυχᾶς of the rivers, as gods θείου γένους.

Daph. Ye springs, and herbage, a pleasant growth, if so be that Daphnis warbles like the nightingales, fatten ye this herd! And if Menalcas shall have driven any *stock* hither, may he, to his satisfaction, pasture all in plenty.

Men. [12] Every where *it is* spring, and every where *are* pastures: and every where udders are full of milk, and the young are suckled, where the fair maiden approaches: but if she should depart, both the shepherd is withered there, and the herbage *too.*

Daph. Sheep *are* there, she-goats with twins *are* there, bees fill their hives there, and the oaks *are* loftier, wherever the handsome Milo sets foot; [13] but should he depart, both he who feeds the heifers, and the heifers *themselves*, are the more dried up.

Men. O he-goat, husband of the white she-goats! [14] where there is endless depth of foliage, O ye flat-nosed kids, come hither to the water. For in that place is he! Go, stump-horn, and say to Milo, that [15] Proteus, even though a god, used to feed sea-calves.

---

[12] Compare Virg. Ecl. vii. 59, 60,
Phillidis adventu nostræ nemus omne virebit
Jupiter et læto descendet plurimus imbri.
Ibid. 55, Omnia nunc rident; at si formosus Alexis
Montibus his abeat, videas et flumina sicca.
Pope Past. i. 69,
All nature mourns, the skies relent in showers,
Hush'd are the birds, and closed the drooping flowers;
If Delia smile, the flowers begin to spring,
The skies to brighten, and the birds to sing.
[13] Virg. Ecl. iii. 100,
Eheu quam pingui macer est mihi taurus in ervo!
Idem amor exitium pecori, pecorisque magistro.
[14] The common reading here was ὦ βάθος, O profunditas, which Casaubon, Reiske, Warton, &c. have altered to ὦ, ubi, so that we must supply δεῦρο, and refer it, I suppose, to ὕδωρ in the next line. Wernsdorf supposes ὦ βάθος ὕλας μυρίον to the "Horrida siccæ Silva comæ," of the he-goat, (cf. Juvenal ix. 13,) and perhaps there is some foundation for this conjecture, to which however the simpler mode of translation above stated seems preferable. For the parallel to the former part of the line, see Virg. Ecl. vii. 7, Vir gregis ipse caper deeraverat.
[15] Horat. Od. i. 2, 7, Omne cum Proteus pecus egit altos
Visere montes.
Cf. Virg. Georg. iv. 395. Hom. Odyss. iv. 448. Wordsworth proposes here to read, καὶ λέγε—Μίλων,
Ὁ Πρωτεὺς φώκας κ. θ. ω. ενεμε.

Daph. Not mine be it to possess the land of Pelops, nor mine to own golden talents, or to outstrip the winds: but I [16] will sing under this rock, holding thee in my arms, looking upon my sheep feeding together, and towards the Sicilian sea.

Men. To trees indeed winter is a dreadful evil, and to waters drought, and to birds the snare, and to wild beasts nets: but to man the yearning for a tender maiden. O Sire, O Jove, not I alone have been in love. [17] Thou too art a lover of women.

These strains indeed then the youths sang alternately: and Menalcas thus commenced his concluding song.

Men. Spare my kids, spare, wolf, my she-goats with young, and do not hurt me, because, small though I am, I tend many. [18] O dog Lampurus, does so deep a sleep hold you? You ought not to sleep soundly while tending *sheep* with a lad. And, ye sheep, neither do you shrink from filling yourselves with the tender herbage. Ye shall be nowise tired of it, when this springs up again. St! feed on, feed on, and, all of you, fill your udders, that the lambs may have a part, and I may lay up the rest in cheese baskets.

Next in turn, Daphnis struck up to sing sweetly.

Daph. [19] Me too, a maiden with meeting eye-brows, having seen yesterday from her cave, as I drove past *it* my heifers, kept declaring to be beautiful, beautiful. Nor indeed did I even answer her a rude word, but kept trudging on my way, looking downwards. [20] Sweet is the voice of the heifer, sweet

---

[16] Græf. reads σύννομε Μῖλον, ὁρῶν τὰν Σικελὰν ἐς ἅλα. But Kiessling thinks, with reason, that a much slighter alteration will render the passage clear, viz. τὰν Σικελάν τε ἅλα. Or we may understand, as Reiske suggests, ἐς in the sense of πρὸς or παρά. "Apud Siculum mare."

[17] Compare the 56th Epigram of Callimachus, ed. Ernesti, i. 324.

[18] Λάμπουρε, "*fire-tail.*"

[19] Meeting eyebrows were considered a beauty among the ancients. Compare Anacreon xxvii. ad pictorem. Ov. Art. Amat. iii. 201,

  Arte supercilii confinia nuda replentes.

And Juvenal Sat. ii. 93,

  Ille supercilium madidâ fuligine tactum
  Obliquâ producit acu.   J. W.

[20] τὸ πνεῦμα, the breath of the pipe. So Idyll ix. 7, 8, and Theocr. Epigr. v. 4, καροδέτῳ πνεύματι. Warton, says Polwhele, thinks Milton had Theocritus in view, when he wrote those lines of Paradise Lost, Book iv. Sweet is the breath of morn, her rising sweet

  With charm of earliest birds, &c.

E

the breath *of the pipe;* and sweetly too the calf lows, and sweetly also the cow: and sweet is it [21] in summer-time to sleep in the open air beside running water. [22] The acorns are an ornament to the oak, apples to the apple-tree, and to the cows the calf, the cows themselves to the herdsman.

Thus sang the youths, but the goatherd addressed them as follows:

Goatherd. Something sweet is thy mouth, and lovely thy voice, O Daphnis. 'Tis better to hear thee sing than [23] to sip honey. Take the pipe, for thou hast won in singing. And if at all you desire to teach me too to sing, while I feed my goats along with you, I will give you, as the price of your teaching, yon hornless she-goat, which always fills the milk-pail above the brim.

As then the youth was delighted, and leapt up, and shouted as victorious; so would a fawn leap upon its dam. And as the other smouldered away, and was cast down in heart by chagrin, so also would a nymph grieve, [24] when betrothed. And from this time, Daphnis became first among shepherds, and, while yet in earliest youth, wedded a Naiad nymph.

IDYLL IX.

THE PASTOR, OR THE HERDSMEN.

ARGUMENT.

The scene is laid in Sicily. Daphnis and Menalcas are challenged by a companion shepherd to contend with one another in singing. They sing in alternate strains, and each carries off a prize; Daphnis a crook,

---

[21] Virg. Ecl. v. 46, Quale sopor fessis in gramine, &c.
[22] Ibid. 32, Vitis ut arboribus decori est, ut vitibus uvæ,
   Ut gregibus tauri, segetes ut pinguibus arvis,
   Tu decus omne tuis.
[23] Than to sip honey.] Polwhele compares Septuagint Cantic. iv. 11, Κηρίον ἀποστάξουσι χείλη σου, νύμφη. μέλι καί γάλα ὑπὸ τὴν γλῶσσαν σου.
[24] γαμεθεῖσ', desponsata. Her grief must be supposed to arise from the impending loss of girlish freedom. Comp. Trach. Sophoc. 144,
   ἕως τις ἀντὶ παρθένου γυνὴ
   κληθῇ, λάβῃ τ' ἐν νυκτὶ φροντίδων μέρος.

and Menalcas a muscle-shell. It seems clear that the whole Idyll is put in the mouth of a shepherd, who narrates the alternate strains of Daphnis and Menalcas, just as Melibæus (Virg. Ecl. vii.) those of Corydon and Thyrsis. Warton observes that Menalcas in his song assumes the character of the Cyclops.

DAPHNIS. MENALCAS.

SING a pastoral strain, Daphnis, and do you first begin the song; begin *you* the [1] song first, and let Menalcas follow after, when you have put the calves to the heifers, and the bulls to the barren cows. And let them feed together, and stray among the foliage, [2] not at all forsaking the herd : but do you sing me a bucolic strain in the first place ; and in the next, in turn let Menalcas answer.

Daphnis. Sweetly indeed the calf lows, and sweetly too does the heifer ; and sweetly also the pipe *sounds*, and the herdsman, and sweetly I too. And by the cool water-side I have a couch of leaves; and on it have been strown beautiful skins from white heifers, all of which, to my sorrow, as they nibbled the [3] arbute-tree, the south-west wind dashed from the mountain peak. And I care as much for the parching summer [4] as lovers care to hear the words of a father or mother.

Thus sang Daphnis to me. And Menalcas thus.

Menalcas. Ætna *is* my mother, and I inhabit a fair cave in the hollow rocks: and I have in sooth whatever things appear in a dream, [5] many sheep and many goats ; of which the skins

---

[1] For instances of this figure, called by the Latins " Iteratio," see Virgil Ecl. v. 51. Milton Lycidas, 37,
  But oh the heavy change now thou art gone,
  Now thou art gone, and never must return.
Virg. Ecl. iii. 58, Incipe Damœta; tu deinde sequere, Menalca.

[2] ἀτιμαγελεῦντες ; a cognate word, ἀτιμαγέλης, " neglecting the herd, feeding alone," occurs, Idyll xxv. 132.

[3] κόμαρος, the strawberry or arbute tree. Comp. v. 128.

[4] A similar boast of indifference occurs, Ecl. vii. 51,
  Hic tantum Boreæ curamus frigora, quantum
  Aut numerum lupus, aut torrentia flumina ripas.
Wordsworth reads with two MSS. ἐρῶν τὸ, i. e. Quantum amans *curat* audire patris aut matris monita. But Toup's conjecture, ἐρῶντε, which we have followed, is generally received.

[5] Virg. Ecl. ii., Mille meæ Siculis errant in montibus agnæ.
Two lines below compare Virg. Ecl. vii. 49,
  Hic focus et tædæ pingues, hic plurimus ignis
  Semper.

lie at my head, and beside my feet. And on a fire of oak-boughs entrails are boiling, and on the fire are dry beech-fagots when it is winter; and in truth not even have I a care for winter, as much as a toothless person has for nuts, when [6] fine meal is at hand.

These indeed I applauded; and straightway gave *as* a present, to Daphnis on one hand a crook, which a field of my father's had raised for me, self sprung, and such as not even perhaps a carpenter would have found fault with; and to the other [7] a beautiful spiral cockle-shell, the flesh of which I myself had eaten, after I had [8] lain in wait for it on the Icarian rocks, having divided [9] five shares for five of us; and he (Menalcas) blew upon the shell.

Pastoral Muses, all hail! and bring to light the song, which formerly I sang in the presence of those herdsmen. [10] Never raise a pimple upon the tip of your tongue. [11] Cicala is dear to cicala, and ant to ant, and hawks to hawks: but to me the Muse and song: of which, I pray, may all my house be full,

---

[6] ἀμύλοιο, sc. ἄρτου, a cake of not ground, i. e. the finest meal. Aristoph. Pax, 1195. Chapman indicates "pap," as the fare of this toothless individual.

[7] Lucretius, quoted by Polwhele,

Concharumque genus parili ratione videmus
Pingere telluris gremium, qua mollibus undis
Littoris incurvi bibulam pavit æquor arenam.

[8] Icaria, one of the Sporades, north-east of Myconos, and south-west of Samos, in the Ægean Sea. Now Nicaria.

[9] πέντε ταμών, for εἰς πέντε μέρη ταμών—ὁ δ' ἐγκαναχήσατο. Cf. Idyll xxii. 75, where Amycus κόχλον ἑλὼν μυκάσατο κοῖλον.

[10] The sense is, "It is no untruth, nor need you fear lest pimples should rise on your tongue to convict you of falsehood." This was as common a superstition, as it is now, with the ancients. Pimples on the nose or tongue were supposed to indicate falsehood. Compare Idyll xii. 23,

ἐγὼ δὲ σὲ τὸν καλὸν αἰνίων
ψεύδεα ῥινὸς ὕπερθεν ἀραιῆς οὐκ ἀναφύσω.

Horace alludes to such marks, in Od. ii. 8, 1,

Ulla si juris tibi pejerati
Pœna, Barine, nocuisset unquam,
Dente si nigro fieres, vel uno
Turpior ungui.

[11] A common proverb. Aristot. Eth. N. κολοιὸς ποτὶ κολοιόν, "Birds of a feather flock together." Ecclesiasticus xiii. 16, "All flesh consorteth according to kind, and a man will cleave to his like." xxvii. 16. "The birds will return to their like." Cf. Juvenal xv. 163.

for neither [12] sleep, nor spring on a sudden, is more sweet, nor flowers to bees, than *are* the Muses dear to me : for whomsoever they behold with pleasure, such hath [13] Circe never at all hurt with her draught.

IDYLL X.

THE WORKMEN, OR REAPERS.

ARGUMENT.

In this Idyll, which is strictly pastoral, Milo and Battus, two reapers, converse over their work. Now Battus, being enamoured of a female flute-player, Bombyce, the daughter of Polybutas, or as some suppose his handmaiden, works but slackly in consequence. Whereupon Milo asks him why he reaps so lazily, and Battus confesses to him his love; and recites a ditty composed for his mistress. Milo then opposes to this song, another of his own, containing precepts on the art of reaping, having first applauded Battus for the fitness and beauty of his composition.

MILO AND BATTUS.

You labouring ploughman, what has befallen you now, wretched man? Neither can you [1] draw the swathe straight,

---

[12] Pope Past., Not bubbling fountains to the thirsty swain,
   Not balmy sleep to labourers faint with pain,
   Not showers to larks, or sunshine to the bee,
   Are half so charming as thy sight to me.

οὐτ' ἔαρ ἐξαπίνας—Wordsw., seeing that the sense requires a dative here, instead of ἐξαπίνας conjectures εὐξαμένοις valdè exoptantibus, and compares with the reading Theocr. ix. 2, and Bion vi. 1, which see.

[13] The draughts of Circe, or spells of unlawful pleasure, are mentioned by Horace, Epist. I. ii. 23, " Sirenum voces et Circæ pocula nosti;" and chiefly in the Odyssey, lib. x. Milton introduces her as the mother of *Comus*, in his Masque so named. The sentiment here expressed with regard to the favourites of the Muses, is fully worked out by Horace, Od. iv. 3, Quem tu, Melpomene, &c.

[1] ὄγμον, says the Scholiast, was properly said of reapers who, as they advance one after another in long order, while they reap, draw, as it were, a furrow, which is called elsewhere αὖλαξ. The root is ἄγω, (cf. Butm. Lexilog. under the word ὀχθῆσαι, L. and S.) the verb ὀγμεύω is used in a metaphor from this sense of ὄγμος, in Sophocl. Philoct. 163. Two lines below the reader may compare Virgil Georg. iii. 466, who, describing a sickening sheep, says,

as of old you used *to draw it;* nor do you reap in a line with your neighbour, but are left behind, as a sheep, whose foot a thorn has wounded, *is left* by the flock. A fine sort of reaper you will be, won't you, at evening, and after mid-day, seeing that now, when you begin, ² you do not make a gap in the swathe?

Battus. Milo, you who reap till late at even, fragment of stubborn rock, did it never befall you to long after one of the absent?

Milo. Never! And what business has a labouring man with longing after those that are without?

Batt. Did it never then chance to you to lie awake through love?

Mil. No, and I trust it never may. ³ It's bad to give a dog a taste of guts.

Batt. Well, but I, Milo, have been in love hard upon eleven days.

Mil. You evidently draw from the cask! ⁴ but I have not vinegar enough.

Batt. ⁵ Therefore all before my doors is unweeded since sowing time.

Mil. And which of the damsels is ruining you?

Batt. The maiden of Polybotas, ⁶ who lately used to play to the reapers in the fields of Hippocoon.

   Videris, aut summas carpentem mollius herbas
   Extremamque sequi, aut medio procumbere campo
   Pascentem.

² ἀρχόμενος (τοῦ ἔργου, sc.) τᾶς αὐλ. ἀποτρώγειν. So Catull. xxxiii. 7, Quare, si sapiet, viam vorabit.

³ χαλεπὸν, &c. One of the proverbs you would expect in a reaping field. Horat. Serm. II. vi. 81, " Ut canis, a corio nunquam absterrebitur uncto." One of our vulgar expressions to the same point is, " Don't let the cat to the cream."

⁴ ἅλις ὄξος. Some would read ὄξους, but Reiske shows from Apollon. Rhod. ii. 424, Callim. H. in Jovem, 84, that ἅλις was used with a nominative or accusative as well as a genitive. The point of the passage is that Milo, who is heart-whole, comically congratulates Battus on his having his fill of love, and deplores his own loveless state, ironically of course. Battus stands by, a very skeleton from sleepless nights and wasting love. He has drawn from a cask with a vengeance.

⁵ Virg. Ecl. ii. 70, Semiputata tibi frondosâ vitis in ulmo est. Battus answers, that he is so much occupied with love, that he does not even remove the sweepings from the yard of his house.

⁶ This verse occurs before, Idyll vi. 41. πολυβώτα, genitivus Doricus, filia Polybotæ. Cf. ii. 66, ἁ τῶ' ὑβούλοιο. J. W.

Mil. ⁷ The god has found out the sinner! you have what you have been long wanting. ⁸ The long-legged grasshopper will lie with you all night.

Batt. You are beginning to jeer at me. But not ⁹ only Plutus is blind, but also the reckless Love. Do not say any thing boastful.

Mil. I do not boast at all. ¹⁰ Only do you lay low the crop; and strike up some loving ditty on the maiden; so will you work more pleasantly; and in fact in former times you used to be musical.

Batt. Pierian Muses, sing with me of the slim damsel: for, O goddesses, ye make all things beautiful, whichsoever ye shall have touched.

¹¹ Graceful Bombyce, all call thee Syrian, *and* shrivelled, and sun-burnt; but I alone *call you* ¹² honey-complexioned. The violet too is dark, ¹³ and the inscribed hyacinth; yet still they are gathered the first in garlands. The she-goat follows

---

⁷ A proverb directed against those who boast, and then fall into the dangers which they have been rejoicing to have escaped.

⁸ μάντις—καλαμαία, a kind of locust or grasshopper with long thin fore-feet, which are in constant motion. Perhaps, mantis religiosa, or mantis oratoria, Linn., also καλαμαία and καλαμῖτις. "If you marry," says Milo, "this old and loquacious damsel, you will have a cicada or locust to disturb you all night." Chapman translates μάντις, a "tree-frog."

⁹ αὐτός, i. q. μόνος or ἰδίᾳ. Cf. Matt. Gr. Gr. § 468, 5.

¹⁰ Soph. Ajax, 384, μηδὲν μέγ' εἴπῃς.

¹¹ Σύραν. Syrian—on account of her dark complexion. "Gipsy," perhaps.

¹² μελίχλωρον, *olive*, as we call it, "a brunette." On this difference between the world's notion and the lover's, see Lucret. lib. iv. 1153. Horat. Serm. I. iii. 38,

Illuc prævertamur, amatorem quod amicæ
Turpia decipiunt cæcum vitia, aut etiam ipsa hæc
Delectant.

For a parallel to the next line, see Virg. Ecl. x. 38,

Quid tum si fuscus Amyntas
Sunt nigræ violæ, sunt et vaccinia nigra.

And Theocr. Id. xxiii. 29.

¹³ Cf. Mosch. Idyll iii. 6. The legend ran that Hyacinthus was accidentally slain by Apollo's disc, and that his blood produced a flower, on whose leaves the initial letter of his name was inscribed. Ovid. Met. x. 162. Virg. Ecl. iii. 106. Georg. iv. 186. Vid. Ecl. ii. 18, Alba ligustra cadunt: vaccinia nigra leguntur.

[14] the cytisus, the wolf the she-goat, *and* the [15] crane the plough: but I am maddened after you. [16] I would I had as much as they say Crœsus of yore possessed; then both of us wrought in gold should be dedicated to Aphrodite; you holding the flute indeed, and either a rose, yes, or an apple; and I *wearing* [17] a new dress, and new Amyclæan shoes on both feet. O graceful Bombyce, [18] thy feet indeed are well turned, and thy voice is soft. Thy manners however I am not able to express.

Mil. Surely the ploughman has escaped my notice *while* making beautiful songs; how well has he measured the form of his harmony! [19] Alas me! for the beard which I have nursed in vain. Consider now also the strains of the divine Lytierses.

[20] O fruitful Demeter, rich in ears of corn, may this field be well tilled, and fruitful in the highest degree.

[14] Cf. Idyll v. 128. Virg. Ecl. ii. 63,
  Torva leæna lupum sequitur, lupus ipse capellam,
  Florentem cytisum sequitur lasciva capella
  Te, Corydon, o Alexi: trahit sua quemque voluptas.
Compare Georg. ii. 431, Tondentur cytisi.

[15] Cf. Georg. i. 120, Strymoniæque grues. Hesiod. O. et D. 448.

[16] Cf. Virg. Ecl. vii. 31, 32,
  Si proprium hoc fuerit, lævi de marmore tota
  Puniceo stabis suras evincta cothurno.
And Ibid. 36, Nunc te marmoreum pro tempore fecimus; at tu
  Si fœtura gregem suppleverit, aureus esto.

[17] σχῆμα. Dr. Wordsworth proposes to read XHIMA, h. e. καὶ εἷμα, for σχῆμα, unnecessarily, for σχῆμα may mean a dress as well as εἷμα. Aristoph. Acharn. 64, ὠκβάτανα τοῦ σχήματος. Besides καὶ can hardly precede δέ where μέν goes before. See a writer in the Classical Museum, vol. ii. 294. But why should we not adopt Græfius's explanation of this somewhat difficult passage, and suppose καινός to be used doubly with reference to σχῆμα and ἀμύκλας. ἀμύκλαι were costly shoes used in Laconia, and so called from Amyclæ, the town where their inventor lived?

[18] Horat. Od. II. iv. 21, Brachia et vultum, teretesque suras Integer laudo. Solomon's Song vii. 1, How beautiful are thy feet with shoes! Some think that Bombyces' feet are called ἀστραγάλοι in point of whiteness. Dice were called ἀστράγαλοι. If this were adopted as the true meaning, we have a parallel in Solomon's Song v. 15, His legs are as pillars of marble, set upon sockets of fine gold.

[19] Compare Idyll xiv. 28, εἰς ἄνδρα γενειῶν. Hor. ii. Sat. iii. 35, Sapientem pascere barbam. Lytierses was a son of Midas, king of Phrygia.

[20] Here we have certain invocations of Ceres and reapers' saws strung

Bind up, reapers, the sheaves, lest haply a passer-by should say, [21] good-for-nothing fellows, this hire too is thrown away.

Let the swathe of your mown-grass look to the north or west: thus the ear fills out. [22] Threshers of corn should avoid sleeping at mid-day: then, most of all, chaff comes from the stalk.

Reapers ought to begin at the rising of the crested lark, and to cease when it goes to rest: but to keep holiday during the heat.

The life of the frog is to be prayed for, my boys. He does not care for one to pour out liquor; for it is at hand for him in abundance.

It is better, miserly bailiff, to cook the lentil. [23] Don't cut your hand in splitting the cummin.

These *couplets* it behoves men labouring in the sun to sing: and 'tis meet that you should tell, O rustic, your starved love to your mother lying awake in bed in the morning.

IDYLL XI.

CYCLOPS.

ARGUMENT.

This Idyll commences with a preface to Nicias, a physician of Miletus, (to whom Theocritus inscribes the 13th Idyll, and of whom he makes

---

together. Compare Virg. Geor. i. 347, Et Cererem clamore vocent in tecta, &c. Cf. Callim. H. in Cer. ii. 127. H. in Dian. 130.

[21] σύκινοι, good for nothing—Men of fig-wood (not worth a fig?) Aristoph. Acharn. 108, speaks of πρίνινοι γέροντες, from πρῖνος, "hearts of oak."

[22] Understand μέμνασο or ὅρα in such cases. Matt. Gr. Gr. § 546. Compare at this place Milton's L'Allegro,
> To hear the lark begin his flight
> And startle, singing, the dull night,
> From his watch-tower in the skies,
> Till the dappled dawn doth rise.

[23] Misers were called bean-splitters. The cummin seed was too small for even them to split. Our Lord uses the word in rebuking the minute exactness of the Pharisees in matters indifferent, St. Matt. xxiii. 23.

favourable mention in Idyll xxviii. 6, and Epigr. vii. 3,) respecting the power of song in relieving the pains of disappointed love. The Cyclops is represented as using this solace for his hopeless passion for Galatea. Polyphemus, sitting on a rock overhanging the sea, beguiles his hours with song. He accuses the fair one of pride, and scorn for his deep devotion to her; and boasts of the gifts of fortune, which he can show, in lieu of gifts of beauty and personal grace. At last he seems to recover from his infatuation, perceiving the vanity of his hopes. Virgil has had this Idyll in his eye, while writing Eclogues ii. and ix.: and Bion perhaps gathered from it some ideas for the first part of his 15th Idyll. Compare Ovid Met. xiii. 755, &c., and Callimach. Epigr. xlix. p. 316 (Ernesti).

[1] THERE is no other remedy for love, O Nicias, either [2] *in the way* of salve, as it seems to me, or of plaster, except the Muses: but this is a light and sweet *thing* amongst men, yet 'tis not easy to find. But methinks you know it well, *as* being a physician, and in truth *a man* especially beloved by the nine Muses.

Thus, for instance, the *famous* Cyclops our countryman, the ancient Polyphemus, used most easily to pass his time, when he was enamoured of Galatea, just as he was now getting a beard about his mouth and temples. And he was wont to love, not at all with roses, or apples, or locks of hair, but with undone fury: and he held all things secondary *to his fury*. [3] Ofttimes his sheep went back by themselves to the fold from the green herbage; whilst he, singing his Galatea, pined away there, on the sea-weedy shore, from break of day, having beneath his breast a most hateful wound *inflicted* by mighty

---

[1] Horat. Od. IV. ii. 35, Minuentur atræ carmine curæ.

[2] οὔτ' ἔγχριστον. Compare Æsch. Prom. V. 488, (and Pearson on the Creed, Art. ii. p. 89,) οὐκ ἦν ἀλέξημ' οὐδὲν, οὐδὲ βρώσιμον οὐ χριστὸν, οὐδὲ πιστὸν. The Greeks had divers remedies and medicines. χριστά, unguents, παστά or πλαστά, plasters, πιστά or πότιμα, liquids, βρώσιμα, esculents, and ἐπῳδαί, incantations, charms, &c. Pope, Past. ii., calls " Love the sole disease thou canst not cure."

[3] αὐταὶ, suâ sponte. Virg. Ecl. vii. 11, Huc ipsi potum venient per prata juvenci. iv. 21, Ipsæ lacte domum referent distenta capellæ, Ubera. Pope Past. iii. 78,

> The shepherds cry, Thy flocks are left a prey!—
> Ah, what avails it me the flocks to keep,
> Who lost my heart, while I preserved my sheep?

Ovid. Met. xiii. 62,

> Quid sit amor sentit, nostrique cupidine captus
> Uritur, oblitus pecorum, antrorumque suorum.

Venus, [4] since she had fastened an arrow in his heart. [5] But he found his remedy, and sitting upon a high rock, looking towards the sea, he was wont to sing such strains as this.

'O fair Galatea, why dost thou spurn thy lover? [6] More white than cream-cheese to look upon, more tender than a lamb, more frisky than a calf, more sleek than an unripe grape? And you come hither just so, when sweet sleep possesses me, but you are straightway gone, when sweet sleep leaves me; [7] and you fly *me*, like a sheep when it has spied a gray wolf. [8] I for my part became enamoured of you, damsel, when first you came with my mother, desiring to cull from the mountain hyacinthine flowers; and I was acting as your guide. But to stop, when *once* I had beheld you, and afterwards, and even at present, from that time I am unable. Yet you do not care, no, by Jove, not a whit. I know, graceful maiden, on account of what you avoid me, [9] because a shaggy eyebrow stretches all over my forehead, from one ear to another, as one great one; and one eye is upon *my brow*, and a broad nostril over the lip.

Yet this same I, being such *as you see*, [10] feed a thousand

---

[4] Κύπριδος ἐκ μεγάλας. Idyll ii. 30, ἐξ Ἀφροδίτας, and vii. 55, τό οἱ ἧπατι: Here we must either, as Jacobs thinks, retain τό, supposing it to mean " quoniam," or read τά οἱ, i. q. ἃ οἱ, according to the oldest form of the article, τὸς, τὰ, τὸν. Matt. Gr. Gr. § 65, 3. See Wordsw. at xiv. 56.

[5] Cf. Callimach. Epig. xlix., and Ovid. Met. xiii. 778,
   Prominet in pontum cuneatus acumine longo,
   Collis: utrumque latus circumfluit æquoris unda.
   Huc ferus ascendit Cyclops, mediusque resedit.

[6] Cf. Ov. Met. xiii. 789—804, where Galatea is called splendidior vitro, tenero lascivior hædo, &c., and Virg. Ecl. vii. 37,
   Nerine Galatea, thymo mihi dulcior Hyblæ
   Candidior cycnis, hederâ formosior albâ.
Ovid imitates this and the next line in the verses beginning,
   Mollior et cycni plumis, et lacte coacto.

[7] Hor. Od. i. 15, 29, Quem tu, cervus uti vallis in alterâ
   Visum parte lupum graminis immemor
   Sublimi feries mollis anhelitu.

[8] Virg. Ecl. viii. 37,
   Sepibus in nostris parvam te roscida mala,
   Dux ego vester eram, vidi cum matre legentem.

[9] Hirsutumque supercilium, promissaque barba. Virg. Ecl. viii. 33.

[10] Virg. Ecl. ii. 21,
   Mille meæ Siculis errant in montibus agnæ
   Lac mihi non æstate novum, non frigore defit.
Compare Ov. Met. xiii. 821—830. Hom. Odyss. ix. 219, &c.

sheep, and from these, milking them, I drink the best milk. And cheese fails me not, either in summer, or in autumn, or in the depth of winter; but the baskets are always overburdened. I am skilled too in playing on the pipes, as no one of the Cyclops here; singing thee, [11] my dear sweet-apple, and myself at the same time, [12] oftentimes early in the night. And I am rearing for you eleven fawns, all of them [13] wearing collars, and four cubs of a bear. Nay, then, come you to me, and you shall have nothing worse; and suffer the pale-green sea to roll up to the beach: [14] you will pass the night with me in my cave more sweetly. [15] There are laurels and tapering cypresses, *there* is black ivy, and the vine with its sweet fruit; there is cool water, which wooded Ætna sends forth for me, a divine drink, out of white snow: (who would prefer to these delights to dwell in sea or waves?) But if in truth I seem to you to be rather shaggy, I have oak-branches *near*, and unresting fire under the embers. And I could endure to be scorched by you even to my *very* soul, [16] and that single eye, than which nothing is more dear to me. [17] Woe is me, that my mother

---

[11] γλυκύμαλον, cf. Callim. H. in Cerer. 29, a term of endearment.

[12] νυκτὸς ἀωρί, Idyll xxiv. 38, Aristoph. Ecclesiaz. 741: see Pierson on Mœris, p. 32, who quotes three passages from the Orators, and two from elsewhere, and states that he has met but one example of ἀωρί not followed by νυκτὸς or νυκτῶν. τοὶ ἕνδεκα νεβρώς. Cf. Virg. Ecl. ii. 40,
    Præterea duo, nec tutâ mihi valle reperti,
    Capreoli, sparsis etiam nunc pellibus albo.

[13] μαννοφόρως, bearing collars, th. μάννος, a necklace. Propert. IV. viii. 24, Armillati colla Molossa canes. Others read μανοφόρως, i.e. μηνοφόρους, moon-marked, which Reiske holds to be the true reading. καὶ σκύμνως. Compare Ovid. Met. xiii. 836, Villosæ catulos summis in montibus ursæ.

[14] ὀρεχθῆν—In the parallel passage of Virg. Ecl. ix. 44, Bentley reads "incani" for insani, as the literal rendering of γλαυκὰν. Virg. Ecl. i. 80, Hic tamen hanc mecum poteris requiescere noctem. Chapman compares with this invitation, Kit Marlow's Shepherd's song, beginning,
    Come live with me and be my love,
    And we will all the pleasures prove, &c.

[15] Compare Hom. Odyss. ix. 183—187, from which Theocr. has taken the ground-work of this passage; and comp. Odyss. ix. 219, 223, 233, &c. at 51, 52.

[16] Catull. iii. 5, Quem plus illa suis oculis amabat.

[17] Pope, Past. ii. 45, expresses the same kind of sentiment:
    Oh, were I made, by some transforming power,
    The captive bird, that sings within thy bower.
    Then might my voice thy listening ears employ,
    And I those kisses he receives enjoy.

did not bring me forth having gills, in which case I should have come down to you, and have kissed your hand, if you would not your lips, and I should be [18] bringing you either white lilies, or the soft poppy with red petals. But the one springs in summer, and the other in the winter, so that I should not have been able to bring you all these together.

Now indeed, dear maiden, yes, now on the spot I will learn to swim, if so be [19] that any foreigner arrive hither, sailing in his ship, that I may learn what possible delight it is to you to dwell in the water-depths. Mayest thou come out, Galatea, and having come forth, forget (as I *do* now sitting here) to go away home: [20] and mayest thou wish to feed flocks with me, and to milk along *with me*, and to press cheese, infusing sharp runnet. My mother [21] alone wrongs me, and I find fault with her: not a kind word ever at all has she spoken to you on my behalf, and this too, though she sees me becoming thin day after day. I will say that my head and both my feet are throbbing, that she may be pained, since I too am pained.

[22] O Cyclops, Cyclops, whither hast thou flown in reason? If thou wouldst forthwith weave baskets, and mowing the young shoots, bear them to the lambs, perhaps thou wouldst have thy senses in a far greater degree. [23] Milk the ewe that is

So Shakspeare, Romeo and Juliet, Oh that I were a glove upon that hand, &c.

[18] Virg. Ecl. ii. 45, 46,   Tibi lilia plenis
           Ecce ferunt nymphæ calathis, tibi candida Nais
           Pallentes violas et summa papavera carpens.

[19] The Cyclops are represented by Hom. Odyss. ix. 125, as knowing nothing of navigation. οὐ γὰρ Κυκλώπεσσι νέες πάρα μιλτοπάρηοι. Virg. Ecl. ix. 39, Huc ades, O Galatea, quis est nam ludus in undis:
           Huc ades: insani feriant sine littora fluctus.

[20] Virg. Ecl. ii. 28, O tantum libeat mecum tibi sordida rura,
           Atque humiles habitare casas, &c.
ταμισον: coagulum. See Tibull. II. iii. 17, Et miscere novo docuisse coagula lacte.

[21] μόνα, in Wordsworth's judgment, is faulty, because Galatea clearly wronged the Cyclops, and so too did the Cyclops himself, (see 72). Wordsw. suggests κόρα, "o virgo, mater me lædit," and points out the same emendation of an unsound passage in Bion xv. 15, where for Μῶνος Ἀχιλλεὺς, read, κῶρος—puer Achilles.

[22] Ibid. 69, Ah! 'Corydon, Corydon, quæ te dementia cepit.

[23] Callimach. Epigr. xxxiii. 5, 6,
    Χ' ἁμὸς ἔρως τοιός δε. τὰ μεν φεύγοντα διώκειν
    Οἶδε, τὰ δ' ἐν μέσσῳ κείμενα παρπέταται.
Hor. Sat. I. ii. 108, Transvolat in medio posita, et fugientia captat.

close at hand! Why dost pursue the one that flies you? [24] Haply you will find another Galatea even more beautiful. [25] Many damsels bid me sport with them in the night season, and all of them titter whenever I listen to them. Plainly even I appear to be somebody on the land.

Thus in sooth Polyphemus used to beguile his love by singing; and [26] he passed his days more easily than *if* he had given money *for a cure*.

IDYLL XII.

AITES.

ARGUMENT.

This Idyll, which is of a lyric, not a Bucolic character, has been suspected to be not the work of Theocritus. It is an expression of love towards a youth on his return to his friend after three days' absence. The poet goes on to hope that this love may be mutual and perpetual. It is ended with a strain in honour of the Megarensians, on account of their having instituted annual kissing-matches at the tomb of Diocles. For the different opinions of commentators, &c., on the authorship of this Idyll, see the edition of Kiessling, London, 1829, at the head of the 12th Idyll.

HAST thou come, dear youth, after three nights and mornings? Hast thou come? [1] Yet those who long, grow old in a day. As much as spring is sweeter than winter, as much as the apple than the sloe, as much as a sheep *is* more woolly than its lambkin, as much as a virgin is better than a thrice-

---

Ovid. Met. xiv. 28, Melius sequerere volentem
    Optantemque eadem, parilique cupidine captam.
[24] Ecl. ii. 73, Invenies alium, si te hic fastidit, Alexim.
[25] Horat. Od. I. ix. 19, Lenesque sub noctem susurri,
    Compositâ repetantur horâ.
At τὶς in the next line, compare Juvenal Sat. i.,
    Aude aliquid brevibus Gyaris et carcere dignum
    Si vis esse *aliquid*.
[26] ἢ for ἢ εἰ, which should perhaps be written.
[1] Hom. Od. τ. 360, αἶψα γὰρ ἐν κακότητι βροτοὶ καταγηράσκουσι.
Virg. Ecl. vii. 43, Si mihi non hæc lux toto sit longior anno.

wed wife, as much as a fawn is swifter than a calf, as much as a clear-voiced nightingale most musical of all birds together; so much have you gladdened me ² *by* having appeared: and I have run *to thee*, as some traveller runs to the shelter of a shady beech when the sun is scorching. ³ Would that the loves might breathe upon both of us evenly, and we might become 'a song' ⁴ to all who shall come after.

'In truth, a certain pair of men were thus affected one toward another; the one ⁵ a lover (εἴσπνηλος), *as* one, who spoke the Amyclæan dialect, would say; and the other again the Thessalian would call thus, ⁶ 'the beloved' (ἀΐταν). And ⁷ they loved each other with equal yoke. Surely then, I wot, were golden men of yore, when he that was loved requited that love.' Yes, would that this might be, O father Jove, would it might be, O undecaying immortals; and ⁸ two hundred generations afterwards some one might bring word to me, unto

---

² For a similar grouping of similitudes. See Pope Past. iii. 43—46,
    Not bubbling fountains to the thirsty swain;
    Not balmy sleep to labourers faint with pain;
    Not showers to larks, nor sunshine to the bee,
    Are half so charming as thy sight to me.
Drummond of Hawthornden, from whom Warton thinks Pope took the idea of this passage, comes very near Theocritus.
    Cool shades to pilgrims, whom hot glances burn,
    Are not so pleasing as thy safe return.
Virg. Ecl. v. 16, Lenta salix quantum pallenti cedit olivæ,
    Puniceis humilis quantum saliunca rosetis,
    Judicio nostro tantum, &c.
And for the sentiment of the eighth line, see Horat. Od. iv. 5,
    Vultus ubi tuus
    Affulsit populo, gratior it dies
    Et soles melius nitent.
³ Tibull. II. i. 80,   At ille
    Felix, cui placidus leniter afflat amor.
⁴ Propert. i. 15, 24, Tu quoque uti fieres nobilis historia.
⁵ Amyclæ was a city of Laconia having a temple of Apollo, south of Sparta. εἴσπνηλος, from εἰσπνέω, is a Laconic word, used by Callimach. Fragm. 169, p. 505, (Ernesti).
⁶ ἀΐτης, a Thessalian word, which Welcker thinks is a form of ἤθεος.
⁷ ἴσῳ ξυγῷ. Pliny Epist. III. ix. 8, Cum uterque pari jugo, non pro se, sed pro causâ niteretur. χρύσειοι πάλαι ἄνδρες. Comp. Aristoph. Nub. 1024; Horat. Od. I. v. 9, Qui nunc te fruitur credulus *aureâ*; and Virg. Georg. ii. 538, Aureus hanc vitam in terris Saturnus agebat.
⁸ Virg. Æn. iv. 387, Audiam; et hæc manes veniet mihi fama sub imos. ἀνέξοδον. Cf. Virg. Æn. vi. 426, Evaditque celer ripam irremeabilis undæ. And ibid. 128,

Acheron, whence we return not, 'Thy love and that of thy graceful loved one is *even* now in the mouths of men, and especially among the youths.' But in truth, of these things indeed the celestials will be arbiters, as they choose; yet I, in praising thee *as* the beautiful, [9]shall not breed fib-marks on the top of my nose. For even if you should have pained me at all, you have immediately made *the hurt* innocent, and doubly gratified me, so I have departed having good measure.

[10]O Nisæan Megarensians, excelling at the oars, may ye dwell happily, since ye have [11]honoured especially the Attic stranger Diocles, the lover of youths. Ever about his tomb in crowds, in earliest spring, youths contend to bear off the prize of kisses. And whoso shall have pressed most sweetly lip to lip, goes back to his mother loaded with garlands. Happy he, who is arbiter of those kisses for the lads. Surely, methinks, he oft [12]invokes the gladsome Ganymede, that he may have a mouth like the Lydian stone, by which money-changers try gold, whether it be base or pure.

Facilis descensus Averni
* * * * * * * *
Sed revocare gradus, superasque evadere ad auras
Hoc opus, hic labor est.

[9] ἀραιῆς, Koehler, Dahl., Kiessling, read ὀκραιῆς, which makes a much better sense. Compare Idyll ix. 30, and the passages there quoted. ψεύδεα = signa mendacii. Wordsw. would have ἀραιῆς retained, but translated not as "exilis," but "teneræ."

[10] *Nisæan*, of Nisæa, the sea-port and arsenal of Megara.

[11] Diocles, an Athenian, became a hero of the Megareans, for dying in defence of a youth in battle. See Scholiast. A festival was held in the spring to his memory, and the youth who gave the sweetest kiss received a garland.

[12] He invokes Ganymede, that he may have as serviceable a mouth for testing rival kisses, as the Lydian stone is useful to money-changers, to test pure and alloyed gold. Wordsw., in a long note, suggests the reading ἔχῃ τύπον for ἐτήτυμον, i. e. whether it have a false stamp.

IDYLL XIII.

HYLAS.

ARGUMENT.

The poet premising somewhat about the power of love over gods and men, opens the subject of the rape of Hylas with a description of the love and care of Hercules for the lad. When the Argonauts had put to shore at the land of the Cyanians, on the coast of the Propontis, Hylas was sent by Hercules to fetch water. Whilst drawing from the fountain, in a lovely spot, he is drawn in by the Nymphs, who are captivated by the exceeding beauty of the boy. Hercules, suspecting some mishap from the delay of Hylas, sets out in quest of him; and as his fruitless search detains him a long time, he is left behind by the Argonauts, who suppose he has quitted them purposely. The hero goes afoot to Colchis. This Idyll is Epic in its character, but with such a touch of Bucolic sweetness about it as to win it a high place among the Idylls of Theocritus. Note the description of the fountain, vs. 40, and the anxiety of the Nymphs to console the lad, 54—59.

Not for us alone, as we used to suppose, *my* Nicias, did he beget Eros, to [1] whomsoever of the gods this child was once born: nor to us first, who are mortals, [2] and do not see the morrow, do the things that are beautiful appear to be beautiful. But even the [3] brazen-hearted son of Amphitryo, who sustained *the attack of* the fierce lion, was enamoured of a lad, [4] the graceful Hylas, that wore the curly locks, and he taught

---

[1] Compare the lines of Virg. Georg. iii. 242, beginning, Omne adeo genus in terris hominum, &c. The father of Cupid is unknown. Compare Meleager Epigr. xci.,

Πατρὸς δ' οὐκέτ' ἔχω φράζειν τίνος· οὔτε γάρ αἰθήρ
Οὐ χθών φησι τεκεῖν τὸν θρασὺν· οὐ πέλαγος.

[2] Comp. Callim. Epigr. xv. Eurip. Alcest. 783,
κοὐκ ἔστιν οὐδεὶς ὅστις ἐξεπίσταται
τὴν αὔριον μέλλουσαν εἰ βιώσεται.

[3] Cf. Hom. Il. ii. 490. Horat. Od. I. iii. 9,
    Illi robur et æs triplex
    Circa pectus erat.
Mosch. iv. 44, infr., πέτρης ὅγ' ἔχων νόον ἠὲ σιδήρου καρτερὸν ἐν στήθεσσι.

[4] Virg. Georg. iii. 6, Cui non dictus Hylas puer? Val. Flacc. Argon. iii. 545, *seq.*, who represents him to have been caught while hunting. Propert. I. xx. 15, *seq.* 45,
    Cujus ut accensæ Dryades candore puellæ,
    Miratæ solitos destituere choros
    Prolapsum leviter facili traxere liquore :
    Tum sonitum rapto corpore fecit Hylas.
Herodot., vii. 193, says this happened at Pagasæ in the bay of Magnesia

him every thing, as a father *would* his own child, by having learned which he had himself become good and illustrious: and he was never apart from him, not even if mid-day were rising, nor when the white-horsed *chariot of* Aurora was mounting to the halls of Jove, nor when the chirping young birds looked to their nest, their mother having fluttered her wings upon her dusky perch: in order that the boy might be ⁵ shapen *with care* according to his mind; and drawing well with him, might turn out a perfect man. ⁶ But when Jason, son of Æson, was sailing in quest of the golden fleece, and the nobles were following along with him, chosen out of all cities, ⁷ because there was some help in them, there came also to rich ⁸ Iolchos the much-enduring son of Alcmene, heroine of ⁹ Midea.

And with him Hylas went down to the well-benched Argo, which vessel touched ¹⁰ not the jostling Cyanean rocks, but

⁵ πεπoναμένος, educatus. Matthiæ. Eur. Iph. Aul. 207. Dissen: Pindar Ol. vi. 11.—J. W. αὐτῷ δ' εὖ ἕλκων, a metaphor taken from beasts of burden, and αὐτῷ said as if it were σὺν αὐτῷ, (Toup.) Hercules is represented never leaving the side of Hylas, in order that the boy, drawing the plough straight on, might turn out well. Others read αὐτῶ, and understand τὸ ἦθος, "drawing his morals from him." Koehler reads αὐτῶ δ' ἐξ ἕλκων, i. e. ἕλκων ἐξ αὐτοῦ ab ipso sumens exemplum. Wordsw., αὐτῶ δ' ἐξ αἴκλων, ejus ex consortio, propriè mensâ communi, in virum fortem evaderet. αἴκλον was the evening meal at Sparta.

⁶ Virg. Ecl. iv. 34, Alter erit tum Tiphys, et altera quæ vehat Argo Delectos heroas.

⁷ ὧν ὀφέλός τι, i. e. ὅτι τούτων ἦν ὀφέλος τι. Il. xiii. 236, αἴκ' ὄφελός τι γενώμεθα.

⁸ Iolchos, or Colchis, the seat of government of Æetes, father of Medea, situate on the Euxine.

⁹ Of Midea, a city of Bœotia, mentioned by Hom. Il. β. 507, in catalogue of ships, bestowed by Sthenelus on Atreus and Thyestes, uncles of Eurystheus.

¹⁰ Κυανεᾶν—συνδρομάδων. Milton Parad. L.,
Harder beset,
And more endangered, than when Argo pass'd
Through Bosphorus, betwixt the jostling rocks.

The jostling rocks, κυάνεαι, νῆσοι, were supposed to close on all who sailed between them. Eurip. Med. 2. Androm. 796. Συμπληγάδας. They were two small islands opposite the Thracian Bosphorus. Ovid. Trist. I. x. 34, Transeat instabiles strenua Cyaneas.—Phasis, a river of Colchis.—διεξάϊξε—μέγα λαῖτμα. It seems clear in this passage that βαθὺν—Φᾶσιν must be taken parenthetically, and μέγα λαῖτμα be referred to διεξάϊξε. Lobeck, at Soph. Ajax, vs. 475, 476, p. 267—269, brings forward several instances of the construction of the verb and its dependent noun being interrupted by an intervening secondary clause. Hesiod. Theog. 151. Eur. Ion, 700.

shot through, (and ran into deep Phasis :) like an eagle, a great surge, from out which at that time low rocks stood. [11] And what time the Pleiads rise, and far-away spots are feeding the young lamb—spring having now turned—then the [12] godlike flower of heroes began to recollect the voyage, and having taken their seats in the hollow Argo, came to the Hellespont, [13] at the third day's blowing of the south wind. And they found an anchorage within the Propontis, where oxen widen the furrows of the Cyanians, as they [14] rub the ploughshare. Having landed then on the shore, they busily prepared a feast [15] at evening by pairs : and many of them strewed for themselves one couch-on-the-ground. For by them lay a broad meadow, suitable for beds of leaves. [16] Thence they cut for themselves the sharp flowering-rush and low galingal. And the auburn-haired Hylas had gone to fetch water for supper, for both Hercules himself and the staunch Telamon, (both which comrades used alway to [17] feed at one table,) with a brazen vessel ;—and quickly he spied a fountain in a

[11] Lambs born mostly in November and December were weaned and sent to feed apart after four months ; this would be about April, and the rising of the Pleiads from April 22nd to May 10th, brought in fine weather commonly. Virg. Georg. iv. 231, 232,

Taygete simul os terris ostendit honestum
Pleias.

[12] ἄωτος. This word (cf. Id. ii. 2) is used for any thing best of its kind. Pindar, Ol. Od. ii., μουσικῆς ἄωτον· ἡρώων ἄωτον. Ibid., στεφάνων ἄωτον. Hom. Il. ix. 657, λίνοιο λεπτὸν ἄωτον. Something like it is Æsch. Prom. v. 7, ἄνθος πυρός. Virg. (Ecl. iv. 34) calls them " delectos heroos."

[13] νότῳ—ἀέντι. Dative for genitive. Matt. Gr. Gr. § 562, 2. The dative absolute is used instead of the genitive, as the subject of the participle may be considered as that in reference to which the action of the verb takes place. Herodot. vi. 21. Thuc. viii. 24. Xenoph. H. Gr. III. ii. 25.

[14] Virg. Georg. i. 46, Et sulco attritus splendescere vomer.

[15] δειελινοί, at evening. Adject. for adv. Matt. Gr. Gr. § 446, 8. Hom. Il. a. 497, ἠερίη. Il. β. 2, παννύχιοι. Il. a. 423, Ζεὺς χθιζὸς ἔβη. Horat. Epod. xvi. 51, Nec vespertinus circumgemit ursus ovile.

[16] βοότομον, " butomus," the flowering rush. Theophr. κύπειρον, (5, 45,) galingal. Fawkes considers the former to be the same with the " carex acuta," mentioned by Virg. Georg. iii. 231.

[17] δαίνυντο τράπεζαν, a sort of cognate accusative, or blending, as some say, of two ideas, i. e. δαινύμενον ἔχειν τράπεσδαν, and δαίνυσθαι. Soph. Ajax, 30, πηδᾶν πεδία. Theoc. Id. xv. 122. Apoll. Rhod. gives an account of this, i. 1207 ; and Propert. I. xx. 23,

At comes invicti juvenis processerat ultra
Raram sepositi quærere fontis aquam.

low-lying spot; and around it grew many rushes, and the pale-blue [18] 'swallow-wort,' and green 'maiden-hair,' and blooming parsley, and couch-grass stretching through the marshes: and in the midst of the water, Nymphs were making ready a dance, sleepless Nymphs, dread goddesses to rustics, [19] Eunica and Malis, and Nychea with a look like spring.

In sooth [20] the boy was holding over *the fountain* an urn that might contain a copious draught, hastening to plunge it; when they all clung to his hand: for love for the Argive boy had encircled the tender hearts of them all: and [21] he fell sheer into the black water, *like* as when a ruddy star hath fallen from the sky sheer into the sea, and a sailor has said to his [22] shipmates, 'Loosen the ship's tackle, my lads, here's a breeze for sailing!' The Nymphs indeed holding on their knees the weeping boy, began to console him with gentle words; [23] whilst the son of Amphitryon, disturbed about the lad, went, with his well-bent bow and arrows [24] after the Scythian fashion, and the club which his right hand ever used to hold. Thrice indeed

---

[18] χελιδόνιον,' swallow-wort or celandine. ἀδίαντον, a water-plant, "capillus Veneris," "maiden-hair." Theophr. ἄγρωστις, (Odyss. vi. 90,) triticum repens.

[19] Cf. Aves Aristoph. 1169, πυρρίχην βλέπων, bellicum intuens. Matt. Gr. Gr. § 409, 2. Æsch. S. c. Theb. 500. Chapman quotes here a rich parallel from Kit Marlow.

[20] Comp. Propert. I. xx. 43,

Tandem haurire parat demissis flumina palmis,
Innixus dextro plena trahens humero.

[21] ἀθρόος. Virg. Georg. i. 365, Sæpe stellas—videbis
Præcipites cœlo labi.
See too Hom. Il. δ. 45. Ov. Met. ii. 319,

Volvitur in præceps, longoque per aera tractu
Fertur, ut interdum de cœlo stella sereno
Etsi non cecidit, potuit cecidisse videri.

[22] ὅπλα, generally ship's tackle, specially her cordage, cables, &c., as Ezech. Spanheim shows in Callimach. H. to Delos, 315. It seems in all its senses to resemble "arma" in Latin. Virg. Æn. iv. 574, Solvite vela citi. Ov. Fast. iii. 586, Findite remigio, navita dixit, aquas.

[23] For a rather diffuse parallel, compare Valer. Flacc. Arg. iii. 570.

[24] Μαιωτιστί, in Scythian fashion. The lake Mæotis is in Scythia, near the mouth of the Phasis. The Scholiast tells us Hercules learned the use of the bow from Teutarus, a Scythian, the herdsman of Amphitryon Æn. viii. 219, Hic vero Alcidæ furiis exarserat atro

Felle dolor: rupit arma manu, nodisque gravatum
Robur—

he [25] shouted Hylas to the full depth of his throat, and thrice, I wot, the boy [26] heard: and a thin voice came from the water; but though very near he seemed to be afar off. [27] And as when a well-bearded lion, some savage lion on the mountains, upon hearing a fawn crying afar off, hastes from his lair towards a most ready meal, in such wise Hercules kept moving about among the impassable briers through regret for the lad, and kept ranging over much space.

Hapless are they who love! How he toiled in roaming over [28] mountains and thickets! and Jason's *enterprise* was all secondary to it.

The ship indeed was waiting with its sails floating in air; and the youths of [29] them that were present, kept washing the hatches at midnight, in expectation of Hercules: he however was going madly wherever his feet led him, for a cruel god was tearing his heart inwardly. [30] Thus indeed most beauteous Hylas is numbered *one* of the blest *immortals*. But the heroes began to revile Hercules as a deserter of the ship, because he had withdrawn from Argo of the thirty benches. And he came a-foot to Colchis, and to [31] inhospitable Phasis.

[25] Virg. Ecl. vi. 43,
   His adjungit, Hylan nautæ quo fonte relictum
   Clamassent, ut littus Hyla, Hyla, omne sonaret.
Spenser, Faery Queen, b. iii. c. 2,
   And every wood, and every valley wide,
   He fill'd with Hylas' name, the Nymphs eke Hylas cried.
[26] Propert. I. xx. 49, 50,
   Cui procul Alcides iterat responsa, sed illi
   Nomen ab extremis fontibus aura refert.
[27] Compare Hom. Il. xviii. 318. Lucret. ii. 355. Ov. Met. v. 164.
[28] ἀλώμενος is joined with an accusative. Eurip. Helen. 539. Bion, Id. i. 20, has ἀνὰ δρυμοὺς ἀλάληται.
[29] Instead of the obscure τῶν παρεόντων, Græfius suggests τῶν ποδεώνων, i. e. the sheets or ropes fastened to the corners of the sails by which they are tightened or slackened. The line will then stand,
   Ναῦς μένεν ἁρμεν' ἔχοισα μετάρσια τῶν ποδεώνων.
Navis stabat antennas habens intentas (vel expansas) ex pedibus. Compare Virg. Æn. v. 830,
   Unà omnes fecere pedem, pariterque sinistros
   Nunc dextros solvere sinus: unà ardua torquent
   Cornua, detorquentque: Ferunt sua flamina classem.
But perhaps the most simple and likely emendation is that of Wordsworth, who for τῶν παρεόντων reads ἑτῶν παρεόντων, sociis præsentibus.
[30] Virg. Æn. vii. 211,   Regia cœli
   Accipit, et numero divorum altaribus addit.
[31] ἄξενος. Ovid. Trist. III. ii. 7, Inhospita littora Ponti.

IDYLL XIV.

THE LOVE OF CYNISCA, OR THYONICHUS.

ARGUMENT.

Æschines, jilted by a maiden of whom he was enamoured, declares to Thyonichus the causes of their quarrel. This leads to an explanation of his heart-sickness, and especially to an account of the banquet, at which their quarrel had arisen. After this Æschines declares to his friend his purpose of crossing the seas, to find relief for his griefs. Thyonichus approves and urges him to go and serve in the armies of Ptolemy; of which monarch a graceful eulogy follows. It seems hence not unlikely that this Idyll, which is not of the pastoral kind, was either composed at Alexandria, or at any rate intended for the eye of the monarch.

ÆSCHINES. THYONICHUS.

Æschines. GOOD morrow to Sir Thyonichus.
Thyonichus. [1] Well, the same to you, Æschines.
Æsch. How late you are!
Thyon. Late? And what is your care, pray?
Æsch. I am not in the best condition, Thyonichus.
Thyon. Therefore I suppose you are lean, [2] and that upper lip is covered, and your locks are unkempt. Such a sort of [3] fellow was a Pythagorean, that arrived here but lately, pale and [4] unsandaled, and he said that he was an Athenian. In truth that man too, methinks, was longing for baked flour.

Ibid. IV. iv. 55,   Euxini littora Ponti
    Dictus ab antiquis Axenus ille fuit.

[1] ἀλλὰ τὺ αὐτόν. So Reiske reads instead of the common τοι αὐτῷ, which will not stand. τὸ αὐτὸν, i. e. volo et ego te ipsum salvere. Reiske also conjectures ἄλλα τοιαῦτα Αἰσχίνᾳ, sc. βούλομαι γίγνεσθαι. Better perhaps is τὺ αὐτὸς, "immo te ego ipse."

[2] Juvenal ix. 12,   Vultus gravis, horrida siccæ
    Silva comæ: nullus totâ nitor in cute.

[3] Pythagorean tenets and Athenian citizens were objects of special ridicule to the luxurious and easy Sicilian. Idyll iv. 21, is an instance of this. Compare Aristoph. Nub. 103, 104, τοὺς ὠχριῶντας, τοὺς ἀνυποδήτους λέγεις.

[4] Κἀνυπόδατος. Ezech. Spanheim, in Callim. H. in Cerer. 125, shows that this was the custom of mourners, and persons engaged in solemn sacrifice, &c. Compare Bion, Idyll i. 21, Venus Adonidem lugens, ἀσάνδαλος dicitur. Cf. 2 Sam. xi. 30. Ezechiel xxiv. 17.

Æsch. [5] You are always joking, good sir : but me the graceful Cynisca wrongs ; [6] and I shall go mad without one knowing it, within a hair's breadth.

Thyon. You are ever thus, good Æschines, [7] mild or sharp, wanting every thing on the spur of the moment ; but tell me, however, what news ?

Æsch. The Argive, and I, and Apis, the Thessalian driver of steeds, and Cleonicus, the soldier, were drinking at my country place. I had killed a couple of young fowls and a sucking pig, and had broached for them the fragrant Thracian [8] wine, almost four years old, as mild as if from the wine-press. [9] A Colchian mushroom had been brought out : 'twas a sweet drink. And when *the cup* was now making way, it pleased us [10] that neat wine should be poured forth to the health of whomsoever each chose, only he was bound to say to whose. We indeed began to drink naming *our loves*, as it had been determined. But she said nothing, though I was present. What mind, think you, had I *then?* [11] 'Won't you speak ? you have seen a wolf,' said some one sportively, 'as the wise man said.' Then she fired up ; you might have lighted

[5] παίσδεις ἔχων. For this redundancy of the participle, see Matt. Gr. Gr. § 567, last clause, p. 986.

[6] θρὶξ ἀνὰ μέσσον. Only a hair's breadth. Prov. Plaut. Mostell I. i. 60, Plumâ haud interest patronus, an cliens, probior siet.

[7] Martial. xii. 47, Difficilis, facilis, jucundus, acerbus es idem. Terent. Heautont. III. i. 21.

[8] Bibline is the name of a district of Thrace, the wine of which was esteemed highly for its sweetness and lightness. Hesiod O. et D. 587.

[9] βολβός Κολχείας, is the reading preferred by Kiessling, and translated here. Wordsworth, in a long and learned note, suggests for βολβός τις κοχλίας to read βολβός, κτείς, κοχλίας, a mushroom, a cockle, a shell-fish : comparing Horat. Sat. II. iv. 33,

Ostrea Circeiis, Miseno oriuntur echini,
Pectinibus patulis jactat se molle Tarentum.

[10] Compare Idyll ii. 152, οὕνεχ' ἔρωτος Ἀκράτω ἐπεχεῖτο.

[11] Λύκον εἶδες ; These words are those of one of the guests, following up the words of Æschines, "Won't you speak?" There is a joke upon the word Λύκος, (wolf or Lycus,) which shows the guest to have been aware of Cynisca's passion, and to have been at the same time apt at proverbs. See Virg. Ecl. ix. 53, Vox quoque Mærim

Jam fugit ipsa : Mærim lupi videre priores.

St. Ambrose in Hexaem. on St. Luke x. 3, writes, Lupi, siquem priores hominem viderint, vocem ejus feruntur eripere. See Wordsw. note at this passage. In the next line Wordsw. would read for Χ' ἤφθα, κ' ᾔθετο from αἴθεσθαι.

even a lamp with ease from her. 'Tis Lycus, *yes*, Lycus it is, son of Labas our neighbour, tall and delicate, and to the fancy of many, beautiful. His was that much talked-of love with which she was pining away: and this had been thus quietly whispered in my ear before: however I had not inquired into it, [12] to no purpose being a bearded man. And now then we four were in the depth of our cups, when the Larissæan began to sing 'My Lycus,' from the beginning, a kind of Thessalian ditty, misguided mind *as he had*. But Cynisca on a sudden began to weep more warmly than a maiden of six years beside her mother, longing for her bosom. Then I, *the hot fellow*, whom you know, Thyonichus, struck her [13] with my fist on the side of the face, ay and another blow again: and she, having drawn her robes up around her, went away out quickly. Do not I please you, my pest? Is another sweeter to you [14] in the bosom? Go, caress another lover: for him those tears of thine flow [15] like sweet apples. And like as a swallow flies back quickly to gather victuals, [16] fresh sustenance for her young nestlings; *nay*, more swiftly ran she from her soft seat, right

[12] μάταν εἰς ἄνδρα γενειῶν, εἰς ἄνδρα, i. q. pro viro, as Plaut. Menæchm. II. ii. 14, pro sano loqueris. See vs. 50, εἰς δέον, in the same construction. Compare Idyll x. 40, ὤμοι τῶ πώγωνος. The meaning of the sentence is, I have not shown myself a man, because I did not examine the matter.

[13] πὺξ ἐπὶ κόρρας "Ηλασα—ἐλαύνω is properly used of a blow given. Hom. Il. ii. 199. Theocr. Id. xxii. 104. Callim. H. in Cerer. 92, ἤλασε κάπρος. Odyss. xix. 393, σῦς ἤλασε λευκῷ ὀδόντι.—ἐπὶ κόρρης πατάσσειν. Demosth. 562, 9. Ovid. Amor. I. vii. 3,
   Nam furor in dominam temeraria brachia movit:
   Flet mea vesanâ læsa puella manu.
Horat. Od. I. xvii. 24, Nec metues protervum
                Suspecta Cyrum, ne mali dispari
                Incontinentes injiciat manus.
κάλλαν αὖθις, understand πληγήν. Compare Æsch. Agam. 1386, τρίτην ἐπενδίδωμι.

[14] ὑποκόλπιος. Juvenal ii. 120, Ingens Cœna sedet, gremio jacuit nova nupta mariti.

[15] τὰ σὰ δάκρυα μᾶλα—μᾶλα for ὡς μᾶλα. Mosch. iv. 56, 57, θαλερώτερα μήλων. Kiessl. Dr. Wordsworth naturally thinks this absurd, and would read δάκρυσι for δάκρυα, h. e. Illi tuæ genæ lacrimis madent. But a writer in Class. Museum, vol. ii. 294, suggests καλὰ for μᾶλα, where the adjective would be an emphatic predicate, "Your tears are very pretty to him." Or καλά, as Briggs says, might stand for καλῶς.

[16] Cf. Hom. Il. ix. 323. Virg. Æn. xii. 473,
   Nigra velut magnas domini cùm divitis ades
   Pervolat, et pennis atria lustrat hirundo.

through the vestibule and folding-doors, [17] wherever her feet bore her. In truth there is a saw spoken, [18] 'The bull has gone to the wood.' 'Tis twenty now, and eight and nine and ten days beside ; to-day is the eleventh, add two: and 'tis two months since we have been parted one from the other, and, [19] after the Thracian custom, I have not shaven myself. And to her now Lycus is [20] every thing, and to Lycus at night the door is opened. [21] But I am neither worthy any account, nor am I numbered, wretched Megarensian, *being* in most dishonoured plight. And if indeed I could love no more, then every thing would go on as it ought: but now, [22] at last, as the mouse, so the saying is, Thyonichus, I have tasted pitch. And what is the remedy for hopeless love, I know not: only Simus, he who was enamoured of the daughter of Epichalcus, *Simus*, my equal in age, sailed abroad and came back heart-whole. [23] I too will sail across the sea : I shall be neither the worst, nor perhaps the foremost, but an ordinary kind of soldier.

Thyon. Would that indeed what you desire could turn out to your mind, Æschines ! But if in sooth you are thus deter-

---

[17] ἁ πόδες ἆγον. Horat. Epod. xi. 20, Ferebar incerto pede. Cf. Idyll xiii. 70.

[18] This proverb is said of those that return not : as the bulls which take shelter in the wood, cannot be caught again. Scholiast. Wordsw. would read τι, βέβακεν ταῦρος ἀν' ὕλαν. He quotes very appositely Soph. Œd. Tyrann. 476—478.

[19] The Thracian mode of shaving was so imperfect, that, in Greek judgment, it passed for unshavenness. The words imply, "Nor have I been shaven even so far as to look like a Thracian." Hom. Il. iv. 533, calls the Thracians ἀκρόκομοι. Cf. Herodot. i. 122.

[20] πάντα. See Matth. Gr. Gr. § 438, p. 724, (edit. 1832,) for this use of πάντα.

[21] An allusion to the Pythian response to the Megarensians, seeking to know their rank among Greek states.

ὑμεῖς δ' ὦ Μεγαρῆες οὔτε τρίτοι, οὔτε τέταρτοι
οὔτε δυωδέκατοι, οὔτ' ἐν λόγῳ, οὔτ' ἐν ἀριθμῷ.

Cf. Callim. Epigr. xxvi.

[22] The proverb of the mouse touching pitch is applied to things troublesome to be retained, yet hard to get rid of. Compare Ecclus. xiii. 1.

[23] For the benefits of this cure for heart-ache, compare Propert. iii. 21,

Magnum iter ad doctas proficisci cogor Athenas :
Ut me longa gravi solvat amore via.

In the next line for ὁμαλὸς δέ τις ὁ στρατιώτας, Wordsworth proposes ὁμαλὸς δὲ τις οἱ, illi : that is, to Simus : which seems highly probable. "Not a very bad, nor a first-rate soldier, but much such another as Simus."

mined to go abroad, Ptolemy is the very best of pay-masters to a free-man.

Æsch. And in other respects, what kind of man is he?

Thyon. The very best to a free-man; indulgent, fond of the Muses, given to love, pleasant in the extreme. He knows him who loves him, still better him that loves him not: gives much to many: not refusing, when asked; as a king should be. But it is not right to ask on every occasion, Æschines. So that if you are minded to clasp the top of your mantle upon your right shoulder, and [24] standing firm on both *feet* will have the nerve to bide the onset of the bold warrior, off with all speed to Egypt! We all become old men, beginning from the temples, and time that maketh gray creeps on by degrees to the chin. Those must do something, [25] whose knee is fresh and active.

IDYLL XV.

THE SYRACUSAN WOMEN; OR, ADONIAZUSÆ.

ARGUMENT.

This Idyll describes a festival in honour of Adonis, kept at the cost of Arsinoe, with great pomp, at Alexandria; and it affords the poet an opportunity for lauding the queen, and through her, king Ptolemy also. Two Syracusan women who have Alexandrian husbands, in a low rank of life, start out with their maids to the palace, to see the show. The Idyll has three scenes, so to speak—first, the dialogue between Gorgo and Praxinoe, at the house of the latter;—then their adventures in the way to the palace;—and lastly, the interior of the palace, and the battle of words between these women and a stranger, which is hushed by the song of a female minstrel in honour of Adonis: when this is ended, they return home. The poem is true to life in its lighter and more homely parts; and is also remarkable for the graceful introduction of praise of the royal family.

---

[24] ἐπ' ἀμφοτέροισι (understand ποσί). Tyrtæus i. 53,
Ἀλλά τις εὖ διαβὰς μενέτω ποσὶν ἀμφοτέροισι
Στηριχθεὶς ἐπὶ γῆς, χεῖλος ὀδοῦσι δακών.
[25] Horat. Epod. xiii. 4, Dumque virent genua.
Aristoph. Acharn. 218, νῦν δ' ἐπειδὴ στερρὸν ἤδη τοὐμὸν ἀντικνήμιον.

IDYLL XV.

CHARACTERS.

GORGO. PRAXINOE. OLD WOMAN. FIRST STRANGER. SECOND STRANGER. SINGING WOMAN.

Gorgo. Is Praxinoe within?
Praxinoe. Dear Gorgo, how late *you are!* *I am* at home. 'Tis a wonder you have come even now. [1] See for a chair for her, Eunoe: and put a cushion on it.
Gorg. [2] It does very well.
Praxin. Be seated.
Gorg. Oh! my unbroken spirit, with difficulty have I reached you in safety, Praxinoe, the crowd being great, and the chariots many. Every where there are [3] booted men; every where cavaliers; and the road is toilsome, and you live too far from me.
Praxin. For this reason that [4] madman came to the extremity of the world, and took [5] a den, not an habitation, in order

---

[1] ὄρη δίφρον. Compare Hom. Odyss. viii. 443, Αὐτὸς νῦν ἴδε πῶμα. Somewhat less simple is the phrase in Iliad ii. 384, εὖ δέ τις ἅρματος ἀμφὶς ἰδών. J. Wordsworth compares Cic. ad Attic. v. 1, Antecesserat Statius ut prandium nobis *videret*. Terent. Heautont. III. i. 50, Asperum, pater, hoc est: aliud lenius, sodes, vidè. Soph. Aj. 1165. Juvenal viii. 96.

[2] ἔχει κάλλιστα, it does excellently well. The Latins use "rectè" thus. Terent. Eun. II. iii. 50, Rogo num quid velit. Recte, inquit. Abeo. Horat. Epist. i. 7, 16, 62, At tu quantumvis tolle. Benignè. Valken. quotes here Plauti Stichus I. ii. 37, P. Mane pulvinum. An. Bene procuras mihi: satis sic fultum est mihi.

[3] κρηπῖδες (the abstract for concrete) for κρηπιδηφόροι, or κεκρηπιδωμένοι. So Eurip. Phœn. ἀγεμόνευμα for ἡγεμών. Troad. 420, νύμφευμα for νύμφη. Iph. in Aul. 189, ἀσπὶς for ἀσπιδοφόροι and λόγχη, for λογχηφόροι. Œd. Col. 1312. Markland ad loc. Of the same nuisance as that which she complains of, Juvenal says, Et in digito clavus mihi militis hæret. In the next line, Wordsworth suggests in place of the corrupt ἔμ' the reading ἄμ' for ἄμα, præterea or simul. And *besides* you live far off. He compares Soph. Alet. vii. 3. Thuc. i. 37, καὶ ἡ πόλις ἄμα αὐταρκῆ θέσιν κειμένη.

[4] πάραρος, like παρήορος, (from ἀείρω,) strictly of a horse which draws by the side of a regular pair; (2). lying beside, at the side of, or out of the way; and so (3) beside oneself. Understand νόον. Compare Il. xxiii. 603. Archiloch. Fragm. 63. Il. iii. 108, ταῦθ' is for διὰ ταῦτα.

[5] ἰλεόν, (i. q. εἰλεόν or εἰλύον,) a lurking-place. Callim. H. in Jovem 25, ἰλυοὺς ἐβάλοντο κινώπετα. Martial. Epigr. xi. 19,
 Donasti, Lupe, rus sub urbe nobis: in quo nec cucumis jacere rectus, Nec serpens latitare torta possit.

that we might not be neighbours to each other; a jealous pest, ever the same for strife.

Gorg. Don't say such things, my dear, of your goodman Deinon, in the presence of the little one. See, ma'am, how he is looking at you!

Praxin. Never mind, little Zoppy, sweet child! I don't mean [6]papa!

Gorg. The infant understands you, [7]by'r Lady. Pretty papa!

Praxin. That papa indeed lately, (and we call every thing lately, you know,) going to buy [8]nitre and ceruse from a stall, even came and brought me *mere* salt, [9]the great big oaf.

Gorg. Ay; and my husband, Diocleidas, is just the same, [10]a ruin of money. For seven drachmæ yesterday he bought five fleeces, *mere* dog's-hair, *mere* pluckings of old wallets; all filth: trouble on trouble. But come, don your [11]fine robe and your clasped kirtle. Let us go to *the palace* of the king, rich Ptolemy, to be spectators of the 'Adonis.' I hear that the queen is getting up a charming kind of affair.

Praxin. In the house of a fortunate person all is flourish-

---

[6] ἀπφῦς. On this passage, compare Juvenal xiv. 47, Maxima debetur puero reverentia, &c. Callim. H. in Dian. 6, ἄππα. Like the Hebrew and Chaldaic Abba, and our "Papa." Hom. Il. v. 408, οὐδέ τι μιν παῖδες ποτὶ γούνασι παππάζουσιν. Persius, Sat. iii., Et similis regum pueris pappare minutum. In point of fact, it is only one of the forms which are the first utterances of the lisping child, just as μάμμα, mamma, for μήτηρ, which are to be referred to common nature, rather than to any origin in language.

[7] τὰν πότνιαν. Proserpine, by whom, as well as Ceres, Sicilian women would swear.

[8] Nitre and paints of various colours ministered much to the dress and cheeks of Greek women. Pollux vii. 95. Ov. Medicam. fac. v. 73,

Nec cerussa tibi, nec nitri spuma rubentis
Desit.

[9] A long lazy loon.

[10] φθόρος for φθορεύς. Cf. Callim. H. in Apoll. 113, ἵν' ὁ φθόρος, Cicer. Verr. Act. i. 1, Pernicies provinciæ. Terent. Adelph. II. i. 34, Pernicies adolescentium.

[11] ἀμπέχονον, a fine upper robe. περοναρτίδα, (cf. 34, ἐμπερόναμα,) a robe fastened to the shoulders with a buckle, woollen in texture, sleeveless; closed on the right side, but on the left only kept together by a few clasps, hence called σχιστὸς χιτών, &c. Liddell and Scott, Lex. in voc. It was a Dorian garment. Cf. Herodot. v. 87, 88. Virg. Æn. iv. 139, Aurea purpuream subnectit fibula vestem.

ing. What [12] you have seen, that you might tell, when you have seen it, to them that have not seen it.

Gorg. It must be time to be off: to the idle 'tis ever holiday.

Praxin. Eunoe, [13] bring hither the towel, and place it in the middle again, good-for-nothing hussey: the cats want to sleep softly. Come, stir, bring water quickly. I want water first. See how she brings the towel. Well, give it me! Don't pour in too much water, wasteful! wretched creature, why are you wetting my kirtle? That will do. [14] I am washed enough to satisfy the gods. Where is the key of the large press? Bring it hither.

Gorg. Praxinoe, that pelisse with ample folds greatly becomes you; tell me [15] how much did it stand you in from the loom?

Praxin. Don't mention it, Gorgo! more than two pounds of good silver. But I had set even my life upon the bargain.

Gorg. Well, it turned out to your wishes.

Praxin. Yes, you have said well. Bring me my cloak and my parasol. Put it about me becomingly. I won't take you, child. [16] Bugbear! Horse bites! Cry as much as you please: but we must not have you become 'lame. Let us be moving. Phrygian slave, take and play with the little man. Call the dog in. Shut the hall door.

---

[17] Good gods! what a crowd! how and when must we pass this nuisance? They are numberless and measureless as

[12] The reading which has been translated here, is that approved by Kiessling, ὧν ἴδες, ὧν εἴπαις καὶ ἰδοῖσα τὺ τῷ μὴ ἰδόντι, where the second ὧν stands for τούτων, the relative anciently serving as the demonstrative pronoun not uncommonly. Wordsw., ὧν ἴδες ὧν εἴποις κατιδοῖσα τὺ τῷ μὴ ἰδόντι. For ὧν—ὧν, repeated, see ii. 82, ὡς—ὡς, iv. 39, ὅσον—ὅσσον. W.

[13] τὸ νᾶμα, as was shown by Ahlward, is for νῆμα, mantele, for νῆμα signifies quicquid ex filis conficitur; this supplies a better sense than if we took it to mean "water." In vs. 28, Praxinoe says that the cats are snoozing on the towel before the fire." αἶρε, affer, fetch hither. J. W. Cf. Soph. Ajax, 545.

[14] Praxinoe says that she has washed enough to satisfy even the gods, the chief lovers of purity.

[15] "Costing how much, did it come to you from the loom?" Praxinoe had bought the wool and other articles for it, and made it herself.

[16] μορμώ, a word used to frighten children. μορμύσσεται is used Callim. H. in Dian. 70, qu. v., and μορμώ, Aristoph. Eq. 693, Ach. 582, Vesp. 1038.

[17] Ὦ θεοί. Di boni, quid turbæ est! Terent. Heaut. Act. 2. For the

ants. Many good works have been done [18] by you, O Ptolemy. Since your sire *has been* among the immortals, no evildoer assaults the passenger, creeping up in the [19] Egyptian fashion. Even as formerly men wholly made up of deceit used to sport, like to each other in evil tricks, [20] all worthless. Sweetest Gorgo, what is to become of us? Here are the warhorses of the king. My good man, don't trample on me. The chesnut charger has reared upright. See, how fiery he is. Impudent Eunoe, will you not fly? He will make an end of his leader. I am very much delighted, that my child remains in the house.

Gorg. Courage, Praxinoe: we are now in the rear of them. And they have fallen [21] into their rank.

Praxin. I too am collecting myself at length. From a child I have been very much afraid of a horse, and the [22] cold snake. Let us hasten on. What a vast crowd is pouring upon us!

Gorg. From court, good mother?

Old Woman. I am, my daughters.

Gorg. Then is it easy to pass in?

O. Wom. By trying the Greeks came into Troy. Fairest of daughters, by trying, in truth, all things are accomplished.

---

simile of the ants, see Idyll xvii. 107. Æsch. Prom. V. 451, ἀείσυροι μύρμηκες, and Horat. Sat. I. i. 33. Virg. Æn. iv. 401, Ac veluti ingentem formicæ, &c.

[18] Ptolemy Philadelphus deified his father Ptolemy Soter, son of Lagus, and his mother Berenice. Compare Idyll xvii. 16, 123, οὐδεις κακοεργὸς. See Herodot. i. 41, μή τινες κατ' ὁδὸν κλῶπες κακουργοὶ ἐπὶ δηλήσει φανέωσι ὑμῖν. And Baehr's note thereupon. J. W.

[19] Propert. III. xi. 33, Noxia Alexandria, dolis aptissima tellus. Cic. pro Rabir., Illinc (Alexandriæ) omnes præstigiæ—illinc inquam omnes fallaciæ, &c. Aristoph. Nub. 1138, ὥστ' ἴσως βουλήσεται Κἂν ἐν Αἰγύπτῳ τυχεῖν ὢν μᾶλλον ἢ κρῖναι κακῶς. Æsch. Fragm. 309, δεινοὶ πλέκειν τοι μηχανὰς Αἰγύπτιοι.

[20] ἐρειοί, a dubious word, expressive of some sort of contempt for Egyptians. Dr. Wordsworth suggests Ἔπειοι, i. e. "all rogues like Epeus, the builder of the fatal Trojan Horse." Æn. 264, Et ipse doli fabricator Epeus. ἕλειοι, dwellers in the marshes, the common receptacle for Egyptian rogues, is the best conjecture. Some read ἀεργοί, comparing St. Paul to Titus i. 12, γαστέρες ἀργοί. τί γενώμεθα—Cf. Blomf. Gloss ad Æsch. 144. J. W. Below compare Virg. Æn. x. 892, Tollit se, arrectum sonipes.

[21] ἐς χώραν, i. e. εἰς τὴν τάξιν αὐτῶν. Schol. So χώραν λαβεῖν, Xenoph. Callim. in Del. 192, πόδες δὲ οἱ οὐκ ἐνὶ χώρᾳ.

[22] Virg. Ecl. iii. 93, Frigidus, o pueri, fugite hinc, latet anguis in herbâ. Comp. Ecl. viii. 71, Sciunt quid in aurem rex reginæ dixerit.

Gorg. The old woman has departed, having delivered oracles.

Praxin. [23] Women know every thing: even how Jove wedded Juno.

Gorg. Observe, Praxinoe, what a throng around the doors!

Praxin. Prodigious! Give me your hand, Gorgo. And do you, Eunoe, take the hand of Eutychis! Keep close to her, that you may not be lost. Let us all go in together. Hold tight to us, Eunoe. Oh! wretched me! my fine summer veil has been torn in two at last, Gorgo. By Jove, if you would be in any degree blest, good sir, keep off my robe.

Stranger. It is not in my power indeed: but still I will keep off.

Praxin. The crowd is all in a heap. They push like boars.

Strang. Courage, madam, we are all safe.

Praxin. [24] Next year and afterwards, dear sir, may you be prosperous, for taking care of us as you did. What a good compassionate man! Our Eunoe is being hustled. Come, wretched girl, burst through. Well done. We are all inside, [25] as the man said, when he shut in his bride.

Gorg. Praxinoe, come hither! first observe the embroidery; how fine and elegant! [26] you would say 'twas the robes of goddesses.

Praxin. Our lady Minerva: what clever spinsters wrought them! What fine artists [27] have painted these life-like pic-

---

[23] So Plautus Trinummus I. ii. 171, Sciunt quod Juno fabulata est cum Jove, neque facta neque futura tamen illi sciunt. Comp. Hom. Il. xiv. 295, where it appears that the immortals had not this knowledge.

[24] εἰς ὥρας, "in annum proximum." Comp. Horat. Od. I. xxxii. 2,
    Quod et hunc in annum
    Vivat, et plures.
φιλ' ἀνδρῶν. Ran. Aristoph. 1081, ὦ σχέτλι' ἀνδρῶν.

[25] A proverb of the bridegroom, who, when he has shut himself and his bride (ἀποκλάξας) in the nuptial chamber, says from his heart, ἐνδοῖ πᾶσαι. κατεκλάξατο is so used, Idyll xviii. 5.

[26] Theocrit. seems to have had an eye to the Odyss. x. 222, 223, in this passage. Wordsw. suggests, and finds Hermann to have hit upon the same idea, the reading for περονάματα—χερνάματα, h. e. "the handiwork."

[27] Cicero in Hortensio apud Nonium Marcell. v. 'inanima,' "Cum omnis," ait, "solertia admiranda est, tum ea quæ efficit, ut, inanima

tures? How true *to nature* they stand, and how true they move! They are breathing, and not inwoven. Man is a clever kind of contrivance. And how admirably is he *represented* as reclining on a [28] silver couch, just shedding the first down from his temples, the thrice beloved Adonis, who is beloved even in Acheron.

2nd Stranger. Ye wretched women, stop prating incessantly, like turtles. They will wear us out, pronouncing all *their words* broadly.

Gorg. Mother earth, where does the man come from? And what is it to you, if we are praters? [29] When you have acquired a right, order us! Do you order Syracusan women? And that you may know this too, [30] we are Corinthians by descent, as was also Bellerophon. We speak in the Peloponnesian dialect. And 'tis lawful, I suppose, for Dorians to speak in the Doric.

Praxin. O Proserpine, may there never arise but one to be my master. I do not care, [31] don't give me scant measure.

quæ sint, vivere ac spirare videantur." Virg. Æn. vi. 848, Æra spirantia. Propert. III. vii. 9, 'Signa animosa.' Horat. ii. Sat. vii. 98,
                                Velut si
          Re verâ pugnent, feriant, vitentque moventes
          Arma viri.
Our own poets speak of 'breathing marble.' See too Shaksp. Winter's Tale, act v. scene 3, "Life lively mocked." On the contrary, Antony and Cleopat. act iii. sc. 3,
          Her motion and her station are as one:
          She shows a body rather than a life;
          A statue than a breather.
σοφόν τι χρῆμ'. Ovid. ex Pont. II. vii. 37, Res timida est omnis miser. Martial. x. Epigr. 59, Res est imperiosa timor, &c. Senec. Ep. 25, Homo sacra res. Cic. ad Quint. Fratr. ii. 13, Callisthenes quidem vulgare, et notum negotium.

[28] Comp. Idyll xx. 21. Hom. Odyss. x. 318, πρίν σφωϊν ὑπὸ κροτάφοισ·ν ἰούλους Ἀνθῆσαι. Virg. Æn. viii. 160, Tum mihi prima genas vestibat flore juventas. Æn. x. 324, Flaventem primâ lanugine malas.

[29] πασάμενος. Kiessling aptly compares Plaut. Pers. II. iv. 2, Emere oportet, quem tibi obedire velis, and Sophocl. Œd. Colon. 839, μὴ 'πίτασσ' ἃ μὴ κρατεῖς. Add to these Plaut. Trinumm. IV. iii. 54.

[30] Archias, the Corinthian, led a colony to Sicily and founded Syracuse. Hence it is called in Idyll xvi. 83, Ἐφυραῖον ἄστυ. It was founded about B. C. 733. See Thuc. vi. 3, (Arnold).

[31] This passage is despaired of by Kiessling—it seems to have been rendered not a whit clearer by the numbers of annotators who have touched it. We must understand χοινίκα—χοινίκα ἀπομάξαι, to give

Gorg. Hush, Praxinoe, the sister of the Argive woman, a very skilful songstress, who also excelled in the dirge of [32]Sperchis, is going to sing the Adonis. She will sing something fine, I am very sure. She is just now bridling up.

Singing Woman. [33]Mistress, that hast loved Golgus, and Idalium, and lofty Eryx, Aphrodite, sporting in gold, how lovely to thee, in the twelfth month, did the soft-footed Hours bring back Adonis from ever-flowing Acheron ; dear Hours, tardiest of the immortals: yet they come objects of longing, ever [34]bringing something for all mortals: Dionæan Venus, thou indeed hast made, as the story of men *runs*, Berenice immortal instead of mortal, having distilled [35]ambrosia into the bosom of a woman : and paying grateful offerings to thee, O thou of many names, of many temples, Arsinoe, the daughter of Berenice, resembling Helen, cherishes Adonis with all good things. Beside him lie fruits in their season, whichsoever the topmost branches bear. And beside him tender [36]quick-growing plants, kept in silver baskets, and golden caskets of [37]Syrian unguent, and honey-cakes, as many as women shape in a mould, mixing all kinds of flowers with the white fine-meal : all shapes as many as *are made* of sweet honey, and those *that are wrought* in moist oil, fowls and creeping

---

scant measure; hence, κενεάν ἀπομάξαι, to lose one's labour. Græfius would read γενεάν. Wordsworth thinks the text may stand as it is, μάκτραν, a kneading-trough, being the ellipse,—or else that ἀποκλάξῃς should be read, and λάρνακα understood. Don't lock the empty chest. Don't command me, over whom you have no right. It might possibly mean, " Don't treat me as a slave, when I am as free-born as yourself." ἑνός, i. e. Ptolemy.

[32] Sperchis.] Herodot. vii. 134.

[33] Golgus, a city of Cyprus. Idalium, a grove and mountain of the same. Eryx, a mountain in Sicily sacred to Venus. Erycina ridens, Horat. Od. I. ii. 32. Ibid. III. xxvi. 9, O quæ beatam Diva tenes Cyprum. Catull. lxiii. 96, Quæque regis Golgos, quæque Idalium frondosum.

[34] The Hours, and their functions. Idyll i. 150. Moschus ii. 160. Ovid. Met. ii 25.

[35] Berenice, cf. Idyll xvii. 36. Ambrosia was thus used by Cyrene. Virg. Georg. iv. 415, for the same purpose. And Ovid Met. xiv. 606,

Ambrosiâ cum dulci nectare mistâ
Contigit os, fecitque Deum.

[36] κῆποι here mean lettuce and other quick-growing plants in pots. Hence, proverbially, pretty things that fade.

[37] Ovid. Heroid. xv. 76, Non Arabo noster rore capillus olet. Said of Syrian unguents.

things, are present here for him. And verdant canopies, weighed down with soft dill, are constructed; and the [38] boy loves are fluttering about overhead, even as young nightingales, perching on the trees, flit about, making trial of their wings, from bough to bough. O the ebony, O the gold, O ye two eagles of [39] white ivory bearing to Jove, the son of Saturn, a lad as cup-bearer. And above are purple rugs, softer than sleep, [40] as Miletus will say, and whoso feeds flocks in the Samian land. Another couch is strown for the beautiful Adonis. One Venus occupies, the other rosy-armed Adonis, the bridegroom of eighteen or of nineteen years. [41] His kiss does not prick; still his lips are reddish all round. Now, indeed, adieu to Venus, enjoying her own husband. [42] And at dawn we in a body, along with the dew, will carry him out to the waves foaming on the shore: and having unbound our hair, and having loosened to the ancles the folds of our robes, with bosoms suffered to appear, will begin the clear-sweet song.

Alone of the demigods, as 'tis said, thou comest, dear

[38] Compare Bion Epit. Adon. 80, ἀμφὶ δέ μιν, κ. τ. λ., and Ovid. Amor. iii. El. 9, Ecce puer Veneris, &c. Images of the Loves always graced this festival.

[39] Ganymede. Æn. i. 28, Rapti Ganymedis honores. V. 255,
Quem præpes ab Idâ
Sublimem pedibus rapuit Jovis armiger uncis.
Ovid. Fast. vi. 45, Rapto Ganymede dolebam. Spenser, Faery Queen B. iii. canto ii. Hor. Od. IV. iv. 3, Expertus fidelem
Jupiter in Ganymede flavo.

[40] ἄνω, understand τοῦ κλιντῆρος. Milesian and Samian wools were the finest. The testimony of the natives of these therefore would be highly valued. Virg. Georg. iii. 306, 307, Quamvis Milesia magno.
Vellera mutentur Tyrios incocta rubores.
μαλακώτεροι ὕπνω. Cf. Idyll v. 58. Virg. Ecl. vii. 45, Somno mollior herba. Our own poets use the phrase "downy sleep."

[41] οὐ κεντεῖ. Though his beard is πυῤῥος, reddish, his touch is not rough, but soft. Tibull. I. viii. 32,
Cui levia fulgent
Ora, nec amplexus horrida barba terit.

[42] Respecting the Adonia, see Smith's Dict. Gr. and R. Ant. p. 12. We have allusion to Adonis or Tammuz, Milton's Paradise Lost, i. 455,
Thammuz came next behind,
Whose annual wound in Lebanon allured
The Syrian damsels to lament his fate
In amorous ditties, all a summer's day,
While smooth Adonis from his native rock
Ran purple to the sea, supposed with blood
Of Thammuz yearly wounded.

Adonis, both hither and to Acheron: neither did Agamemnon enjoy this *privilege*, nor the great Ajax, hero of grievous wrath, nor Hector, the most honourable of the twenty sons of Hecuba, nor Patrocles, nor Pyrrhus having returned from Troy, nor those who were yet earlier *in date*, the Lapithæ and [43] Deucalions, nor the descendants of Pelops, and Pelasgi, [44] eldest rulers of Argos. Be prosperous now, dear Adonis, and mayest thou give pleasure [45] next year; both now thou hast come, O Adonis, and whenever thou mayest arrive, thou wilt come, dear.

Gorg. Praxinoe, the affair is very clever. The female is fortunate in having so much knowledge—most fortunate, in that she sings sweetly. However, it is time even for home: Diocleidas is without his dinner. [46] And the man is vinegar all *over:* and, if he is hungry, don't go near him. Farewell, beloved Adonis, and go to those who rejoice *at your coming*.

IDYLL XVI.

THE GRACES; OR, HIERO.

ARGUMENT.

This poem is written in praise of Hiero, son of Hierocles, tyrant of Syracuse, a ruler of great moderation, and also of warlike renown, acquired in his battles with the Carthaginians. The poet lashes the avarice of most rulers; who, he says, do not favour poets, and so prevent their fame from gaining that immortality, which cannot be attained, save by song. He goes on to praise Hiero as an honourable exception; and afterwards prays for the future safety and fortunes of Syracuse, and of Hiero, its ornament and support. In conclusion he invokes the

---

[43] Δευκαλίωνες, i. e. such as Deucalion. So Plutarch speaks of Πηλεῖς καὶ Ἀγχίσαι καὶ Ὠρίωνες καὶ Ἡμαθίωνες. And Longinus cites a Tragedian speaking of Ἑκτορές τε καὶ Σαρπηδόνες.

[44] Ἄργεος ἄκρα, i. q. αὐτόχθονες.

[45] εἰς νέωτ'. εἰς τὸ ἐπιὸν ἢ νέον ἔτος, v. Hesych. Heinsius, Briggs, Wordsworth, prefer to read at verse 145, τὸ χρῆμα σοφώτερον ἁ θήλεια. Just as at verse 83. σοφόν τι χρῆμ' ἄνθρωπος.

[46] ὄξος ἅπαν. Cf. Idyll iii. 19; xv. 20. Horat. Epist. I. xv. 29, Impransus civem qui non dignosceret hoste.

Graces, to win favour for his strains. The poem was written in the time of the Punic war, after Hiero's treaty with Rome (B. C. 263). In character it is epic and encomiastic.

THIS is ever a care to the daughters of Jove, ever to poets, to hymn immortals, [1] to hymn the glories of brave men. The Muses indeed are goddesses; goddesses sing of gods: but we are mortals here; let *us* mortals sing of mortals. [2] Yet who of as many as dwell under the bright dawn, will open his doors, and graciously welcome in his home our [3] Graces, and not send them away again unrewarded? Whilst they indignantly return home with naked feet, flouting me much, because they have gone on a fruitless journey; and sluggishly again, having thrust their heads upon their [4] starved knees, they abide at the bottom of an empty coffer, where they have [5] a dry seat, whensoever they shall have returned *after a* bootless *errand*. Who of the present generation of men [6] is of such a nature as this? Who, *I mean*, will love one that has spoken well of him? I know not! for no longer, as of old, are men anxious to be celebrated for worthy deeds, but they have been conquered by gains. And every one keeping his hands in his bosom, regards his [7] money, from what source it shall increase; and would not even rub the rust off, or give it to any one; but says immediately, [8] 'The shin is further off than the knee:

---

[1] Hom. Il. ix. 189, ἄειδε δ᾽ ἄρα κλέα ἀνδρῶν· Odyss. viii. 73, Μοῦσ᾽ ἄρ᾽ ἀοιδὸν ἀνῆκεν ἀειδέμεναι κλέα ἀνδρῶν. Horat. IV. viii. 28, Dignum laude virum musa vetat mori.

[2] τίς γάρ. There is an ellipse of τοῦτο θαυμαστόν ἐστιν—γάρ supplying the reason. It is a wonder that mortals sing the praise of mortals, seeing how ill-requited they are.

[3] χάριτας, i. e. his poems. For a similar prosopopœia, see Horat. Epist. i. 20, where he compares his book with a damsel desiring to go forth in public.

[4] ψυχροῖς, starved. Compare Aristoph. Plut. 262,
ὁ δεσπότης γὰρ φησιν ὑμᾶς ἡδέως ἅπαντας
ψυχροῦ βίου καὶ δυσκόλου ζήσειν ἀπαλλαγέντας.

[5] αὔη—ἕδρα. Compare Idyll i. 51; viii. 44.

[6] For τοιός δε ὥστε φιλεῖν τὸν εὖ εἰπόντα. So Sophocl. Œd. Tyr 1493, 1494, τίς οὗτος ἔσται; τίς παραρρίψει τέκνα
τοιαῦτ᾽ ὀνείδη λαμβάνων;

[7] Compare Horat. Od. III. xvi. 17,
Crescentem sequitur cura pecuniam
Majorumque fames.
ὑπὸ κόλπῳ. See Ov. Am. 1. x. 18, Quo pretium condat, non habet ille sinum.

[8] Cicero quotes this proverb, Epist. ad Diversos, lib. xvi. Ep. 23,

let me have something myself. Gods honour poets. And who would listen to another? Homer is enough for all. This is the best of poets, who will carry off nothing from me.' Strange men! now what gain is your countless gold laid up within? Such is not the advantage of wealth to the wise: but *it is rather* to give a part to [9] one's tastes, and a part also to one of the poets: and to do good to many of one's [10] kinsmen, and many too of other men, and ever to perform sacrifices to the gods; [11] and not to be a bad host, but to send away *a guest* having treated him kindly at one's board, whensoever he may choose to depart: but chiefly to honour the sacred interpreters of the Muses, that, though buried in Hades, you may be well spoken of; and may not lament ingloriously in chilly Acheron, like some [12] poor man, having had his hands made callous inside by the spade, bewailing portionless poverty *left him* by his fathers.

[13] In the mansions of Antiochus and king Aleuas, [14] many

Nec tamen te avoco a syngraphâ, γόνυ κνήμης. Athenæus ix. 383, γόνυ κνήμης ἔγγιον. Plaut. Tunica pallio propior. Charity begins at home. Shaksp. Two Gentleman of Verona, act ii. sc. 6, I to myself am dearer than a friend. θεοὶ τιμῶσιν ἀοιδούς, is equivalent to the cant phrase, Providence will take care of poets.

[9] ψυχᾷ—δοῦναι, Genio dare, (Lat.) Horat. Epist. II. i. 144, Floribus et vino Genium memorem brevis ævi. Æsch. Pers. 827, ψυχῇ διδόντες ἡδόνην καθ' ἡμέραν.

[10] πηὸς, "cognatus." See Odyss. viii. 581, where the Schol. observes that it denotes connexion secondary to blood relationship, for which it was never expressly used. See Valken. Phœniss. 431,—derived from πέπαμαι.

[11] Theocrit. had in view Odyss. xv. 68. Compare Pope's Imitation of Horace, Sat. ii. 2,
Through whose free opening-gate
None comes too early—none departs too late, &c.
For patriarchal hospitality, see Genesis xviii., xix.

[12] ἀχήν, needy, a χαίνω, akin to egenus. Æschylus uses the substantive ἀχηνία. Choeph. 301. Ag. 419. Virg. Æn. vi. 436, Nunc et pauperiem et duros perferre labores.

[13] Aleuas, a king of Thessaly, one of a most powerful dynasty, Herodot. vii. 6. Ovid Ibis, 327,
Quosque putas fidos, ut Larissæus Aleuas
Vulnere non fidos experiere tuo.

[14] ἐμετρήσαντο, i. e. μέτρημα ἔλαβον. Fawkes compares ἀρραλιὰν ἔμμηνον with the "Demensum," or monthly measure of Roman slaves Terence Phorm. Act. i. § 1,
Quos ille unciatim vix de demenso suo
Suum defraudans genium, comparsit miser.

serfs had monthly provisions measured out to them: and many calves lowed with horned heifers, as they were driven to the stalls of the Scopadæ: and shepherds would let out to feed along the Crannonian plain, ten thousand choice sheep for the hospitable Creondæ: [15] yet had there been no pleasure to them of these things, after that they had poured out their sweet spirits into the broad bark of hateful Acheron; and, out of mind, having quitted those many and rich resources, they would have lain long ages among the wretched dead, had not the clever bard, [16] the Ceian with his changeful song *set* to his many-stringed lyre, made them illustrious to posterity; [17] for even swift steeds which came to them crowned from the sacred contests, obtained a share in the honour. And who had ever known the nobles of the [18] Lycians, who the sons of Priam

Hesiod, Op. 349, εὖ μὲν μετρεῖσθαι παρὰ γείτονος—Πενέσται.—Thirlw. History of Gr. i. 437. Each of the chief Thessalian cities exercised a dominion over several smaller towns, and they were themselves the seat of noble families, of the line of ancient kings, able generally to draw to themselves the whole government of the nation. Larissa was thus subject to the house of Aleuadæ; Crannon and Pharsalus, to the Scopadæ and Creondæ, branches of the same stock. The vast estates and flocks and herds of these were managed by their serfs, the Penests, who, at call, were ready to follow them to the field afoot or on horseback. Cf. Herodot. vi. 127.

[15] σχεδιάν. Æn. vi. 304, Et ferrugineâ subvectat corpora cymbâ; for the sentiment cf. Tibull. I. iv. 63,

>Carmine purpurea est Nisi coma: carmina ni sint
>Ex humero Pelopis non nituisset ebur.

Hor. IV. viii. 22,   Quid foret Iliæ
>Mavortisque puer, si taciturnitas
>Obstaret meritis invida Romuli.

Add Spenser, "Ruines of Time," quoted by Gaisford.
>For not to have been dipt in Lethe lake
>Could save the son of Thetis from to die,
>But that blind bard did him immortal make,
>With verses dipt in dew of Castalie.

Comp. Hor. IV. ix. 26—28; ii. 3, ad fin.

[16] ὁ Κήιος. Simonides of Cos (B. C. 540) was the friend of Hipparchus the tyrant, Pausanias the Spartan general, and Hiero the Syracusan tyrant. He wrote, in Doric dialect, lyrics, elegies, epigrams, and dramatic pieces.

[17] ἵπποι, the victorious steeds from the games of Greece. Compare Callim. in Cerer. H. 110,
>καὶ τὸν ἀεθλοφόρον καὶ τὸν πολεμήϊον ἵππον.

[18] Nobles of the Lycians,] i. e. Sarpedon, Pandarus, Glaucus. Comp.

with the flowing locks, or Cycnus *called* feminine from his complexion, had not bards hymned the battle-dins of olden *heroes?* Not even Ulysses, though he wandered one hundred and twenty months over all *nations* of men, and went alive to extremest Orcus, and escaped the cave of the destructive Cyclops, would have had lasting renown : hushed too in silence had been the swine-herd Eumæus, and Philætius busied among the heifers of the herd, and great-hearted Laertes himself, had not the [19] songs of a man of Ionia befriended them.

From the Muses comes worthy renown to men ; but [20] the living consume the wealth of the dead : since however the toil is the same to measure waves on the shore, as many as the wind drives to land with the green ocean, [21] or to wash a muddy brick with dark-coloured water, as to get round a man [22] blinded by avarice, farewell to all such : and may they have money untold, and ever may a longing for more possess them.

Il. ii. 875. Cycnus, son of Neptune, was slain by Achilles at Troy. According to Hesiod, he was white-headed, and hence cailed θῆλυς. Compare Ovid. Met. x. 72, &c., Jam leto proles Neptunia Cycnus, Mille viros dederat, &c. At line 51, Ὀδυσεύς. Cf. Horace Epist. I. ii. 19,

Multorum providus urbes
Et mores hominum inspexit, latumque per æquor
Dum sibi dum sociis reditum parat, aspera multe
Pertulit.

[19] Horace Od. IV. ix. 26—28,

Vixere fortes ante Agamemnona
Multi, sed omnes illachrimabiles
Urgentur, ignotique longâ
Nocte, carent quia vate sacro.

Fawkes observes that Theocritus, keeping up his pastoral capacity, honours with princes the swine-herd and the neat-herd.

[20] The living consume, &c.] Compare Horace Od. II. iii. 19,

Exstructis in altum
Divitiis potietur hæres.

Virg. Georg. ii. 108, Nosse, quot Ionii veniant ad littora fluctus.

[21] θολεράν, i. e. unbaked. Whence the proverb of Terence, Phorm. I. iv. 9, Purgem me? Laterem lavem. πλίνθους πλύνειν. Zenob. Diogen. Centur. Suid. Somewhat parallel is Jeremiah xiii. 23, "Can the Æthiopian," &c.

[22] βεβλαμμένον, blinded, stricken. Mente captum. So used Il. xxii. 15, Odyss. xxiii. 14, &c. Two lines below, compare Horace Od. III. xvi. 17,

Crescentem sequitur cura pecuniam
Majorumque fames.

Yet I would prefer [23] to many mules and horses, honour, and the friendship of men. Now I am in quest of one, to whom among mortals I may come with favour, by the help of the Muses; for hard are the ways to minstrels, apart from the daughters of Jove, the mighty counsellor. Not yet hath heaven tired of drawing on months and years; many steeds will yet move the chariot's wheel. Such a man will arise, as shall need me for his bard, when he has achieved as much as mighty Achilles, or strong Ajax in the plain of Simois, where is the sepulchre of Phrygian Ilus. Already [24] now the Phœnicians, dwelling at the very farthest part of Libya under the setting sun, shudder with alarm: already Syracusans carry their lances by the middle, having their arms burdened with wicker shields: and among them Hiero, a match for elder heroes, girds himself, and [25] his horsehair plumes overshadow his helmet.

Oh that, most glorious father Jove, and lady Minerva, and thou, [26] Proserpine, who with thy mother hast obtained by lot the great city of the exceeding-rich Ephyræans, by the waters of Lysimelia, stern necessity would send our enemies out of the island over the Sardinian wave, to announce to wives and children the fate of their dear ones, [27] by *the fact of* their be-

---

[23] Xenoph. Mem. Socr. II. iv. 1, ποῖος γὰρ ἵππος, ἢ ποῖον ζεῦγος οὕτω χρήσιμον, ὥσπερ ὁ χρηστὸς φίλος. Cf. Cic. de Amicit. xv. 17.

[24] So Virg. Æn. vi. 799, Hujus in adventum jam nunc et Caspia regna, Responsis horrent Divûm, et Mæotia tellus. Carthage, as every one knows, was founded by a Phœnician colony [see Æn. i. 338, 339]. This Idyll bears evidence in these lines of having been written during the first Punic war, after the alliance of Hiero with the Romans, B. C. 263. (Vid. Arnold's Rome, ii. 471, 472.)

[25] Virg. Æn. x. 869, Ære caput fulgens cristâque hirsutus equinâ. ἵππουρις and ἱπποδάσεια coupled with κόρυς denote the same in the Iliad, frequently. Two lines above we find a parallel in Virg. Æn. VII. vi. 32, Flectuntque salignas Umbonum crates.

[26] Proserpine and Ceres were specially worshipped by the Syracusans. Syracuse was founded by a Corinthian colony (compare Idyll xv. 91, note). The ancient name of Corinth was Ephyre. Lysimelia, a pool at the mouth of the river Anapus, hard by Syracuse. Sil. Ital. xiv. 51,

    Sed decus Hennæis haud ullum pulchrius oris,
    Quam quæ Sisyphio fundavit nomen ab Isthmo,
    Et multum ante alias Ephyræis fulget alumnis.

[27] ἀριθματοὺς ἀπὸ πολλῶν, i. e. διὰ τὸ εἶναι, κ. τ. λ. The sense is, that the tale of destruction should find its way home in the few that returned safe. Horat. A. P. 206, Populus numerabilis utpote parvus. Cas-

ing numbered by many; and *oh!* might cities be inhabited again by former citizens, *cities* as many as the hands of enemies have laid waste utterly: and *oh that* they might till flourishing fields; and their ²⁸ thousands unnumbered of sheep, fattened upon the herbage, might bleat along the plain, and heifers, coming in herds to the stalls, urge on the traveller by twilight: and oh that the fallow lands might be broken up for sowing, what time²⁹ the cicala, watching the shepherds in the open air, chirps within the trees on the topmost branches; that spiders might distend fine webs in the arms, ³⁰ and not even the name of the battle-cry be *heard* any longer. And may minstrels bear lofty glory for Hiero, even beyond the Scythian sea, and where ³¹ Semiramis having bound a broad wall with asphalt reigned within it. I indeed am *but* one man: yet the daughters of Jove love many others also, to all of whom it is a care to hymn Sicilian ³² Arethusa with her peoples, and

aubon remarks a like phrase among the Hebrews. Isaiah x. 19, "And the rest of the trees of the forest shall be few, (in the original "a number,") that a child may write them." So Cic. Orat. pro lege Manil. c. ix., Tanta fuit clades, ut eam ad aures L. Luculli non ex proelio nuntius, sed ex sermone rumor afferret.

²⁸ Virg. Ecl. ii. 21, Mille meæ Siculis errant in montibus agnæ. "The folds shall be full of sheep, and the valleys also shall stand so thick with corn, that they shall laugh and sing," Psalm lxv. 14. Compare also Ps. cxliv. 13.

²⁹ ἀχεῖ ἐν ἀκοεμόνεσειν. Virg. Ecl. II., Sole sub ardenti resonant arbusta cicadis. With the next clause compare Hom. Odyss. xvi. 34, 35. Hesiod Op. et D. ii. 93. Propert. III. vi. 33, Putris et in vacuo texetur aranea lecto. So Catullus, Carm. XIII. v. 7, Nam tui Catulli
    Plenus sacculus est aranearum.
Virg. Georg. iv. 247, In foribus laxos suspendit aranea casses. Add to these Bacchylides, Fragm. ix., and Tibull. I. x. 49.

³⁰ Comp. Isaiah ii. 4, "Nation shall not lift up sword against nation, neither shall they learn war any more." Theocritus is said to have imitated in some passages of this piece, Isaiah, and the 66th, 72nd, and 144th Psalms.

³¹ Compare Ovid. Met. iv. 57,
    Ubi dicitur altam
  Coctilibus muris cinxisse Semiramis urbem.

³² Arethusa. See Idyll i. 117. Ovid. Met. v. 573—641. Silius xiv. 53, Hic Arethusa suum piscoso fonte receptat Alpheon, sacræ portantem signa coronæ. Milton in Arcades celebrates,
  Divine Alpheus, who by secret sluice
  Stole under seas to meet his Arethuse.
For μέλει, Wordsw. suggests μολοι, obveniat, contingat.

[33] the warrior Hiero. [34] Ye goddesses having your rise from Eteocles, that love Minyan Orchomenus, hated of old by Thebes, inglorious indeed may I remain at home: yet with confidence would I go to men's halls, if they call me, along with my Muses, and I will not leave even you behind. For apart from the Graces what is *ever* beloved by man? May I ever bide with the Graces.

IDYLL XVII.

THE PRAISE OF PTOLEMY.

ARGUMENT.

The poet intending to celebrate Ptolemy Philadelphus, king of Egypt, sets out with the praise of his father, Ptolemy Lagus, to whom after his death a place among the gods had been ascribed; and goes on to eulogize Berenice, the mother of Philadelphus, whom Venus was supposed to have received into her temples to be her πάρεδρος, or assessor. He next proceeds to set forth the fortunes and virtues of Philadelphus himself, beginning with the happy omens which had attended his birth in the island of Cos, and portended his future opulence and power. Then follows an enumeration of the royal territories, and laudation of the royal wealth, augmented as it has been by the blessings of peace. The poet commends in glowing terms the munificence and discernment of Philadelphus in conferring favours, as well as his filial piety shown so eminently. He ends with praise of the queen, the wife and sister of Ptolemy. Reiske, Warton, and others have held this to be a poem of Callimachus; but Eichstadt declares that, while it equals the lightness of the poems of that writer, it surpasses them in jejuneness.

---

[33] Hiero. Silius Ital. xiv. 79, &c., gives a character of the old age of Hiero.

[34] Ω Ετεόκλειοι θύγατρες. i. e. O goddesses, whose worship was originated by Eteocles, son of Cephisus, or Andreus, who first sacrificed to the Charites at Orchomenus in Bœotia. See Pausan. ix. 34, § 5; 35, § 1. Schol. ad Pind. Ol. xiv. 1. Smith's Dict. Gr. R. B. vol. ii. 53. For the grounds of enmity between Thebes and Orchomenus, J. W. refers us to Thirlwall, Hist. Greec. c. iv. vol. i. p. 91, § 9. At the last line compare Milton, L'Allegro,

These delights if thou canst give,
Mirth, with thee I mean to live.

¹ BEGIN we with Jove, and at Jove make an end, ye Muses, whensoever we sing in our minstrelsy the best of immortals. But of men, on the other hand, let Ptolemy be spoken of among ²the first, and *last*, and *at the middle;* for he is the most excellent of men. Heroes, who ³aforetime sprung from demigods, having done noble deeds have met with skilful poets. But I, knowing how to speak well, would *fain* hymn *the praise of* Ptolemy; and hymns are a glory even of the immortals themselves. A wood-cutter having gone to woody Ida, looks around whence to begin his work, though there is abundance at hand. What shall I first recount? for innumerable *glories* occur to tell, with which the gods honoured the best of kings.

From his fathers what a man indeed was Ptolemy son of Lagus ⁴to accomplish a great work, when he had conceived in his mind a counsel which no other man was able to devise. ⁵ Him father *Jupiter* has made equal in honour even to the blest immortals, and for him a chamber of gold has been built in the mansion of Jove; and beside him sits Alexander, kindly disposed *to him,* a god hard upon Persians with variegated turbans. And opposite to them is set the chair of Hercules, slayer of the Centaur, wrought out of solid adamant; where with other celestials he holds feasts, rejoicing exceedingly in his grandchildren's grandchildren, ⁶because the son of Saturn

---

¹ Virg. Ecl. iii. 60, A Jove principium. Ecl. viii. 11, A te principium, tibi desinet. Hom. Il. i. 97, ἐν σοὶ μὲν λήξω, σέο δ' ἄρξομαι.
² Milton's Paradise Lost, v. 165, Him first, Him last, Him midst, and without end. Horat. i Ep. i., Primâ dicte mihi, summâ dicende Camoenâ.
³ πρόσθεν, olim. So "ante," in Latin. Ovid. Fast. i. 337,
   Ante, deos homini quod conciliare valeret
   Far erat.
Three lines below compare with ὕμνοι δὲ καὶ, κ. τ. λ. Horace Epist. II. i. 138, Carmine Dì superi placantur, carmine Manes.
⁴ Compare Callim. H. in Jov. 87, where he says of this same Ptolemy, Εσπέριος κεῖνος γε τελεῖ τὰ κεν ἠοῖ νοήσῃ. So Hom. Od. β. 272, οἷος ἐκεῖνος ἔην τελέσαι ἔργον τε ἔπος τε.
⁵ Ptolemy Philadelphus, son of Ptolemy Lagides, or Soter, (one of Alexander's generals, who obtained Egypt at the division of his empire,) was associated in the government by his sire, to the exclusion of his children by his first wife Eurydice; in return for which Philadelphus deified Lagides and his wife Berenice. Below at line 19, J. W. quotes Juvenal iii. 66, Ite quibus grata est pictâ lupa barbara mitrâ.
⁶ Callim. H. in Dian. 159, γυῖα θεωθείς. Ov. Met. iv. 538, Abstulit

has exempted their limbs from old age, and because, being of his [7] brood, they are styled immortals. For to both the brave son of Hercules is an ancestor, and both [8] reckon up *their descent* to Hercules, as the source. Wherefore likewise when, at length satisfied with fragrant nectar, he goes from the feast to the chamber of his dear spouse, to the one he gives his bow and the quiver under his elbow, and to the other his iron club, studded with knots; and they bear the arms to the ambrosial chamber of white-[9]ancled Hebe, along with their ancestor, Jove's son himself. And among wise women how did far-famed Berenice shine, a great blessing to her parents! Upon whose fragrant breast, indeed, the august daughter of Dione, that occupies Cyprus, impressed her slender hands. Wherefore 'tis said that never did any woman so please her husband, as Ptolemy in fact loved his own wife. She indeed returned his love far more *than other wives*. Thus he could trustfully commit his whole house to his children's care, whensoever lover-like he ascended to the chamber of his *loving* wife.
[10] But of an unloving woman the thoughts are ever on a

illis quod mortale fuit. Soph. Œd. Col. 607, Μόνοις οὐ γίγνεται θεοῖσι γῆρας. The founder of the kingdom of Macedon was Caranus, an Argive, sixteenth in descent from Hercules. From him Philip and Alexander therefore traced their pedigree. See more, as J. W. refers us, in Valkenaer on Herodot. viii. 137.

[7] νέποδες, i. q. τέκνα, a brood. Eustath. (quasi νεόποδες, from νέος.) Compare nepos, nepotes. It occurs in Callim. Frag. lxxvii. 260. Apoll. Rhod. iv. 1745.

[8] Juvenal viii. 131, Tunc licet a Pico numeres genus. Ἡρακλείδας. Hyllus.

[9] Hebe, daughter of Jupiter and Juno, was the fabled wife of Hercules. Odyss. xi. 602, where Ulysses is represented beholding Hercules with καλλίσφυρος Ἥβη, a mythic union of strength and youth.

[10] The meaning of this and the foregoing verses seems—"A husband sure of his wife's love, can trust his children, because they are no bastards, with his interests and fortunes." As Ptolemy, son of Lagus, did, in sharing his kingdom with Philadelphus, his son by Berenice. Horat. Od. Il. v. 21—24,

> Nullis polluitur casta domus stupris:
> Mos et lex maculosum edomuit nefas;
> Laudantur simili prole puerperæ:
> Culpam pœna premit comes.

Compare Martial vi. 7, 24,

> Et tibi, quæ patrii signatur imagine vultus,
> Testis maternæ nata pudicitiæ.

Compare also Juvenal vi. 81; Hesiod O. et D. 235. Catull. lix. 229

stranger; and her parturitions are easy, but the children never like the father. O Lady Aphrodite, excelling the goddesses in beauty, to thee she was a care, and on account of thee beauteous Berenice did not cross mournful Acheron; but having snatched her away ere she had come down to the dark stream, and to the ever-rueful ferryman of the ·dead, thou placedst her in thy temple, and gavest her a share in thine honour. And gentle to all mortals, she ever breathes upon them soft loves, and to one that longs [11] makes his cares light.

[12] O dark-browed Argive lady, thou didst bear Diomed, slayer of hosts, a Calydonian hero, when thou hadst been united to Tydeus. But deep-bosomed Thetis bare the warrior Achilles to Peleus, son of Æacus: and thee, O warrior Ptolemy, distinguished Berenice to a warrior, Ptolemy. [13] And Cos did rear thee, having received *thee* a new-born babe from thy mother, when thou sawest the dawn first. For there the [14] daughter of Antigone, weighed down with throes, called out for [15] Lucina, the friend of women in travail. And she with kind favour stood by her, and in sooth poured down her whole limbs an insensibility to pain, and *so* a lovely boy, like to his father, was born.

[16] And Cos when she beheld him broke forth into joy, and

> Sit suo similis patri
> Manlio, et facilè insciis
> Noscitetur ab omnibus;
> Et pudicitiam suam
> Matris indicet ore.

J. W. aptly compares Shaksp. Much Ado about Nothing, act i. sc. 1, "Truly the lady fathers herself," and Terent. Heaut. V. iv. 17.

[11] κούφας διδοῖ, i. e. κουφιξει. Cf. Idyll xxiii. 9, φίλαμα τὸ κουφίζον τὸν ἔρωτα.

[12] Tydeus, son of Æneus, king of Calydon, flying to Argos, married Deipyle, daughter of Adrastus, who bare him Diomed, called here Calydonian, because of his father's origin.

[13] Ptolemy Philadelphus was born at the island of Cos, whither his mother Berenice had accompanied her husband during the naval campaign of B. C. 309, against Demetrius. Comp. Callim. H. in Del. 165—190.

[14] Berenice was the daughter of Antigone, the daughter of Cassander, the brother of Antipater. See Smith D. G. A. p. 482, vol. i.

[15] Lucina, λυσίζωνος. Call. H. in Jov. 21, ἐλύσατο μίτραν. See Spanheim, note at this passage. To her belonged the influence we moderns ascribe to chloroform.

[16] ὀλόλυξεν, uttered a cry of joy. Eur. Electr. 691. This impersonation of the island is bold and sublime. Polwhele compares with passages of holy writ, e. g. Why hop ye so, ye high hills. Break forth into singing,

said, with fond hands touching the infant: [17]'Blessed, boy, mayest thou be, and mayest thou honour me as much as even Phœbus Apollo honoured Délos of the azure fillet : and in the same honour mayest thou rank the [18]promontory of Triops, assigning equal [19]favour to the Dorians dwelling near, as also king Apollo lovingly paid to [20]Rhenæa." Thus, I wot, spake the island, and the propitious eagle-bird of Jove thrice from on high, above the clouds, screamed with its voice. This methinks is a sign of Jove. To Jove the son of Saturn august monarchs are a care: and chiefly he, whomsoever he shall have kissed at his first birth ; and great fortune attends him. Much land rules he, and much sea. Numberless continents, as well as myriads of races of men, till corn-fields assisted by the moisture of Jove: but no *region* produces so much as low-[21]lying Egypt, when Nile gushing forth breaks up the moist clods. Nor hath any so many cities of men skilled in works. Three hundred indeed of towns have been

---

ye mountains. Theocritus however has a closer parallel here, in Callim. H. in Del. 264, Αὐτὴ δὲ χρυσέοιο ἀπ' οὔδεος εἵλεο παῖδα, spoken of the island Delos. Hom. H. in Apoll. 61, 119, q. v. Virg. Ecl. v. 62,
Ipsi lætitia voces ad sidera jactant
Intonsi montes.

[17] ὄλβιε κῶρε γένοιο, for ὄλβιος, a rare construction in Greek, Eurip. Troad. 1229. In Latin, Tibull. i. 7, 53, Sic venias hodierne. Propert. II. xv. 2, Lectule deliciis facte beate meis. Virg. Æn. ii. 282, Quibus Hector ab oris, expectate venis.

[18] Spanheim, at Callim. H. in Del. 160, says that Triops was king of Cos, and father of Merops, another king of the island ; and that from him the promontory of Cnidos was called Triopium. Comp. H. in Cerer. 31.

[19] The Dorian Pentapolis consisted of five cities, Lindus, Ialysus, Camirus, Cos, and Cnidos. Thirwl. H. of Greece, vol. ii. 88.

[20] Rhenæa, an island close to Delos, to which in the purification of Delos by Pisistratus, and afterwards in the Peloponnesian war, all dead bodies were carried from Delos for burial ; and all births of Delian children arranged to take place there. Cf. Thuc. iii. 104. Polycrates, tyrant of Samos, bound it to Delos and dedicated it to Apollo. See Virg. Æn. iii. 75.

[21] "Ægypti pars depressior." Tibull. i. 7, 23,
Fertilis æstivâ Nilus abundet aquâ
Nile pater quânam possim te dicere causâ
Aut quibus in terris occuluisse caput.

The Delta is here alluded to. See Georg. iv. 287—294, for another account of the Nile. θρύπτει, confringit. Herod. ii. 12, (quoted here by J. W.,) τὴν Αἴγυπτον μελάγγαιόν τε καὶ καταρρηγνυμένην ὥστε ἰοῦσαν ἰλύν τε καὶ πρόχυσιν ἐξ Αἰθιοπίης κατενηνειγμένην ὑπὸ τοῦ ποταμοῦ.

built for him, ay and three thousand over *and above* thirty thousand, and two triads, and besides them thrice nine; in [22] all which magnanimous Ptolemy is sovereign. And in truth he cuts off for his portion a part of Phœnicia and Arabia, and of Syria and Libya, and the black Æthiopians; and he bears sway over all the Pamphylians, and warrior Cilicians, and Lycians, and war-loving Carians, and the island Cyclades, for [23] his ships are the best that sail over the sea; and all sea and land and rushing rivers are ruled over by Ptolemy. And for him many horsemen and many shield-bearers arrayed in gleaming brass rage and roar.

In wealth indeed he outweighs all monarchs, so much every day comes into his splendid house from every quarter, and the peoples go about his works in peace and quietness. For no hostile infantry having crossed the Nile abounding in [24] crocodiles, has raised the battle-cry in strange villages; nor has any armed man leapt ashore from a swift ship against the cattle of Egypt, as a foe: such a hero yellow-haired Ptolemy has established himself in her broad plains, skilful to wield the spear; whose whole care is to protect his patrimony, as a good king's *should be;* and other realms he is himself acquiring. Not however to no purpose, I ween, is the gold in his wealthy house, [25] even as the riches of labouring ants are

[22] $τῶν πάντων$, referred to $πολέων$, but in the neuter gender. Cf. Epigr. i. 3, 4. The whole number is 33,339. Wordsworth refers us for the riches of Ptolemy, to the commentators on Daniel xi. 5.

[23] His ships are the best, &c. Fawkes compares Waller,
Where'er thy navy spreads her canvass wings,
Homage to thee, and peace to all she brings.
Byron, Corsair, opening,
Our flag the sceptre, all who meet obey.
$κελάδοντες$, resonantes. Cf. Idyll vii. 137. Aristoph. Nub. 284, $καὶ ποταμῶν ζαθέων κελαδήματι$.

[24] For the crocodiles of the Nile, see Herodot. lib. ii. Senec. Natur. Quæst. iv. 1, p. 611, Elzev. J. W. At "yellow-haired Ptolemy," compare Horat. Od. IV. xv. 17,
Custode rerum Cæsare, non furor
Civilis, aut vis exiget otium.

[25] Cf. Æsch. Prom. v. 451, $ἀείσυροι μύρμηκες$. Horat. Sat. i. 1, 33.
Magni formica laboris
Ore trahit quodcunque potest, atque addit acervo
Quem struit.
For the next line compare Virg. Æn. x. 619,
Tua largâ
Sæpe manu multisque oneravit limina donis.

ever poured in; but much of it indeed the splendid temples of the gods have, whilst ever and anon he offers first-fruits with other gifts: and much has he bestowed on brave kings, and much on cities, and much on good comrades; nor has any man, skilled to strike up a sweet song, [26] come to the sacred contests of Bacchus, [27] to whom he has not presented a gift worthy of his craft. [28] And the interpreters of the Muses sing the praise of Ptolemy, in return for his beneficence. But what can be more honourable to a man of wealth than to win worthy renown among men? This remains sure even to the sons of Atreus, while those countless acquisitions, as many as they made, when they had taken the mighty house of Priam, have been hidden some where in the [29] mist, from which thereafter there is no longer a return. [30] This man, alone of men of former ages, impresses the foot-prints of his parents, yet warm in the dust, as he treads above them. [31] To his loved mother and father he has placed incense-breathing temples, and has set them up therein conspicuous with gold and ivory, as helpers to all mortals. And many fatted haunches of oxen does he burn, in revolving months, on blood-red altars, himself and his goodly spouse, than whom no nobler woman

---

[26] The festivals of Bacchus celebrated by Ptolemy, and the "sacred contests" here alluded to, appear to have been either dramatic pieces, or the Dionysia at which poets contended with those dramatic pieces.

[27] Ptolemy's munificence drew to his court seven poets, called the Pleiades from their number, Theocritus, Callimachus, Apollonius, Aratus, Lycophron, Nicander, Philicus.

[28] Horat. Od. III. i. 3, Musarum sacerdos. In Cicero's oration for Archias, Ennius is quoted as calling poets "sanctos." Propert. III. i. 3, Primus ego ingredior puro de fonte sacerdos. Virg. Georg. ii. 475,
Me vero primum dulces ante omnia Musæ,
Quarum sacra fero ingenti percussus amore.

[29] ἀέρι: caligine. See Hom. Odyss. ix. 144,
ἀὴρ γὰρ παρὰ νηυσὶ βαθεῖ' ἦν, οὐδὲ σελήνη
οὐρανόθεν προὔφαινε.
Cf. Il. v. 864.

[30] Ovid. Met. vii. 775, Pedum calidus vestigia pulvis habebat. Hom. Il. xxiii. 763, describes the act which gives rise to this metaphor,
αὐτὰρ ὄπισθεν
ἴχνια τύπτε πόδεσσι, πάρος κόνιν ἀμφιχυθῆναι.
ἐκμάσσεται imitatione exprimit.

[31] Ptolemy raised temples in honour of his parents, as well as one to his sister as Venus Arsinoe. χρυσῷ: Signa auro illinebant antiqui. J. W. Vid. not. Wordsw. Theocr. p. 158.

embraces her bridegroom in the palace [32] with bended arm, loving as she does from the heart her brother and husband. Thus too was consummated [33] the holy marriage of the immortals, whom sovereign Rhea bare as sovereigns of Olympus: and Iris, still a virgin, having washed her hands with unguents, strews one couch for Jupiter and Juno to sleep upon. Farewell, O king Ptolemy; but of thee I will make mention like as of other demigods; and methinks [34] I shall speak a word not *to be* spurned by posterity: 'Excellence at any rate one will gain from Jupiter.'

IDYLL XVIII.

THE EPITHALAMIUM OF HELEN.

ARGUMENT.

After the nuptials of Helen and Menelaus, the chief maidens of Sparta, ranging themselves before the bridal chamber, sing an Epithalamium, beginning with the jokes which would naturally be passed at the expense of the bridegroom. Menelaus is next felicitated on the score of the prize of beauty which he has won, while so many of the noblest suitors failed. The poet passes naturally on to a description of Helen's personal and mental graces, and puts into the mouth of the chorus a warm expression of their love and regard for her. This Idyll is of a lyric character, and is amongst the most beautiful of its kind. Some have been led, by its dissimilarity from the other Idylls, to suppose Theocritus not to have been its author. But there is no reason why

---

[32] ἀγοστῷ, with a bent arm, akin to ἀγκῶν.

[33] A comparison is instituted between the marriage of Jove and Juno, and that between Philadelphus and Arsinoe; the brother in each case wedding his sister. Iris is represented as discharging the office which, in Idyll ii. 160 of Moschus, the Hours discharge for Jove and Europa.

[34] φθέγξομαι, &c. The moral sentence that follows is premised by φθέγξομαι, and the sense is, that the observation of excellence in Ptolemy, granted him by the gods, causes the poet to exhort all that his words reach, not to scorn his example, but to seek from Jove, who alone can give it, like excellence. ἕξεις. The second person here is used, as elsewhere, for an indefinite third person. Compare Sophocl. Trachin. 2. Ajax 155. Tacitus German: Nam magnum—haud tueare.

he should not have excelled in this as in more homely styles. He may have borrowed from Stesichorus, but the Epithalamium of that poet not being extant, we have no means of deciding whether, or how far, this was the case. It is of that class of Epithalamia which is called κατακοιμητικὸν, or slumber-inducing.

[1] Whilome in Sparta, at the house of auburn-haired Menelaus, maidens having blooming [2] hyacinth in their tresses, formed the dance in front of a [3] newly-painted nuptial chamber, the twelve first *maidens* of the city, [4] pride of the Spartan women, when the younger son of Atreus, having wedded Helen the beloved daughter of Tyndarus, had shut her within his chamber. And they began to sing, I ween, all beating time to one melody with many-twinkling [5] feet, and the house was ringing round with a nuptial hymn. "Hast thou then fallen asleep thus too early, O dear bridegroom? Art thou

---

[1] It was Brunck's opinion that Theocritus wrote this Idyll with an eye to the Song of Solomon, many passages of which strikingly receive illustration from it. ἔν ποκ' ἄρα Σπάρτᾳ. Callimach. H. in Lav. Pall. ἔν ποκα Θήβαις.

[2] Milton's Paradise Lost iv. 301, "Hyacinthine locks." Odyss. vi. 230,
κὰδ δὲ κάρητος
οὔλας ἧκε κόμας, ὑακινθίνῳ ἄνθει ὁμοίας.
Horace Od. I. iv. 9, 10,
Nunc decet aut viridi nitidum caput impedire myrto
Aut flore, terræ quem ferunt solutæ.

[3] Embroidery, or tapestry, is here spoken of—provided at the husband's expense. Hom. Il. xvii. 36, θαλάμοιο νέοιο. Odyss. xxii. 178. Comp. Idyll xxvii. 36.

[4] μέγα χρῆμα. See Matt. Gr. Gr. § 430, p. 704. Herodot. i. 36. συὸς χρῆμα μέγα. Acharn. Aristoph. 150; Nub. 2. Valken. on Phœn. 206.

[5] περιπλέκτοις, which appears the true reading here, signifies literally "intertwined." Some would read χερσὶ for ποσὶ, bringing Horat. Od. I. iv. 6, Junctæque nymphis gratiæ decentes Alterno terram quatiunt pede, and Ovid. Fast. vi. 329, Pars brachia nectit, Et viridem celeri ter pede pulsat humum, to support the reading. But these do not militate against ποσσί, which is borne out by Euripid. Troad. 2, 3; Iph. in Aulis, 1055—1057.

Gray's Progress of Poesy:
Thee the voice, the dance, obey,
Temper'd to thy warbled lay.
O'er Idalia's velvet green
The rosy-crowned Loves are seen
On Cytheræa's day,
With antic sports, and blue-eyed pleasures,
Frisking light in frolic measures:

then of a nature over sluggish, or art thou fond of slumber? [6] Or wast thou drinking a *draught too* much, when thou didst lay thyself on thy couch? If thou didst want to sleep in season, thou shouldest have done so by thyself, [7] and have suffered the damsel to sport with her maidens beside her fond mother, until morning prime; since both the day after to-morrow, and to-morrow, and from year to year, O Menelaus, she i your bride. Blest husband, some lucky person [8] sneezed on thee, as thou wentest to Sparta, (whither the rest of the nobles *repaired*,) that thou [9] mightest accomplish *thine object.* Alone among demigods thou wilt have Jupiter, son of Saturn, as father-in-law. A daughter of Jove has gone beneath the same coverlet with thee, being such an one as no other of Greek women, that treads the earth. Surely a great thing would she bear to thee, if she bare one like its mother. For we are play-mates all, who had the same course *to run,* [10] when we had anointed ourselves, like men, beside the banks of

> Now pursuing, now retreating,
> Now in circling troops they meet;
> To brisk notes in cadence beating
> Glance their *many twinkling* feet.

Muse of the many twinkling feet. Byron, The Waltz.
Compare Hom. Odyss. viii. 265; Iliad xviii. 491—495.

[6] πολύν τιν', understand οἶνον. Eurip. Cyclops 566, χαλεπὸν τόδ' εἶπας, ὅστις ἂν πίνῃ πολύν. Theogn. v. 509, οἶνος πινόμενος πουλὺς, κακός, ἢν δέ τις αὐτὸν Πίνῃ ἐπισταμένως, οὐ κακὸς ἀλλ' ἀγαθός.

[7] Compare Catull. Carm. Nupt. LX., 20,
Hespere, qui cœlo fertur crudelior ignis?
Qui gnatam possis complexu avellere matris,
Complexu matris retinentem avellere gnatam,
Et juveni ardenti castam donare puellam.
βαθὺν ὄρθρον. Cf. St. Luke Evang. c. xxiv. v. 1, ὄρθρου βαθέος.

[8] ἐπέπταρεν. See Idyll vii. 96, Σιμιχίδᾳ μὲν ἔρωτες ἐπέπταρον. Propert. II. iii. 23,
Num tibi nascenti primis, mea vita, diebus,
Aridus argutum sternuit omen amor.
Catull. xliii. 9. Comp. Xenoph. Anab. III. ii. 9, πτάρνυται τις ἀγαθὸς, homo boni ominis. So Callimach. H. in Lav. Pall. 124, ἀγαθαὶ πτέρυγες. Propert. III. x. 11, Felicibus—pennis. Ovid. Fast. i. 513, Este bonis avibus visi natoque mihique. Virg. Ecl. v. 65, Sis bonus o felixque tuis.

[9] ἀνύσαιο. Comp. Idyll v. 144, ἀνυσάμαν τὸν ἀμνὸν. With χλαῖναν (two lines below) compare Sophocl. Trach. 539,
καὶ νῦν δύ' οὖσαι μίμνομεν μιᾶς ὑπὸ
χλαίνης ὑπαγκά λισμα.

[10] The river Eurotas ran close by Sparta. For the hardy nurture and

Eurotas, four times sixty damsels, a youthful band of maidens; of whom not one *would be* faultless, if haply she should have been compared with Helen. ¹¹ As the rising morn would show out its beauteous face against the night, or *as* bright spring ¹² when winter has relaxed ; so also the golden Helen was wont to shine out amongst us. ¹³ As a tall cypress hath shot up, an ornament to a fertile field or garden, or a Thessalian steed to a chariot, thus also the rosy-complexioned Helen is an ornament to Lacedæmon. ¹⁴ Neither does any damsel weave such work in the wool-basket, nor cut off from the long upright beams a closer warp in the curiously wrought web, having woven it with the shuttle. ¹⁵ No, nor is any *damsel* so skilled to strike the cithern, ¹⁶ singing of Artemis, and broad-chested Athené, as Helen, ¹⁷ in whose eyes are all loves.

exercises of Spartan maidens, see Thirlw. Greece, vol. i. p. 327. Virg. Æn. i. 315,   Virginis os habitumque gerens et virginis arma
         Spartanæ.
¹¹ Ἀὼς ἀντέλλοισα. Comp. Solomon's Song vi. 10, "Who is she that looketh forth like the morning?" Job xli. 18. In this passage, which is unsound as it stands in MSS., we have adopted the reading ἀὼς ἀντέλλοισ' ἅτε καλὸν ἔφηνε προσώπον ποτ' τὰν νύκτ' ᾖ, which Kiessling seems to favour. Chapman quotes an exquisite parallel from Campbell's Gertrude of Wyoming.
         A boy   *   *   *   *   *   *   *
         Led by his dusky guide like morning brought by night.
Wordsworth's suggestion is ποτ' τίν νύξ: Sicut præ te, nox, exoriens Aurora prænitet. As rising morn, compared with thee, O night, shines out with bright countenance. And this seems extremely probable.
¹² χειμῶνος ἀνέντος. Solomon's Song ii. 11, "Lo, the winter is past, the rain is over and gone." χείματος οἰχομένοιο, Meleag. ii. πιείρᾳ μεγάλα ἅτ'. Wordsw. proposes πιείρᾳ ἴλατα ἅτ, ut abies, &c.
¹³ Catull. Epithalam. Pel. 89—90,
         Quales Eurotæ progignunt flumina myrtos,
         Aurave distinctos educit verna colores.
Θεσσαλὸς ἵππος. These were the most approved steeds of Greece. See Sophoc. Electr. 703. Solomon's Song i. 9, "I have compared thee, O my love, to a company of horses in Pharaoh's chariots."
¹⁴ For the full understanding of these verses, read Smith's Dict. Gr Rom. Ant., art. Tela, p. 940—943.
¹⁵ Æn. vi. 647, Jamque eadem digitis, jam pectine pulsat eburno.
¹⁶ Laconian maidens, so skilful at weaving, might fitly hymn Minerva, and, so hardy in nurture, sing the praise of the divine huntress, Artemis. Ov. Fast. iii. 817, Pallade placatâ, lanam mollire puellœ Discant et plenas exonerare colos. Comp. Tibull. II. i. 65.
¹⁷ Burns, "The kind love that's in her e'e." Meleager Epigr. Anthol. xvi. Ζηνόφιλας ὄμμασι κρυπτόμενος. Cf. Musæus, 64.

"O beauteous, O graceful damsel, thou indeed art a matron now; but we in the morning shall proceed to the course and the flowery meads, to cull chaplets breathing sweet *incense*, oft remembering thee, O Helen, as suckling lambs yearning for the teat of their mother. For thee first *of any* having plaited a chaplet of [18] low-growing lotus, we will place it on the shady plane tree; and for *thee* first, taking moist oil from silver flask, we will drop it beneath the shady plane tree, and letters shall be [19] graven on the bark, that any passer-by may recite in Doric: "Reverence me, I am Helen's tree."—Hail, thou bride! Hail, bridegroom, happy in thy father-in-law. May Latona indeed, Latona the nurse of youth, grant to you the blessing of children; and Venus, goddess Venus, that ye may be loved alike one by other; and Jove, Jove the son of Saturn, lasting riches; that they may descend from nobly-born to nobly-born again. [20] Sleep on, breathing into the bosoms each of the other love and desire, and forget [21] not to rise towards morn. We too will return at dawn, as soon as the earliest [22] songster having reared his crested neck, shall have

---

[18] The Lotos, a flower of the Nile, is found composing garlands in Egyptian monuments. Ovid. Trist. III. i. 31,
    Sic nova Dulichio lotos gustata palato,
    Illo, quo nocuit, grata sapore fuit.

[19] Letters graven.] Propert. I. xviii. 22, Scribitur et vestris Cynthia corticibus. Virg. Ecl. x. 53,
    Tenerisque meos incidere amores
    Corticibus: crescent illæ: crescetis amores.
Compare Idyll xxiii. 46.—Pope Past. III. 66, 67,
    Oft on the rind I carved her amorous vows,
    While she with garlands hung the bending boughs.

[20] Catull. lxii. 331, 332,
    Languidulosque paret tecum conjungere somnos
    Levia substernens robusto brachia collo.
Compare Solomon's Song viii. 3, 4, "His left hand should be under my head, and his right hand should embrace me. I charge you, O daughters of Jerusalem, that ye stir not up, nor awake my love until he please."

[21] Idyll xxiv. 7, ὕπνος ἐγέρσιμος.

[22] ὁ πρᾶτος ἀοιδός. Cf. Idyll xxiv. 63, "The feather'd songster chanticleer." Prudentius, Hymn Matutin. Daniels' Thesaurus Hymnologicus i. 119,
    Ales diei nuntius
    Lucem propinquam præcinit.
St. Ambrose calls the cock "præco diei," &c. Ovid, Jam dederat cantus lucis prænuncius ales.

crowed from his roost, [23] Hymen, O Hymenæus, mayest thou joy over these nuptials.

IDYLL XIX.

THE STEALER OF HONEY-COMBS.

ARGUMENT.

This little poem seems to have been wrought out of the fortieth ode of Anacreon, which has been rendered into English by our freshly lost Thomas Moore; to which however it is clearly inferior in the merit of originality and management of subject. Valkenaer thinks it a poem of Bion; but Stobæus (c. 63) quotes the lines as the work of Theocritus. Meleager (Epigr. cviii. Antholog. Jacobs) has taken the same subject for his muse.

[1] THE naughty bee once stung the pilferer Eros, as he was plundering a comb from the hives, and pierced all the tips of his fingers; and he began to lament and blow his hand; and struck the earth, and leaped *aloft*. Then showed he his pain to Aphrodité, and began to complain 'that at any rate the bee is a little creature, and yet what great wounds it inflicts!' And his mother smiling said—How then? are you not a creature resembling the bees? Since little though you be, yet the wounds you inflict, how great are they!

---

[23] Cf. Catull. lx., Hymen o Hymenæ, Hymen ades, o Hymenææ. Milton P. L. IV. " Heavenly quires the hymenæan sung." Chapman quotes at length a parallel from the same, lib. viii.

[1] H. Voss observes that μέλισσα is said collectively, not "a bee," but "the bee," hence τραύματα, not τραύμα, below at line 6.

[2] χὼ τυτθὸς μὲν ἔης—Eo quod tantulus quum sis, quanta facis vulnera. The imperf. ἔης, observes Schæfer, has the force of a present, as at Idyll v. 79, ἦ στωμύλος ἦσθα Κομάτα. Anacr. xxix. 40, τὰ δ' ἦν ἀμείνω. Bion xv. 4, κἦν μοι συρίσδεν, Μύρσων φίλον.

IDYLL XX.

THE HERDSMAN.

ARGUMENT.

The poet in this Idyll introduces a rustic complaining of the scorn and contempt of a city maiden in rejecting his addresses. Having declared the cause of this scorn, he shows how undeserving he is of it, as being neither ugly nor a man of the lowest condition, seeing that gods and goddesses had sought out of his rank of life, objects of love. Heinsius holds this to be a poem of Moschus, but though Valkenaer inclines to the same opinion, the mass of testimony ascribes it to Theocritus.

EUNICA laughed at me when I wished sweetly to kiss her, and, teasing me, said thus:[1] 'Away with you from me! Clown as you are, do you want to kiss me, wretch? I have not learned to kiss bumpkins, [2] but to press city lips. Don't *you* at any rate kiss my fair mouth, no, not in your dreams. What a look you have! what a speech! [3] how rudely you toy! How mincingly you talk! what wheedling words you utter! How [4] smooth is the beard you have! what sweet hair! [5] *Nay,* your lips in truth are diseased, and your hands are black, and you smell foully. Away from me, lest you contaminate me!'

Speaking thus, [6] she spat thrice on her breast, and [7] eyed

---

[1] ἔρρε. Æolic for εἶρε, (says Grævius at Callim. H. in Del. 130,) as φθέρρειν for φθείρειν. Latin. Abin' in malam rem. Terent. Andria II. i. 17. Hom. Iliad viii. 164, ἔρρε, κακὴ γλήνη. Il. xxii. 498, ἔρρ' οὕτως.

[2] θλίβειν χείλεα. Labra suaviter premere. Comp. Idyll xii. 32; Bion i. 44.

[3] ἄγρια παίσδεις. Mosch. i. 11, and see the notes of this transl. on that passage.

[4] Virg. Ecl. viii. 34, Hirsutumque supercilium promissaque barba.— ἀδέα χαίταν. Simple adjectives in υς are often common in gender. Comp. Matth. Gr. Gr. § 119, b. 4. θῆλυς ἐέρση, Odyss. v. 467. Of course the lines 6—8 are ironical.

[5] Aristoph. Nub. 50, ὄζων τρυγός, τρασιᾶς, ἐρίων. A *strong* description of a rustic.

[6] τρὶς εἰς ἑὸν ἔπτυσε κόλπον. Compare ii. 62; Theocr. vi. 39; Soph. Antig. 653.

[7] Comp. Virg. Æn. iv. 363, 364,
    Huc illuc volvens oculos, *totum*que pererrat
    Luminibus tacitis.

me all over from my head to my two feet, making mouths at me with her lips, and looking at me askance. ⁸And she played the woman with much affectation as to her figure, and laughed at me with a mocking and proud kind of laugh. But ⁹quickly my blood boiled up, and I became purple in complexion by reason of my chagrin, as a rose *is* with dew. And she indeed left me and went away. But I bear wrath at my heart, because a worthless mistress has ridiculed me, pleasing though I am.

Shepherds, tell me the truth; 'am I not beautiful?' ¹⁰Has one of the gods, I wonder, made me on a sudden another mortal? ¹¹For formerly a pleasing kind of beauty was blooming upon me, as ivy on the trunk, and used to shade my chin; and my locks poured, like parsley, around my temples, and my white forehead was wont to shine over dark eye-brows; my eyes *were* far more ¹²bright than those of blue-eyed Athené; ¹³my mouth more sweet even than cream cheese; and ¹⁴from my lips flowed a voice more pleasant than from a

---

Hor. Epist. II. ii. 4,   Hic et
    Candidus, et talos a vertice pulcher ad imos
    Fiet.

⁸ Compare Bion xv. 18, where the word is used of Achilles in woman's apparel with Deidamia, καὶ γὰρ ἴσον τήναις θηλύνετο. σεσαρὸς. Comp. Idyll vii. 19. Literally, "of parted lips."

⁹ Compare Callimach. Bath of Pallas, 27,

Ω κῶραι, τὸ δ' ἐρευθος ανεδραμε, πρώϊον οἴαν
   Ἡ ῥόδον ἢ σιβδας κόκκος ἔχει χροίαν.

Cf. Bion i. 35; Moschus iii. 5.

¹⁰ Propert. I. xii. 11, Non sum ego qui fueram. Horat. Od. IV. i. 3, 4, Non sum qualis eram, &c. The poet may allude to Homer; Odyss. xiii. 429.

¹¹ Odyss. xi. 318,

πρὶν σφωΐν ὑπὸ κροτάφοισιν ἰούλους
Ἀνθῆσαι, πυκάσαι τε γένυν εὐανθεῖ λάχνῃ.

Virg. Æn. viii. 160, Tum mihi prima genas vestibat flore Juventa. See too Idyll xv. 85.

¹² χαροπώτορα. Anacreon Od. xxviii. opposes Minerva's bright blue eye to the languishing blue of that of Venus. χάροπος seems originally to have meant a bright fierce-looking eye, without any defined notion of colour. It came to mean such as have a grayish or light blue lustre, darker than, but not differing much from, γλαυκός, and indeed used here with it. Tacitus calls the eyes of the Germans, "truces et cœrulei oculi." See Liddell and Scott, Lexicon.

¹³ Ov. Met. xiii. 795, Mollior et cycni plumis et lacte coacto.

¹⁴ Compare Iliad i. 249, τοῦ καὶ ἀπὸ γλώσσης μέλιτος γλυκίων ῥέεν

honey-comb. And sweet is my melody, both if I warble to the shepherd's pipe, and if I sing to the flute, or the reed, or the [15] flageolet. And all the women along the mountains say that I am handsome, and all *of them* love me ; but the city miss has not kissed me, but has run past me, because I am a rustic ; [16] and she is not yet aware that beauteous Bacchus used to drive the calf in the valleys. Neither did she know that Venus maddened after a herdsman, and tended flocks *with him* on the Phrygian mountains.[17] Adonis, himself, she kissed in the woods, and in the woods she lamented. [18] And who was Endymion? Was he not a herdsman? Yes, and him Selene kissed, as he fed his herds; and coming from Olympus she went up to the Latmian glade, and slept beside the lad. [19] Thou too, Rhea, bewailest thy herdsman. And *hast* not even thou, O son of Saturn, wandered [20] *in the form of* a bird through *love of* a herd-tending boy.

But Eunica alone has not kissed the herdsman, *Eunica* who is superior *no doubt* to Cybele, and Venus, and to Selene.

αὐδή. Cantic., or Song of Solomon, iv. 11, " Thy lips, O my spouse, drop as the honeycomb : honey and milk are under thy tongue."
[15] πλαγίαυλος. Hence flageolet, " quasi dicas plagiaulet." Æmil. Port. Lex. Doric. Comp. Bion iii. 7.
[16] Virg. Ecl. x. 18, Et formosus oves ad flumina pavit Adonis. ii. 60, Quem fugis, ah demens! habitarunt di quoque silvas. Pope II. Past.
59—62,　　See what delights in silvan scenes appear,
　　　　　　Descending gods have found Elysium here.
　　　　　　In woods bright Venus with Adonis stray'd,
　　　　　　And chaste Diana haunts the forest glade.
[17] Ovid Trist. ii. 299,
　　　　　　In Venere Anchises, in Lunâ Latmius heros,
　　　　　　In Cerere Jasion qui referatur erit.
Compare Bion's Idyll on this subject.
[18] Endymion. Cf. Idyll iii. 49, A shepherd, by whose side, as he slept at Mt. Latmus in Caria, Selene, kissing him, lay. See Smith's Dict. Gr. R. Biogr. ii. 16, B. ἵνα. One MS. has ἅμα, which Wordsworth approves. Catull. Com. Berenices, v. 5,
　　　　　　Ut Triviam furtim sub Latmia saxa relegans
　　　　　　Dulcis amor gyro devocet aerio.
Compare, Latmius Endymion non est tibi, Luna, rubori. Ovid. Ant. Am. iii. 85.
[19] Atys, a shepherd of Celenæ in Phrygia, beloved by Rhea or Cybele. Cf. Smith Dict. ii. 417, B. See Ovid Fast. iv. 221—244. And see the poem of Catullus, bearing the name of Atys, and Propert. II. xxiii. 20.
[20] For the legend of Ganymede see Smith Dict. G. R. B. ii. 230, and Virg. Æn. v. 253 ; Ov. Met. x. 255 ; Horat. iv. 4.

Love no longer even thou, [21] 'would-be *Venus*,' thy sweet one either in the city or on the mountain, but sleep alone all night long.

IDYLL XXI.

THE FISHERMEN.

ARGUMENT.

This Idyll contains a conversation of two fishermen by night. Our poet addressing one Diophantus with a few observations on the force of poverty in rousing men to active pursuits, describes the scene of this colloquy, which is laid in a scantily furnished sea-side hut. One of the fishermen calls upon the other to unriddle him the dream which he has dreamed. It was this: that he had in pursuit of his calling caught a golden fish, and thereupon determined with an oath to eschew the trade for the future. Now that the golden hope and his dream have proved alike unreal, he fears lest he ought to consider his oath binding. His comrade bids him be of good cheer, telling him that his oath is clearly no more real than his dream was. This is the only Idyll descriptive of fishermen's life that has come down to us; and it has been suggested, with much reason, that in it Theocritus imitated the θυννοθήρα or Ἁλιεύς of Sophron.

ASPHALION AND A COMRADE.

[1] POVERTY, O Diophantus, alone arouses the arts: she is the teacher of labour; for hard cares do not permit labouring men even to sleep. And even if a man shall have tasted sleep [2] for a little space in the night, solicitudes on a sudden

---

[21] "Would-be Venus." It seems clear that the poet makes his rustic taunt Eunica in these last words, and the suggestion of Wordsworth, τὸν Ἄρεα, "thy Mars," (alluding to Venus' amour with that God,) will give point to an otherwise obscure passage. Theocritus, in the 27th Idyll, in like manner makes a shepherd call himself "Paris," and address his sweetheart as "Helen."

[1] Compare Virg. Georg. i. 145, 146,
 Tum variæ venere artes: labor omnia vincit
 Improbus, et duris urgens in rebus egestas.
Compare Aristoph. Plut. 552—554. Persius Prologus 10, Magister artis, ingenique largitor venter.

[2] For ἐπιψαύσῃσι, Wordsworth suggests ἐπισβέσσῃσι—shall have dis-

present themselves and disturb him. Two old men, [3] hunters of the finny tribe, were reclining together, having strewed for themselves dry sea-weed in their wattled cabin, *and* resting themselves against its wall of leaves; and near them were lying the implements of their handicraft, the wicker baskets, the rods, the hooks, and [4] the gum cistus, covered by sea-weed, fishing lines, and weels, and bow-nets of rushes, cords, and [5] two oars, and an old boat on its rollers. Beneath their heads was a scanty cloak of mat-work, garments, and felt caps. This was to the fishermen their whole [6] stock of implements, this their wealth. And neither had an earthen pot, or a [7] measure; all, all seemed superfluous to them; [8] poverty was a friend to their fishing trade. And no neigh-

---

sipated (his cares), comparing Horat. Od. II. xi. 17, Dissipat Evius curias edaces. ὀλίγον is used here adverbially—νυκτός, the genitive of the part of time. Cf. Idyll xxiii. 32, ἀλλ' ὀλίγον ζῇ.   Hom. Odyss. xix. 515, &c.,

Αὐτὰρ ἐπὴν νύξ ἔλθῃ, ἕλῃσί τε κοῖτος ἅπαντας
Κεῖμαι ἐνὶ λέκτρῳ, πυκιναὶ δέ μοι ἀμφ' ἀδινὸν κῆρ
'Οξεῖαι μελεδῶναι ὀδυρομένην ἐρέθουσιν.

Juvenal xiii. 217, Nocte brevem si forti indulsit cura soporem.

[3] ἰχθύος—for ἰχθυῶν. See Idyll xvi. 72. Mosch. v. 10.

[4] λήδανον was the "gum cistus," which is found on the leaves of λῆδον, an oriental shrub. Some such herbs were used as baits in fishing, as we learn from Oppian Halieut. Various readings have been suggested to simplify the passage. The best is Briggs's δελῆτα for τε λῆδα; as δελέατι becomes δελῆτι. Heysch. It will thus be simply "baits." Wordsworth prefers to erase the comma at τάγκιστρα, and joining τὰ φυκιόεν τά with it; and for τε λῆδα, to read τὰ πῆδα, the oars—a word used by Homer, Odyss. vii. 328, and elsewhere. Then we should construe "the hooks covered with sea-weed, *and* the oars." But see Wordsworth's note.

[5] κωάς τε, is the common reading, but obviously unsound. The fishermen had scanty bed-clothes: if they had had skins or fleeces, they would not let them lie among their implements. The best suggestion seems Kiessling's κῶπα τε, a pair of oars. But if so, Wordsworth's conjecture in the last note is overthrown. J. Wordsworth, however, thinks that κῶας is the true reading, and that it means the skin used as a "seat cover," or "coverlet," as the case might be, of Greek sailors, mentioned by Thirlwall, Greece, vol. iii. 158, note.

[6] πόνος. There is no need here to substitute πόρος, with Schæfer and Brunck. πόνος here signifies "id quo labor fit," as vs. 9, χεροῖν ἀθλήματα—

[7] ἴν must be read here—i. e. a measure whose half was called ἡμίνα, Eustath., ἅπαντα περισσά. Wordsworth suggests οὐ κλίναν, not a bed.

[8] Read πάντ' ἐδόκει τήνοις. ἄγρας πενία σφιν ἑταίρα. Sanctamand. This is the slightest alteration, though Wordsworth's suggestion is ingenious, who reads—παντ' ἐδόκει τήνοις ἃ γρας πέρι, ἃ σφ' ἀγ' ἑταίρους.

bour had they [9]near; but on all sides the sea would gently float up even to [10]the narrow cabin. Not yet was Selené's car accomplishing the mid-way of her course, when their wonted toil began to wake the fishermen, and having thrust away slumber from their eyelids, they proceeded to rouse a song in their minds.

Asph. They were all liars, friend, as many as used to say that the summer nights shorten, when Jove draws out the days to a great length. Already have I seen a myriad dreams, nor *is it* yet dawn. Have I forgotten myself? What is the matter? [11]Are the nights then lagging?

Com. Asphalion, are you blaming the fair summer? For *it is* not the season *which* has of its own accord over-stepped its due course, but your cares, disturbing your sleep, make the night long to you.

Asph. Hast ever learnt, I wonder, to interpret dreams; for I have seen a good one. I would not have you be without a share in my vision; be partner of all my dreams, even as you are of my spoils. For you will not be surpassed in understanding; [12]he is the best diviner of dreams with whom understanding is the teacher. Besides there is leisure too; for what can a man do as he lies on *a bed of* leaves close by the waves, [13]and sleeps uncomfortably on prickly shrubs,

---

Omnia iis videbantur supervacanea præ piscatione et prædâ, quæ eos fecit socios.

[9] i. e. between the cabin and the sea.

[10] θλιβομέναν, pressed *for room.* Theoc. xx. 4, θλίβειν χείλεα, to press the lips. Musæus 114, ἠρέμα μὲν θλίβων ῥοδοειδέα δάκτυλα κούρης. For παντᾶ, (or πενία, which is the reading of MSS.,) Wordsworth would read πνοιᾳ δε, connecting it with θλιβομεναν, which would then signify "fractam vento."

[11] Aristoph. Nub. 2, 3,

τὸ χρῆμα τῶν νυκτῶν ὅσον;
ἀπέραντον. οὐδέποθ' ἡμέρα γενήσεται.

[12] Scaliger reads ὃς γὰρ ἂν εἰκάξῃ—which seems borne out by the following quotations. Cic. de Divin. ii. 5, Qui bene conjiciet vatem perhibebo optimum. Eurip. apud Plutarch, μάντις δ' ἄριστος ὅστις εἰκάζει κάλως. Better perhaps is Wordsworth's τοὔναρ ἵν' εἰκάξῃς.

[13] ἄσμενος ἐν ῥάμνῳ. Such is the common reading, which yields a tolerable sense, viz. that Asphalion cannot comfortably, without fear, sleep on thorns, in a rough and dangerous place. If we adopt any various reading, μηδὲ καθεύδων ἀλλύχνος ἐν ῥάγμῳ, i. e. "without a light, on the sea's edge," is best. This reading has the merit of introducing the words following less abruptly.

[14] and the light is in the Prytaneum, *not here,* [15] for they say that that is ever catching *spoil.*

Com. Tell me, pray, the vision of the night, and say and signify all to *me* your comrade.

Asph. [16] At evening, when I fell asleep over my sea-faring labours, (I was not indeed full of meat; for dining [17] at the proper time, if you recollect, we were sparing of our stomachs,) I *fancied* I saw myself on a rock, busy, and I was sitting and watching for fish, and throwing the sly bait *hanging* from the rod. And one of the fat *fellows* made a bite; (for *even* in sleep every dog scents loaves, and so do I a fish;) and it indeed clung to the hook, and the blood began to flow, and I was getting the rod bent by his movement. *So* stretching out both my hands, I found a struggle about the creature, how I should catch a large fish with hooks rather small for him. [18] Then, reminding him of his wound, 'will you prick me then,' said I : 'Nay, rather you shall be pierced sorely;' and I extended my rod, while he did not escape it. I seemed to have accomplished my labour, I drew ashore a golden fish, altogether wrapt up in the gold. But fear possessed me, lest haply it should be a

---

[14, 15] To this very difficult passage the only light which seems clear, is the explanation of Strothius. The comrade says, (34—37,) Unfold your dream, since we have leisure : we cannot sleep, so comfortless is our couch, and we cannot work because 'tis dark. We have not the same means of dispelling darkness as the rich, or public halls, which can keep their lamps (λυχνια) burning all night; nor is our ἄγρα, our gain from our craft, such as to enable us to get a light for the dark nights. When it is said the light is in the Prytaneum, (the common hall of Athens, Syracuse, and other large towns,) it is implied that *it is* " *not in the fisherman's hut,*" by the same figure as we say " wine is the rich man's drink," i. e. " not for the poor man." And so in the New Testament, St. Matt. xi. 8, " Behold, they that wear soft clothing are in king's houses," i. e. you must not look for them in the desert. The 37th verse implies that public halls can always afford to be lit up. These fishermen, says Chapman, were honest radicals.

[16] δειλινὸν, adverbially. Compare Idyll i. 15; xiii. 69; xxiv. 11.

[17] ἐν ὥρᾳ. Pierson's suggestion, ἀωρί, intempestivè, yields a better sense. For μεμαῶτα, two lines below, Wordsworth reads βεβαῶτα; and at ἐκ καλάμων, in the line below, compare Ovid Met. xiii. 923, Nunc in mole sedens moderabar arundine limum.

[18] For the obscure reading of the books, which has been literally Englished in the text, but yields no adequate sense, Kiessling, after reviewing many other suggestions, proposes εἶθ' ὑπομιμνάσκων τῶ τρώματος ἤρεμα νύξα, καὶ νύξας ἐχάλαξα, καὶ οὐ φεύγοντος ἔτεινα—I gently pricked him, and when I had done so, relaxed my hold on the rod, &c.

fish beloved by Neptune, or perhaps a treasure of blue-eyed Amphitrite. Then softly I disengaged him from the hook, lest ever the hooks should retain the gold from his mouth. [19] And *the fish* indeed I hauled ashore with ropes, and I swore that never in future would I set foot upon the sea, but abide on land and reign over the gold. This *was even what* awoke me: but do you, my friend, resolve my mind henceforward, for I am alarmed at the oath which I have sworn.

Com. Why then fear it not! you have not sworn; for neither did you find, as you saw, a fish of gold. But visions resemble falsehoods. [20] And if in reality, and not in sleep, you shall search these spots, the hope of your dreams requires a fish of flesh, lest you should die by famine, though amid dreams of gold.

IDYLL XXII.

THE DIOSCURI.

ARGUMENT.

This hymn to the Dioscuri is divided into two parts—the first (27—134) in praise of Pollux, the second of Castor. After a proem (1—26) sounding their common praises, a most renowned contest between Pollux and Amycus is described. When the Argonauts touched at the

---

[19] Wordsworth, seeing the absurdity of the text, which makes the fisherman haul ashore a fish, after he has disengaged the hook from the mouth, suggests—καὶ τότε μὲν κιστῇ κατέκλαξα τὸν ἐντ' ἄρρητον. Et tunc ego arcâ eum conclusi tanquam sacrum. This reading he supports by Horat. Sat. I. i. 67, and v. 71; as well as by Ovid Met. ii. 557, clauserat Actæo textâ de vimine cistâ.

[20] Here Bindemann suggests

εἰ δ' ὕπαρ, οὐ κνώσσων τὺ τὰ χωρία ταῦτα ματεύσεις
ἐλπίδα τῶν ὕπνων, ζάτει. κ. τ. λ.

If you in reality, and not in sleep, shall seek in these places the hope raised in your dreams, seek then, &c. A sense which, it will be allowed, is clearer than that of the text. Wordsworth reads ἐλπὶς τῶν ὕπνων, placing a colon at ὕπνων, and then ζάτει, κ. τ. λ., i. e. There is hope in your dreams: seek the fish of flesh. In the next line he reads, with Scaliger, τοῖς for τοι; the article for the possessive pronoun "tuis,"
'Lest you die in famine, and your golden dreams."

shores of the Bebrycians, Pollux and Castor, going in quest of water, find in the region, which abounds in springs, one Amycus of great bodily strength; who gives out to them that they shall then only draw water, when they can conquer him in boxing. Terms are accepted, the Argonauts and Bebrycians convened, and in the conflict Pollux comes off victorious, although there was reason to fear that his adversary's vast strength might overwhelm him. In the remainder of the Hymn is commemorated Castor's fight with Lynceus. The circumstances of which were these. When the Dioscuri had carried off the daughters of Leucippus, Idas and Lynceus, the sons of Aphareus, their betrothed lovers, overtake the ravishers at the tomb of Aphareus. Then Lynceus having in vain tried to persuade the Dioscuri to give back the maidens, challenges Castor to single combat. Castor accepts the challenge, and they fight first with spears, and then with swords, till Lynceus is wounded, and pierced through at his father's tomb, to which he had fled. Idas, grieved at the loss of his brother, seizes a fragment of the tomb to hurl at Castor, but is himself overthrown in the act by a thunderbolt from Jupiter.

[1] WE celebrate the two sons of Leda and Ægis-bearing Jove, [2] Castor and Pollux, formidable to contend in boxing, when he has bound his knuckles over with thongs of ox-hide. We celebrate both twice, and the third time, the male offspring of the [3] daughter of Thestius, twin Lacedæmonian brothers, [4] preservers of men when already at the utmost extremity, and of horses thrown into confusion in the bloody rout, and of ships [5] which, running counter to setting and rising stars of heaven, have chanced upon rough gales. For these having raised a huge wave at the stern of them, or even at the prow, or wheresoever each may choose, are wont to dash it into the

---

[1] For the conflict of Pollux with Amycus, cf. Apollon. Rhod. lib. ii., and Valerius Flaccus iv. Argonaut. 99—334.
[2] Hom. Odyss. xi. 299, Κάστορα θ' ἱππόδαμον, καὶ πὺξ ἀγαθὸν Πολυδεύκεα. Horat. I. xii. 25, 26. Puerosque Ledæ, Hunc equis, illum superare pugnis nobilem. Virg. Æn. v. 405, Tantorum ingentia septem Terga boum plumbo insuto ferroque rigebant.
[3] Κούρης Θεστιάδος, i. e. Leda. Just as in Idyll xv. 110, ἁ Βερενικεία θυγάτηρ. Comp. Hom. Il. iv. 367. Her female offspring is commemorated in Euripid. Iph. Aul. 49.
[4] Horat. Od. I. iii. 2, Sic fratres Helenæ, lucida sidera.—ἐπὶ ξυροῦ εἶναι. Cf. Hom. Il. x. 173; Herodot. vi. 11; Sophocl. Antig. 1009.
[5] Βιαζόμεναι—struggling against. Herodot. ix. 41; Hom. Il. xi. 558, ἐβιήσατο παίδας. Sophoc. Fragm. ap. Stobæum, πάντων ἄριστον μὴ βιάζεσθαι θεούς. Compare St. Matt. xi. 12, ἡ βασιλεία τῶν οὐρανῶν βιάζεται. Chapman Englishes it "star-defying;" setting at a wrong season of the year. The fate of such is given in the poet's 9th Epigram, infra, vs. 5, 6.

hold, and then break up both the sides *of the ship*, whilst all the tackle hangs with the sail, broken off hap-hazard; and *there* [6] *is* a vast rain from the sky, as night steals on, and the broad sea murmurs, [7] struck by the blasts, and by the incessant hail. [8] Yet, notwithstanding, ye, on your part, draw out even from the depths ships with sailors and all, *just* as they think they are going to perish. Then quickly cease the winds and there *is* a clear calm over the sea, and the clouds flee away in different directions; and the Bears shine out again, and in the midst of the [9] 'asses' a dusky crib, indicating [10] that all the weather for sailing is clear and fine. Oh! both of you, helpers to mortals, oh both of you, friends, as horsemen, harpers, wrestlers, minstrels—Shall I begin to sing of Castor, or Pollux first? Celebrating both, I will sing of Pollux first.

Now the ship Argo, I ween, having cleared [11] the rocks

---

[6] Æn. v. 10, 11,
  Olli cæruleus supra caput astitit imber
  Noctem hyememque ferens.
Hom. Il. ii. 413, καὶ ἐπὶ κνέφας ἐλθεῖν. We have here translated the emendation of Kiessling, ἐφερποίσας.

[7] See Virg. Æn. ix. 669, 670,
  Quàm multâ grandine nimbi
  In vada præcipitant; cum Jupiter humidus Austris
  Torquet aquosam hyemem, et cœlo cava nubila rumpit.
Two lines below for αὐτοῖσιν ναύταισιν, compare Eurip. Hippol. 1188, αὐταῖσιν ἀρβύλαισιν, and Bp. Monk's note thereon. Matth. Gr. Gr. § 405, Obs. 3.

[8] Cf. Horat. Od. I. xii. 25, Quorum simul alba nautis Stella refulsit, &c., and Od. I. xiv. 10, Non di, quos iterum pressa voces malo: add to these Od. IV. viii. 32,
  Clarum Tyndaridæ sidus ab infimis
  Quassas eripiunt æquoribus rates.

[9] Cf. Aratus 905, ὄνων φάτνη, two stars in the breast of the crab, of which Pliny, H. N. xviii. 35, says, Sunt in signo Cancri duæ stellæ parvæ. Aselli appellatæ, exiguum inter illas spatium obtinente nubeculâ, quam Præsepia appellant. ἡ Ἄρκτος was the Great Bear, or Charles's Wain; αἱ ἄρκτοι, the Greater and Lesser Bear. Cic. N. D. ii. 41; Virg. Georg. i. 245; Æn. vi. 16.

[10] τὰ πρὸς πλόον εὔδια. Æn. iii. 518, Postquam cuncta videt cœlo constare sereno.

[11] συνιούσας, the Cyanean rocks. See Idyll xiii. 22; Ovid Trist. I. x. 34, Transeat instabiles strenua Cyaneas. Pliny iv. B. 27; Ovid Heroid. Ep. xii. 121, Complexos utinam Symplegades elisissent. Theocritus differs from Apollon. Rhod. II. 565, respecting the site of the Bebrycians, the latter making it on this side the Bosporus in Propontis, while Theoc-

that meet in one, and the mischievous mouth of snowy Pontus, arrived at the country of the Bebrycians, carrying the dear children of the gods; here upon many heroes were descending by one ladder from both the sides of Jason's ship. And having landed on the low beach and [12] sheltered shore they were strewing couches, and [13] rubbing sticks to and fro in their hands. But Castor, manager of steeds, and the dark complexioned Pollux, were both keeping aloof, having strayed from their comrades. And spying on a mountain [14] a wild wood of vast size, they found under a smooth cliff an ever-flowing spring, filled with pure water, and the pebbles beneath seemed like crystal or silver, from the depths; and near *the spot* there had grown tall pines, and poplars, and plane trees, and cypresses with leafy tops, [15] and fragrant flowers, pleasant work for hairy bees, *flowers* as many as, when spring is ending, sprout up along the meadows.

And here a man of overwhelming size would sit and take the air, terrible to look upon, [16] having his ears bruised with hard thumps, [17] and his huge chest and broad back were arched and rounded with iron flesh, like a forged colossus. And on his strong arms the muscles stood out at the surface of the shoulder, like [18] round stones which the river torrent

ritus places it beyond the Bosporus, on the shore of Bithynia, which the Pontus washes.

[12] ὑπήνεμον, sheltered from the wind. Soph. Antig. 411, καθήμεθ' ἄκρων ἐκ πάγων ὑπήνεμοι. Xen. Æc. xviii. 7. Æn. iii. 223, Tum littore curvo exstruimusque toros.

[13] Pieces of wood for striking a light. See Hom. Hymn to Merc. 111. Vid. Apollon. Rhod. i. 1184. Add Sophocl. Philoct. 36, καὶ πυρεῖ' ὁμοῦ τάδε.

[14] Virg. Æn. i. 165—167,
Desuper horrentique atrum nemus imminet umbrâ:
Intus aquæ dulces vivoque sedilia saxo.
Wordsworth compares very aptly some beautiful lines of Ausonius in his Mosella, 60—75.

[15] Compare Idyll vii. 80.

[16] Æn. iii. 621, Nec visu facilis, nec dictu affabilis ulli. Hard thumps, i. e. those of hands covered with the cæstus, which some say Amycus introduced. It is described by Virgil Æn. v. 405, Terga boum plumbo insuto, ferroque rigebant. Ibid. 478, Duros libravit cæstus 436, *duro crepitant sub vulnere malæ.*

[17] Comp. Val. Flacc. Argon. iv. 202, &c., At procul e silvis, &c.

[18] ὀλοίτροχοι, rolling stones thrown from a wall, on besiegers. Herodot. viii. 52. ὀλοοίτροχος, occurs Il. xiii. 137, which place Virgil has copied. Æn. xii. 684.

I

has polished by rolling in its vast eddies; [19] but over his back and neck was hung a lion's skin, fastened on by the paws. And him the prize man Pollux first bespoke.

Poll. Save you, stranger, whoever you are. Who are the mortals to whom this country belongs?

Amyc. How can I be [20] safe, that is, when I see men, whom I have never seen?

Poll. Be of good cheer! deem that you see neither unjust men, nor unjust men's sons.

Amyc. I am of good cheer! And not from you is it meet that I should be taught this.

Poll. You are savage, in every thing malignant and overbearing.

Amyc. I am such as you see me: yes, and I am not setting foot on *your* country.

Poll. Come—and return home again, ay, having met with hospitable *treatment.*

Amyc. Do not either you entertain me, and my entertainment is not in readiness.

Poll. My good sir, would not you at any rate allow us even to drink of this water?

Amyc. You shall learn, when thirst [21] shall dry your relaxed lips.

Poll. Is it silver, or what is the pay, will you tell us, by which we might persuade you?

Amyc. [22] Lift your hands against me in single combat, having stood man against man.

Poll. As a boxer, or even tripping up the heels, and *keeping* eyes right?

Amyc. Having laboured might and main in boxing, spare not your craft.

---

[19] Diomed is thus arrayed, Hom. x. 177, 178. Claudian Rapt. Proserp. i. 16,   Simul procedit Iacchus,
           Crinali florens hederà, quem Parthica tigris
           Velat, et auratos in nodum colligit ungues.

[20] χαίρε—χαίρω πῶς. J. Wordsworth points to similar puns on this word in Alcest. Eurip. 527, and Monk's note, and Matthiæ at Hecuba 424.

[21] τέρσει. We have here translated according to Buttmann's view, who holds it to come as if from a present τέρρω. The aor. imperat. τέρσον occurs, Nicand. Theriac. 96, 693, 709.

[22] So Apollon. Rhod. ii. 14, πρὶν χείρεσσιν ἐμῇσιν ἑὰς ἀνὰ χεῖρας ἀεῖραι.

Poll. [23] Why, who is there with whom I shall match my hands and cæstus?

Amyc. He is near. Don't you see me? The boxer shall be called Amycus.

Poll. Is the prize also ready for which we shall both contend?

Amyc. I will be called thine, or thou shalt be called mine, if I shall have conquered.

Poll. [24] Such as these are the cock-fights of crimson-crested birds.

Amyc. Whether then we be like birds or lions, at all events we will fight for no other prize.

So spake Amycus, and [25] having taken a spiral shell, raised a sound *from it.* And they quickly gathered together to the shade of the plane trees, at the blast of the trumpet, the always long-haired Bebrycians. In like manner too Castor, pre-eminent in fight, went and summoned from the Magnesian ship all the heroes. Now they, when, in fact, they had fortified their hands with coils of ox-hide, and had rolled great thongs [26] around their arms, proceeded to engage in the midst, breathing slaughter one against the other. Hereupon a great struggle arose to them, as they were urgent which of the two should get the glare of the sun at his back. But by skill you over-reached a great hero, O Pollux, and all the countenance of Amycus was being struck with the rays. Then he, in sooth, enraged at heart, was advancing forward, taking aim with his

---

[23] Polwhele compares here the conflict between David and Goliath.

[24] The Scholiast at Aristoph. Aves, (70, 71,) states that in cock-fights it was usual that the vanquished should ever afterwards follow and obey the victors. Here Pollux refers to such a custom. It may be remarked that, after the Persian war, cock-fights were annual occurrences at Athens.

[25] κόχλον ἑλών. Cf. Virg. Æn. vi. 171, Sed tum forte cavâ dum personat æquora conchâ. Ov. Met. i. 333—338, gives a full account of this instrument.

[26] γυῖα. Callim. H. in Dian. 177. Ernesti at that passage shows that γυῖα is said of all the members, especially the hands, and feet, and knees, in which lies the greatest force of the body. Hom. Il. xiii. 61, γυῖα δ᾽ ἔθηκεν ἐλαφρά, πόδας καὶ χεῖρας ὕπερθεν. Here it clearly stands for the lower part of the arm, which was bound with thongs, as the old statues of boxers would show. Compare Smith's Dict. Gr. R. Antiq. pp. 215, 216, art. 'cæstus.' Below at vs. 84, cf. Shakspeare's Love's Labour Lost, iv. 5, Down with them, but be first advised
In conflict that thou get the sun of them.

hands; when the son of Tyndarus hit the tip of his chin as he came on, and he was roused more than before, and dealt his blows [27] at random, and kept rushing on with great force, bending over towards the earth. And the Bebrycians began to shout; but on the other side the heroes were cheering on strong Pollux, though fearful lest haply in a narrow spot [28] a man resembling Tityus should bear down and subdue him. But in truth the son of Jove on his part coming up with him in one place and another kept wounding him with both *hands* in turn, and was checking from his onslaught the son of Neptune, overbearing though he was. And he [29] stood reeling with blows, and spat out gory blood: *and* then all the chiefs raised a shout together, when they saw grievous wounds about his mouth and jaws, and his eyes were straitened for room on his swollen visage.

[30] Him, indeed, the prince (Pollux) disturbed, *by* making feints with his fists on every side; but when at length he perceived that he was distressed, he drove his fist above the middle of his nose right down his brow, and stripped off all his forehead to the bone. [31] But he, having been stricken, measured his length on his back, among the green foliage. [32] Hereupon, a fierce fight arose again, when he had righted

---

[27] Pugnam concussit. Something like this is Virgil's—Nunc dextrâ ingeminans ictus, nunc ille sinistrâ, Æn. v. 458; and Scott's Lady of the Lake, "And shower'd his blows like wintry rain."

[28] Ovid Met. iv. 456,
Viscera præbebat Tityos lanianda, novemque
Jugeribus distentus erat.
Virg. Æn. vi. 595, &c.,
Necnon et Tityon terræ omnipotentis alumnum
Cernere erat, per tota novem cui jugera corpus
Porrigitur, &c.

[29] μεθύων. A metaphor, the idea of which may have arisen from Odyss. xviii. 239, ἧσται νευστάζων κεφαλῇ, μεθύοντι ἐοικώς. So Psalms, "They reel to and fro, and stagger like a drunken man." In the language of the English ring "groggy," as Chapman observes.

[30] χερσὶ προδεικνύς. Some read χεῖρε, unnecessarily, for σκήπτρῳ προδεικνύς occurs in Sophoc. Œd. T. 456, "Feeling his way." As Seneca, "Baculo seniliter prætentare." Virg. Æn. v. 433, Multa viri necquicquam inter se vulnera jactant.

[31] Virg. Æn. 446, Ipse gravis graviterque ad terram pondere vasto,
Concidit.

[32] Ibid. 453, At non tardatus casu, neque territus heros,
Acrior ad pugnam redit, ac vim suscitat irâ.

himself, and they were hurting one another by blows with the hard cæstus. But the ruler of the Bebrycians for his part was directing his fists against the chest, and outside the neck *of his foe*, while Pollux the invincible was disfiguring all *the other's* visage with unseemly blows. And his flesh (i. e. that of Amycus) was sinking through sweat, and from being huge he had become on a sudden a little man; but the other, as he tasted toil, was bearing limbs ever stronger, and still improving in healthy colour.

Now how at last the son of Jove overthrew [33] the athlete, declare, thou goddess! for thou knowest; and I, the interpreter of others, will speak as much as thou desirest, and as is agreeable to thyself. In truth, *Amycus* for his part being desirous to do some great deed, seized with his left hand the left hand of Pollux, bending slantwise with a lunge; and with the other *hand* making his assault, raised [34] his broad fist from his right side, and he would have hit and injured the king of the Amyclæans, but he in turn came up secretly from under with his head, and then with his strong hand struck him under the left temple, and fell on his shoulder; then the dark blood poured out rapidly from his gaping temple: [35] and with his left hand he struck his mouth, and the thickset teeth rattled; whilst he kept maiming his face with ever sharper blows, until he had smashed his cheeks; but then all on the [36] ground he fell senseless, [37] and lifted up both hands at once, as renouncing the victory, for he was nigh unto death.

[33] ἀδηφάγον, "gluttonous." Cf. Philoct. Sophocl. 313, where the word is applied to νόσον. It is elsewhere an epithet of ἵπποι, ζῶα, &c., and seems to stand for an expression of the good keep which is commonly connected with brute strength. See Pierson on Mœris Atticist. pp. 89, 90, With the next line compare Virg. Æn. vii. 645, Et meministis enim, divæ, et memorare potestis.

[34] Compare Æn. v. 443—445,
Ostendit dextram insurgens Entellus, et altè
Extulit: ille ictum venientem a vertice velox
Prævidit, celerique elapsus corpore cessit.

[35] Æn. v. 469, 470,
Crassumque cruorem
Ore ejectantem mixtosque in sanguine dentes.

[36] ἀλλοφρονέων (Hom. Il. xxiii. 698) is explained οὐκ ἐν αὑτῷ ὤν, ἀλλ' ἐξιστάμενος τῇ διανοίᾳ.

[37] The worsted combatant in encounters of this kind used to signify his discomfiture by holding up his hands, or by falling on the ground.

To him then, though thou wast victor, O boxer Pollux, thou didst nothing madly violent; and he sware to thee a great oath, calling his sire Neptune from the deep *to witness*, that never more would he be vexatious to strangers. And thou indeed, O king, hast been celebrated by me. But I will sing of thee too, Castor, son of Tyndarus, swift on horseback, brandisher of the lance, clad in brazen mail.

The two sons of Jupiter indeed had caught up, and were carrying off, two daughters of Leucippus: ay, and in sooth these two, [38] two brethren, sons of Aphareus, wooers about to marry, Lynceus and the stout Idas, were pursuing at full speed. But when they reached the tomb of the deceased Aphareus, from their chariots all at once rushed, one against the other, burdened with spears and hollow shields. Then spake Lynceus to them from out his helmet, shouting loudly. 'Fair sirs, why long ye for battle? And how *is it* ye are wrongful in the case of the betrothed of others; and [39] *why* are naked swords in your hands? To us, look you, Leucippus promised these his daughters long before any; to us this marriage *stands* upon oath. But ye, in no seemly manner, in the case of the brides of others, [40] by oxen, and mules, and by goods not your own, have perverted the man; and by gifts have stolen our *affianced* brides. In very truth I myself have often said the following words before the face of both of you,

---

See Lambert Bos.; Antiq. Græc. 53, where much information respecting pugilistic encounters among the ancients may be found.

[38] Idas and Lynceus, sons of Aphareus and Arene; or, as she is called vs. 206, Laocoosa. Theocr. has related their story with great variations Lynceus was the same to whom Horat. alludes Epist. I. i. 18, Non possis oculo quantum contendere Lynceus. For the full history, see Smith's Dict. G. R. B. ii. 561, 562; Ovid Met. viii. 304; Fast. v. 699—720, where the scene is laid at Aphidna. Propert. I. ii. 15.

[39] Horat. Epod. vii. 1, 2,

        Quò, quò scelesti, ruitis ? aut cur dexteris
        Aptantur enses conditi ?

The daughters of Leucippus, brother of Aphareus, were Phœbe and Hilaira.   Non sic Leucippus succendit Castora Phœbe
        Pollucem cultu non Hilaira soror.

I. Propert. ii. 15. ἰδνόω, to betroth for presents. Odyss. ii. 53, ὥς κ
αὐτὸς ἐεδνώσαιτο θύγατρα.

[40] The Dioscuri and Aphareidæ appear by some accounts to have been engaged in a plunder of cattle conjointly, and after gaining their object the former ch ted the latter of their share.

even though I am not a man of many speeches :—Not so, kind sirs, is it fitting that princes should woo spouses, for whom bridegrooms are already provided. [41] Wide, look you, is Sparta, and wide equestrian Elis, and Arcadia rich in flocks, and the cities of the Achæans, Messene and Argos, and all the Sisyphian coast-land, where myriads of damsels are nurtured under the care of their parents, lacking neither figure nor mind. 'Tis easy for you to wed of these whichsoever you may choose, since many would wish in sooth to be fathers-in-law to the noble; and ye are distinguished among all heroes, and *so are* your fathers, and your mother's race at the same time by descent. Nay, friends, suffer this marriage to be consummated for us, and for you two let us all look out another *bridal.*—Many such words I was wont to say, but a blast of wind would bear them away to the moist wave, and favour did not follow my speeches. [42] For ye two were inexorable and harsh. But yet even now be persuaded, for ye both [43] are kinsmen to us on the father's side. But if your heart yearns for war, and it must needs be that, [44] having made mutual strife break forth, we end our feuds with bloodshed, Idas, indeed, and his cousin, brave Pollux, shall hold off their hands, having kept from the battle; but let us two, I and Castor, being the younger, decide *the issue* in fight, and let us not leave to our parents exceeding grief. One corpse is enough from one house, but the others shall feast all their friends as

---

[41] The various parts of the Peloponnese are enumerated. Σίσυφις, Corinthian; so called from the fabled king Sisyphus. Odyss. xi. 593. Two lines below compare Virgil Æn. xii. 24,

Sunt aliæ innuptæ Latio et Laurentibus agris
Nec genus indecores.

[42] ἀκηλήτω. Sophoc. Trach. 999, τόδ᾽ ἀκήλητον μανίας ἄνθος καταδερχθῆναι: unappeasable.

[43] Aphareus and Tyndarus were brothers, sons of Gorgophone, the former by her first husband Perieres, the latter by Æbalus, the second husband of Gorgophone. Thus their children, the Dioscuri and Aphareidæ would be cousins. For λῦσαι there is another reading λοῦσαι. Wordsworth thinks that this is a mistake of transcribers for δεῦσαι—rigare hastas sanguine. Virg. Æn. xii. 308, Sparso rigat arma cruore. Cf. Hom. Il. ρ. 51.

[44] Virg. Æn. ii. 129, vocem rumpit. iv. 553, Tantos illa suo rumpebat pectore questus. αναρῥήσσειν is used as here, Pindar Fragm. 172; Aristoph. Eq. 626. Below compare Æn. xii. 78, Teucrûm arma quiescant, et Rutilûm : nostro dirimamus sanguine bellum.

bridegrooms instead of corpses, and shall wed these maidens; 'tis meet, look you, to remove great strife by a little evil.'

He spake, and his words in truth the god was not about to render idle. For they two, indeed, who were elder in age, put off their arms from their shoulders upon the ground; whilst Lynceus, advanced to the mid space, brandishing his strong lance under the topmost [45] rim of his shield; and in like manner brave Castor brandished his pointed spear, and the plumes of the crests of both kept nodding. First of all, indeed, with lances [46] they were busied in aiming at each other, if haply they saw any part of the body exposed. But, in truth, the points of their spears, ere they had wounded one *or the other*, were broken, having stuck fast in their [47] mighty shields. Then they two, having drawn their hangers from the scabbards, again proceeded to deal out slaughter one against the other, and there was no withdrawal of battle. Oft, indeed, Castor pierced into the broad shield and [48] horse-plumed helmet, and oft the [49] keen-eyed Lynceus struck the other's shield, and the point reached [50] as far as the purple crest. Now of this man's hand, as he brought his sharp sword in the direction of his (Castor's) left knee, Castor lopped off the extremity, having removed from under *the blow* with his left foot; and he, having been wounded, cast away his sword, and speedily set off to fly to the tomb of his father, where brave Idas was reclining, and beholding the battle of men akin to each other. But the son of Tyndarus having rushed after him, thrust his broad blade right through his flank and navel, and the steel

---

[45] The parts of the shield were ἄντυξ, or ἴτυς περιφέρεια, or κύκλος, the rim; (Hom. Il. xviii. 479;) ὀμφαλός, the boss; (cf. Hom. Il. vi. 118, ἀσπὶς ὀμφαλόεσσα;) τελαμών, the thong, or shoulder-strap; πόρπαξ, the ring, by which it was held, for which ὄχανον, a handle, was substituted.

[46] πόνον εἶχον. Cf. Idyll vii. 139. Cf. Virgil Æn. ii. 748,

Partes rimatur apertas
Quà vulnus lethale ferat.

[47] δεινοῖσι. Il, vii. 145. The epithet is worthy to be applied to shields, if, as Kiessling suggests, we remember, Æsch. S. c. Theb. 372, &c., the devices on the shields of the seven chiefs. Reiske conjectures ἐν ἰτέινοισι.

[48] ἱππόκομος. Il. xii. 339; Idyll xvi. 81, which see.

[49] Cf. note at vs. 140, above; Pind. Nem. x. 116, κείνου γὰρ ἐπιχθονίων πάντων γένετ' ὀξύτατον ὄμμα. Horace Epist. I. i. 28, Non possis oculis quantum contendere Lynceus.

[50] ὅσον. Compare Idyll i. 45.

quickly scattered in different ways his intestines within, and Lynceus lay bowed to the earth, and down his eye-lids, I ween, a heavy slumber coursed.

⁵¹No, nor did Laocoosa see even the other of her sons consummate a marriage dear to him at his father's hearth; for of a truth he on his part, Messenian Idas I mean, having broken off a column standing out from the sepulchre of Aphareus, was in act to throw it speedily at his brother's murderer; ⁵²but Jupiter bore aid, and dashed out of his hands the wrought marble, and burnt him up with his blaze of lightning. Thus to fight with the sons of Tyndarus ⁵³is no light matter. Both they themselves are mighty, and were born of one who is mighty.

Hail, children of Leda! and may ye ever send worthy fame to my hymns, for friendly, I wot, are all poets to the Tyndaridæ, and Helen, and to other heroes, who sacked Troy, in aid of Menelaus. For you, ye princes, the Chian bard wrought glory, when he had sung the city of Priam, and the ships of the Greeks, and the Ilian battles, and Achilles, ⁵⁴tower of war. And to you, in my turn also, I bear propitiatory offerings of sweet Muses, such as they themselves provide, and according as my means are; and to the gods the ⁵⁵noblest of honours is song.

---

⁵¹ Compare with this Eurip. Phœnissæ, 336—350. (Dindorf.) Just above, for the death of Lynceus, compare Virg. Æn. x. 745,
Olli dura quies oculos, et ferreus urget
Somnus: in æternam clauduntur lumina noctem.
⁵² Ovid Fasti, v. 712,
Ibat in hunc Idas; vixque est Jovis igne repulsus,
Tela tamen dextræ fulmine rapta negant.
⁵³ οὐκ ἐν ἐλαφρῷ. So Herodot. i. 118, οὐκ ἐν ἐλαφρῷ ποιεῖσθαι. Compare Iphig. in Aul. Eurip. 969; Helen. 1227, ἐν εὐμαρεῖ; and Electr. 530.
⁵⁴ πύργον αὐτῆς. Odyss. xi. 555. Eurip. Alcest. 311, παῖς—πατὴρ ἔχει πύργον μέγαν.
⁵⁵ Compare Idyll xvii. 8.

IDYLL XXIII.

THE LOVER; OR, LOVE-SICK

ARGUMENT.

This Idyll represents the ungovernable love of a young man for a friend, who despised him, in consequence of which he at last hangs himself. The other, nowise moved, goes to the baths, and is there slain by a statue of Eros which falls upon and crushes him. Virgil has taken the idea of his second Eclogue partly from this. Compare also Ovid Met. xiv. 698.

[1] A CERTAIN love-sick man was enamoured of a hard youth, in beauty fair, but in disposition no longer on a par. He hated him that loved him, and had not even a jot of mildness, and he knew not Eros, what god he was, and [2] what sort of bow and arrows he holds in his hands, how grievous shafts he hurls against boys; but in all respects, whether in speeches or in approaches, *he was* unbending. Nor was there any solace of the fires of love, not quivering of lip, nor bright flash of eyes, [3] nor rosy cheek, nor word, nor kiss that relieves love. [4] But as a beast of the forest watches the hunters, so would he do all things against the man: and fierce were his lips, and sternly looked his eyes; [5] they had fate upon them: and his countenance answered to his bile, and the colour fled from it, [6] clad in arrogance from his

---

[1] πολύφιλτρος, suffering from many love-charms. Hence enamoured, love-sick. Virg. Ecl. II. i., Formosum pastor Corydon ardebat Alexin, &c.

[2] Mosch. i. 21, τοὶ πικροὶ κάλαμοι, τοῖς πολλάκι κἠμὲ τιτρώσκει. Ovid. Met. v. 380, 381, Et arbitrio matris de mille sagittis
   Unam, seposuit, sed quâ nec acutior ulla,
   Nec minus incerta est.

[3] ῥοδόμαλον. Compare Idyll vii. 117; Tibull. III. iv. 34.

[4] Compare Apollon. Rhod. i. 1243.

[5] εἶχον ἀνάγκαν. Heinsius reads εἶδεν ἀνάγκαν, "she looked necessity," but the reading of the text seems best. For ἀνάγκη, necessitas, see Horat. Od. I. iii. 35, Tarda necessitas lethi; I. xxxv. 17, Te semper anteit sæva necessitas.

[6] Ov. Met. xiv. 714, Spernit et irridet, factisque immitibus addit Verba superba ferox. περικείμενος. The construction is like the Homeric ἀλκήν, ἀναιδείην ἐπιειμένος. Il. i. 149; viii. 262, &c. Perhaps the comma should be removed after χρώς in the preceding line.

wrath. But even under these circumstances he was beautiful, [7] *and* from his wrath the lover was the more inflamed. [8] At last he could not endure so great a blaze of Cytherea, but went and [9] began to bewail at the cruel dwelling, and kissed the door-post, and thus lifted up his voice:—

Cruel and morose youth, offspring of an evil lioness, [10] flinty youth, and unworthy of love, I have come bringing thee this last present, my rope; since no longer do I wish to pain thee, lad, angered as thou art, but I am going whither thou hast devoted me; where, 'tis said, the road is common, and [11] where oblivion is the remedy, for them that love. [12] But even though I should have taken it all to my lips, and have drained *the cup*, not even thus shall I quench my yearning thirst. But now I add farewell to your vestibule—I know what is coming.

[13] Both the rose is lovely, and time withers it. And the violet is beautiful in spring, yet quickly it grows old. White is the lily; when it falls, it withers: the snow too is white, and it melts after it has become frozen. And

---

[7] Compare Martial, Ep. v. 47,
>Basia dum nolo, nisi quæ luctantia carpsi:
>Et placet ira mihi plus tua, quàm facies.

Chapman compares Shakspeare's Twelfth Night,
>"O, what a deal of scorn looks beautiful
>In the contempt and anger of his lip!"

[8] Ov. Met. xiv. 716,
>Non tulit impatiens longi tormenta doloris
>Iphis, et ante fores hæc verba novissima dixit.

[9] An allusion to the custom referred to in Idyll iii. Horat. Od. I. xxv. 1, Parcius junctas quatiunt fenestras, &c.

[10] λάϊνε. See Idyll iii. 18, τὸ πᾶν λίθος. Ibid. 39, ἀδαμάντινα. Tibull. I. vi. 32.

[11] Here some read τὸ λάθας. Cf. Virg. Æn. vi. 714,
>Lethæi ad fluminis undam
>Securos latices, et longa oblivia potant.

Hor. Od. I. xxviii. 15, Omnes una manet nox,
>Et calcanda semel via lethi.

[12] Comp. Song of Solomon viii. 6, 7, "Love is strong as death: jealousy is cruel as the grave, the coals thereof are coals of fire, which has a most vehement flame. Many waters cannot quench love, neither can the floods drown it."

[13] Virg. Ecl. ii. 18, Alba ligustra cadunt, vaccinia nigra leguntur. Tibull. I. iv. 29, Quam citò purpureos deperdit terra colores:
>Quam citò formosas populus alta comas.

For παχθῇ, (line 31,) Wordsworth suggests θαλπῇ, cum sol eam calefaciat, or cum nix calefiat, as Soph. Antig. 415.

the beauty of childhood is fair, yet it lives but a short space. That time shall come when even you will love; when, scorched at your heart, you shall weep briny tears. Nay, do you, boy, even now for this last time, do a pleasant act, [14] whensoever, having gone forth, you shall have beheld me suspended at your vestibule, pass me not by, wretch as I am, but stand and weep *though* briefly; and having shed the libation of a tear, loose me from the rope, and place about me garments from your limbs, and cover me, and for the last time [15] kiss me, and make the dead man a present of your lips. Be not afraid of me. I cannot live, no, not if, having been reconciled, you shall kiss me. And hollow me out a tomb, [16] which shall bury my love. And if you depart, [17] shout this over me thrice: 'O friend, thou liest low.' Yes, and if you will, say this too: 'And for me a beautiful companion has perished.' And write this inscription, which I will engrave for [18] you in verses: 'Traveller, this man Love slew; pass not by, but stop and say this, He had a cruel comrade.'

Thus having said, he took up a stone, and having planted it against a wall even to the middle of the door-posts, a dreadful stone, he proceeded [19] to attach to them the slender rope,

[14] Ov. Met. xiv. 733, &c.,
  Dixit et ad postes, ornatos sæpe coronis,
  Cum foribus laquei religasset vincula summa
  "Hæc tibi serta placent, crudelis et improba," dixit, &c.

[15] See Bion, i. 45, &c., ἔγρευ τυτθὸν Ἄδωνι, τὸ δ' αὖ πύματόν με φίλασον.

[16] Propert. I. xvii. 19, 20,
  Illic si qua meum sepelirent fata dolorem,
  Ultimus et posito staret amore lapis. Cf. Virg. Ecl. v. 42.

[17] Prop. I. vii. 23, 24,
  Nec poterunt juvenes nostro reticere sepulchro;
  Ardoris nostri magna poeta, jaces.

[18] Ovid. Trist. III. iii. 71—74,
  Quosque legat versus oculo properante viator
  Grandibus in tumuli marmore cæde notis:
  Hic ego qui jaceo, tenerorum lusor amorum,
  Ingenio perii Naso poeta meo.
Comp. Idyll xvii. 47; Tibull. III. ii. 27. But Wordsworth's reading, τοίχοισι, is far more probable, and rests on good ground.

[19] For ἀπ' αὐτῶν, which must refer to the beam above the doors, Vossius would read ἄνωθεν (as Æsch. Agam. 884, πολλὰς ἄνωθεν ἀρτάνας ἐμῆς δέρης ἔλυσαν). But Kiessling thinks ἀπ' αὐτῶ "unicè verum."

and began to throw the noose around his neck; and *then* he rolled the stepping-stone from under his foot, and hung, a corpse. But the other in his turn opened the doors, and beheld the dead man suspended from his own hall-*door;* nor was he overcome in his spirit, nor did he weep [20]for the slaughter of a young man : but yet more, he polluted for the dead man all the youthful garments, and proceeded to go to the contests of the wrestlers, and to seek, afar off, pleasant baths ; and he came to the god whom he had insulted, for Eros was standing on a stone basement above the waters. [21]And the statue leaped forth and slew the wretched youth, and the water became purpled, but the voice of the lad kept coming to the top. Rejoice, ye that love, for he who hated has been slain ; and ye, beloved youths, be affectionate, for the god knows how to punish.

IDYLL XXIV.

THE LITTLE HERCULES.

ARGUMENT.

In this Idyll the first achievement of the boy Hercules is recounted, his victory, to wit, over the hostile dragons sent against him by Juno. Alcmena, terrified by this prodigy, (62,) sends for Teiresias, the seer, to explain it, and to point out means of appeasing the wrath of the gods. He comes, and unfolds the labours, the earthly and the heavenly glory which should attend the child, when grown to man's estate. He also orders the dragons to be burned, and the house to be purified. There follows an enumeration of the masters, whose training conduced to make Hercules a worthy hero. The end of the poem, which we may suppose to have gone deeply into the history of his training, has been lost. .Valkenaer thinks that this Idyll, and the

---

[20] νέον φόνον for φόνον τοῦ νέου. Pind. Ol. ii. 78, νέα ἄεθλα for ἄεθλα τῶν νέων. But J. Wordsworth shows by a number of passages, that νέον stands here, by a sort of euphemism, for νεόκοτον, " strange, unwonted." ἐπὶ νεκρῷ. A better reading is suggested, ἔτι, by Kiessling, which we have adopted.

[21] Polwhele in his notes compares (as regards the manner of death) Callimachus, Epigr. vii., which see ; and also gives a version of the same by Duncombe.

25th, and the Megara of Moschus, are the three parts of one poem, the Heraclea of some nameless author. Reiske supposed Idylls 24th and 25th to be parts of the Heraclea of Pisander; but Kiessling points out that the non-preservation of the customs of the heroic age in these two Idylls disproves this theory. We may safely, with Warton, reckon it among the Idylls of Theocritus.

ONCE upon a time Alcmena of [1] Midea, having washed both Hercules, now ten months old, and Iphiclus, younger by a night, and having filled them with milk, had laid them down in a [2] brazen shield, which, a noble *piece of* armour, Amphitryon had taken as spoil from fallen Pterelaus. And the woman, touching the head of her children, spake *thus:* 'Sleep, my babes, a sweet sleep, and one from which ye may awake; sleep, my lives, two brothers, secure children, happily may ye sleep, and happily arrive at morn.' Thus having said, she rocked the great shield, and sleep took possession of them.

But what time [3] the Bear revolves at midnight toward the setting, opposite Orion himself, and he displays his broad shoulder, then in sooth Juno of many schemes set in motion two dreadful monsters, dragons bristling with azure coils, against the broad threshold, where the door-posts of the chamber are hollow, having urged them by threats to devour the babe Hercules.

These twain then having uncoiled themselves, were rolling their ravenous bellies along the ground; and [4] from their eyes, as they went, evil fire was glancing, and they were spit-

[1] Midea. See Idyll xiii. 20.

[2] Meursius (at Callim. H. in Jov. 48) tells us that the shield was often the cradle of a hero's child, the father praying his offspring might be thereby inspired with a taste for war. He quotes a fragment of the Andromeda of Ennius, "Nam ubi introducta est, puerumque ut laverent, locant in clypeo." Pterelaus, king of the Taphians, was subdued by Amphitryon, who made war upon him in behalf of Electryon, the father of Alcmena. He had one golden hair, which Neptune had given him, till which was taken, he was to be immortal. This his daughter Comætho gave to Amphitryon. See Smith Dict. G. R. B. i. 152, *Amphitryon.*

[3] Anacr. iii. 1—3, Μεσονυκτίοις ποθ' ὥραις Στρέφεται ὅτ' Ἄρκτος ἤδη κατὰ χεῖρα τὴν Βοώτου. Hom. Odyss. v. 274, Ἄρκτον—ἥ τ' αὐτοῦ στρέφεται, καὶ τ' Ὠρίωνα δοκεύει, i. e. keeps his head turned towards Orion. The same is meant here by κατ' αὐτόν.

[4] Compare Æn. ii. 210, Ardentesque oculos suffecti sanguine et igni. And compare the whole passage. Milton, in his description of the old serpent, speaks of "eyes that sparkling blazed." P. L. ix. 496. For ἐρχομένοις, Pierson suggests δερκομένοις, ingeniously.

ting forth noxious venom. [5]But when at length, licking their forked tongues, they had come nigh the boys, then, I wot, as Jove knoweth all things, the dear children of Alcmena awoke, and a light was raised all over the chamber. In truth, the one, namely Iphiclus, forthwith shouted out, when he perceived the evil monsters above the hollow shield, and saw their ruthless fangs; and kicked away with his feet the fine coverlet, being eager to escape: but the other, Hercules, opposing them, held fast to them with his hands, and bound both in a firm grasp, having seized them by the throat, where baneful poisons, such as even the gods abhor, are wrought by murderous serpents. [6]And they two, on the other hand, began to wind with their coils around the child, late-born, *still* a suckling, ever tearless under his nurse's care: but again they began to uncoil, since they were wearied in their spines, in trying to find a riddance from his constraining grasp. And Alcmena heard a cry, and awoke first. 'Rise, Amphitryon, for timid fear possesses me: rise, [7]nor put your sandals on your feet. Hear you not how greatly the younger of the children is crying? [8]Or perceive you not that, some where in the early night, these walls also around are all plain to be seen, without *the aid of* clear dawn? There is some strange thing, I know, in the house, there is, dear husband.'

Thus said she: and he, having complied with his wife's *request*, descended from his couch, and rushed in quest of his curiously-wrought sword, which was [9]always suspended for him upon a peg, above his cedar couch. In truth he was reaching after his new-spun belt, lifting in the other hand a large scabbard, a work wrought of the lotus; when, I wot,

---

[5] Virg. Æn. ii. 211, Sibila lambebant linguis vibrantibus ora.

[6] Virg. Æn. ii. 214, Corpora natorum serpens amplexus uterque, Implicat; and 217, Spirisque ligant ingentibus.

[7] I. Tibull. iii. 91, Tunc mihi, qualis eris, longos turbata capillos
Obvia nudato, Delia, curre pede.

[8] Here, as in ℣. 22 above, there seems to have been a supernatural light intended. Compare Hom. Odyss. xix. 37—39, where Telemachus from the flood of light draws the inference ἦ μάλα τις θεὸς ἔνδον. And compare Plaut. Amphitr. V. i. 44, Ædes totæ confulgebant tuæ, quasi essent aureæ.—ἀωρί. Cf. xi. 40. John Wordsworth suggests for ἄτερ ἄπερ, tanquam, sicut.

[9] ἄωρτο, the epic plusq. perf. of ἀείρω. Il. iii. 272; xix. 253. Matt. Gr. Gr. p. 233. Kiessl.

the spacious chamber was filled again with gloom. Then at length he shouted to the servants [10] snoring heavily in sleep: 'Bring fire with all speed, having snatched it from the hearth, my servants, and force back the strong bolts of the doors: rise, ye patient-hearted servants, [11] the master calls.' [12] The servants then speedily came forward with blazing lights, and the chamber was filled with the bustling of each. In good truth, I ween, when they saw the suckling Hercules tightly holding two monsters in his tender hands, they shouted out, clapping their hands together: but he began to point out the serpents to his sire Amphitryon, and to leap aloft with joy in his boyishness, and laughingly he laid before his father's feet the dire monsters stupified with death. Alcmena indeed then took to her bosom, dry by reason of fear, Iphiclus in passionate distress; and Amphitryon placed the [13] other boy under his coverlet of wool, and again returned to his couch and was mindful of slumber. The cocks a third time now were proclaiming the last of dawn: then [14] Alcmena having summoned Teiresias the soothsayer, telling all things true, recounted to him the strange matter, and bade him answer how it was likely to end. 'And do not,' *said she*, [15] 'if the gods intend any thing adverse, hide it from me through scruples: for that 'tis impossible for men to escape whatever the Fate [16] forces down the spindle, I teach thee, prophet son of Eueris, very

[10] Comp. Æn. ix. 326, Exstructus toto *proflabat pectore* somnum. Cf. Æsch. Choeph. 612.

[11] αὐτὸς properly means oneself as opposed to others. Hence it implies emphasis, without opposition; the master, for instance, as in the Pythagorean αὐτὸς ἔφα, Ipse dixit. Cf. Aristoph. Nub. 219; Ran. 520; Liddell and Scott Lex.

[12] Hom. Il. xviii. 525, οἱ δὲ τάχα προγένοντο.

[13] χλαῖναν. Comp. Idyll xviii. 19; vii. 36.

[14] Teiresias the soothsayer, son of Eueris; stricken with blindness, because he had seen Minerva at her bath. Cf. Callimach. H. in Lavacr. Pallad. 91. Propert. IV. x. 57,
  Magnam Tiresias aspexit Pallada vates
  Fortia dum, positâ Gorgone, membra lavat.

[15] Compare Eli's abjuration of Samuel, I. iii. 17, "I pray thee hide it not from me," &c. The poet here passes abruptly from his own person to that of Alcmena.

[16] κλωστήρ is the same as "fusus." Virg. Georg. iv. 349,
  Carmine quo captæ dum fusis mollia pensa
  Devolvunt.
Virg. Æn. i. 22, Sic volvere Parcas.

wise though thou art!' Thus spake the queen. And he answered thus: 'Cheer up, lady, mother of noblest progeny, [17] of the blood of Perseus; [18] for, by my dear light, long since gone from mine eyes, many Achaian women shall ply the soft yarn with the hand about the knee, [19] at even-tide singing of Alcmena by name: [20] thou shalt be a glory to the women of Argos. This thy son, being such a hero, is about to ascend to the star-bearing heaven, [21] a hero with a broad chest, to whom both all monsters and *all* other men shall be inferior. To him it is fated, after he has accomplished twelve labours, to dwell in the halls of Jove: but all his mortal parts [22] the Trachinian pyre shall have. And he shall be called son-in-law of the *very* immortals, who set on these skulking monsters to destroy the babe. [23] In truth, that day shall come, when the sharp-toothed wolf, having seen the kid in his lair, shall not be willing to harm it. But, lady, let the fire be in readiness, look you, under the ashes, and make ye ready dry logs

---

[17] Of the blood of Perseus. She was daughter of Electryon, son of Perseus.

[18] Compare Idyll xi. 53, and Gray's Bard, "Dear as the light that visits these sad eyes." Remembrance of lost blessings is keener than the sense of possession. Chapman compares Milton, Paradise Lost, B. iii. 33—37.

[19] Virg. Georg. i. 390, Nec nocturna quidem carpentes pensa puellæ. Macaulay's Lays of Ancient Rome,
> And as she twirled the distaff
> With solemn steps and slow,
> She sung of great old houses,
> And of fights fought long ago.

[20] Compare Odyss. xxiv. 196—199. Ovid. Ep. ex Pont. IV. viii. 47.

[21] ἀπὸ στέρνων πλατύς. See Idyll xvi. 49, θῆλυς ἀπὸ χροιᾶς.

[22] The body of Hercules was burnt on a pyre at the top of Œta, a mountain of Thessaly. Trachinian is the same as Thessalian, from Trachis, a city of Thessaly, called after Hercules, Heraclea. Hence the name of the tragedy of Sophocles, "Trachiniæ." Comp. Spanheim's note at Callim. H. to Dian. 159. Below at γαμβρὸς δ ἀθανάτων, the plural is for the singular, Juno being the goddess indicated.

[23] Theocritus may have read Isaiah xi. 6, "The wolf also shall dwell with the lamb, and the leopard shall lie down with the kid; and the calf, and the young lion, and the fatling together; and a little child shall lead them." Cf. also lxv. 25. Virg. Ecl. iv. 22, Nec magnos metuent armenta leones. Cf. Ecl. v. 61. Lactantius, lib. vii. 24, quotes the Erythræan Sibyl,

σαρκοβόρος τε λέων φάγετ' ἄχυρον παρὰ φάτναις
σὺν βρέφεσίν τε δράκοντες ἀμάτορσι κοιμήσονται.

of [24] aspalathus, or paliurus, or of bramble; or the brittle wild-pear wood shaken by the wind: and at midnight, when they wished to destroy thy child, burn these two dragons upon the wild cleft-wood. [25] Then at morn let one of the attendants, having gathered the ashes of the fire, carry and throw it thoroughly every whit across the river, upon the rugged rocks, over the boundary, and return home without turning back: but first of all [26] purify the house with clear sulphur, and next remember to sprinkle with a green branch [27] plenty of pure water, mixed, as is usual, with salt; and to sacrifice to supreme Jove a boar pig, that ye may ever be superior to your enemies.'

Teiresias spake, and withdrew with his ivory seat, though he was bent with the weight of many years. And Hercules was reared under his mother's care, like a [28] young plant in a garden, being called *the son* of Argive Amphitryon. Letters [29] aged Linus, son of Apollo, a sleepless guardian, a hero, taught the boy: and to bend the bow, and to be a good shot with arrows, [30] Eurytus, rich in broad lands from his forefathers. [31] Eumolpus, son of Philammon, made him a

---

[24] Aspalathus.] Cf. Idyll iv. 57, Rose of Jerusalem.—Paliurus.] Virg. Ecl. v. 39, Spinis surgit paliurus acutis. All kinds of thorns were considered efficacious for dispelling evil agency. Ovid Fast. ii. 28, Februa poscenti pinea virga data est. ἀχερδος. Odyss. xiv. 10. Soph. O. C. 1596. A wild prickly shrub.

[25] Ecl. viii. 101, Fer cineres Amarylli foras; rivoque fluenti,
Transque caput jace, ne respexeris.

Cf. Æsch. Choeph. 93, ἀστρόφοισιν ὄμμασιν, and Blomf. Glossary at that passage.

[26] For the use of sulphur in purifications, see Tibull. I. v. 11, Ipseque te circum lustravi sulfure puro. Compare also Odyss. x. 527, &c.

[27] ἐστεμμένον might be translated "brimming." It seems to convey the idea of excessive fulness. Compare ἐπιστεφέας, Il. i. 471; viii. 232. Compare also Idyll ii. 2.

[28] In a garden.] Cf. Hom. Il. xviii. 57; Odyss. xiv. 175. In the Psalms, too, we have children compared to olive branches.

[29] Linus. Virg. Ecl. iv. 56,

Nec Linus; huic mater quamvis, atque huic pater adsit,
Orphei Calliopea, Lino formosus Apollo.

Cf. Smith Dict. Gr. R. Biogr. p. 787, vol. ii.

[30] Eurytus (Odyss. viii. 224; Il. ii. 730) was of Æchalia in Thessaly. Cf. Smith Dict. G. R. B. ii. 113.

[31] Eumolpus, son of Philammon. Philammon was the son of Phœbus and Chione. Ov. Met. xi. 317, Carmine vocali clarus citharâque Phil-

minstrel, and moulded both his hands upon a cithern of boxwood. And in how many ways men of Argos, throwing *their adversaries* from their legs with a cross-buttock, trip up each other in wrestling, and in how many ways boxers *are* formidable in the cæstus, and what tricks adapted to their art men ready for every kind of contest have invented, *by* falling forward to the earth, all *these* he learned under the teaching of [32] Harpalycus of Phanote, son of Mercury, whom not though beholding him afar off, could any one withstand, as he contended in the games. Such a scowl rested on his awe-inspiring visage. Moreover, with feelings of love, Amphitryon himself was wont to teach his son to drive steeds in the chariot, and turning safely [33] round the post, to guard the box of the nave of the wheel, since full oft in equestrian Argos he had carried off prizes in contests of speed; and his chariots on which he used to mount, [34] still unbroken, burst their reins by reason of age. But to aim at *his* man with outstretched spear, keeping his back under cover of his shield, and to bear up against sword-wounds, and to marshal a phalanx, and in making his attack to measure again and again the ambuscades of the enemy, and to cheer on the cavalry, Castor the horseman taught him, having come an exile from Argos, what time [35] Tydeus was holding the whole inheritance and broad vineyard, having received equestrian Argos from Adrastus. Among the demigods was no other warrior like to Castor, before old age wore out his youthful vigour.

ammon. The Eumolpus who is said to have instructed Hercules in music was son of Musæus, a pupil of Orpheus. Ov. Met. xi. 93,
    Cui Thracius Orpheus
    Orgia tradiderat cum Cecropio Eumolpo.
Cf. Smith Dict. G. R. B. ii. 92.

[32] Harpalycus, the tutor of Hercules in wrestling, (109, 110,) boxing, (111,) pancratiasm, (112,) was the son, it would seem, of Mercury, and a native of Panope, or Phanote; which, according to Strabo, (ix. 538,) is synonymous, and is in the region of Lebadeia in Bœotia. Cf. Ovid Met. iii. 19; Hom. Odyss. xi. 580.

[33] περὶ νύσσαν. Compare the advice of Nestor to Antilochus, (Il. xxiii. 334—337,) to near the post as closely as possible, yet without grazing it. Cf. Hor. Od. I. i. 4, Metaque fervidis Evitata rotis, &c.

[34] So skilful had been the charioteering of Amphitryon, that though his chariot's thongs, or reins, failed at last through age, no breakage had ever damaged them.

[35] Æneus, king of Calydon, after the death of Athæa, married Perebœa,

K 2

Thus indeed his loving mother [36] had Hercules brought up. And a couch was made for the lad near his father, [37] a lion's skin, *a couch* very agreeable to himself: and [38] his dinner was roast-meat and a huge Dorian loaf in a bread basket; it would be safe to satisfy a digger and delver. But [39] at the close of day he was wont to take a little supper, uncooked; and he was clad in unembroidered garments [40] above the calf of the leg.

IDYLL XXV.

HERCULES THE LION-SLAYER, OR, THE WEALTH OF AUGEAS.

ARGUMENT.

In this fragmentary poem we find Hercules in the land of Elis, in the neighbourhood of the famous stables of Augeas. Having arrived thither, he is led to the king by an old rustic. The king has retired into the country to visit his herds. A description of a vast herd returning from pasture is finely interwoven, (84—137,) and Hercules is exhibited repelling with ease the assault of the finest bull of the herd, a proof of valour which excites the admiration of the king and his son. This son of Augeas, as they travel by the same road, begs Hercules to recount to him, by what means he slew the Nemean lion. The hero, complying, narrates the whole exploit. Some have doubted whether Theocritus wrote this poem. It is variously assigned by such,

---

daughter of Hipponous, by whom he had Tydeus. Tydeus, when grown up, was banished, and fled to Adrastus, king of Argos, and marrying his daughter Deipyle, begat Diomed.

[36] παιδεύσατο, h. e. "educendum curavit."

[37] The custom of sleeping on skins occurs Virg. Æn. vii. 87.

Cæsarum ovium sub nocte silenti
Pellibus incubuit stratis, somnumque petivit.

[38] For a notion of the appetite of Hercules, see Eurip. Alcest. 750—760; Aristoph. Vesp. 60; Ran. 62; Av. 1690; Pax, 741. Dorian bread was of the commoner and less fine kind.

[39] ἐπ' ἄματι, post diem. In the same sense is ἐπὶ τῇ τελευτῇ τοῦ βίου, "at the close of life."

[40] Virg. Æn. i. 317, describes Harpalyce, a Thracian princess of manly hardihood, as "nuda genu."

to Pisander, a contemporary of Tyrtæus, to some unknown poet earlier than the date of Theocritus, and to some Alexandrine Rhapsodist. Hermann deems it not unworthy of Theocritus. Old editions have prefixed to this Idyll a poor attempt of some nameless grammarian to furnish a beginning.

* * * * * * * * * *

And to him spake the old man, a husbandman [1] in charge of the tillage, having ceased from the work which lay on his hands : 'Stranger, I will readily tell over to you *all* that you ask, since I stand in awe of the dread vengeance of [2] Hermes by the wayside. For they say, that, most of *all* the gods of heaven, he is incensed, if so be that any one spurn a traveller very anxious *to know* the way. The fleecy flocks indeed of king Augeas [3] feed not all on one pasture, or one spot ; but some, I ween, pasture round about on the banks of [4] Elisus, others beside the sacred stream of divine [5] Alpheus, others again hard by [6] Buprasium teeming with grapes, and others also here. Now separately, for each of these, folds have been built. But for all the herds, overflowing though they are, still there are here pastures ever rich, along the wide standing-waters of [7] Menius ; [8] for dewy meads and water-pastures luxuriate in fragant herbage in abundance, which in sooth increases the strength of horned heifers. And here, to your right hand, appears their stall, all of it quite on the other side of the flowing river, in that quarter where the planes grow all

---

[1] ἐπίουρος, Etym. M. 362, 29, ὁ ἐφεστηκὼς φύλαξ ; from ὁρῶ, ἐπίορος, and by epenthesis, ἐπίουρος.

[2] ἐνόδιος, said specially of Mercury, who had his statues in the crossways. Valkn. Diatr. 138. In Aristoph. Plut. 1159, we find him called ἡγεμόνιος, the guide and protector of travellers, and these two epithets are coupled together in his case by Arrian de Venat. c. 35, 'Ερμοῦ ἐνοδίου καὶ ἡγεμονίου.

[3] βόσκονται ἴαν βόσιν. Cf. Matth. Gr. Gr. § 421, obs. 3, p. 680.

[4] Elisson, or Elissa, was a river of Elis, not far from Olympia. (Strabo.)

[5] Alpheus, a river of Elis. Compare Idyll iv. 6.

[6] Buprasium, a city of Elis, mentioned by Homer, Il. ii. 615, where the forces of the Epeans, who occupied the north of Elis, as it would seem, are being enumerated. See also Il. xi. 759, and Il. xxiii. 631. Augeas ruled over the Epeans. Cf. vs. 166.

[7] Μηνίου. Heyne suggests Πηνεοῦ, (as in Pindar Ἀλφεοῦ for Ἀλφειοῦ,) which Kiessling approves. The Peneus was a river of Elis.

[8] Nonnus. Dionys. b. 3, 15. ἐαριναῖς ἐγέλασσε λελουμένον ἄνθος ἱεραῖς. εἰαμεναί, Il. iv. 483, derived pernaps from ἧμαι, low, flooded meadows.

the year long, and the green wild olive, a sacred holy-grove of [9] pastoral Apollo, a most perfect god, stranger.

'And right forwards are built very spacious dwellings for us husbandmen, who zealously guard for the king his great and untold wealth, sometimes casting [10] the seed into thrice-ploughed fallows, and in like manner into four times ploughed. Now his boundaries the diggers and delvers know, who, hard-working *fellows*, come to the wine vats, when the ripe summer season shall have arrived. For in truth all this is the plain of prudent Augeas, and *these* his wheat-bearing [11] acres and wooded orchards, even to the extreme points of the mountain ridge having-many-springs, which we ply with our labour all day long, as is the law for servants, whose life is a-field. But tell you also me, [which likewise will be better for yourself,] [12] being in need of what have you come here? Either, I suppose, you seek Augeas, or one of his servants, whom he has. Now I, look you, can fully tell you every particular, as I know them accurately; for I think that you at any rate come not of evil people, nor are yourself like unto evil men, such a noble figure is conspicuous about you: surely, methinks, *of* such *a stamp* are the sons of immortals among mortal men.' And him the valorous son of Jove addressed in answer: 'Yes, old man, I would wish to see Augeas, ruler of the Epeans, for *it was* even a want of this *which* brought me here. But if now he is abiding in the city among his citizens, engaged in caring for his people, and is deciding questions of law, prythee, aged sir, bid you one of

---

[9] Pastoral Apollo.] Compare Callim. H. in Apoll. 47,
Φοῖβον καὶ Νόμιον κικλήσκομεν, ἐξέτι κείνου,
ἐξοτ᾽ ἐπ᾽ Ἀμφρύσῳ ζευγίτιδας ἔτρεφεν ἵππους.
Virg., Georg. iii. 2, calls Apollo, Pastor ab Amphryso.
The wild olive, ἀγριέλαιος or κότινος, bore the leaves which composed the crown of the victor at the Olympic games.

[10] Virg. Georg. i. 47, 48,
Illa seges demum votis respondet avari
Agricolae, bis quae solem, quae frigora sensit.
Virg. Georg. i. 398, Namque omne quotannis
Terque quaterque solum scindendum.

[11] γύαι, from γύης, ὁ. Elmsl. Soph. O. C. 58. Eurip. Bacch. 13. Heracl. 839. Vid. Valkenaer ad Phoeniss. Eurip. vs. 648.

[12] Compare Virg. Æn. vii. 197,
Quae causa rates aut cujus egentes
Littus ad Ausonium tot per vada caerula vexit?

the servants to be my guide, whosoever *is* the most honourable [13] manager over these lands, to whom I might say somewhat, and *from whom* I might learn somewhat, when he speaks. For God, in sooth, hath made one man in need of one, and another of another.'

And him the old man, trusty husbandman *as he was*, answered yet again: 'By the advice, stranger, of some one of the gods you come hither. Since to you every business, which you wish, quickly finds its accomplishment. For hither hath come but [14] yesterday from town Augeas, dear son of the Sun, with his child, the strong and noble Phyleus, to visit after many days the property, which he has in countless extent in the country. Thus, I suppose, even to princes their house seems to be safer, to their mind, if they manage it themselves. But let us go to him by all means; and I will be your guide to my stall, where we shall find the king.'

Thus having spoken, he began to lead the way; but [15] in mind he at least was pondering much, as he saw the lion's skin, and the club, which filled his hand, whence the stranger could be: and he was eager to question him. But again through fear he was keeping within his lips his speech as it rose, lest he should address to him, in his haste, any inopportune word: for 'tis hard to know another man's mind. And as they approached, [16] the dogs quickly noticed them from afar

---

[13] αἰσυμνήτης, a manager, from αἴσια νέμειν, to give each his due. Here the person indicated seems to be the Latin "villicus." αἰσυμνήτης stands for the elective prince of the Mitylenæans in Aristot. Politic. III. xiv. 8. Cf. Smith, D. G. and R. Antiq. pp. 32—36.

[14] χθιζὸς, elegantly for χθές. So Il. A. 497, ἠερίη δ' ἀνέβη μέγαν οὐρανόν. See below at vs. 223. Horat. Epod. xvi. 51, Nec vespertinus circumgemit ursus ovile.

—From town.] Elis was not built in Homer's day, much less that of Hercules. There is no doubt an anachronism, unless we suppose, with Warton, that ἄστυ here stands for the palace or seat of government.

[15] Polwhele remarks, that the ancients never inquired the names of their stranger guests, instancing the Phæacians of the Odyssey, and the Germans of Tacitus, De Mor. G. c. 21.

[16] Compare Homer Odyss. xiv. 29, 30,

ἐξαπίνης δ' Ὀδυσῆα ἴδον κύνες ὑλακόμωροι
Οἱ μὲν κεκλήγοντες ἐπέδραμον—

Comp. Odyss. xvi. 5. "Princes of old made much of dogs. Telemachus is attended by two house dogs, Odyss. ii. Achilles has nine at his board, Il. xxiii. Two attend Evander, Æn. 8, and Syphax in Livy."—Warton.

off, in both ways, by their scent of flesh, and by the sound of feet. And barking furiously they rushed from different sides on Hercules, son of Amphitryon: but about the old man, barking without need or cause, they kept fawning on the other side. These indeed he for his part proceeded to frighten into retreating, by stones, merely lifting them from the ground; and sharply with his voice did he threaten every one of them, and check their barking, though he rejoiced in his heart that they protected his stall, yes, when he was absent; then spake he such words as these: 'Strange! what an animal this is, that the gods our rulers have made to be with men: how sagacious! if it had but a mind, so far intelligent, within, as to know with whom 'twere right to be angry, and with whom not, then no other of brutes had vied with it for the meed of honour. But, as it is, 'tis a very wrathful kind *of beast*, and [17] savage to no purpose.'

He spoke; and speedily they came in their progress to the stall. The [18] Sun indeed at that time had turned his steeds towards the west, bringing on eventide: and the fat sheep arrived, coming up from pasture to their [19] folds and pens. Next full myriads of heifers were seen, one after another, coming, like rainy clouds, as many as in the heaven are being driven forward, either by force of the south wind, or of Thracian Boreas: of which there is no numbering, as they move in air, no, nor cessation; for so many does the violence of the wind roll after the first, and the rest too rise and swell upon others again: so many herds of heifers, *I say*, were coming up ever and anon behind. Then in sooth all the plain was filled, and all the ways, with the cattle coming in, while the fertile fields were full of lowings, and the stalls easily crowded with trailing-footed oxen; the sheep too were folding themselves in the pens. [20] Here, indeed, no man, though they

---

[17] ἀρρηνὲς, savage, (a collateral form of ἀρρην, from ῥὴν, L. and S.,) ἄγριον, δύσχερες. Hesych.

[18] Compare Hom. Odyss. xvii. 170,

Ἀλλ' ὅτε δὴ δειπνηστὸς ἔην, καὶ ἐπήλυθε μῆλα
Πάντοθεν ἐξ ἀγρῶν.

Virg. Georg. iv. 433, Vesper ubi e pastu vitulos ad tecta reducit.

[19] αὔλια, shelters for the smaller stock; σηκούς, for the larger. Cf. 99, 18, 61, 76, 169, (for αὔλια,) of this Idyll; for σηκοὶ, see vs. 98.

Hom. Il. iv. 433, ὥστ' ὄϊες πολυπάμονος ἀνδρὸς, ἐν αὐλῇ
Μυρίαι ἑστήκασιν ἀμελγόμεναι γάλα λευκόν.

[20] '*Though they were numberless*,' is to be understood, says Kiessling,

were numberless, stood inactive by the oxen, in lack of work:
but one was fitting with well-cut thongs wooden logs about the
cows' feet, for the purpose of standing close beside to milk
them. Another, again, was putting the dear calves to
their own mothers, all eager *as they were* to drink of the
pleasant milk: another was holding a milk-pail; another was
[21] thickening a rich cheese; another was driving in the bulls,
apart from the cows. And Augeas was going over all the ox-
stalls, and noting what fruits of his possessions his herdsmen
were making for him. And with him his son as well as mighty
and wise Hercules were following, as the king went round his
large property. Hereupon the son of Amphitryon, though hav-
ing in his bosom a spirit unbroken [22] and sternly fixed for ever,
yet was vastly astonished on seeing the countless tribe of oxen,
I ween. For no one would say, or [23] have supposed, that the
stock of one man, no, nor of ten others, ay, such as were rich
in flocks beyond all other men, was so great. Since Phœbus
had presented to his son this special gift, to be rich in cattle
above all men; yes, and he kept altogether prospering for
him all his beasts to the uttermost; [24] for no disease, of
those which destroy the labours of herdsmen, assailed his
herds. But ever more in number, ever finer sprang up horned
heifers duly from year to year: for of a truth all were
[25] mothers of live offspring, far beyond others, and all of fe-
male offspring. And together with these, three hundred bulls
were ranged in rows, white-legged and crumple-horned; nay,

of the cattle. Harles refers the words to the men, and illustrates the number of servants by Dido's Feast, Virg. Æn. i. 701.

[21] The first meaning of τρέφω is, to thicken, congeal, or curdle, hence τροφαλίς, Aristoph. Vesp. 338, fresh cheese. Odyss. ix. 246, Αὐτίκα δ' ἥμισυ μὲν θρέψας λευκοῖο γάλακτος. Cf. Il. v. 902. Virg. Ecl. i. 35 and 82, Pressi copia lactis. For the next line compare Virg. Georg. iii. 212, Aut intus clausos satura ad præsepia servant.

[22] θυμὸς ἀρηρώς. Odyss. x. 553, οὔτε φρεσὶν ᾗσιν ἀρηρώς.—ἔθνος, used of bees, Iliad ii. 87; of birds, v. 459; of flies, v. 469.

[23] ἐώλπει, arbitratus fuisset. Compare Mosch. ii. 146, ἐέλπομαι εἰσοράασθαι. Idyll iv. 55—80, ἔολπα. Spero is so used by the Latins. Æn. i. 543, At sperate deos memores fandi atque nefandi. Ecl. viii. 26, Quid non speremus amantes. Æn. xi. 275.

[24] νοῦσος—αἴτε. A rare construction. See Porson's note at Eurip. Orest. 910, αὐτουργὸς, οἵπερ. Porson ap. Monk Eurip. Hippol. 78. Virg. Æn. viii. 427, Fulmen—quæ plurima—

[25] Genesis xxxi. 38, "These twenty years have I been with thee: thy ewes and thy she-goats have not cast their young."

there were other two hundred red; and all such as were even already full-grown. And other twelve again beside these were feeding, [26] sacred to the Sun, and in colour they were like swans, *so* white *were they*, and they were conspicuous among all the trailing-footed oxen, which also were feeding on the verdant herbage apart from the herd in the pasture; so exceedingly were they exulting over themselves.

And whensoever swift wild beasts chanced to sally forth from the bushy thicket into the plain, for the sake of heifers afield, these *were they*, I wot, *that* would rush first to the conflict, guided by their scent of the skin; and bellow fearfully, [27] looking slaughter in their visages. And chief of them indeed both in strength, and in his natural force and high courage, *was* huge Phaethon: whom in sooth herdsmen were all [28] wont to liken to a star, because as he moved he shone out greatly among other oxen, and was very conspicuous. Now he in fact, when he beheld the dry hide of a fierce-eyed lion, upon this rushed against wary Hercules himself, *so as* to bring against his sides his head and sturdy forehead. But, as he approached, [29] the hero quickly seized his left horn with his broad hand, bent his neck, [30] hard though it was, down to the earth beneath; and then thrust him back again, having pressed heavily with his shoulder; so the bull, having the tendons of the muscles strained, stood right up on his haunches. Then marvelled both the king himself, and Phyleus, his warlike son, and the herdsmen over [31] crumple-horned kine, as they beheld the immense strength of the son of Amphitryon. Then they two, Phyleus and strong Hercules, began to proceed to the city, having left there behind *them* the fruitful fields. But as soon as they had set [32] foot on the highway,

[26] Sacred to the Sun.] Herodot., ix. 93, mentions a flock of sheep in Ionia sacred to Phœbus. Cf. Hom. Odyss. xii. 123.

[27] φόνον λεύσσοντε. Compare Idyll xiii. 45, and see Matt. Gr. Gr. § 409, 2, p. 653.

[28] Hom. Il. vi. 295, ἀστὴρ δ' ὥς ἀπέλαμπεν, sc. πέπλος. Kiessling.

[29] ἄναξ. Thus Homer calls all his heroes. In later poets the term is applied to the sons or near kinsmen of sovereigns.

[30] Hercules seizing the bull's left horn forces his head down to the ground; then pressing with his shoulder, he shoves him back. The bull in vain strains every nerve against Hercules, but unable to repel him, is at last forced right up on his haunches by the efforts of his antagonist.

[31] So Archilochus (Fragm. viii.) has βοῦς κορωνός.

[32] The meaning seems to be, that as soon as they had got over the

having got over [33] with active feet a narrow path which in sooth extended through the vineyard from the ox-stalls, not being in any way very distinguishable amid green foliage, here then, I say, the dear son of Augeas addressed the offspring of highest Jove, as he came on behind him, having slightly bent his head over his right shoulder :

[34] 'Stranger, I am just now pondering in my mind, that I have certainly heard long ago some famous story about thee. For there came hither on his way from Argos, one, [35] quite a young man, an Achæan from [36] Helice by the sea-shore, who in truth, look you, was also discoursing among many of the Epeans, that one of the Argives in his presence had destroyed a wild beast, a savage lion, a monster of evil to rustics, having a hollow den [37] in the grove of Nemean Jupiter. I know not accurately, whether he was from [38] sacred Argos, on the spot, or an inhabitant of the city of Tiryns, or Mycenæ. Thus he at least used to say : but by birth he reported that *the hero* was (that is, if I recollect rightly) [39] of the lineage of Perseus. I deem that none other of the [40] Ægialæans, but you, has had

by-path, where Hercules and Phyleus could not walk abreast, and make any way, being at last on the high road, Phyleus made room for Hercules beside him, in order that they might converse without difficulty.

[33] καρπαλίμοις ποσί. Il. xvi. 342.

[34] Read with Briggs, whom Kiessling approves,
ξεῖνε πάλαι τινὰ πάγχυ σέθεν πέρι μῦθον ἀκούσας
ὡσείπερ, &c.

[35] ὡς νέος ἀκμήν. ἀκμήν, in later writers, stands for ἔτι. See Pierson, Mœris, 79. Only once so in Xenophon, Anab. iv. 3, 26.

[36] Helice by the sea-shore.] Cf. Idyll i. 125, a city of Achaia, on the Peloponnesian coast of the "Corinthiacus Sinus." Spanhem. ad Callim. H. in Del. 100, who quotes Ovid Met. xv. 293,
Si quæras Helicen et Burim Achaïdas urbes,
Invenies sub aquis.

[37] In the grove of Nemean Jupiter.] The Nemean games were held in a grove in Argolis, between Cleonæ and Phlius. Strabo viii. 6, p. 210 (Tauchnitz). It appears that Hercules either revived these ancient games, or introduced the alterations by which they were henceforth celebrated in honour of Jupiter. Of the Nemean lion, vid. Trachin. Sophocl. 1092, 1093.

[38] Argos was sacred to Juno. Iliad iv. 52. Ov. Met. vi. 414. Fast. vi. 47. Virg. Æn. i. 24, Memor Saturnia belli
Prima quod ad Trojam pro caris gesserat Argis.
Her temple there was called Heræum.

[39] ἐκ Περσῆος. The line ran thus, Perseus, Alcæus, Amphitryo, Hercules. Cf. Idyll xxiv. 72.

[40] Ægialæans, the inhabitants of the sea-coast of Achaia and Argolis,

the courage to do this deed, and the wild beast's' hide, which envelopes your sides, very clearly bespeaks the work of your hands. Come now, tell me first, (that I may know in my mind, O hero, whether I guess rightly or not,) if even you are that hero, [41] of whom the Achæan from Helice told us, his hearers, and I judge of you rightly. And tell me how you yourself slew this dreadful wild beast, and how it came into the land of well-watered Nemea. For such a monster you could not find, though you desired to see it, in [42] Apis; since it surely rears none such, but *only* bears, and wild boars, [43] and the destructive seed of wolves. Whereat they used to wonder then, as they heard the story, and some too even thought that the traveller was telling a falsehood, giving freely of a false tongue to please present *company.*'

Thus having spoken, Phyleus [44] made way from the middle of the road, that it might suffice for them to walk together upon, and also, I ween, that he might more easily hear Hercules speak, who, having accompanied him, addressed him in such a speech as follows.

'O son of Augeas, as to that which you asked me first, you have yourself, and very easily, guessed aright. And concerning this monster, I will tell you each particular, how it was accomplished, since you desire to hear ; that is to say, except whence it came ; for that, though there be many Argives, no one can clearly state : /only we conjecture that some one of the

---

before the Ionians settled there. Eustathius says the whole Peloponnese was so called.

[41] ὅν ἔειπεν. Compare Sophoc. Electr. 984. Eurip. Med. 250,
λέγουσι δ' ἡμᾶς, ὡς ἀκίνδυνον βίον
ζῶμεν.
De quo referebat.

[42] Apis and Ἀπία γῆ — "The Peloponnese," especially "Argolis,"' (Æsch. Suppl. 262,) said to be so called from Apis, a mythical king of Argos. Compare Horat. Od. I. xxii. 13,
Quale portentum neque militaris
Daunia in latis alit æsculetis.

[43] ἔρνος, Lucret. iii. 741, Triste leonum seminium. Virg. Georg. ii. 151, Sæva leonum semina. In Il. xvii. 53, ἔρνος appears in its proper sense, a shoot or scion, used of plants; here in its secondary meaning, or second intention. Below, (vs. 188,) J. Wordsworth compares Æsch. Choeph. 260. Prom. v. 294.

[44] ἐξερωέω, a rare word; it occurs Hom. Il. xxiii. 468, αἱ δ' ἐξηρώησαν, ἐπεὶ μένος ἔλλαβε θυμόν.

immortals, [45] angry on account of sacrifices, inflicted the pest on the men descended from Phoroneus. For overwhelming, like a river, all [46] the men of Pisa, the lion kept ravaging them furiously, and most of all the [47] Bembinæans, who were dwelling near to him, being in most intolerable plight. Now this conflict Eurystheus imposed on me to accomplish first of all, for he desired that the savage beast might kill me. But I took my supple bow, and hollow quiver filled with arrows, and set forth: and in my other hand *was* my stout club, bark and all, of the shady wild olive, of a good size: which I myself having found under sacred Helicon, had pulled up whole with its thick roots. But when I had come to the place where the lion was, then it was that, having taken my bow, and applied the string to the [48] hooked tip, I forthwith set upon it a baneful arrow. And moving my eyes every where, I proceeded to look out for the destructive monster, if haply I might spy him, and that too before he had caught sight of me. [49] 'Twas mid-day, and no where was I able to discern tracks of him, or to hear his roar. No, nor was there any man, *set* over cattle, or *engaged* in tillage, to be seen throughout the arable land, whom I could question: but pale fear was keeping each in his dwelling. I had not however stayed my steps, reconnoitring a woody mountain, ere I even beheld him, and straightway began to make trial of prowess. In truth, he was [50] going before evening to his den, having fed on flesh and blood; and he had got his squalid mane, and grim visage, and chest, bespattered about with gore; and was licking his

---

[45] ἱρῶν μηνίσαντα. Just as in Hom. Il. i. 65, εἴτ' ἄρ' ὅγ' εὐχωλῆς ἐπιμέμφεται, εἴθ' ἑκατόμβης. See also Iliad ix. 529. Soph. Aj. 176.—Phoroneus was the son of Inachus, king of Argos, and the Phoroneans are therefore identical with the Ægialeans, vs. 174.

[46] Men of *Pisa*,] a town of Elis, celebrated for the Olympic games.

[47] Bembinæans,] the people of a village near to Nemea, mentioned by Strabo, viii. 6, p. 210, Tauchnitz, referred to at 169.

[48] κορώνη. τὸ ἄκρον τοῦ τόξου, εἰς ὃ ἡ νευρὰ δέδεται. Hesych. The word occurs, Hom. Il. iv. 111. Odyss. xxi. 138, 165, αὐτοῦ δ' ὠκὺ βέλος καλῇ προσέκλινε κορώνῃ.

[49] Warton compares here Apollon. Rhod. iv. 1247. Four lines below, compare Ovid. Met. viii. 298,

      Diffugiunt populi: nec se, nisi mænibus urbis
      Esse putant tutos.

[50] προδείελος, before eventide. Compare l. 56 of this Idyll and the note there.

jaws with his tongue. But I quickly hid myself amid shady bushes on a woody hill-top, awaiting when he might come *upon me:* and I hit him, as he drew nearer, on his left flank, *but* [51] to no purpose; for in no wise did the barbed missile penetrate through his flesh, but glancing back fell on the green herbage. Then speedily did he raise in astonishment his blood-red head from the ground, and ran over it on all sides with his eyes, making his observations, and, in yawning, [52] he gave *me* a view of his gluttonous teeth. Now at him I proceeded to shoot another arrow from the string, being vexed that before it had escaped fruitlessly from my hand, and I hit him between the breasts, where the lung is seated. But not even so did the painful arrow pierce beneath the hide, but fell before his feet, absolutely to no purpose. Again the third time I was preparing, though grievously disgusted in mind, to draw *my bow anew,* when the furious beast caught sight of me, [53] as he glared around with his eyeballs: and [54] he rolled his great tail about the hollow of the knee, and quickly bethought him of battle: his whole neck was swollen with rage, and his tawny mane [55] bristled, as he chafed; whilst his back-bone became curved, like a bow, as he gathered himself up from all sides towards his flanks and loins. And as, when a chariot-maker, skilled in many works, [56] bends shoots of the easily

[51] τηϋσίως, the Homeric word for μάταιον. Vid. Odyss. iii. 316; xv. 13. Hymn to Apoll. 540. (Either Ionic for ταύσιος, or αὔσιος = μάταιος, or from ἀύω, ἀϋτέω, noisy. L. and S.)

[52] Compare here Homer Il. xx. 165—168, 169,

λέων ὣς
Σίντης, ὅν τε καὶ ἄνδρες ἀποκτάμεναι μεμάασιν·
* * * * * * * *
ἔρχεται· ἀλλ' ὅτε κέν τις 'Αρηϊθόων αἰζηῶν,
δουρὶ βάλῃ, ἐάλη τε χανὼν, περὶ τ' ἀφρὸς ὀδόντας
γίγνεται.

[53] Æn. ix. 793, where the lion is represented at bay, "asper, acerba tuens." πᾶς δέ οἱ αὐχήν. Compare Job xxxix. 19, "Hast thou given the horse strength? hast thou clothed his neck with thunder?"

[54] Compare Il. xx. 168—173, above, and Hesiod, Scnt. 426—432.

[55] ἔφριξαν. So the Latins use "horrere." Horat. Epod. v. 27,
Horret capillis, ut marinus, asperis
Echinus, aut currens aper.
Æn. vi. 419, Horrere videns jam colla colubris. Æn. i. 635, Horrentia centum Terga suum.

[56] Comp. Hom. Il. xxi. 37,
ὅδ ἐρινεὸν ὀξέϊ χαλκῷ
τάμνε, νέους ὄρπηκας, ἵν' ἅρματος ἄντυγες εἶεν.

cleft wild fig-tree, having first warmed them in the fire, *to be* wheels for the chariot-seat on its axles, the thick-barked fig-shoot is apt to fly from out his hands in the bending, and leaps to a distance with one bound, so upon me sprang [57]all-at-once the fierce lion from afar, eager to glut himself on my flesh: but I in one hand was holding before me my arrows, and my double-folded cloak from my shoulders, while with the other, having raised my dry club above his temple, I struck him [58] upon the head, but broke my sturdy olive club right in twain, there upon the shaggy skull of the enormous beast. Ay, and he fell, even before he reached me, from on high upon the earth, and stood upon trembling feet, nodding with his head: for dimness had come over both his eyes, the brain having received a concussion within the skull from the violence. Now when I observed him to be stunned by severe pain, ere at least he had recovered himself and breathed afresh, being beforehand I struck him on the nape of his sturdy neck, having cast on the ground my bow and well-sewn quiver: and I proceeded to throttle him vigorously, having set my strong hands firmly together behind him, lest he should lacerate my flesh with his claws; [59]and with my heels I kept strenuously pressing to the ground his hinder feet, having mounted upon him: while with *his* sides I kept protecting *my* thighs, until I had strained his shoulders to the uttermost, having lifted him upright, [60]breathless as he was: and Hades received a monster soul.

And then, in fact, I began to deliberate how I should draw

The ὄρπηξ was more commonly used for the rails of the chariot. ἄντυγες. Cf. Dict. G. R. Ant. p. 55, b.

[57] ἀθρόος. Comp. Idyll xiii. 50.
[58] ἤλασα. Idyll xiv. 35.
[59] Hercules as it were rides the lion; so that his thighs are, as it were, shielded by the sides of the lion.
[60] ἄπνευστον. Cf. Ovid, Epist. ix. 61,

Nempe sub his animam pestis Nemeæa lacertis
Edidit: unde humerus tegmina lævus habet.

And Sophocl. Trachin. 1089, &c. The souls of beasts descended to the shades, according to Homer and Virgil. Virg. Æn. vi. 285, enumerates animals beheld by Æneas in the shades, Multaque prætereà variarum monstra ferarum. Orion (Odyss. xi. 572,) is described hunting in Orcus the shades of wild beasts which he had slain on the barren mountains.

the shaggy hide from off the limbs of the dead beast, [61] a very laborious task : for it was not able to be cut with steel, nor with stones, though I tried, no, nor with wood. Thereupon one of the immortals put it into my mind to devise, *how* to rip up the skin of the lion with his own claws. With these I speedily flayed him, and placed *the skin* around my limbs, that it might be to me a defence against skin-wounding Enyalius. Such, look you, friend, was the destruction of the Nemean monster, after he had first brought many deaths upon sheep and men.'

IDYLL XXVI.

THE BACCHANALS.

ARGUMENT.

This poem narrates the slaughter of Pentheus, king of Thebes. While Agave his mother, with her sisters, Ino and Autonoe, is celebrating the orgies of Bacchus, Pentheus is spied by the Bacchants, concealed amongst some shrubs. Hereupon they make an attack upon the unfortunate offender, and, under the influence of Bacchic phrensy, seize him and mangle him. At the close of the poem, our poet prays the gods that it may be permitted him to live purely and safely, and adds an encomium on Bacchus and Semele. The subject has been treated by Euripides and by Lucius Accius, his translator. See also Ovid's Metamorph. iii. 701—733.

INO and Autonoe, and [1] apple-cheeked Agave, led three [2] companies, themselves being three, to a mountain. And they

---

[61] ἀργαλέον—μόχθον, accusative in apposition with the sentence. Cf. Virg. Æn. vi. 222, Pars ingenti subiere feretro, Triste ministerium.
Comp. Matth. Gr. Gr. § 432—434.—σιδήρῳ. Harles argues from the use of this metal, and not χάλκος, here, that the author of this Idyll disregards the manners of the heroic age. But Kiessling shows that both were in use, by the references, Il. iv. 485; Odyss. i. 483, 484 ; ix. 391. For ὕλη, (275,) Wordsworth suggests ἀλλῇ, h. e. Nullâ aliâ ratione.

[1] Apple-cheeked.] Hesychius thinks μαλοπάρηος is equivalent to λευκοπαρηός, albis geris prædita; but it is clear from Id. vii. 117, xxiii. 8, and xxix. 16, as well as the Scholiast on Hom. Il. xxii. 68, that the word equals ῥεθομάλις, or ἀπαλοπάργος, generally rosy-cheeked.

[2] Virg. Ecl. v. 30, Daphnis thyasos inducere Baccho. Cf. Eurip.

indeed having plucked wild foliage of a ³ bushy oak, and green ivy, and asphodel that *grows* over the ground, had reared ⁴ in an open meadow twelve altars, the three for Semele, the nine for Bacchus: and, when they had taken in their hands ⁵ from the *mystic* chest curiously-wrought sacred images, had laid them down silently upon the ⁶ newly plucked altars, as Bacchus himself was wont to teach, as himself was well pleased *it should be*. But Pentheus was beholding all from a high rock, creeping under an ancient mastich tree, a shrub of the country. Autonoe first spied him, and raised a fearful cry, and rushing in suddenly, with her feet disturbed the orgies of frantic Bacchus: and these, ⁷ uninitiated persons behold not. Maddened indeed both she, and maddened, I ween, straightway also others. Pentheus was flying affrighted; while they kept pursuing, having drawn-up-tight their robes by the waist to the knee. Now Pentheus spake thus, 'What want ye, women?' But Autonoe said this, 'Soon shalt thou know, ere thou hast heard it.' His mother, on the one hand, roared out, as she seized the head of her son, *deeply* ⁸ as is the roar of a lioness with cubs: and Ino on the other hand brake his great shoulder

Bacch. 679. Propert. iii. 17, 24, Pentheos in triplices funera grata greges. —ἐς ὄρος. The mountain was Cithæron, according to Euripides; Parnassus, according to Æschyl. Eumen. 26.

³ λασίας, bushy. So Callim. H. ad Dian. 192, ἡ δ' ὁτὲ μὲν λασίησι ὑπὸ δρυσὶ κρύπτετο κούρη.

⁴ καθαρῷ, open. So Virg. Æn. xii. 771, *Puro* ut possent concurrere campo.

⁵ Reiske understands this of the curiously wrought images of Bacchus and Semele, drawn on this occasion from the cista or mystic chest or vase, mentioned Catull. Nupt. Pel. et Thet. 260, 261,

Pars obscura cavis celebrabant orgia cistis,
Orgia, quæ frustra cupiunt audire profani.

For πεπονάμενα, Wordsworth proposes to read ποπανεύματα, baked flat cakes used at sacrifices.

⁶ νεοδρέπτων, newly plucked. As these altars were composed of boughs, poetic liberty uses the material of the altars for the altars themselves.

⁷ βέβηλοι, profani. Horat. Od. III. i. 1, Odi profanum vulgus. Callim. H. to Apoll. 2, and Spanheim's note there. Ovid. Met. vii. 156, Et monet arcanis oculos removere profanos.

⁸ Horat. Od. III. ii. 41, Quæ velut nactæ vitulos leænæ,
Singulos eheu lacerant.

Callim. H. to Ceres, 52, ἠὲ κυναγὸν Ὄρεσιν ἐν Τμαρίοισιν ὑποβλέπει ἔνδρα λέαινα Ὠμοτόκος. Cf. Eurip. Bacch. 1137; Ovid Met. iii. 725.

L

with the shoulder-blade, when she had trampled on his belly: and the same was Autonoe's manner of acting: and the rest of the women tore in pieces the remainder of his flesh, and arrived at Thebes all of them stained with blood, bearing from the mountain [9] not Pentheus but πένθημα. I care not [10] for it, nor let another think of being hostile to Bacchus, not even though one has suffered worse treatment than this, and is but nine years old, or even entering on his tenth year. But may I be pure and holy, and please the pure and holy. From Ægis-bearing Jove this omen hath honour, namely, [11] 'To the sons of the pious comes the better fortune, and to the impious not so.'

Hail to Bacchus, whom on snowy [12] Dracanus supreme Jupiter deposited, having relieved his vast thigh: and hail to beauteous Semele, and her Cadmeian sisters, objects of love and care to many heroines, who at the instigation of Bacchus performed this deed, undeserving of blame: let no one blame the *acts* of the gods.

IDYLL XXVII. ν

THE [1] FOND DISCOURSE OF DAPHNIS AND THE DAMSEL.

ARGUMENT.

In this truly pastoral Idyll, the herdsman Daphnis is represented as striving to win a maiden, who is tending her goats. His efforts at

---

[9] *Not Pentheus, but πένθημα,*] i. e. grief, a source of mourning. The pun is untranslateable. For instances of it, see Eurip. Phœniss. 598, 599. Soph. Ajax 430. Æschylus calls Helen 'Ελέναυν. Shakspeare is fond of these "concetti." He makes a strange prince say of Rome, This is Rome, and room enough. He makes a pun on Hotspur's name, calling him, when dead, Coldspur. Cf. Bacch. 367, Πενθεὺς δ' ὅπως μὴ πένθος εἰσοίσει δόμοις.

[10] *I care not for it.*] The sense appears to be, 'This treatment of Pentheus shakes not my reverence for Bacchus: whom I advise none to offend or quarrel with; even though a harder case of punishment should come under his notice, e. g. a child of nine or ten years punished by the Bacchants, for chance privity to the orgies.'

[11] Melancthon called this verse the best in Theocritus.

[12] Dracanus, a promontory and city of Samos.

[1] ὀαριστύς. Juno, in Homer Il. xiv. 216, receives from Aphrodite a

wooing and the damsel's coyness are very graphically pictured. There has been much dispute as to the authorship of this Idyll, which some ascribe to Moschus; others, to an imitator of Theocritus; whilst Warton, Eichstadt, and others, agree in determining that it is not the work of Theocritus.

Daphnis. [2] The prudent Helen Paris, another herdsman, carried off: my Helen here is kissing me, the herdsman, rather.

Damsel. Brag not, little satyr, 'tis said the kiss is an empty favour.

Daph. [3] There is even in empty kisses sweet delight.

Dams. I wipe my mouth, and spit out your kiss.

Daph. Dost wipe thy lips? Give me them again that I may kiss.

Dams. 'Tis good for you to kiss heifers, not [4] an unwedded girl.

Daph. Boast not: for soon youth passes by you, like a dream.

Dams. The bunch of grapes is *still* a bunch of raisins, and the withered rose will not perish *wholly*.

Daph. Come under the wild olives, that I may tell thee a tale.

Dams. I don't choose: before now you have cajoled me by sweet tales.

Daph. Come beneath the elms, that you may hear my pipe.

Dams. Satisfy your own taste: nothing sorry [5] pleases me.

Daph. Fie, fie, regard, yes, even thou, maiden, the wrath of the Paphian goddess.

Dams. Farewell to her of Paphos! Only be Diana propitious!

cestus, or girdle. ἔνθ' ἔνι μὲν φιλότης, ἐν δ' ἵμερος, ἐν δ' ὀαριστὺς. Compare Il. xxii. 126.

[2] Cf. Idyll xviii. 25, &c. Bion xv. 10. Horat. Od. I. xv., Pastor cum traheret per freta navibus, &c. Homer always represents Helen as right-minded, and sensible of her error. Il. iii. 171; vi. 344.

[3] This line occurs in Idyll iii. 20.

[4] Comp. Hom. Odyss. vi. 106, παρθένος ἀδμής. Two lines below Wordsworth reads ἔσται for ἐστι.

[5] ὀιζυον. So Virg. Ecl. iii. 27, Stridenti miserum stipulâ disperdere carmen. Calpurn. Sic. iii. 59,
    Torrida Mopsi
Vox, et carmen inops et acerbæ stridor avenæ.

Daph. Say not so; lest she smite you, and you come into an inextricable net.

Dams. Let her smite as she will! On the other hand, Diana aids me. Lay not your hand upon me. [6] *If you do*, I will tear your lip too.

Daph. You do not escape Love, whom never did other maiden escape.

Dams. I do escape him, yes, by Pan! But you ever bear the yoke.

Daph. I fear lest, in truth, he shall give thee to a worse man.

Dams. Many were my wooers: but not one pleased my taste.

Daph. I too, *as* one of many, come hither as your suitor!

Dams. And what can I do, kind sir? Marriages are full of trouble.

Daph. Nor care nor grief hath marriage, but dancing!

Dams. Well, but in sooth they say that women fear their husbands.

Daph. Rather they always rule them! Whom do women fear?

Dams. I fear to be in labour: Lucina's dart is painful.

Daph. But your queen is Diana, [7] that helps in hard labours.

Dams. But I fear to be a mother; lest I should lose my fair complexion.

Daph. Yet, if you shall have borne dear children, you will see a new light in your sons.

Dams. And what [8] nuptial gift bring you me, worth marrying for, if I should consent.

---

[6] Horat. Epod. iii. 19, Manum puella suavio opponat tuo,
   Extremâ et in spondâ cubet.
Warton reads καὶ εἰσέτι χεῖλος ἀμύξεις; Will you again assail my lips with bites? Wordsworth, καὶ εἴγ' ἔτι χεῖλος, ἀμύξω. Ne mihi injicias manum, et si insuper labium tuum (injeceris) mordicabo.

[7] μογοστόκος, an epithet of Lucina, in Hom. Il. xvi. 187, xix. 103. Here of Diana. Horat. Carm. Sec. 15, 16,
   Sive tu Lucina probas vocari
   Seu Genitalis.
Cf. Odyss. iii. 22, 2.

[8] ἕδνον, the bridegroom's present to the bride, in Homer frequently, and in Æsch. Prom. Vinct. 560. Compare Idyll xxii. 147.

Daph. You shall have all the herd; all the groves, and pasture.

Dams. [9] Swear not to go away after wedding, deserting me against my wish?

Daph. I will not indeed, no, by Pan; even though you should wish [10] to drive me off.

Dams. Are you going to build me a nuptial chamber, and build me a house and stalls?

Daph. I am building thee chambers: and the flocks I tend are beautiful.

Dams. And what, what story should I tell my aged father?

Daph. He will approve your marriage, when he has heard my name.

Dams. Say that name of thine: even a name often pleases.

Daph. I am Daphnis; and my sire Lycidas, and my mother Nomæa.

Dams. You come of gentle blood! but I am no worse than you.

Daph. Neither are you honourable in the highest degree; for your sire is Menalcas.

Dams. Show me your grove, where your stall stands.

Daph. Come hither and see how my tall cypresses bloom.

Dams. Feed ye, my she-goats: I shall go see the works of the herdsman.

Daph. [11] Graze well, my bulls, whilst I show the máiden the groves.

[12] * * * * * * * * * * *

Thus they indeed, delighting in young limbs, were whispering one to the other. [13] A stolen embrace was springing up. And she indeed, when she had arisen, I wot, went forward to tend her flocks, showing shame in her eyes; but her heart was warmed within: and he *proceeded* to his herds of oxen, rejoiced at his marriage.

---

[9] She fears what Simætha found too true, Idyll ii. 40.

[10] διώκειν, fugare.

[11] καλὰ νέμεσθε. So Idyll iii., τὸ καλόν is used adverbially. ἵνα "dum," de tempore. Hom. Odyss. vi. 27, "quo tempore." So ὅπου, Xenoph. Cyr. III. iii. 6. Kiessling.

[12] I hesitate not to leave untranslated these verses, following Polwhele's example. J. B. For a sufficiently close rendering, see Chapman's version.

[13] φώριος εὐνά. Bion, xv. 6, λάθρια Πηλείδαο φιλάματα, λάθριον εὐνάν. Virg. Æn. iv. 171, Nec jam furtivum Dido meditatur amorem.

IDYLL XXVIII.

THE DISTAFF.

ARGUMENT.

This sweet ditty was written to commend an ivory distaff, which the poet, about to sail to Miletus, intended as a present for Theugenis, the wife of Nicias the physician. Under the semblance of teaching the distaff what sort of a mistress it is about to have, he cleverly and gracefully praises a most honourable matron and her husband. The Idyll is of the lyric class; the metre Choriambic; a favourite of Alcæus, and one which Horace imitates in the 18th Ode of the first book.

Nūllām | Vărĕ săcrā | vītĕ prĭūs | sĕvērĭs ār | bŏrēm.

O DISTAFF, [1] practised in wool-spinning, gift of blue-eyed Minerva, labour at thee is fitting to wives who are prudent-housekeepers. Attend me confidently to the famous city of [2] Neleus, where is [3] the temple of Venus, green by reason of the soft reed. For thither we ask of Jove a favourable voyage, that [4] I may be gratified by the sight of my friend Nicias, and be loved by him in turn; *Nicias*, a sacred scion of the Graces of lovely voice; and may present thee, that wast wrought of much worked ivory, to the hands of the wife of Nicias, as a gift. With her you will finish off much work for men's robes, and many [5] gauze-like garments, such as women wear. For twice in the same year will the mothers of lambs yield their soft fleeces to be shorn in the pastures, even for the sake of Theugenis of the beautiful ancle. So industrious

---

[1] Idyll xv. 80, ποῖαί σφ' ἐπόνασαν ἔριθοι; Pierson in Mœr. Atticist. says that συνέριθος and φιλέριθος are used in much the same senses. συνέριθος, Leonid. Epigr. cxxiii. 3.

[2] Νείλεω. Neleus, son of Codrus, leaving Athens, went to Ionia, and built or restored Miletus, Ælian V. H. viii. 5. The εἰ in Νείλεω must be considered a peculiarity of Dialect. Wesseling defends it at Herodot. ix. 97.

[3] Athenæus, b. 13, p. 372, Τὴν ἐν Σάμῳ Ἀφροδίτην, ἥν οἵ μὲν ἐν καλάμοις καλοῦσιν. "Yon deep bed of whispering reeds."

[4] Futures middle for passive. See Matt. Gr. Gr. § 496, 8.

[5] ὑδάτινα = Thalassina, fine gauzy Milesian textures. See Ovid. Art. A. iii. 177, Hic undas imitatus habet quoque nomen ab undis,
 Crediderim nymphas huc ego veste tegi.
Virg. Georg. iii. 316, Quamvis Milesia magno
 Vellera mutentur Tyrios incocta rubores.

is she, and loves all that ⁶discreet *women love*. Now, I should not wish to present thee, as thou art from our land, to slack and idle houses. ⁷For thy country is that which ⁸Archias from Ephyre founded of old, the richest part of the island, Trinacria, a city of men in repute. Now indeed, keeping the house of a man who has learnt many saving medicines to ward off from men grievous diseases, you will dwell in lovely Miletus, among Ionians; that among townsfolk Theugenis may have a good distaff, and you may ever and anon put her in mind of a friend who loves the song. For looking at you, one shall say this to another: 'Sure there is great grace with a trifling gift: and all the gifts from friends are precious.'

IDYLL XXIX.

LOVES.

ARGUMENT.

In the Idyll, which is of the lyric character, our poet blames the inconstancy and fickleness of a beautiful youth, and urges him to con-

---

⁶ Penelope, Helen, (Hom. Odyss. iv. 130,) Lucretia were all industrious workers in wools. Polwhele here quotes Epitaph. Spon. Miscell. Antiq. Erudit. p. 151,
> HIC . SITA . EST . AMYMONE.
> MARCI . OPTIMA . ET . PULCHER
> RIMA . LANIFICA . PIA . PUDICA.
> FRUGI . CASTA . DOMISEDA.

St. Paul, Ep. to Tit. ii. 5, σώφρονας, ἁγνας οἰκούρους.

⁷ ἀκιρῶς. According to Liddell and Scott, Lex., this is the same as ἀκιδνος, weak, faint, &c. It is only found here, and as a various reading, Hesiod, O. et D. 233.—ἰβολλόμαν, the earliest form of ἰβουλόμην.

⁸ Corinth, or Ephyre, was the mother country of Syracuse, which was founded by Archias. See Idyll xv. 91, xvi. 83, and notes there.—μυελόν, medullam, the marrow, i. e. the richest land. Callim. H. to Del. 48, μαστὸν παρθενίης. Virg. Æn. iii.,
> Quæ vos a stirpe parentum
> Prima tulit tellus, eadem vos *ubere læto*
> Accipiet reduces.

Varro de R. R. I. vii. 10, Cæsar—campos Roseæ Italiæ dixit esse *sumen*.

sult his good name by better faith in future. The metre is Æolic.
ξ ⏑ – ⏑ ⏑ – ⏑ ⏑ – ⏑ ⏑ – ⏑. See Hermann, Element. Doctr. Metr. p. 360, seq.

¹ 'WINE,' dear youth, 'and truth,' is the saying; and we must be true *as* drunkards. And I indeed will tell what lies in the depths of my heart. You choose not to love me with your whole soul, I know it: ²for the half of life, which I have, lives *in* thy beauteous form, and the rest has perished. And whensoever you choose, I pass a day like the gods; but when you choose not, *I am* wholly in gloom. How is this seemly, ³to consign him that loves thee to cares? Nay, if you would be persuaded at all by me, the younger by the elder, then you yourself would be better circumstanced, and commend me for it; build one nest in one tree, where no savage reptile shall reach. But now you occupy one branch to-day, and another to-morrow; and you seek one after another. And suppose any one shall have seen and praised ⁴your fair face, to him then you straightway become a friend of more than three years' date; whilst you place your first admirer in the third rank. You seem to savour of arrogant men. Nay, prefer, as long as you live, to have always one like *yourself*. For if you thus do, you will be well-reported of by the citizens; and Love would not be troublesome to you, *Love*, who easily subdues the minds of men, and hath wrought me into softness from being iron-hearted. But *be this as it may*, ⁵I approach thee closely by thy tender lip.

⁶Remember that last year thou wast younger, and that we

¹ "In vino veritas," Erasmus. Cf. Horat. Od. I. xviii.
² Horat. Od. II. xvii. 5,
　　　　Ah! te meæ si partem animæ rapit
　　　　Maturior vis, quid moror altera;
　　　　Nec carus æque nec superstes
　　　　Integer?
³ διδῶν, Doric for διδόναι, or διδοῦν.
⁴ ῥέθος, a face, Soph. Antig. 529. Cf. Idyll xxvi. 1.
⁵ πεδέρχομαι for μετέρχομαι: so in line 37, πέδα for μέτα. Æschylus has several such Doricisms or Æolicisms, see Prom. Vinct. 269, Choeph. 589, 590, &c.
⁶ Hermann ad Viger. p. 926, pronounces μέμνασο to be the true substitute for the hopelessly corrupt reading ὀμνάσθην, which none can render. Wordsworth suggests a much slighter alteration, ἀμνασθῆν, the Æolic 1st aorist infinitive for ἀναμνησθῆναι, as μεθυσθῆν for μεθυσθῆναι in Alcæus Mus. Crit. i. 425; Fragm. 3. He suggests likewise that ὅτι γηραλέοι πέλομες, depends not on ὀμνασθῆν, but ἀποπτύσαι. i. e. Re-

are old, before you spurn us, and wrinkled; and to have youth recalled is impossible; for it hath wings on its shoulders. and we are [7]too slow to catch the flitting *runaways*. Considering this, you must [8]be more agreeable, and return my love, who love you without guile, that so, when you get your mannish chin, we may be to each other fast friends like Achilles. But if you commit these *words* to the winds to bear away, and say in your heart, 'Good fellow, why do you trouble me?' now let me go for love of thee, even after the golden apples, and in quest of Cerberus, guardian of the dead; but then, not even though you called me, would I come forth at the hall-doors, having ceased from violent love.

IDYLL XXX.

THE DEATH OF ADONIS.

ARGUMENT.

When Venus, on the death of Adonis, had bidden a boar, the author of the crime, be brought before her, the animal tries to excuse his sin, by pleading, that he had been smitten by love of the beauteous youth, and had therefore longed to kiss his limbs. Then he surrenders himself to Venus, that she may inflict upon him the penalty due to his guilt. The goddess, taking pity, orders him to go free. In consequence of which, the boar thenceforth voluntarily attends Venus.

The argument, no less than metre, of this Idyll prove it Anacreontic: but though Warton deems it the work of Anacreon, or an imitator, it seems to have had a place among the Idylls of Theocritus, from the very oldest edition. Porson says of it, ad Aristoph. Lysistr. 1246, "Idyllium Theocriti falsò inscriptum." The metre runs $\cup\_\cup\_\cup\_\cup\_\cup\_$. Herm. Elem. Doctr. Metr. p. 475.

WHEN Cytherea beheld Adonis already dead, with locks unkempt, and his cheek pale, she bade the Loves bring the

---

member that last year you were younger, before you spurn me, because I am old and wrinkled. For a parallel on the whole passage, (26—30,) see Horace's beautiful Ode to Ligurinus, lib. IV. x.

[7] βαρδύτεροι. Cf. Idyll xv. 104.

[8] ποτιμώτερον, a metaphor from mellow and mild wines.

wild boar before her. And they forthwith on wings, [1] having traversed all the wood, found out the [2] hateful boar, and bound him once and again. And one, having tied him with a rope, was dragging on his captive; while another, driving him in the rear, kept striking him with his arrows. Now the beast was advancing timidly, for he was afraid of Cytherea. Then Aphrodité said to him, 'Thou worst of all wild beasts, didst thou wound this thigh? Hast thou stricken [3] my lover?' But the beast answered thus, 'I swear to thee, Cytherea, by thyself and thy lover, and these my bonds, and these my hunters, I did not wish to wound thy beauteous lover! but I gazed on him [4] as though *I had been* a statue, and not being able to endure my warmth, I was mad to kiss the limb which he had bare; and *then* [5] my tooth hurt him. Take these, O Venus, *and* punish them, wrench out (for why do I carry them beyond the due number?) these passionate teeth. But if these do not satisfy thee, *then take* these my lips also; for why did they dare to kiss?'

But Venus pitied him, and bade the Loves to loose his bonds. Thenceforth he was wont to attend her, and would not go to the woods; [6] and having approached the fire, kept burning his loves.

[1] For this transitive use of an intransitive verb, compare Virg. Æn. iii. 191, Vastumque cavâ trabe currimus æquor.

[2] στυγνὸν τὸν ὗν ἀνεῦρον, must mean " Found the boar sad," as J. W. shows by reference to Æsch. Agam. 625, &c. It cannot have the same force as τὸν στυγνὸν ὗν ἀνεῦρον. Wordsworth suggests στυγνοί, i. e. " Sadly found out the boar."

[3] ὁ ἀνήρ, is "amator," just as " vir " is used by Terence Andria III. i. 2, Fidelem haud fermè mulieri invenias virum: and Hecyra, I. i. 2.

[4] ἄγαλμα might be referred to Adonis as an accusative, or as a nominative to the boar, which is much the most agreeable to the sense of the passage.

[5] κραντήρ, the wisdom teeth were so called. In Latin, "genuini." They are those teeth which come last and complete the set, from κραίνω. Shakspeare, in his Venus and Adonis, makes the same excuse for the boar.

[6] Bindemann, whom Kiessling approves, takes this passage to mean that the boar, approaching the funeral pile of Adonis, thrust himself upon it, and so made an end of his love. Scaliger would read ἔκλαιε, kept lamenting his wretched love. May not the fire be that of Venus ever present, and the boar's constant attendance the means of keeping up his warmth of love? I see Chapman inclines to this idea, explaining it, "He became one of Aphrodité's train, and his contemplation of the charms of Beauty might burn out his recollection of beauty's paramour."

A FRAGMENT FROM THE BERENICE.

This fragment from the Berenice, as it is inscribed, is given by Athenæus vii. 284, A. Casaub., and mentioned by Eustathius ad Hom. Iliad v., ἱερὸν ἰχθύν, p. 1067, 41. Berenice, called θίος in verse 3, is the Queen of Egypt, wife of Ptolemy Lagidas, who was divinely honoured by her son Ptolemy Philadelphus, (Idyll xv. 106—108, xvii. 34, &c.,) and was supposed to vouchsafe most benignantly all the blessings of plenty.

AND if a man asks good sport and wealth for himself, [1] whose subsistence is from the sea, and his nets are his ploughs, then let him slay [2] at nightfall to this goddess a sacred fish, which men call 'white,' for it is the sleekest of all others; and *then* he will set his nets, and draw them up out of the sea full.

[1] Compare Theocr. Idyll vii. 60, ὅσαισί περ ἐξ ἁλὸς ἄγρα.
[2] ἀκρόνυχος. Reiske has confounded this with ἀκρώνυχος, or ἀκρώνυξ —summis unguibus. The Scholiast rightly explains it ἑσπερινός, Nicand. Theriac. 762. Compare Ajax, Sophocl. 283, and Lobeck's note on the words ἄκρας νυκτός.
[3] φιαρός is used, Theocr. xi. 21, of Galatea, q. v.

EPIGRAMS

OF

THEOCRITUS THE SYRACUSAN.

I.

THESE [1] dewy roses and yon thick [2] creeping-thyme are dedicated to the Heliconian *Muses*. And the dark-leaved bays to thee, O Pythian Pæan : for the [3] Delphic rock hath given thee this for an ornament. And this [4] white he-goat with the horns, browsing the extremity of a branch of the turpentine tree, shall stain *thy* altar.

II.

[5] DAPHNIS the fair-complexioned, that did modulate pastoral hymns with beautiful pipe, dedicated to Pan these *gifts;* his reed-pipe with stops, his shepherd's crook, his sharp dart, his fawn's skin, *and* [6] the wallet, in which he once used to carry apples.

[1] Roses were sacred to the Muses, Anacreon, Ode 53. Sappho, Fragm. 2. Polwhele.

[2] ἕρπυλλος. Virg. Ecl. ii. 11, Allia, serpyllumque, herbas contundit olentes. Georg. iv. 31.

[3] Δελφὶς πέτρα. (See Soph. Œd. Tyr. 463. Eurip. Androm. 998.)

[4] ὁ μαλός, white. Hesych. Others, (as if it were μαλλὸς,) shaggy. We have translated ἀγλάϊσε as if transitive, with Brunck. Kiessling renders it, " Delphica petra hoc decore nituit."

[5] Daphnis, in this Epigram, dedicates to Pan his pipe, his crook, and dart, in token of bidding adieu to music, hunting, and love.

[6] An allusion to the custom of lovers, to carry apples to their mistresses. Compare Idyll ii. 120 ; iii. 10 ; xi. 10. Kiessl. Compare also Virg. Ecl. iii. 70.

III.

DAPHNIS, you sleep on leaf-strown ground, [1] resting your wearied body; and the [2] poles are fresh fastened along the mountains. But Pan is in chase of you, and [3] Priapus, who has saffron-berried ivy bound about his lovely head, advancing to the interior of the cave with one bound. But do you take flight, fly, having [4] shaken off the lethargy of sleep, *that is* stealing over you.

IV.

[5] WHEN you have turned down yon lane, goatherd, where the oaks *are*, you will find [6] a fresh-carved image of fig-wood, [7] with three legs, with the bark on, and without handles, but with creative phallus able to accomplish works of Venus: and an enclosure duly sacred surrounds it, and an ever-runing stream from the hollow rocks luxuriates on all sides in laurels and myrtles, and fragrant cypress: where the grape-begetting vine sheds itself around with its tendrils, and ver-

---

[1] Compare Idyll i. 16, 17.

[2] στάλικες, the poles on which hunters fastened their nets. Daphnis, weary of hunting, had ceased from snaring wild beasts, when, lo! he falls himself into the snare of Pan and Priapus. The poet works upon the ground of Pan's love for Daphnis.

[3] See Tibull. I. iv. 1,

> Sic umbrosa tibi contingant tecta, Priape,
> Ne capiti soles, ne noceantve nives.

Catull. xix. 10,

> Florido mihi ponitur picta vere corolla
> Primitu', et tenerâ virens spica mollis aristâ.

[4] ὕπνου κῶμα, a lethargic sleep. For a like construction, see Virg. Georg. i. 134, Frumenti herba. Ecl. v. 26, Graminis herbam. Soph. Trach. 20, εἰς ἀγῶνα μάχης. It is difficult to decide between the various readings suggested in place of καταγρόμενον. Wordsworth approves of κατειβόμενον, " pouring down," which is not unlikely to be right, as in the MSS. ᾱγ and ει are written with the same mark over them.

[5] A shepherd describes a statue of Priapus, and the fair spot where it stands dedicated to the god: and at the same time he vows an ample sacrifice to him, if he will free him from love of Daphnis, with whom he is smitten. Failing this, he would fain have his love returned, and in this case he promises three victims to the god.

[6] Horat. Serm. I. viii. 1, Olim truncus eram ficulnus, inutile lignum.

[7] Since Priapus is generally represented as standing on one foot, or a stake rather, Jacobs proposes to read ἀσκελές.

nal blackbirds, with sweet-voiced songs, chaunt various-noted melodies: yellow nightingales respond with their plaints, warbling with their throats the sounds of music. Prythee, take your seat there, and supplicate the graceful Priapus, that I may discourage the loves of Daphnis: and *say* that I will straightway sacrifice a fine he-goat: but if he shall have refused, I am willing, *after* having succeeded in this, to pay three victims. [1] For I will offer a heifer, a shaggy he-goat, and a lamb which I am keeping in the stall: and may the god hear propitiously.

V.

ARE you willing, *I ask you* by the Nymphs, to sing me some sweet *trifle* on the [2] double flutes? And I will take up [3] a harp, and begin to strike it somewhat: and the cowherd Daphnis shall charm us at the same time, singing to the breathing [4] of a wax-bound pipe. Then standing near a leafy oak, behind the cave, would we rob of sleep [5] the goat-footed Pan.

VI.

AH! thou wretched Thyrsis, what boots it thee, if thou waste with tears thy two eyes in lamentation! The young she-goat [6] is gone, the pretty kid is gone to the shades; for a ruthless wolf crushed her with his talons. And [7] the dogs

---

[1] ῥέξω. So Virgil Ecl. iii. 77, Cum *faciam* vitulâ pro frugibus, ipse venito. Σακίταν. See Idyll i. 10.

[2] "Sometimes one person played two flutes (αὐλοὶ) at once. See a painting from Pompeii, and Dict. Gr. and Rom. Antiq. v. tibia." Liddell and Scott, Lexicon.

[3] "A harp." πακτίδ', from πήγνυμι. It appears to have been an ancient kind of harp with twenty strings. Sophocl. Fragm. 227, uses the word.

[4] "καροδίτῳ πνεύματι, i. e. δόνακι κηροπλάστῳ: fistulâ." Briggs.

[5] Αἰγιβάταν, capripedem, a dubious reading is αἰγιβόταν, a goatherd. Jacobs remarks, from a comparison of this passage with Idyll i. 15, that shepherds and cowherds had less reverence for Pan than the goatherds, whose tutelary god he was.

[6] οἴχεται is a 'vox solennis' of the dead common in pastoral and other poets.

[7] Briggs observes, "It was late for the dogs to bark, when the kid was devoured."

then give tongue. What boots it, when, gone as she is, nor a bone nor ash is left of her?

VII.

UPON A STATUE OF ÆSCULAPIUS.[1]

THE son of Pæan came even to Miletus, [2]to dwell along with a man that heals diseases, Nicias *by name:* [3]who ever day by day approaches him with sacrifices, and has had this statue carved out of [4]fragrant cedar, having promised the highest price to Eetion, because of his skilful hand; and he has thrown all his art into the work.

VIII.

THE EPITAPH OF ORTHON.

STRANGER, Orthon, a man of Syracuse, gives thee this charge: Walk no where, in your cups, of a wintry night. For such is the fate, which I have met: and [5]instead of my ample father land, I lie having wrapped myself in foreign soil.

IX.

GOOD man, [6]be careful of your life, nor be a voyager out

---

[1] This is an Epigram on a statue of Æsculapius by the hand of Eetion, set up by Nicias the physician of Miletus, concerning whom see Idylls xi., xiii., xxviii.

[2] συμφέρομαι is used elsewhere in this sense. Philoct. Sophocl. 1084, ἀλλ' ἐμοὶ καὶ θνῄσκοντι συνοίσει.

[3] ἐπ' ἆμαρ ἀεί, "Quotidie." So Soph. Œd. Col. 682, κατ' ἦμαρ αἰεί. ἱκνεῖσθαι for ἱκετεύειν frequently occurs, as here, in Sophocles.

[4] Fragrant cedar,] often used for these purposes. See Virg. Æn. vii. 177, where in the palace of Picus are to be seen,
   Veterum effigies ex ordine avorum
      Antiquâ e cedro.

[5] Warton remarks that the ancients held it a misfortune, if a man was buried under only a little earth. γῆν ἐπιέσσασθαι, to shroud oneself in, or be buried in, earth. Pindar, Nem. ii. 21. Xenoph. Cyrop. vi., where Panthea assures Abradates that she would prefer, with him, κοινῇ γῆν ἐπιέσασθαι, μᾶλλον ἢ ζῆν μετ' αἰσχυνομένου αἰσχυνομένη. For ἀντὶ δὲ πολλᾶς, Wordsworth suggests ἀντὶ φίλης δὲ.

[6] The four last lines of this Epigram were introduced into the text

of season: since life is not long to a man. Wretched Cleonicus, you, on the other hand, were in haste to go *as* a merchant from [1] Cœlesyria to fruitful [2] Thasos. *Ay*, a merchant, O Cleonicus; but crossing ocean just about the [3] very setting of the Pleiad, you went down along with the Pleiad.

X.

UPON A STATUE OF THE MUSES.

To you, goddesses, Xenocles dedicated this marble statue, in gratitude [4] to Nine altogether: a musician, no one will say otherwise, and enjoying repute on the score of this talent, he is not forgetful of the Muses.

XI.

AN EPITAPH ON EUSTHENES THE PHYSIOGNOMIST.

This monument is of Eusthenes: *he was* the philosopher [5] who judged men by their features; being clever at learning even the mind from the eye. Worthily have his friends buried him, though a foreigner, in a foreign *land:* [6] and to

---

by Grævius, from a very ancient Palatine codex. To illustrate the Epigram, see Hesiod, O. et D. 616.

[1] κοίλης Συρίης, Cœlesyria, so called from its lying as it were in a valley between Libanus and Antilibanus. It is here that the Oròntes (Pharphar) rose.

[2] Thasos, an isle in the Ægean Sea, very fertile. Dionys. 523, ὠγυγίη τε Θάσος, Δημήτερος ἀκτή.

[3] Setting of the Pleiad.] Compare Callimach. (Ernesti) Epigr. xix.
φεῦγε θαλάττῃ
Συμμίσγειν ἐρίφων, ναυτίλε, δυομένων.
Where, however, Blomfield and others remark, that, according to Ptolemy and Horace, there was danger in sailing in the season "Orientis hædi."

[4] ἐννέα πάσαις, nine in all. This is a common signification of πᾶς. Mosch. i. 6, ἐν εἴκοσι πᾶσι μάθοις νιν. Callim. in Dian. 105, πέντ' ἔσαν αἱ πᾶσαι. A Latin poet, Gratius Faliscus, author of a poem on the chase, has a parallel usage of " omnes."
    Accessere tuo centum sub nomine Divæ
    Centum *omnes* nemorum, centum de fontibus *omnes*
    Naiades.

[5] What the ancients meant by φυσιογνώμων appears in Aristot. Prior Analyt. ii. 28.

[6] χυμνοθέτης. We have translated the reading of D. Heinsius and

lyric poets he was wondrously dear. The philosopher in death hath all it was fitting he should have; even though he was[1] powerless, I wot he found friends-to-care-for-him.

XII.

UPON A TRIPOD DEDICATED TO BACCHUS BY DEMOTELES.

DEMOTELES, [2]the leader of the choir, who set up the tripod, O Dionysus, and [3]thee the sweetest of gods, was pretty-[4]well-in-merit among boys; but in the choir of men he gained victory, seeing both the beautiful and the becoming.

XIII.

UPON AN IMAGE OF THE HEAVENLY APHRODITE.

[5] OUR Venus *is* not the vulgar: propitiate the goddess by having called her 'heavenly,' the offering of chaste Chrysogona in the house of Amphicles, with whom she had both children and life in common; and ever it was better to them [6]from year to year, [7]as they began with thee, O divine lady; for if they care for the immortals, mortals find advantage *in it* themselves.

Toup. But the majority of editors consider the passage corrupt. Three MSS. read αὑτῆς, and for δαιμονίως φίλος ἦν ΑΛΙΜΩΝ ΩΣ, against sense and metre, Wordsworth proposes a very desirable emendation grounded upon this, i. e. ΩιΔΙΜΟΝ, i. q. ἀοίδιμον, ὡς φίλος ἦς. If we accept this, the meaning of the passage will be, they buried him, a stranger, in a foreign land; and *as one* worthy to be sung of by its (ξείνης) minstrels, how dear he was to them.
[1] For ἄκικυς, Heinsius reads ἄοικος—κηδεμόνας. The poet says that Eusthenes had neither wife, children, nor relations, yet his worth and genius found him friends to mourn and bury him.
[2] ὁ χορηγός, not the provider of the chorus, whose office every reader of the Greek theatre, and of the Midias of Demosthenes, knows; but the choir-leader, as is seen by verses 3 and 4.
[3] σέ, that is, thy statue.
[4] μέτριος ἦν, " modicam laudem adeptus est."—χορῷ—'Ανδρῶν. See Idyll xvii. 112.
[5] Plato, in his Symposium, says there were two Venuses; one, the daughter of Cœlus, who is called Οὐρανία, Urania: the other, the daughter of Jupiter and Dione, who is known as Πάνδημος, or popular.
[6] εἰς ἔτος. Understand ἐξ ἔτεος. Comp. Idyll xviii. 15.
[7] ἐκ σέθεν ἀρχομένοις. "A te omnia auspicantes inde felicitatis fructum retulerunt." Briggs.

XIV.

AN EPITAPH OF EURYMEDON.

You left an infant son; and yourself too in life's prime, Eurymedon, found a tomb here, in death. For you indeed there is [1]a seat amid godlike men; but him citizens will honour, remembering his sire as worthy.

XV.

UPON THE SAME.

Traveller, I shall know, whether you pay any more *honour* to the good, *than the bad,* or if even the coward gets likewise an equal share from you. You will say [2] Hail to this tomb, for it lies light upon the sacred head of Eurymedon.

XVI.

UPON A STATUE OF ANACREON.

Stranger, regard this statue [3]carefully, and say, when you have returned home, [4]'In Teos, I saw a likeness of Anacreon, [5] pre-eminent, if ever man was, among bards of old.' And by having added also, that he delighted in the young, you will truthfully describe the whole man.

XVII.

UPON EPICHARMUS.

Both the inscription is Doric, and the man, he who in-

---

[1] ἕδρα, "statio." Compare Callim. H. in Del. 233, and Spanheim and Ernesti thereupon. κείνη δ' οὐδέποτε σφετέρης ἐπιλήθεται ἕδρης.

[2] χαιρέτω, i. e. if you are favourable to the good, you will say, "Hail to this tomb," &c.

[3] σπουδᾷ, attento animo. Briggs.

[4] Teos, a city near Colophon, the birth-place of Anacreon and Erinna. Horat. Epod. xiv. 10, Anacreonta Teium. Od. I. xvii. 18, Et fide Teiâ Dices, &c.

[5] τῶν πρόσθ' εἴ τι περισσόν. Understand ὄντος περισσοῦ. Compare Idyll vii. 4, and notes there. Apollon. Rhod. iii. 347, Παναχαιίδος εἴ τι φέριστον ἡρώων.

vented comedy, [1]Epicharmus. O Bacchus, to thee[2] the Pelorians, who are settled in the city of Syracuse, set him up here in brass instead of in his true nature, inasmuch as they are mindful to pay the price of his labours to a *fellow* citizen, [3]for he had abundance of wealth; for many saws useful for life *and conduct* taught he to their children. Great gratitude *is due* to him.

XVIII.

THE EPITAPH OF CLEITA, NURSE OF MEDEIUS.

THE little Medeius raised this monument by the way-side to his [4]Thracian nurse, and inscribed it 'Of Cleita.' The woman will enjoy his thanks in requital for her having reared the boy. Why not? [5]She has yet *another* name, Useful.

---

[1] Epicharmus, though born at Cos, was carried, when three months old, to Megara, about B. C. 540. From about B. C. 484 to his life's end he dwelt at Syracuse. He was the great comic poet of the Dorians.

[2] ἐνίδρυνται Πελωρεῖς τᾷ πόλει. Reiske asks with reason what had the Pelorians, dwellers about the promontory of Pelorum, to do with Syracuse. Tyrwhitt and Jacobs read for Πελωρεῖς τᾷ—πεδωριστᾷ πόλει, excelsâ urbe — but Syracuse is low. Wordsworth proposes to read πεδοικισταί, coloni, inquilini, Doric for μετοικισταί, just as we have πέδα for μέτα in Idyll xxix. 25—38, and very frequently in Æschylus πεδάορος, πεδάρσιος, &c. (See Blomf. in Gloss. Prom. v. 277, 735, 952.) The Syracusans, it will be remembered, were a Corinthian colony, and ἐνίδρυνται is properly used of colonists. This suggestion, therefore, is especially to the purpose. In his addenda, Wordsworth prefers πεδοικιστᾷ to agree with πόλει.

[3] A curious reason for honouring him. To clear the Syracusans of such a charge, some editors have read ῥημάτων, for χρημάτων, but "a heap of words" is no stronger ground for a statue of him at the people's expense than a heap of gold. Wordsworth has probably come very near the truth, when he suggests,

ξῶρον παρεῖχε, χρὴ μὲν ὧν μεμναμένους
τελεῖν ἐπίχειρα.

Donum nobis dedit, (see 9, 10,) oportet igitur nos ejus benè memores eum remunerari.

[4] Thracian nurses seem to have been in esteem. See Idyll ii. 70. Callimachus has an Epigram somewhat similar to this.

[5] ἔτι χρησίμη καλεῖται — If we read the words as they stand, the Epitaph turns on the nurse's name, Cleita, (famous,) and her surname, given for her useful qualities, χρησίμη. But some MSS. read τελευτᾷ for καλεῖται, and Wordsworth suggests that the passage should be read τί μὰν; ἔτι χρήσιμ' οὐ τελευτᾷ. Quidni ita faceret? Nam ipsa

XIX.

UPON ARCHILOCHUS.

STAND and behold the ancient poet, [1] Archilochus, him of the Iambics, whose [2] infinite renown has reached both to the west and to the east. Of a truth, I ween, the Muses and Delian Apollo were wont to love him: so melodious was he, and skilful both in making Iambics and singing to his lyre.

XX.

UPON A STATUE OF PISANDER, WHO COMPOSED "THE LABOURS OF HERCULES."

FOR you this man, [3] Pisander from Camirus, first of the former poets, wrote the exploits of Jove's son, the lion-subduer, the quick-of-hand; and declared how many labours he had accomplished. And this very man, that you may duly know it, the people set up here, having made him of brass, [4] many months and years afterwards.

XXI.

UPON HIPPONAX, THE POET.

HERE lies [5] Hipponax the poet. If thou art worthless,

quidem periit, sed ejus officia adhuc utilia, (her rearing of the boy,) non perierunt. Though the nurse is dead, her care of him keeps her memory alive. Wordsworth suggests also χρησίμ᾽ οὐκ ὀλεῖται — Utilia non peribunt.

[1] Archilochus of Paros, one of the first Ionian lyric poets, and the first Greek poet who composed Iambics on fixed rules. He flourished 714—676 B. C. The biting character of his Iambics is marked by Horace A. P. 79, Archilochum proprio rabies armavit Iambo.

[2] μυρίον. Infinite. So in Idyll viii. 50, ὦ βάθος ὕλας Μυρίον.

[3] Pisander, a poet of Camirus in Rhodes, who flourished about B. C. 648—605, was author of a poem, in two books, on "The Labours of Hercules." Vid. Müller's History of Greek Lit. ix. § 3.

[4] Theocritus publishes the fact, that the inhabitants of Camirus neglected the memory of their bard until long after his death.

[5] Hipponax of Ephesus was the third Iambic poet of Greece, after Archilochus and Simonides. His date B. C. 546. Horace, Epod. vi. 14, "Aut acer hostis Bupalo," alluding to the savage Iambics which he launched at Bupalus and Anthermus, brothers and statuaries of Ephesus, who had made his image ridiculous. They were driven by his satires to hang themselves.

come not nigh his tomb; but if thou art both [1]good, and come of good *stock*, sit down boldly, and sleep, if thou wilt.

XXII.

AN EPIGRAM OF THEOCRITUS UPON HIS OWN BOOK.

[2]The Chian *Theocritus* is another; but I, Theocritus who wrote these *Idylls*, am a Syracusan, one of the commonalty, [3]son to Praxagoras and well-known Philina, and I have never [4]claimed to myself another's muse.

XXIII.

This bank allows the same to strangers as to citizens. Deposit *your money*, and take it up again, [5]a calculation being duly made. Let some one else make excuses; but [6]Caicus tells back the monies of others, even by night if they wish it.

XXIV.

[7]The inscription will declare what is the tomb, and who under it: I am the grave of her that was called Glaucè.

---

[1] κρήγυός. Vid. xx. 19, and Hom. Il. i. 106.
[2] The Chian namesake of our poet was an orator and sophist, and perhaps historian of the time of Alexander the Great. This Epigram is probably the work of some grammarian who wished to mark the difference between the two persons. See Smith's Dict. Gr. Rom. Biog. vol. iii. pp. 1031, 1032.
[3] Some have supposed, from Theocritus seeming to represent himself under the character of Simichidas, or son of Simichus, Idyll vii. 21, that he was son of Simichus: but it seems better to consider that he used that name as an assumed one, just as Virgil does Tityrus. And indeed this Epigram seems to establish his parentage.
[4] "Alienæ laudis appetens nunquam fui." Briggs. "I never flirted with another's muse." Chapman.
[5] ψήφου. The ancients used pebbles and counters in casting up accounts. ψήφου πρὸς λόγον ἐρχομένης, is in Latin "rationibus rectè subductis."
[6] Caicus is of course the manager of the bank, which never fears a run upon it.
[7] This Epigram (Anthol. Pal. vii. 262,) is printed among those of Theocritus only in Wordsworth's edition. He is led to print it there by the reasons given for ascribing it to Theocritus in the Anthologia Palat.

THE IDYLLS
OF
BION THE SMYRNÆAN.

IDYLL I.

THE EPITAPH OF ADONIS.

I WAIL for Adonis; beauteous Adonis is dead. 'Dead is beauteous Adonis;' the Loves join in the wail. Sleep no more, Venus, in purple vestments; rise, wretched *goddess*, in thy robes of woe, [1] and beat thy bosom, and say to all, 'Beauteous Adonis hath perished.' I wail for Adonis: the Loves join in the wail. Low lies beauteous Adonis on the mountains, having his white thigh smitten by a tusk, a white tusk, and he inflicts pain on Venus, as he breathes out his life faintly; but adown his white skin trickles the black blood; and his eyes are glazed neath the lids, and the rose flies from his lip; and round about it dies also the kiss, which Venus will never relinquish. To Venus, indeed, his kiss, even though he lives not, is pleasant, yet Adonis knew not that she kissed him as he died.

I wail for Adonis: the Loves wail in concert. A cruel, cruel wound hath Adonis in his thigh, [2] but a greater wound doth Cytherea bear at her heart. Around that youth [3] indeed

---

[1] And beat thy bosom.] See Ovid Met. x. 720,
   Utque æthere vidit ab alto
   Exanimem, inque suo jactantem sanguine corpus
   Desiluit, pariterque sinus, pariterque capillos
   Rupit et indignis percussit pectora palmis.

[2] φέρει ποτικάρδιον ἕλκος. Ov. Met. v. 426,
   Inconsolabile vulnus Mente gerit tacitâ.

[3] Faithful hounds whined.] Senec. Hippolyt. 1108,
   Mæstœque domini membra vestigant canes.
Ossian, "His dogs are howling in their place."

faithful hounds whined, and Oread Nymphs weep; but Aphrodité, having let fall her braided hair, wanders up and down the glades, sad, unkempt, ⁴unsandaled, and the brambles tear her as she goes, and ⁵cull her sacred blood: then wailing piercingly she is borne through long valleys, crying for her ⁶Assyrian spouse, and calling on her youth. But around him dark blood was gushing up about his navel, and his breasts were empurpled from his thighs, and to Adonis the parts beneath his breasts, white before, became *now* deep-red. Alas, alas for Cytherea, the Loves join in the wail. She hath lost her beauteous spouse, she hath lost with *him* her divine beauty. Fair beauty had Venus, when Adonis was living; but with Adonis perished the fair form of Venus, alas, alas! All mountains, and the oaks say, 'Alas for Adonis.' ⁷And rivers sorrow for the woes of Aphrodité, and springs on the mountains weep for her Adonis, and ⁸flowers redden from grief; whilst Cytherea sings mournfully along all ⁹woody-mountain-passes, and along cities. Alas, alas for Cytherea, beauteous Adonis hath perished. And Echo cried in response, 'Beauteous Adonis hath perished.' ¹⁰Who would not have lamented the dire love of Venus? alas! alas! When she saw, when she perceived the wound of Adonis, which none might stay, when she saw gory blood about his wan thigh, unfolding wide her arms, she sadly cried, 'Stay, ill-fated Adonis, Adonis, stay: that I may find thee for the last time, that I may enfold thee around, and mingle kisses with kisses. Rouse thee a little, Adonis, and again this last time

⁴ ἀσάνδαλος, unsandaled, betokening haste or severe distress. See Theocr. Id. xxiv. 36.
⁵ Cull her sacred blood.] See for the same bold metaphor, Æsch. S. c. Theb. 718, ἀλλ' αὐτάδελφον αἷμα δρέψασθαι θέλεις. Virgil Æn. xi. 804,
    Hasta sub exsertam donec perlata papillam
    Hæsit, virgineumque altè bibit acta cruorem.
⁶ Assyrian spouse.] Adonis was son of Cinyras and Myrrha. Cinyras is variously called king of Cyprus, Arabia, and Assyria.
⁷ Rivers sorrow.] Compare Mosch. iii. 2 and 28.
⁸ And flowers redden.] Cf. Theocr. xx. 16, καὶ χρέα φοινίχθην ὑπὸ τῶλγεος, ὡς ῥόδον ἔρσα. Briggs reads for πτόλιν, νάπος from the Aldine Edit.
⁹ κνημός is used in Homer Il. for the woody passes of Ida. πούς, the base of the mountain. κνημός, from κνήμη, (the leg between ancle and knee,) the part just above the base.
¹⁰ Milton's Lycidas. Who would not sing for Lycidas, &c.

kiss me: kiss me just so far as there is life in thy kiss, [11]till
from thy heart thy spirit shall have ebbed into my lips and
soul, and I shall have drained thy sweet love-potion, and
[12]have drunk out thy love: and I will treasure this kiss, even
as *if it were* Adonis himself, since thou, ill-fated one, dost flee
from me. Thou flyest afar, O Adonis, [13] and comest unto
Acheron, and its gloomy and cruel king; but wretched I
live, and [14] am a goddess, and cannot follow thee. Take,
Proserpine, my spouse: for thou art thyself far more power-
ful than I, [15] and the whole of *what is* beautiful falls to thy
share; yet I am all-hapless, and feel insatiate grief, and
mourn for Adonis, since to my sorrow he is dead, and I am
afraid of thee. Art thou dying, O thrice-regretted? [16] Then
my longing is fled as a dream; and widowed is Cytherea,
and idle are the Loves along my halls: and with thee has my
charmed-girdle been undone; nay, why, rash one, didst thou
hunt? Beauteous as thou wert, wast thou mad enough to
contend with wild beasts?' Thus lamented Venus; the
Loves join in the wail. Alas, alas for Cytherea, beauteous

[11] The last kiss was wont to be given to the dearest one, when "in articulo mortis;" and it was a fancy of old, that the survivor drew in, with the last breath of the dying, their passing life. Virg. Æn. iv. 684, Extremus si quis super halitus errat, Ore legam. Seneca, Herc. Oct. 1339, Spiritus fugiens meo Legatur ore. Cicero, Ut extremum filiorum spiritum ore excipere liceret.

[12] ἐκ δὲ πίω τὸν ἔρωτα. Virg. Æn. iv. 749,
    Necnon et vario noctem sermone trahebat
    Infelix Dido, longumque bibebat amorem.

[13] Acheron, and its gloomy and cruel king.] Virgil Georg. iv. 469, 470, Manesque adiit, regemque tremendum,
    Nesciaque humanis precibus mansuescere corda.
Job xviii. 14, "His confidence shall be rooted out of his tabernacle; and it shall bring him to the king of terrors."

[14] And am a goddess.] Compare Spenser's Fairy Queen,
    O what awails it of immortal seed
    To been ybred, and never born to die;
    For better I it deem to die with speed,
    Than waste with woe and wailful miserie.

[15] τὸ δὲ πᾶν καλὸν. Catull. iii. 13,
    At vobis male sit, malæ tenebræ
    Orci, quæ omnia bella devoratis
    Tam bellum mihi passerem abstulistis.

[16] ὡς ὄναρ ἔπτη. Compare Job xx. 8, "He shall flee away as a dream, and shall not be found; yea, he shall be chased away as a vision of the night."

Adonis has perished. The Paphian goddess sheds as many tears as Adonis pours forth blood: and these all, on the ground, become flowers: [17] the blood begets a rose, and the tears the anemone. I wail for Adonis: beauteous Adonis hath perished. Lament no more, Venus, thy wooer in the glades: there is a goodly couch, there is a bed of leaves ready for Adonis; this bed of thine, Cytherea, dead Adonis occupies; and though a corpse, he is beautiful, a beautiful corpse, as it were sleeping.

Lay him down on the [18] soft vestments in which he was wont to pass the night: in which with thee along the night he would take his holy sleep, on a couch all-of-gold; yearn *thou* for Adonis, sad-visaged *though he be now:* and lay him [19] amid chaplets and flowers; all with him, since he is dead, [20] ay, all flowers have become withered: but sprinkle him with myrtles, sprinkle him with unguents, with perfumes: perish all perfumes, thy perfume, Adonis, hath perished. Delicate Adonis reclines in purple vestments; and about him weeping Loves set up the wail, [21] having their locks shorn for Adonis:—and one was trampling on his arrows, another on his bow, and [22] another was breaking his well-feathered

[17] The blood begets a rose, &c.] Cf. Ovid Met. x. 731—737.

[18] Soft vestments.] Indicative of rank and luxury. Compare St. Luke vii. 25, "Behold, they which are gorgeously apparelled, and live delicately, are in king's courts." In the next line τὸν ἱερὸν ὕπνον ἐμόχθει, "divinum illum soporem tecum elaborabat," certaminibus nimirum amatoriis. Briggs.

[19] βάλλε δ' ἐνὶ στεφάνοισι, &c. See Milton's Comus at the end,

Beds of hyacinths and roses,
Where young Adonis oft reposes,
Waxing well of his deep wound,
In slumber soft; and on the ground
Sadly sits th' Assyrian queen.

[20] I must here refer the reader to the beautiful lines from Ben Jonson's "Sad Shepherd," quoted by Chapman in his translation of this passage.

[21] κειράμενοι χαίτας ἐπ' Ἀδώνιδι. For this ancient custom, see Homer, Il. xxiii. 135; Odyss. iv. 197; Sappho, Epigr. 2. Ovid and Statius have illustrations of the same practice. In sacred Scripture, Ezechiel says, in a description of a great lament, "They shall make themselves utterly bald for thee," xxvii. 31.

[22] Ovid imitates this passage in his death of Tibullus, Amor. iii. 9, 7,
Ecce puer Veneris fert eversamque pharetram,
Et fractos arcus, et sine luce facem

quiver; and one has loosed the sandal of Adonis, while another is carrying water in golden ewers, and a third is bathing his thighs; and another behind *him* is fanning Adonis with his wings.

The Loves join in the wail for Cytherea herself: Hymenæus has quenched every torch at the door-posts, and shredded the nuptial wreath; and no more is [23] Hymen, no more Hymen the song *that is* sung, alas! alas! is chanted: alas, alas for Adonis, wail the Graces, far more than Hymenæus, for the son of Cinyras, saying one with another, 'Beauteous Adonis hath perished;' and far more piercingly speak they, than thou, [24] Dione. The Muses too strike up the lament for Adonis, and invoke him by song, but he heeds them not; not indeed that he is unwilling, but Proserpine does not release him. Cease, Cytherea, thy laments, refrain this day from thy dirges. [25] Thou must wail again, and weep again, another year.

IDYLL II.

EROS AND THE FOWLER.

A BIRD-CATCHER, yet a boy, hunting birds in a leafy grove, spied Eros, [1] from whom men-turn-away, perched on the branch of a box-tree; and when he had observed *him*, in delight because in sooth it seemed to him a great bird, [2] fitting

---

Below at Χὼ μὲν ἔλυσε πέδιλον, for this office of respect, see St. John i. 27; Acts xiii. 25.

[23] οὐκ ἔτι δ' Ὑμὰν. Compare Lamentations v. 15, "The joy of our heart is ceased; our dance is turned into mourning." For Hymenæus, see Theocr. xviii. 58; Catull. 62; and in its primary sense, Hom. Il. xviii. 493.

[24] Dione was the mother of Aphrodité, but here we are to understand the daughter under the mother's name.

[25] Compare Theocr. Idyll xv. 143, 144.

[1] ἀπότροπον, explained by Hesych., "quod aversetur aliquis." It is so used Œd. Tyr. 1313, 1314, ἰὼ σκότου νέφος ἐμὸν ἀπότροπον. Briggs here conjectures ὑπόπτερον, "alatum."

[2] The ancient mode of catching birds with rods was this. Reeds smeared with bird-lime were joined together lengthwise, till they struck the wings of the bird, which meanwhile was being charmed by the song of the fowler hid amid the bushes. (Schwebel.)

together one on another his rods all at once, he proceeded to lay a trap for Eros, as he hopped [3]hither and thither. And the lad, being chagrined that no success befell him, threw down his rods, and went to an old rustic, who had taught him this art; and spoke to him, and showed him Eros perching. [4]But the old man, gently smiling, wagged his head, and answered the boy: 'Beware of thy sport, and come not at yon bird; fly far *from it;* 'tis an evil brute; happy will you be, [5]so long as you shall not have caught it; but if you shall have reached to man's stature, yon bird that now flees, and hops away, will come himself of his own accord, on a sudden, [6]and settle upon your head.'

IDYLL III.

THE TEACHER TAUGHT.

THE mighty Venus stood beside me, *when I was* yet [1]in youth's prime, leading with her fair hand infant Eros, nodding towards the ground; and addressed me as follows, 'Prythee, good herdsman, take and teach Eros to sing.' Thus said she, and herself went away; but I, witless as I was, began to teach Eros, as though he wished to learn, as many pastorals as I knew; namely, how [2]Pan invented the cross-flute, how

[3] τᾷ καὶ τᾷ. Mosch. i. 16,
καὶ πτερόεις ὡς ὄρνις ἐφίπταται αλλοτ' ἐπ' ἄλλους
ἀνέρας ἠδὲ γυναῖκας.
Cf. Theoc. xv. 119.

[4] ὁ πρέσβυς μειδιόων κίνησε κάρη. Ecclus. xii. 18, "He will shake his head, and clap his hands, and whisper much, and change his countenance."

[5] εἰσόκα, here "quamdiu," as Iliad vii. 604. It often signifies "usque dum," "until," Mosch. iv. 13. The word has therefore the two-fold force of donec. ἐς μέτρον. So St. Paul's Ep. to Ephes. iv. 13. Hesiod has the line, ἀλλ᾽ ὅταν ἡβήσειε, καὶ ἥβης μέτρον ἵκοιτο, ε. 131.

[6] This little Idyll has been imitated successfully by Spenser in the third Eclogue of his Shepherd's Calendar, verse 60 to the end.

[1] The reading here was ὑπνώοντι, clearly corrupt. We have translated the best emendation, that of Herelius, ἔθ᾽ ἡβώοντι.

[2] Virgil Ecl. ii. 32, Pan primus calamos cerâ conjungere plures Instituit. πλαγίαυλος tibia obliqua, seems to have been the same as the σύριγξ or fistula. ὡς αὐλὸν 'Αθάνα. Pindar says Minerva invented the αὐλὸς, "tibia recta," or "longa," after the Gorgon had been slain by

Athena the pipe, how ³Hermes the lyre, and how sweet Apollo the cithern. These I began to teach him; but he did not take heed to my words, but himself kept singing me love-ditties, and teaching me ⁴the desires of mortals and immortals, and his mother's doings. And I forgot indeed all *the strains* which I was teaching Eros, but whatsoever love-ditties Eros taught me, I learned *them* all.

IDYLL IV.

THE POWER OF LOVE.

THE Muses fear not the savage Eros, but love him from their hearts, and follow him close behind. And if haply one follow them having an unloving spirit, out of that man's way they fly, and are not willing to teach him. But if a man agitated in mind by Eros sing sweetly, to him every one of them hasten ¹in flowing stream. I *am* witness that this statement is ²universally true; for if indeed I sing of any other mortal or immortal, my tongue ³stutters, and sings no longer as before; but if again I warble any ditty to Eros, and to Lycidas, ⁴why then the strain flows joyously through my lips.

Perseus through her aid, Pyth. Od. 12. Ovid makes Minerva say, in Fast. lib. vi., Prima terebrato per rara foramina buxo
　　　　　Ut daret effeci tibia longa sonos.
Comp. Callim. H. in Dian. 244.
　³ Hermes the lyre.] Horat. (Od. I. x. 6) calls him, Curvæque lyræ parentem. Ἑρμάων, Doric for Ἑρμῆς. Hes. Fr. 9, 1.
　⁴ Compare Virgil Georg. iv. 345,
　　　　Inter quas curam Clymene narrabat inanem
　　　　Vulcani, Martisque dolos et dulcia furta
　　　　Eque Chao densos Divum referebat amores.
　¹ ἐπειγόμεναι, προρέοντι, "hastening flow forth;" for the translation in the text thanks are due to Chapman.
　² πᾶσιν, as neuter, "in all things," "altogether." This usage of the word is very common in Herodotus.
　³ βαμβαίνει. Agathias, Epigr. xiii, χείλεα βαμβαίνει φθέγματι γηραλέῳ.
　⁴ καὶ τόκα. Ruhnken prefers αὐτίκα. But Iliad ix. 674; Theocr. Id. xxiv. 20, quoted by Schæfer, amply justify the common reading.

IDYLL V.

LIFE TO BE ENJOYED.

[1] I KNOW not how, nor is it fitting I should, to labour at what I have not learned. If my ditties are beautiful, then these only, which the [2] Muse has presented to me aforetime, will give me renown. But if these *be* not to men's taste, what boots it me to labour at more? For if indeed Saturn's son or shifting fate had given to us a twofold life-time, so that one term might be spent on pleasure and delights, and the other in toil, 'twere possible perhaps *for one*, having first laboured, at some after-period to receive the fruits. But since the gods have allowed *but* one time for living to come to men, [3] and this a short space, and too brief for all, [4] how long, ah wretched men, do we toil over labours and works? And how far are we to throw *our whole* souls upon gains and upon arts, longing ever for much more wealth? Surely we have all forgotten that we were born mortal, and how brief a time we have had assigned to us by fate.

---

[1] In the Florilegium of Stobæus, this first line is given as Bion's, and prefixed to this Idyll. Brunck and Winterton omit it or write it separately.

[2] Pierson and others read Μοῖσα here for Μοῖρα, the common reading. But the latter has to support it, Horace Od. II. xvi. 37—40,
> Mihi parva rura et
> Spiritum Graiæ tenuem Camenæ,
> Parca non mendax dedit et malignum
> Spernere vulgus.

[3] μῇονα πάντων, "non potens omnia complecti." Hor. Od. II. ii. 11,
> Quid æternis minorem
> Consiliis animum fatigas.

Job xiv. 1, "Man that is born of a woman is of few days, and full of trouble."

[4] ἐς πόσον, κ. τ. λ. Compare here St. James iv. 13, 14; and for the moral of this earnest and beautiful pleading of natural religion, refer to Psalm xc. 12, "So teach us to number our days, that we may apply our hearts unto wisdom."

IDYLL VI.

CLEODAMUS AND MYRSON.

Cleodamus. [1] OF spring, good Myrson, or winter, or autumn, or summer, what is pleasant to you? And what do you desire most to come? Is it summer, when all things, as many as we labour at, are completed? Or sweet autumn, when hunger comes *but* lightly on men? Or is it even [2] idle winter? since 'tis e'en in winter that many, while they warm themselves, [3] are overpowered by laziness and sloth. Or is beauteous spring more agreeable to you? Tell me what your inclination prefers; for our leisure has given us leave to speak.

Myrson. For mortals to judge divine works is unmeet; for all these are holy and sweet; yet for your sake, Cleodamus, I will speak out which is to me more sweet than *all the* rest. I would not it were summer, [4] for then the sun scorches me. I would not *it were* [5] autumn, for *then* ripe fruits breed disease. I dread to endure terrible winter, its falling snow and frosts. Come spring to me thrice-welcome in the [6] whole year, when there is neither frost, nor does sun oppress us. In spring every thing is fruitful. All sweet things burst forth in spring, [7] and night is equal to men, and morning the same.

---

[1] Εἴαρος. ἐπὶ is understood, according to Briggs. Brunck reads Μόρσων for Μύρσων, the former being used by Theocritus. In verse 4 we find λιμός, feminine. It is common.

[2] χεῖμα δύσεργον, that is, unsuited for rustic pursuits. Virg. Georg. i. 299, Hiems ignava colono. G. Wakefield interprets it, "Bruma intractabilis." See Georg. i. 211.

[3] Cf. Virg. Georg. i. 303, Invitat genialis hiems curasque resolvit.

[4] Virg. Ecl. vii. 46, Jam venit æstas Torrida.

[5] Horace Sat. ii. 6, 19, Auctumnusque gravis Libitinæ quæstus acerbæ. In the next line some place a full stop after φέρειν, and construe, winter *is* terrible to bear.

[6] Λυκάβαντι, from Λυκάβας, an Homeric word, signifying the year: from λύκη, lux, and βαίνω. πάντ' εἴαρος. Compare Theocr. xi. 58; Virgil Ecl. iii. 57, Nunc frondent silvæ, nunc formosissimus annus.

[7] The vernal equinox. Virg. (Georg. i. 208) says of the autumnal equinox, Libra die somnique pares ubi fecerit horas.

VII.

ON HYACINTHUS.

PERPLEXITY seized on [1]Phœbus experiencing so great grief; he began to seek every remedy, and strove to obtain a cunning art. And with ambrosia and nectar he anointed, he anointed all the wound; but for the fates all remedies are remediless.

VIII.

FRIENDSHIP.

BLESSED *are* they who love, [2]whensoever they are loved equally in return. Blest was [3]Theseus, when Pirithous was with him, even though he had descended to *the abode* of relentless Hades. Blest was Orestes among the [4]churlish inhospitables, because Pylades had chosen common paths with him. [5]Achilles, grandson of Æacus, was fortunate in his friend's life-time, blessed was he in his death, because he warded off from him dire fate.

---

[1] τον Φοῖβον is no doubt the true reading, though one editor has ἀμφασία δὲ Βίων' ἕλε: another, τὸν βίον ἕλεν: and another, Παιῶν' ἕλε, (i. e. Ipse Deus medicinæ obstupuit). But bearing the story of Hyacinthus in mind we need no alteration. The fair youth, son of Amyclas, king of Sparta, and of Diomedè, was unintentionally slain by Apollo's discus. The hopelessness of the passionate god's attempts to undo the mischief are touched upon in this fragment. For more particulars see Ovid Met. x. 184, &c.

[2] Whensoever, &c.] Theocr. Idyll xii. 15,
ἀλλήλους δ' ἐφίλησαν ἴσῳ ζύγῳ· ἦ ρα τοτ' ἦσαν
χρύσεοι οἱ πάλαι ἄνδρες, ὅτ' ἀντεφίλησ' ὁ φιληθείς.

[3] Compare Horat. Od. IV. vii. 27, 28,
Nec Lethæa valet Theseus abrumpere caro
Vincula Pirithoo.

[4] The churlish inhospitables.] 'Αξείνοι. Allusion is here made to the fierce character of the barbarians dwelling on the east coast of the sea called first from them Axenus, the inhospitable; but afterwards Euxine, from the civilization introduced by Greek settlers. For χαλεποῖσιν, Briggs suggests Χαλύβεσσιν. The Chalybes were a nation of Asia Minor, bordering on Pontus. Æsch. Prom. V. calls them ἀνήμεροί γαρ, οὐδὲ πρόσπλαστοι ξένοις.

[5] The friendship of Pylades and Orestes is commemorated in more than one Greek tragedy: Achilles and Patroclus appear as fast friends in the Iliad. See Ovid. Ep. ex Ponto II. iii. 41—46; and for some excellent remarks on this beautiful trait of the Heroic ages, see Thirlwall's Greece, vol. i. c. vi. 77.

IX.

It is not well, my friend, on every occasion to have recourse to a craftsman, nor at all in every matter to have need of another, but [1] do you even yourself fashion a Pan's pipe; and it is an easy task for you.

X.

May Eros invite the Muses, may the Muses bring Eros: and to me, always yearning after it, may the Muses give song, the sweet song, than which [2] no charm is sweeter.

XI.

[3] From the frequent drop, as the saying *is*, ever falling, even the stone is bored into a hollow.

XII.

But I will go *on* my way to yon slope, [4] warbling at the sands of the shore, whilst I supplicate cruel Galatea: for I will not relinquish my sweet hopes even till extreme old-age.

XIII.

Neither leave me unrewarded, since even Phœbus gave a reward to song. And honour makes the things *we do* better.

XIV.

[5] Beauty is woman's grace: but man's is courage.

---

[1] τεχνᾶσθαι, may be the infinitive for the imperative here.
[2] No charm, or remedy. Comp. Theocr. Idyll xi. 1, for the same sentiment.
[3] So Ovid., Quid magis est durum saxo? quid mollius undâ?
   Dura tamen molli saxa cavantur aquâ.
And again, Gutta cavat lapidem, non vi sed sæpe cadendo. Lucret. lib. iv. ad fin., Nonne vides etiam guttas in saxa cadentes
   Humoris, longo in spatio pertundere saxa?
[4] Warbling.] I have translated Brunck's reading, ψιθυρίσδων, as ψιθυρίσδω seems condemned by the futures before and after it. In the next line ψάμαθον τε καὶ ἠϊόνα, is an instance of Hendiadys. See Theocr. i. 1.
[5] See Anacreon, Ode II., γυναιξὶν οὐκ ἔτ' εἶχεν
   τί οὖν δίδωσι; κάλλος, κ. τ. λ.

IDYLL XV.

THE EPITHALAMIUM OF ACHILLES AND DEIDAMIA.[1]

MYRSON. LYCIDAS.

Myrson. Are you willing now, Lycidas, sweetly to sing me [2]a Sicilian melody, delightsome, charming the mind, *and* amorous, such as the Cyclops Polyphemus sung on the seashore to Galatea?

Lycidas. And if, Myrson, it be agreeable to me to sing to my pipe, then what shall my song be?

Myrs. I admire, Lycidas, the Scyrian strain, sweet love, the stolen kisses, the [3]stolen embrace of the son of Peleus. How he, a boy, put on *a maiden's* mantle, and how he belied his form, and how among the daughters of Lycomedes, Deidamia, [4]holding him in her arms, gratified Achilles, son of Peleus.

Lycid. Once *on a day*, the herdsman carried off Helen; and led her to Ida, a sore grief to Ænone; then Lacedæmon was wroth, and gathered all the Achæan host. Nor did any man of Hellas, of Mycenæ, or Elis, or of the Laconians, stay behind in his home, [5]bearing as vengeance dread war. But only

---

[1] The Scyrian strain.] Lycomedes king of the Dolopians, in the island of Scyros, near Eubœa, was father of Deidamia, and grandsire of Pyrrhus, or Neoptolemus. This fragment relates to the sojourn of Achilles, in maiden's guise, among the daughters of Lycomedes at Scyros, whither he had been brought by his mother Thetis, as she knew the Trojan war must be fatal to him. Among his female companions he was called Pyrrha from his golden locks. His sex and hiding-place were discovered by a stratagem of Ulysses.

[2] Σικελὸν μέλος. Virg. Ecl. iv. 1, Sicelides Musæ. Mosch., Σικελικαὶ Μοῖσαι. All marking Sicily as the land of pastoral poetry "par excellence."

[3] λάθριον εὐνάν. Compare Theocr. xxvii. 67, ἀνίστατο φώριος εὐνά.

[4] For the unintelligible reading, ἀπαλέγοισα
      'Αηδήνη τ' ἁπαστὸν 'Αχιλλία Δηιδάμεια—
we have ventured to translate, as at least sense, Ruhnken's conjecture,
      ἀγκὰς ἔχοισα
      Πηλείδην ἀγάπαξεν, κ. τ. λ.
which is approved by Valkenaer and Jacobs, and is by far the best. For the several conjectures of Toup, Wakefield, and Briggs, see Briggs' Bucolici Græci, p. 361.

[5] φέρων δισσὶν ἀνὰν ἄρνα, is hopeless. Scaliger amended it thus, φέρων τισὶν αἰνὸν *Άρνα, to which Lennep. prefers τίσιν, vindictam, which Brunck follows. This has been translated in the text above. Ruhnken's

Achilles was lying concealed among the daughters of Lycomedes, and was learning skill in wool, instead of arms, and in his white hand was holding a maiden's [6]task; and in appearance he was as a girl; for he was equally womanish with them, and as fresh a colour as theirs blushed on his snowy cheeks; and he was wont to walk with the step of maidenhood, and to cover his hair with a veil; yet had he the spirit of Mars, and possessed the love of a man, and from dawn to nightfall would he sit beside Deidamia; and at times indeed he would kiss her hand, and often [7]would he raise her beauteous mouth, and the sweet tears would flow forth. But with no other of like age did he eat; and he kept doing every thing in eagerness for a sleep in common. Then he spoke also a word to her, 'With one another other sisters slumber, but I remain alone, and thou sleepest [8]apart *from me;* we two, virgins of like age, we twain beautiful. Yet sleep we alone in our several beds, and this evil and troublesome partition-wall [9] wickedly separates me from you. For not of you am I—' [10]

suggestion φέρων φθισάνορ' Ἄρηα, is elegant and has claims to be received. Wakefield, φέρων δυσόμιλον Ἄρηα. Jacobs, φυγὼν δυσμικτὸν Ἄρηα. Briggs, φέρον δὲ ξυνὸν Ἄρηα.

[6] The reading here was κόρον, scopam, a broom; but this was a slave's work. See Eurip. Hec. 362; Androm. 166. In the next line, at Θηλύνετο, compare Theocr. xx. 14.

[7] στόμ' ἀνὰ καλὸν ἄειρε. Ursinus corrected this to σῶμ'; which, however, yields not, I venture to think, a better sense. The line is corrupt, no doubt. Scaliger proposed to read, understanding it of weaving, στάμονα καλὸν ἄειρε τὰ δ' ἀδέα καιρέ' ἐπῄνει, "and would often lift the beautiful warp, and praise the scented threads (or thrums)." Briggs reads, τὰ δ' εὔχροα δακτυλ' ἐπῄνει, "would praise her fresh-coloured fingers." In this translation I have adopted Brunck's ἐπέρρει, as the slightest alteration.

[8] For νύμφα, read with Briggs νόσφι. Two lines below, κατὰ λέκτρα is used distributively, like κατὰ σφίας, in the Iliad. κατ' ἄνδρα, man by man, Herodot. &c.

[9]
ἁ δὲ πονηρὰ
νύσσα γὰρ δολία———

The awkwardness of δὲ and γὰρ coming thus together, and the offence against metre in the last syllable of νύσσα, have suggested the reading νύσσα καὶ ἀργαλέα, which I have followed. One reading (Brunck's) is

ἁ δὲ πονηρὰ
νύσσα, καὶ δολία με τροφὸς ἀπὸ σεῖο μερίζει.

The duenna is thus introduced into the passage.

[10] The remainder of this Idyll is lost.

XVI.

TO THE EVENING STAR.

HESPER! [1]golden light of the lovely Foam-born! Hesper, *dear* friend, sacred ornament of dark night, hail, thou friend, [2]as much more faint than the moon, as thou art eminent above the stars; and give thou me, as I go a merry-making to a shepherd, light instead of the moon: because she, beginning *her course* to-day, went down too quickly. I am not going forth for theft, nor to molest a wayfarer in the night: but I am a lover; and 'tis meet to return a lover love for love.

XVII.

LOVE RESISTLESS.

GENTLE Cyprus-born *goddess*, child of Jove and the sea, why art thou so wroth with mortals and immortals? I have said but little; *rather*, why dost thou so much hate them, and why, prythee, shouldest thou have given birth to Eros, so great a plague to all, cruel as he is, without natural affection, in mind nowise resembling his form? And to what end hast thou given him to us [3]winged and a far-darter, that we might not be able to escape him, bitter as he is.

---

[1] Hom. Il. xxii. 318, speaks thus of Hesperus,
"Ἕσπερος, ὃς κάλλιστος ἐν οὐρανῷ ἵσταται ἀστήρ.
And Virgil (Æneid viii. 589) of Lucifer,
Lucifer undâ
Quem Venus ante alios astrorum diligit ignes
Extulit os sacrum cœlo, tenebrasque resolvit.
[2] So Statius Silv. ii. 82,
Quantum præcedit clara minores
Luna faces, quantumque alios premit Hesperus ignes.
Cf. Horat. I. xii. 48. In the next line, for κῶμον ἄγοντι, compare Theocr. Idyll iii. 1.
[3] πτανὸν. Compare an epigram of Archias,
φεύγειν δὴ τὸν Ἔρωτα κένος πόνος· οὐ γὰρ ἀλύξω
πεζὸς ὑπὸ πτηνοῦ πυκνὰ διωκόμενος,
which Fawkes renders,
Of shining Love 'tis vain to talk,
When he can fly, and I but walk.

THE IDYLLS

OF

MOSCHUS THE SYRACUSAN.

IDYLL I.

LOVE A RUNAWAY.

[1] 'My son Eros,' Venus was loudly calling, 'Eros, if any one has seen straying in the cross-roads, he is my runaway: the informer shall have a reward. The kiss of Venus *shall be* your pay; and if you shall have brought him, not the [2] bare kiss, but, stranger, you shall have even more: now the lad is very notable; you would know him among [3] twenty together: in complexion indeed *he is* not fair, but like to fire; and his eyes are piercing and fiery-red: evil his heart, pleasant his speech. For he does not speak the same as he thinks; his voice *is* as honey, [4] but if he be wroth, his mind is ruthless;

---

[1] "Ben Jonson in his Masque, 'The Hue and Cry after Cupid,' has imitated Moschus in this Idyll very closely. The proclamation, however, is addressed by the Graces to the softer sex, with one of whom Aphrodite supposes young Love to be concealed." Chapman. Heindorf, in his edition, separates τὸν Ἔρωτα τὸν υἷεα by a comma before and after, so that the words may be read as part of the cry of Venus. ἐβώστρει, made proclamation after, Hom. Odyss. xii. 124. So βοᾷ is used by Euripides, Phœn. 1161, βοᾷ πῦρ καὶ δικέλλας, which Valkenaer renders " clamando petit."

[2] γυμνὸν τὸ φίλαμα. Theocr. Idyll iii. 20; xxvii. 4.

[3] ἐν εἴκοσι πᾶσι: inter viginti omnino, "amongst as many as twenty." The alteration to παισὶ weakens the force.

[4] Compare Plaut. Truc. I. ii. 76,
     In melle sunt linguæ vestræ sitæ, atque orationes
     Lacteque : corda felle sunt lita, atque acerba aceto.
Heskin quotes a rhyming distich,
        Mel in ore, verba lactis,
        Fel in corde, fraus in factis.

deceiving, telling truth in nothing, wily child, he [5]sports cruelly. His head has goodly curls, but [6]impudent is the face he wears: his little hands are tiny, 'tis true, yet they shoot far; shoot even to Acheron, and to the king of Hades. *He is* naked indeed so far as his body is concerned, but his mind is [7]shrouded. And *being* winged, as a bird, he flies upon now one party of men and women and now another, and settles on their inmost hearts. He has a very small bow, and upon the bow an arrow: small *is* his arrow, yet it carries even to the sky: and a golden quiver above his back, and within it are the bitter shafts, with which he often wounds even me. All, all is cruel; but far most a little torch that he has, [8]with which he kindles the sun himself. If you at any rate shall have caught him, bind and bring him, and do not pity him. And if ever you shall have seen him weeping, beware lest he beguile you; and if he smile, do you drag him on: and if he should desire to kiss you, avoid it; his kiss is mischievous, [9]his lips poison. But should he say, 'Take these, I present thee all the arms I have,' do not touch them, deceitful gifts; for they have all been dipt in fire.'

IDYLL II.

EUROPA.

VENUS once sent upon Europa a sweet dream, what time the [1]third portion of night sets in, and dawn is near; what time

---

[5] ἄγρια παίσδει. Compare Virgil, Ecl. iii. 8, Transversa tuentibus hircis. Æn. ix. 794, Asper, acerba tuens. Geor. iii. 149, Asper acerba sonans: all illustrative of the frequent poetic use of adjectives neuter, plural and singular, for the adverb. Cf. Matth. Gr. Gr. 446, § 7, 8.

[6] ἰταμὸν, (from εἶμι, ἴτης,) bold: in a bad sense, generally. Cf. Aristoph. Ran. 1292, ἰταμαῖς κυσίν.

[7] ἐμπεπύκασται. Hom. Il. iii. 298, πυκιναὶ φρένες. πυκινὸς νόος; μήδεα πυκνὰ; elsewhere. Proverbs v. 6, "Lest thou shouldest ponder the path of life, her ways are moveable, that thou canst not know her."

[8] I have followed the reading of Luzacius, τᾷ ἅλιον αὐτὸν ἀναίθει. Hermann retains the common reading τὸν ἅλιον; but punctuates thus,
πολὺ πλεῖον δὲ οἱ αὐτῷ
βαιὰ λαμπὰς ἰοῖσα· τὸν ἅλιον αὐτὸν ἀναίθει.

[9] φάρμακον ἐντί. Others read φαρμακόεντα.

[1] From Homer's day the Greeks divided "night" into three watches,

sleep sweeter than honey settling on the eyelids, limb-relaxing though it is, fetters down the eyes with soft bond; ²what time moreover the tribe of truthful dreams is roving abroad. Then as she slumbered in a chamber next the roof, the daughter of Phœnix, yet a maiden, Europa, fancied ³that two continents were contending for her, Asia and the opposite coast, and they were in shape as women. Now of these the one had the form of a foreign woman, whilst the other in truth resembled a native, and hugged *her* more closely *as* her own child; and kept saying that she was her mother, and that herself had nurtured her. But the other, using violence with strong hands, was drawing her away, nothing loth: for she said that 'twas fated by ægis-bearing Jove that Europa should be her prize.

She then started in affright from ⁴her strown couch, quaking at heart, for she had beheld the dream as a real appearance; and seating herself she kept silence a long time, yet still had she before her waking eyes both the women. And late at length the maiden uplifted a timid voice, 'Who of the celestials has sent upon me such phantoms? What manner of dreams *are these which* have exceedingly scared me, as I slumbered right sweetly in my chamber on my strown couch? And who was that foreign woman, whom I beheld in my sleep? How did a yearning toward her strike me at heart! How graciously did she too welcome me, and regard me as her own child! But may the blessed *gods* decide the dream to me for good.' Thus saying, she sprang up; and went to seek her dear companions, in the prime of life, her equals in years, well-pleasing, and nobly-born, with whom she was ever wont

(Il. x. 253; Od. xii. 312,) just as they did "day" also. The first part of the day was called ἠώς, which the time here mentioned (the πύματον λάχος of Apollon. Rhod. i. 1022) immediately precedes. The Latins called it cockcrow, "gallicinium," ἀλεκτοροφωνία. See art. Dies, 339, i. Smith's Dict. Gr. and Rom. Ant.

² εὖτε καὶ ἀτρεκέων. Hor. Sat. I. x. 32,
Vetuit me tali voce Quirinus,
Post mediam noctem visus, cùm somnia vera.
ἔθνος ὀνείρων. So Hom. Odyss. xxiv. 12, δῆμον ὀνείρων. ποιμαίνεται, ovium ritu vagatur.

³ ἠπείρους δοιάς. So Æsch. Persæ, 186.—Ἀσίδα τ' ἀντιπέρην τε. ἀντιπέρην is an adverb. Supply τὴν ἀντιπέρην οὖσαν ἤπειρον.

⁴ Eurip. Orest. 313, μένε δ' ἐπὶ στρωτοῦ λέχους. Soph. Trach. 916, στρωτὰ—φάρη. τὸ γὰρ ὡς ὕπαρ εἶδεν ὄνειρον. The order seems to be εἶδεν γὰρ τὸ ὄνειρον ὡς ὕπαρ.

to sport, [5]when she was making ready for the choir, or when she might be washing her skin at the mouths of [6]the Anaurus, or whensoever [7]she might be culling odorous lilies from the mead. And these quickly showed themselves to her, and they had each in their hands a basket for-holding-flowers; and they proceeded to go to the meadows by-the-shore, where too they were ever wont to gather themselves in one troop, delighting both in the growth of the roses and in the roaring of the sea. But Europa herself was carrying a basket wrought of gold, *and* admirable, a great wonder, a great work of Hephæstus, which he had bestowed on [8]Libya as a gift, when she went to the bed of the Earth-shaker; and she gave it to very-beauteous Telephassa, who was of near kin to her; and upon Europa, yet unwedded, her mother, Telephassa, bestowed it as a famous present. Whereon many sparkling curious-works had been wrought; on it indeed was wrought [9]of gold Io the daughter of Inachus, while still a heifer, and she had not the figure of a woman. And frantic she was going afoot over the briny paths, like unto one swimming; and a sea had been wrought of dark blue. And aloft, upon the brow of the shore, were standing two men together, and they were watching the sea-traversing heifer. On it moreover was [10]Jupiter, son of Saturn, patting gently with his hand the heifer daughter of Inachus, whom

[5] Compare Callimach. H. in Apoll. 8, Οἱ δὲ νέοι μολπήν τε καὶ ἐς χορὸν ἐντύνεσθε.

[6] There is an Anaurus in Thessaly, and one in Dardania. It is suggested, that as neither of these will suit the locality of Europa's story, we must read ἀναύρῳ in its first sense—a river or a torrent: as in Anacr. Od. vii., διὰ δ' ὀξέων ἀναύρων—

[7] Horat. III. xxvii. 29 speaks of Europa as
  Nuper in pratis studiosa florum,
  Debitæ nymphis opifex coronæ.

[8] Libya, a daughter of Epaphus and Memphis; the mother by Neptune of Agenor, Belus, and Lelex. Agenor is by most of the poets called the father of Europa, though Homer makes her the daughter of Phœnix. Telephassa was daughter-in-law to Libya.

[9] Horace (de Art. Poet.) calls her "Io vaga." Virgil places the legend of Io on the shield of Turnus, Æn. vii. 789—791,
  At levem clypeum sublatis cornibus Io
  Auro insignibat: jam setis obsita, jam bos,
  Argumentum ingens, et custos virginis Argus.

[10] ἐν δ' ἦν Ζεὺς Κρονίδης, ἐπαφώμενος ἠρέμα χερσί. The old reading left out Κρονίδης, and ended the line with χειρὶ θείῃ. Briggs proposes ἐπαφῶν μόνον ἠρέμα χειρὶ θείῃ, as Æsch. Prom. V. 874, ἐπαφῶν ἀταρβεῖ χειρὶ, καὶ θιγὼν μόνον.

beside seven-mouthed Nile he was transforming again to a woman from a horned cow. Of silver indeed was the stream of Nile; and the heifer, I ween, of brass; but Jove himself was fashioned of gold. ¹¹ And about the crown of the rounded basket Hermes had been formed; and near to him Argus had been *represented* stretched, distinguished by his sleepless eyes; and from his deep-red blood was springing up a bird exulting in the many-hued colour of his wings, having spread wide the plumage of his tail, and like some ship speeding through the sea, he was covering all round with feathers the rims of the golden basket. Such was very-beauteous Europa's basket.

Now these, when in truth they had entered the flowery meads, were then pleasing their fancy each with various kinds of flowers; one of them was plucking odorous narcissus, another hyacinth, another the violet, and another the creeping thyme: and on the ground were falling many leaves of spring-nursed ¹² meadows. But others again were culling in rivalry incense-laden tufts of yellow crocus; in the midst however stood the princess, gathering with her hands the beauty of the bright-red rose, ¹³ like as foam-born *Venus* shone conspicuous among the Graces. Not long however was she destined to please her fancy on flowers, or to ¹⁴ preserve, I wot, her virgin zone undefiled. For of a truth the son of Saturn, when he observed her, had then been smitten at heart, subdued by the unforeseen darts of Venus, who alone can overcome even Jove: wherefore now, both as desiring-to-

---

¹¹ δινήεντος. The reading δινωθέντος "tornati" is suggested as more probable, Virgil's line, Lenta quibus torno facili superaddita vitis, being adduced in support of this emendation. The story of Argus is found in Ov. Met. i. 625—627,

Centum luminibus cinctum caput Argus habebat:
Inde suis vicibus capiebant bina quietem:
Cætera servabant, atque in statione manebant.

¹² Wakefield suggests λειρώδων. Briggs, μηκώνων, because λειμώνων has occurred so recently. Briggs quotes Propert. I. xx. 37,

Et circumriguo surgebant lilia prato
Candida purpureis mista papaveribus.

¹³ So Virg. Æn. i. 499,

Exercet Diana choros, quam mille secutæ
Hinc atque hinc glomerantur Oreades: illa pharetram
Fert humeris gradiensque deas supereminet omnes.

¹⁴ ἔρυσθαι, i. q. ἐρύεσθαι. Hom. Od. v. 484, ὅσον τρεῖς ἄνδρας ἔρυσθαι. ἄχραντον. Compare Eurip. Iph. in Aul. 1574, ἄχραντον αἷμα καλλιπαρθένου δέρης.

avoid the wrath of jealous Herè, and wishing to beguile the young fancy of the maiden, he concealed the god, and transformed his body, [15] and became a bull; not such a one as feeds in the stalls, nor indeed such a one as cleaves a furrow, dragging the curved plough; nor like one that grazes in the herds, no, nor of such a kind as the bull that is tamed and draws the heavy-laden wain. But of a truth the rest of his body was chestnut-coloured, whilst a silvery ring was gleaming on his mid forehead, and his eyes were [16] sparkling from under, flashing through desire; and horns equal one to the other were branching up from his head, like orbs of the horned moon, her disc cut in half; so came he into the meadow, and did not alarm the maidens by his appearance: [17] but a longing to draw near to him arose in all, and to touch the lovely bull; for his divine scent from afar surpassed even the sweet odour of the meadow. And he stood before the feet of faultless Europa, and began to lick her neck, and to soften the maiden's *heart*. Then would she stroke him, and gently with her hands wipe off from his lips much foam, and she kissed the bull. But he [18] lowed softly: you might say that you heard a [19] Mygdonian flute, uttering distinctly a clear sound; then he bent the knee before her feet, and began to look keenly on Europa, with his neck turned towards her, and to display to her his broad back. Then she bespoke her maidens with-thick-falling hair thus, 'Come, dear playmates of like age, that we may delight ourselves in sitting on the bull here; for in sooth he will spread his back beneath us,

[15] Ov. Met. ii. 850,
Induitur tauri faciem, mixtusque juvencis
Mugit et in teneris formosus obambulat herbis.
See also the remainder of the 2nd Book in illustration of this Idyll.
[16] ὅσσε δ' ὑπογλαύσσεσκε. So Brunck reads in preference to the corrupt ὑπογλαύκεσκε.
[17] Ov. Met. ii. 858, &c., Miratur Agenore nata,
Quòd formosus erat, quòd prælia nulla minetur.
[18] Lowed softly.] Compare Nonnus, lib. i.,
Σιδονίης ποτὲ ταῦρος ἐπ' ἠόνος ὑψίκερως Ζεὺς
ἱμερόεν μύκημα νόθῳ μυκήσατο λαιμῷ.
[19] Mygdonian flute,] or pipe. Mygdonian stands for "Phrygian." The Mygdones, a Thracian tribe, settled in Phrygia. The Phrygian pipe had two holes above and terminated in a horn bending upwards. (See Tibull. II. i. 86. Ov. Met. iii. 533, Adunco tibia cornu.) It thus approached the nature of a trumpet, producing slow, grave, solemn tones. Smith, Dict. Gr. R. A., Tibia, p. 969.

and take us all up, even as a ship; mild *is* he to look upon, and gentle, nor is he at all like to other bulls; [20] and a right mind, as of a man, surrounds him, and he wants but speech.' Thus saying, [21] she took her seat smilingly on his back; and the rest were about to do so; when straightway the bull sprang up, having carried off her whom he wished, and speedily he came to the sea. But she having turned her round began to call her dear companions, outstretching her hands; and they could not reach her, for having set foot on the strand he ran forward as a dolphin, and the Nereids emerged from out the brine, ay, the whole of them, I wot, arrayed themselves in line, [22] sitting on the backs of whales. And moreover heavily-roaring Earth-shaker himself above the sea, levelling the waves, led the briny way for his brother; and [23] the Tritons, dwellers in deep-flowing ocean, were gathered round him, sounding on long conches a nuptial melody.

But she truly, sitting on the bull-like shoulders of Jupiter, with one hand indeed kept holding the bull's long horn, whilst in the other hand she was drawing back the folds of her purple-flowing robe, in order that the countless spray of the hoary brine might not wet the skirt of it when drawn towards

---

[20] Theocr. Idyll xxv. 79—83, puts similar language, respecting a dog, into the mouth of the steward of Augeas.

[21] Ovid. Met. ii. 868,

Ausa est quoque regia virgo,
Nescia quem premeret, tergo considere tauri.

Horat. III. xxvii. 25,

Sic et Europe niveum doloso
Credidit tauro latus, et scatentem
Belluis pontum, mediasque fraudes
Palluit audax.

[22] Virg. Æn. v. 822, &c.,

Tum variæ comitum facies, immania cete
Et senior Glauci chorus, Inousque Palemon
Tritonesque citi.

For the next line see Milton's Comus, "By the earth-shaking Neptune's mace."

[23] Milton, *ibid.*, "By scaly Triton's winding shell." Virg. Æn. vi. 171,

Sed tum forte cavâ dum personat æquora conchâ
Æmulus, exceptum Triton submerserat.

Valkenaer in this passage has restored the reading of the Codices. βαρύθροοι αὐλητῆρες, "loud-voiced minstrels." Triton was a son of Neptune and Amphitrite. He was his father's trumpeter—his trumpet a conch-shell. Four lines below we have translated the reading of Auratus ὄφρα μὴ ὤην Δεύοι εφελκομένην.

her. Now the deep robe of Europa had been formed into
loose folds at the shoulders, like the sail of a ship, and was
wont to lighten the maiden. But when at length she was far
from her fatherland, and [24] there appeared neither any sea-
dashed shore, nor tall mountain, but air indeed above, and
boundless ocean beneath, peering round about her, she gave
vent to words like these: 'Whither bearest thou me, divine
bull? Who art thou? Or how dost thou traverse the way
[25] with untiring feet, and yet not shudder at the sea? For by
swift ships the sea is overrun, but bulls dread the briny path.
What kind of drink is sweet to thee? what food wilt thou get
from the sea? Art thou in truth, I wonder, some god? For
[26] thou dost *acts* beseeming the gods. Neither do marine
dolphins walk upon land, nor bulls in any wise on the sea.
But thou rushest unwetted over land and sea, and thine
[27] hoofs are oars to thee. Nay, haply also lifted aloft above
the azure air, thou wilt take flight, resembling swift birds.
Ah me! ill-fated assuredly in a high degree; [28] even I who,
having left afar my father's house, and followed this bull, am
pursuing a strange voyage, and roaming alone. But mayest
thou, earth-shaking regent of the hoary sea, graciously light
upon me! I hope to behold this god directing my voyage, as
my forerunner. For not without a god's *help* do I traverse
these watery paths.' Thus spake she; and her the broad-
horned bull addressed thus: 'Take heart, maiden, fear not
ocean's billow: I myself, look you, am Jove, though near at
hand I seem to be a bull; yes, for I am able to appear whatso-
ever I choose. Now desire of thee hath impelled me to

[24] Virg. Æn. iii. 192,
    Postquam altum tenuere rates, nec jam amplius ullæ
    Apparent terræ, cœlum undique, et undique pontus.
Cf. Lucret. iv. 435. Horat. iii. 27. Ovid. Trist. I. ii. 23.
[25] ἀργαλέοισι πόδεσσι. Briggs suggests ἀργαλέην σὺ. One MS. has ἀργαλέην γε.
[26] We have translated the reading given by Briggs, as restored by
Gaisford, ἐπεοικότα, which yields a better sense than ἀπεοικότα.
[27] So Seneca Hippolyt., Ungulà lentos imitante remos. For the
line above see Matt. Gr. Gr. 594, 4. When a preposition should stand
twice with two separate nouns, it is often put only once, and then with
the second. So in Latin, Horat. iii. 25, 3, Quæ nemora aut quos agor
in specus. Cf. Bion, Id. v. 11, καμάτως κ' εἰς ἔργα πονεῦμες.
[28] Horace, Od. III. xxvii. 49, Impudens liqui patrios Penates: and for
Jove's answer see the same ode, Uxor invicti Jovis esse nescis. Mitte
singultus.

measure so much sea, taking the appearance of a bull: but Crete shall receive thee presently, *Crete*, which reared even myself; where shall be thy nuptials: and by me thou shalt bear illustrious sons, who shall all of them be sceptre-bearers among the dwellers upon earth.

So said he: and what he said found fulfilment: Crete indeed at length appeared: and Jove again assumed his own form. And he loosed her girdle, and the [29] Hours prepared her bed, and she who was aforetime a maiden became presently bride of Jove. [30] And she bore sons to Jove and became a mother forthwith.

[In connexion with this Idyll, Ovid Met. vi. 103, and Fast. v. 605—612, may be read with advantage. See Chapman's notes.]

IDYLL III.

THE EPITAPH OF BION, A LOVING HERDSMAN.

PLAINTIVELY groan at my bidding, ye woodland dells, and thou Dorian water, and weep, rivers, the lovely Bion; now wail at my bidding, ye plants, and now, groves, utter a wail; now may ye flowers breathe forth your life in sad clusters; [1] blush now sorrowfully, ye roses, now, thou anemone; [2] now,

---

[29] The Hours are (in Greek poets) ministers of the gods, Il. viii. 433, xxi. 450; the companions of the sun, Ov. Met. ii. 25. In Theocr. i. 150, the beauty of a cup is ascribed to its having been washed in their fountain. In Idyll xv. 103, they bring back Adonis to Venus year by year, from Acheron. In nature or art alike they are interested in the perfection of beauty.

[30] Minos, Sarpedon, and Rhadamanthus were her sons. She afterwards married Asterion, king of Crete, who brought up her sons, and whom one of them, Minos, succeeded.

[1] See Bion's Lament for Adonis, 36, ἄνθεα δ' ἐξ ὀδύνας ἐρευθαίνεται. Moschus seems here to allude to this passage.

[2] βάμβαλε, lisp. This is an emendation of Heindorf for λάμβανε, the common reading. A kindred form, βαμβαίνω, occurs in Bion iv. 10, —αἴ αἴ. Comp. Theocr. x. 28, καὶ ἁ γραπτὰ ὑάκινθος. The legend ran, that when Hyacinthus had been accidentally slain by Apollo's disc, his blood produced a flower on whose leaves the initial letters of his name were inscribed. Ov. Met. x. 162,

    Ipse suos gemitus foliis inscribit, et " ai ai "
    Flos habet inscriptum, funestaque littera ducta est.

hyacinth, speak thy letters, and with thy leaves lisp 'ai,' 'ai,' more than is thy wont: a noble minstrel is dead.

Begin Sicilian Muses, begin the lament.

Ye nightingales, that wail in the thick foliage, tell the news to the Sicilian waters of [3] Arethusa, that Bion the herdsman is dead, that with him both the song is dead, and perished is Doric minstrelsy.

Begin, Sicilian Muses, begin the lament.

Plaintively wail beside the waters, Strymonian swans, and with mournful voices sing a sorrowful ode, with as sweet a sound as *was that* of old, *wherewith* he used to sing to your lips. [4] And tell, again, to Æagrian maids, tell to all Bistonian nymphs, that the Dorian Orpheus has perished.

Begin, Sicilian Muses, begin the lament.

That darling of the herds no longer sings: no longer does he warble, as he reclines beneath the solitary oaks: but in Pluto's *realm* he chants [5] a song of forgetfulness. And voiceless are the hills; and the heifers, which roam with the bulls, lament and will not go to pasture.

Begin, Sicilian Muses, begin the lament.

Thy sudden fate, O Bion, even Apollo bewailed, and the Satyrs grieved, and the dark-robed Priapi; and Pans sigh for thy melody, whilst the fountain nymphs through the wood mourned *for thee*, [6] and their tears became waters; and Echo

According to other traditions, the flower sprang from the blood of Ajax. See Sophocl. Ajax 430 (Lobeck); Ov. Met. xiii. 395, who combines the two legends, and Virg. Ecl. iii. 106. The hyacinth, we know, has no such inscription on its leaves.

[3] The nymph Arethusa, pursued by the river-god Alpheus, was changed by Artemis into a stream, which, flowing beneath the sea, rose again near Syracuse. See Virg. Æn. iii. 694—696. Virgil alludes to the land of pastoral song, Sicily, under this name, Ecl. xi., Extremum hunc Arethusa mihi, &c.

[4] A verse would seem to have slipped out here, which should have made mention of Thracian Orpheus, and so have connected Strymon, Bagria. and the Bistones with this song.—The Dorian Orpheus. So Propert. IV. i. 64, says of himself "Umbria Romani patria Callimachi."

[5] A song of forgetfulness.] Compare Theocr. i. 63.

[6] καὶ ὕδατα δάκρυα γέντο. "Et lachrymæ in rivos abeunt." Briggs suggests reading ὕδασι. Et undis lachrymæ obortæ sunt. Comp. Bion 34, καὶ Παγαὶ τὸν Ἄδωνιν ἐν ὤρεσι δακρύοντι. Spenser, Shepherd's Calendar, November,

    The floods do gasp, for dried is their source,
    And floods of tears flow in their stead perforce.

amid the rocks laments, because thou art mute, and mimics no more thy lips; and at thy death the trees have cast off their fruit, and the flowers have all withered; good milk hath not flowed from ewes; nor honey from hives; but it has perished in the wax wasted with grief; for no longer is it meet, now that thy honey is lost, to gather that.

Begin, Sicilian Muses, begin the lament.

[7] Not so much did the dolphin lament beside the shores of the sea, nor so sang the nightingale ever on the rocks, no, nor so much complained the swallow along the high mountains, [8] neither did Ceyx wail so much over the griefs of Halcyon.

Begin, Sicilian Muses, begin the lament.

Neither did Cerylus sing so much in the gray-green waves, nor so much [9] did the bird of Memnon, fluttering around his tomb, deplore the son of Aurora in the valleys of the East, as they have bewailed Bion, having perished.

Begin, Silician Muses, begin the lament.

Nightingales, and all swallows, which once he was wont to delight, which he was teaching to speak, sitting on the branches *of trees*, kept wailing opposite to each other, whilst the other birds kept responding, 'Grieve, ye doves, but we *will do so* too.'

Begin, Sicilian Muses, begin the lament.

---

[7] The dolphin's delight in song, commemorated in the fable of Arion, (Herod. i. 23; Pausan. iii. 25; Virg. Ecl. viii. 54,) is applied by Moschus here to the sorrow of all things for the hushing of Bion's song. For traits of the dolphin's musical taste and benevolence, see Pliny, N. H. ix. 8.

[8] Ceyx perished by shipwreck, and his wife, finding his lifeless body on the strand, threw herself into the sea. The gods in pity changed them both into the birds called Halcyons. Ov. Met. xi. 410. Comp. Virg. Georg. i. 399. Κηρύλος, Att. Κειρύλος, a sea-bird, according to some, the male Halcyon. Aristot. H. A.

[9] Μέμνονος ὄρνις. Aurora besought Jove to make her lover Tithonus immortal. She forgot to stipulate for immortal youth. She therefore had an infirm, though immortal, paramour. But while he was yet young she bore him two sons, of whom Memnon was one. Memnon was slain at Troy by Achilles, and Aurora obtained from Jove a promise that his memory should have more than mortal honours. Accordingly from his funeral pyre there rose a flight of birds, which having thrice flown round the flames, divided themselves into two bodies, and fought so fiercely that above half perished in the fire. These birds, called Memnonides yearly returned to Memnon's tomb, and renewed the encounter. See O. Met. xiii., Terque rogum lustrant, et consonus exit in auras
  Plangor.
See also Pliny, x. 36.

Who shall sing to thy pipe, O thrice-regretted? And who shall apply his lip to thy reeds? Who so bold? For even yet they breathe of thy lips and thy breath: and Echo amid the reeds feeds upon thy songs. To Pan I bear [10]the pipe: haply even he would fear to set his mouth to it, lest he should carry off a second prize after thee.

Begin, Sicilian Muses, begin the lament.

[11]Galatea too weeps for thy lay, *she* whom of old thou didst delight, as she sat in thy company along the sea-beach. For not like Cyclops didst thou sing: from him indeed the fair Galatea used to fly; but thee she was wont to regard [12]with more sweetness than the sea. And now, forgetful of the wave, she sits on the lonely sands, and even yet leads thy ... to pasture.

Begin, Sicilian Muses, begin the lament.

All along with thee, O herdsman, have perished the Muses' gifts, charming kisses of maidens, lips of boys: and around thy tomb weep sad-visaged Loves. Venus loves thee far more than the kiss, with which lately she kissed dying Adonis. This is a second grief to thee, most musical of rivers! This, [3]O Meles, is a fresh grief; to thy sorrow perished Homer aforetime, that [14]sweet mouth of Calliope, and men say thou didst deplore thine illustrious son in streams of much weeping, and didst fill all the sea with thy voice: now again thou weepest another son, and pinest over a fresh woe. Both *were* beloved by the fountains; the one indeed was wont to drink of the Pegasean spring; the other, to enjoy a draught of the Arethusa. And the one sang the fair daughter of Tyndarus, and the mighty son of Thetis, and Menelaus, son of Atreus: but the other would sing not of wars, nor tears, but Pan; and would sound *the praise* of herdsmen, and feed the herd

---

[10] Πανὶ φέρω τὸ μέλιγμα. μέλιγμα is equivalent to "fistula," the effect for the cause. In Meleager's epigrams, as Wakefield observes, Anacreon is called τὸ μέλισμα, that is, "auctor τοῦ μελίσματος."

[11] The poet here alludes to Bion's Idyll on Galatea, a fragment only of which is extant.

[12] Compare Theocr. Idyll xi. 43; Virgil Ecl. ix. 39.

[13] Meles, a river of Ionia, washes the walls of Smyrna, where Bion was born. Here also was supposed to have been the birth-place of Homer: hence called Melesigenes.

[14] Compare here Theocr. Idyll vii. 37, καὶ γὰρ ἐγὼ Μοισᾶν καπυρὸν τι να—

as he sang: and he was wont to fashion Pan's-pipes, and to milk the sweet heifer, and to teach the lips of youths, and to cherish Eros in his bosom, [15]and rouse a passion in Aphrodité.

Begin, Sicilian Muses, begin the lament.

Every famous city laments thee, O Bion, *as do* all the towns: [16]Ascra indeed wails for thee, far more than for Hesiod: not so much does Bœotian Hylæ regret Pindar; nor so much did pleasant Lesbos weep about Alcæus: no, nor hath the Ceian town wept for her bard so much. Paros regrets thee more than Archilochus; and Mitylene yet plaintively utters thy melody instead of Sappho's. All, as many as have a clear-sounding voice, *all* singers of pastorals by the Muses' favour, weep for thy fate, now thou art dead. [17]Sicelidas, the glory of Samos, weeps; and among the Cydonians, he who was aforetime cheerful to look on with his smiling eye, Lycidas, yet sheds tears as he wails: whilst among the citizens of Cos, Philetas mourns beside the river Halens; and among Syracusans, Theocritus: but I sing for thee a strain of [18]Ausonian sorrow, *I*, no stranger to the pastoral song, but heir to the Doric Muse, which thou didst teach thy scholars: honouring me, to others indeed thou didst leave thy wealth, but to me thy song.

Begin, Sicilian Muses, begin the lament.

Alas, alas, when once in a garden the mallows have died, or the green parsley, or blooming crisp dill, they live again after, and spring up another year. But we, the great, and brave, or wise *of* men, after we have once died, unheard of in hollow

---

[15] καὶ ἤρεθε τὰν Ἀφροδίταν. Comp. Theocr. Idyll xxi. 21.

[16] Ascra, a town of Bœotia, or according to Hesiod, who was its chief glory, a village at the foot of Helicon in the Thespian region. O. et D. 638.—Hylæ, a city of Bœotia. Pindar was born either at Thebes or Cynocephalæ, B. C. 522. Alcæus, a native of Lesbos. Simonides, of Ceos, B. C. 556. Archilochus, of Paros. See Theocr. Epigr. xix. Sappho, (of the same date with Alcæus, B. C. 628—570,) was one of the two leaders of the Æolian school of poetry, Alcæus being the other. She was a native of Mytilene.

[17] Σικελίδας. See Theocr. Idyll vii. 40. Lycidas: Theocr. vii. 12. The Cydonians inhabited the south of Crete. Philetas: ibid. 40. Τριοπίδαις. Triops was a king of the island of Cos. Cf. Theocr. xvii. 68. The river Halens is mentioned in the Thalysia referred to above.

[18] Αὐσονίκας ὀδύνας. The Sicilian Sea was called Ausonius Pontus, from Auson, a son of Ulysses and Calypso. Therefore as Moschus was a Syracusan, he calls his song Ausonian.

earth, sleep a right long and boundless slumber, from which none are roused.[19] And in the earth thou indeed wilt be covered in silence, but it has seemed good to the Nymphs that the frog should croak for ever. Yet I envy him not: for *'tis* no pretty song he sings.

Begin, Sicilian Muses, begin the lament.

Poison came, O Bion, to thy lip: thou knewest poison. How did it find access to thy lips, yet not become sweet ? or what mortal *was* so far ruthless, as to mix for thee, or to give thee the poison, if thou didst speak ? He shunned the *power of* song.

Begin, Sicilian Muses, begin the lament.

But justice has overtaken all. And I, shedding tears over this woe, bewail thy fate; yet were I able, like [20] Orpheus, having gone down to Tartarus, like Ulysses once, or as Alcides in days of yore, I too would haply descend to the home of Pluto, that I might see thee, and, if thou singest to Pluto, that I might hear what thou singest. Nay, but in the presence of the damsel (Proserpine) warble some Sicilian strain, sing some pleasant pastoral. She too, being Sicilian, [21] sport-

---

[19] Cf. Job xiv. 7—10, "There is hope of a tree, if it be cut down, that it will sprout again, and that the tender branch thereof will not cease. Though the root thereof wax old in the earth, and the stock thereof die in the ground ; yet through the scent of water it will bud, and bring forth boughs like a plant. But man dieth, and wasteth away : yea, man giveth up the ghost, and where is he?"

Spenser, Whence is it that the flow'ret of the field doth fade
        And lyeth buried long in winter's bale?
        Yet soon as spring his mantle hath displayed,
        It flow'reth fresh, as it should never fail,
        But thing on earth that is of most avail,
        As virtue's branch and beauty's bud,
        Reliven not for any good.

Catull., Soles occidere et redire possunt:
        Nobis cum semel occidit brevis lux
        Nox est perpetua una dormienda.

[20] Alcides went alive to Tartarus by command: Odysseus, to obtain information needful to him: but Orpheus went down to recover his wife. His story is beautifully told in the fourth Georgic of Virgil. See also Pope's Ode on St. Cecilia's Day. Chapman.

[21] Proserpine, daughter of Ceres, was carried off by Pluto. The legend is to be found in Hesiod Theog. 914; Callimach. H. in Cerer. 9, and Spanheim, on that passage; Ovid. Met. v. 565; Fast. iv. 422. Milton alludes to it thus:

ed on the Ætnæan shores, and knew the Doric song: nor will thy strain be unhonoured; and as of old to Orpheus, sweetly singing to his lyre, she gave Eurydice to return, so will she send thee, Bion, to thy hills. Yes, if even I could avail aught by singing to my pipe, I too would sing before Pluto.

IDYLL IV.

MEGARA, THE WIFE OF HERCULES.

My mother, why dost thou thus wound thy spirit, being sad beyond measure, and *why* is the former bloom no longer preserved on thy cheeks? Why, I pray thee, art thou vexed so much? Is it in sooth because thine illustrious son suffers countless annoyances from [1] a man of no account, even as a lion from a fawn? Alas me! why then have the immortal gods thus so far dishonoured me? why then did my parents beget me to a fate thus adverse? Ill-fated *am I*, who, since I have come to the bed of a faultless hero, whom I did honour indeed like my own eyes, ay, even now both worship and reverence him in my heart. But than him has no other of living beings been more ill-starred, or tasted so many cares in his own thoughts; wretched man, who with the [2] bow and arrows, which Apollo himself had provided for him, dire weapons either of one of

> Not that fair field
> Of Enna, where Proserpine, gathering flowers,
> Herself a fairer flower, by gloomy Dis
> Was gather'd, which cost Ceres all that pain
> To seek her through the world; nor that sweet grove
> Of Daphne by Orontes, and th' inspired
> Castalian spring, might with this Paradise
> Of Eden strive.   Parad. Lost. Book iv.

[1] Eurystheus, to wit. Megara was the daughter of king Creon of Thebes, and wife of Hercules, (Hom. Od. xi. 269. Eurip. Herc. Fur. 9, &c.,) by whom he had several children; whom after his battle with the Minyans he slew, with two of the children of Iphiclus, under the influence of madness sent by Juno.

[2] τόξοισιν. By this name is understood, bow, arrows, and quiver. πᾶσα ἡ τοξικὴ σκευή. Apollodorus says Mercury gave Hercules his sword, Apollo his bow, Vulcan his mail, Minerva his cloak, whilst his club he himself cut in the Nemean grove.

the Fates, or of Erinnys, ³slew his own children, and robbed them of their dear life, as he raged about his house, and it was full of slaughter. Them indeed I, wretched *woman*, beheld with mine own eyes, stricken by their father; and this hath befallen no other even in a dream: nor was I able to succour them, though they loudly called upon their mother; for resistless evil was nigh. ⁴And even as a bird laments over her nestlings as they perish, which while still in infancy a fierce snake devours amid the thick bushes, while she, kind mother, hovers over them shrieking very shrilly, yet is not able, I ween, to succour her children ; for in truth, she herself hath a great dread of coming nigher to the ruthless monster; so I, most wretched mother, wailing for mine own offspring, with frantic feet kept running to and fro through my house frequently. Yes, and would that dying along with my children I too had lain low, having through my heart a poisonous arrow, thou, Artemis, mighty ruler to women, the gentler beings. So, when they had mourned for us, would our parents with their own hands have placed us on a common pile with many funeral honours; and having collected into one golden urn the bones of all, would have buried us, where we first were born. But now they indeed inhabit horse-breeding Thebes, ploughing the deep rich ⁵clods of the Aonian plain; but I at Tiryns, Juno's rocky city, wretched woman that I am, am ever in the same manner wounded at heart by many griefs; and there is present to me no rest from tears. But my husband indeed I behold with mine eyes *only* for a brief space in our house; for a work is prepared for him of many labours, at which he toils, as he roams over land and sea, yes, for he has within his

---

³ Eurip. Herc. F. says that Megara was slain along with her children; he follows Stesichorus and Panyasis. Plutarch and Pausanias coincide with Moschus.
⁴ Compare for this beautiful passage, Hom. Il. ii. 308. Virg. Geor. iv. 512,
        Qualis populeâ mœrens Philomela sub umbrâ
        Amissos queritur fœtus ; quos durus arator
        Observans nido implumes detraxit: at illa
        Flet noctem, ramoque sedens miserabile carmen
        Integrat, et mœstis latè loca questibus implet.
⁵ Aonian plain.] Bœotia was by its ancient inhabitants called Aonia. Tiryns, a town of Achaia, not far from Argos, was the native place o. Hercules, hence called Tirynthius.

breast a strong heart of iron or stone; [6] but thou meltest away like water, weeping both at night, and as many days as *come* from Jove. None other, however, of my kinsfolk can stand by and comfort me; for it is not a wall between houses that shuts them in; no! but all dwell right beyond the [7] piny Isthmus: nor have I to whom, having looked, as an ill-fated woman, I could unfold my heart, except at least, 'tis true, my sister Pyrrha: but she herself, too, is grieving more about her husband, thy son, [8] Iphiclus; for most woeful children of all I deem that you have borne both to a god and a mortal man.

Thus in sooth spake she: and [9] the warmer tears poured the more down from her eyelids on her lovely bosom, as she called to mind her children, and her own parents afterwards. And in like manner Alcmena was [10] bedewing her white cheeks with tears; and deeply while she groaned even from her heart, with wise words thus did she reply to her dear daughter-in-law:

[11] 'Unhappy in thy children, why then, I pray, hath this fallen upon thy sharp thoughts? how *is it that* thou wishest to disturb us both, by speaking of our unceasing sorrows? for not now have they been wept for the first time. Are not the *woes* enough, in which we are involved as they arise, ever and anon, each second day? Yes, fond indeed of laments

---

[6] So the Hebrew sacred writers. Joshua vii. 5, "Wherefore the hearts of the people melted, and became as water." Psalm xxii. 14, "I am poured out like water: my heart also in the midst of my body is like melting wax." lviii. 6, "Let him fall away like water that runneth apace."

[7] The Isthmus Corinthiacus is here meant. κατ' ἐξοχὴν. Pine trees were common in that maritime country, and a garland of pine leaves formed the victor's crown at the Isthmian games in honour of Neptune, to whom the pine was sacred.

[8] Iphiclus, the half-brother of Hercules, married, secondly, Pyrrha, youngest daughter of Creon, king of Thebes. Apollod. ii. 4, § 11, θεῷ τε καὶ ἀνέρι. Jupiter and Amphitryon.

[9] Of the numerous emendations of the probably corrupt μήλων, Wakefield's μᾶλλον seems most intelligible. Briggs suggests δήλως. If we read the verse as it stands in Heskin's edition, μήλων, we should construe, "and moist tears were pouring down her cheeks from her eyelids on her fair bosom;" but this is hardly Greek.

[10] Wakefield suggests here ἐμίαινεν, quoting Virg. Æn. xii. 67, Stat. Theb. ix. 713, and Young's line, "And lights on lids unsullied with a tear."

[11] Δαιμονίη παίδων, rightly explained by Schwebel, κακόδαιμον παίδων ἕνεκα.

would be the man, who [12] would wish to add to the number of our woes. Cheer up then! such fate as this we have met by Heaven's *behest;* and in truth I see thee, dear child, labouring under unabating griefs: yet I am ready to pardon your woe; for in fact I suppose [13] even of joy there is satiety. And I very exceedingly lament and pity thee, for that thou hast partaken of our dismal destiny, which also hangs heavily over our heads. For be Proserpine and richly-robed Demeter witnesses, (by whom with great hurt to himself would any of our foes swear wilfully a false oath,) that in mine heart I love thee not a whit less, than if thou hadst come from out my womb, and wert to me in mine house a [14] late-born daughter: nor do I imagine that, for thine own part, this at any rate altogether escapes thee. Wherefore say not ever, [15] my young shoot, that I care not for thee, not even if I wail more constantly than fair-haired Niobe: for 'tis no cause of blame for a mother to weep over an afflicted son: since for ten months did I labour, before even I first beheld him, whilst I had him in my womb, and he brought me near to [16] *Hell's* gate-keeper Pluto; so severe throes did I endure when about to travail hard with him. But now my son is gone to accomplish a fresh toil on a foreign land, nor know I, ill-starred *woman,* whether I shall welcome him again having returned hither, or not. And besides also a fearful dream has scared me during sweet sleep; and I fear exceedingly, having seen a hurtful vision, lest it betide something untoward to my children. For my son, stout Hercules, seemed to me to hold in both his hands a well-made spade, with which he was delving,

---

[12] ὅστις ἀριθμήσειεν, understand ἄχεα, Qui numeret dolores ultra nostros, or construe as if it were ὅστις ἐπαριθμήσειεν ἡμετέροις ἀχέεσσι, which has been done in this translation. Two lines above, Polwhele compares Matt. v. 34, "Sufficient for the day is the evil thereof."

[13] "And if there is a satiety of joy, much more of grief." These words are an excuse for sorrow finding vent. Moschus imitates Hom. Iliad xiii. 636, πάντων γὰρ κόρος ἐστὶ· καὶ ὕπνου καὶ φιλότητος
μολπῆς τε γλυκερῆς, καὶ ἀμύμονος ὀρχηθμοῖο.

[14] τηλυγέτη—ἡ τελευταία τῷ πατρὶ γενομένη: one born at the end, last. An Homeric word, from τῆλε, of same root as τέλος; and γίνομαι. See Butm. Lexil. p. 510—512. Ed. 1836.

[15] ἐμὸν θάλος. So Meleager Epigr. 109, αἱ αἱ, ποῦ τὸ ποθεινὸν ἐμοὶ θάλος.

[16] πυλάρταο. So Hom. Il. viii. 365, εἰς Ἀϊδός περ ἰόντα πυλάρταο ρατεροῖο.

as *one* that had taken *the work* for hire, a dyke at the outskirt of some flourishing field, stripped, without cloak, and well-girdled tunic: but when he had arrived at the end of all the work, labouring at the strong fence of a levelled plot for vines, in truth, he was about, having placed his [17]shovel upon the projecting raised bank, to put on the garments, in which he had been clad before; when, on a sudden, above the deep trench there blazed up a fierce fire, and a vast flame was gathering round him: but he kept ever drawing back with swift feet, desiring to escape the destructive weapon of Hephæstus; and continually in front of his person he was brandishing, as a [18]shield, his spade: and with his eyes he kept looking around hither and thither, lest in truth the hostile fire should burn him. High-souled Iphiclus, desiring, as methought, to lend him help, tripped and fell upon the ground, ay, before he came *up to him:* nor could he raise himself erect again, but lay [19]still, like a feeble old man, whom even against his will joyless age has forced to fall; and there he lies fixedly on the ground, till some passer-by maintaining [20]ancient reverence for the hoary beard, has upraised him by the hand; so on the ground had spear-brandishing Iphiclus [21]fallen. But as I beheld my two sons in sore distress, I did weep, till sound sleep at length was dispelled from mine eyes, and forthwith bright dawn came. Such dreams, dear one, have thoroughly affrighted my mind all night long: [22]but may they all turn from our house upon Eurystheus; and may my spirit become a prophet to him, nor fate accomplish otherwise aught else.

[17] λίστρον, a hoe or shovel for levelling. Hom. Odyss. xxii. 455. ἄνδηρον is used by Theocr. v. 93.

[18] γέρρον, an oblong wicker shield covered with ox-hide, such as the Persians wore. Herod. vii. 61. See Thirlwall, H. of Greece, vol. ii. p. 255, note 1.

[19] ἀστεμφὲς, immobiliter. Theocr. Idyll xiii. 37, ἀστεμφεῖ Τελαμῶνι, Telamoni invicto.

[20] ὄπιδα προτέρην πολιοῖο γενείου, for προτέρην, senilem, Valken. reads στυγερὴν, Jacobs κρατερὴν or κρυερὴν, Wakefield τρομερὴν, while Briggs suggests προπετῆ, prostrate. But surely προτέρην, "elder" or "ancient," will yield as good a sense as either.

[21] λελίαστο. Hom. Il. xx. 430, λιαζόμενον προτὶ γαίῃ.

[22] πρὸς Εὐρυσθῆα τράποιτο. So Virg. Georg. iii. 513, Dii meliora piis, erroremque hostibus illum. Æn. ii. 190, Quod dii prius omen in ipsum Convertant.

IDYLL V.
THE CHOICE.

WHEN the breeze gently strikes the gray-green sea, [1] I am roused in my fearful mind, and no longer is land dear to me, [2] but the calm *sea* attaches me *to it* far more : but whensoever the hoary deep has resounded, and the sea-water foams up [3] into an arch, and the waves rage afar, I look out for land and trees, and flee the brine : and welcome to me is earth ; then does the shady wood delight *me*, where though the wind should blow violently, [4] yet the pine tree sings. Surely a hard life lives the fisherman, whose house is his bark, the sea his occupation, fish his slippery prey. But sweet to me is sleep beneath a leafy plane, and I should love to hear the sound of the fountain hard by, which, as it babbles, delights, not alarms, the rustic.

IDYLL VI.
"LOVE THEM THAT LOVE YOU." [5]

PAN loved his neighbour Echo, and Echo was [6] enamoured of the frisky Satyr, while the Satyr was mad after Lyda : as Echo Pan, so did the Satyr inflame Echo, and Lyda the

[1] Animo timido *ad navigandum* sollicitor.
[2] ποτάγει. Briggs suggests πείθει δε, as does also Jacobs.
[3] κυρτὸν, i. e. κατὰ τὸ κυρτόν, archedly. τὰ δε κύματα μακρά. Compare Hom. Iliad. iv. 422, and Virg. Georg. iii. 237,

  Fluctus ut in medis cæpit cum albescere ponto,
  Longius ex altoque sinum trahit, utque volutus,
  Ad terras immane sonat per saxa, nec ipso
  Monte minor procumbit : at ima exæstuat unda
  Vorticibus, nigramque altè subjectat arenam.

[4] ἁ πίτυς ἄδει. Cf. Theocr. Id. i. 1 ; Virg. Eclog. viii. 22,
  Mænalus argutumque nemus, pinosque loquentes
  Semper habet.

[5] Heskin gives Theocr. Id. vi. 17, as the heading of this Idyll. καὶ φεύγει φιλέοντα, καὶ οὐ φιλέοντα διώκει. Horace, Od. I. xxxiii. 5,
  Insignem tenui fronte Lycorida
  Cyri torret amor : Cyrus in asperam
  Declinat Pholoen, &c.

[6] ᾖρα and ᾖρατο. Theocr. (vii. 96) and Bion (vi. 8) have the same variations of the form of this verb—Σκιρτητᾶ Σατύρω. So Virg. Ecl v. 73, Saltantes Satyros imitabitur Alphesibæus.

Satyr: and love was smouldering *in each* in their turns. For as strongly as any one of them hated the lover, so strongly in like manner was he, loving, hated, and was suffering [1] a requital. These lessons speak I to all them that love not, [2] 'Cherish them that love you, that if ye love, ye may be loved again.'

IDYLL VII.

ALPHEUS.

[3] ALPHEUS, when he glides along the sea, past Pisa, comes to Arethusa, bringing his waters [4] laden with wild-olives, bearing as a dower fair leaves and flowers and sacred dust; and he enters the waves deeply and runs in under the sea beneath, and water mingles not with waters; and the sea is not conscious of it, as the river passes through. Love, knavish boy, plotter of ill, teacher of fearful things, has taught through his spell even a river to dive.

AN EPIGRAM

ON EROS PLOUGHING.

[5] HAVING laid aside torch and bow, mischievous Eros took up an ox-goad, and he had a wallet slung-on-his-shoulders;

[1] πάσχε δ' ἅ ποίει, is another reading; but ἄποινα, which has good authority, is more elegant.

[2] Cf. Theocr. xxiii. verse the last. Shelley has translated this Idyll. See notes to Chapman's translation.

[3] The legend of Arethusa ran thus: Heated with the chase, she bathed in the Alpheus; and while so engaged, frightened by a strange murmur in the stream, she sprang to the shore in terror. The river-god pursued her through all Arcadia, where at eventide, feeling her strength fast failing, she called Artemis to aid, by whom she was changed into a fountain. Alpheus, resuming his watery form, would fain mingle his stream with hers. But she fled under the earth through the sea, till she rose again in Arcadia, followed by Alpheus still. The Greeks believed that offerings thrown into the Alpheus at Elis rose again at Ortygia near Syracuse. See Pausan. v. 7, § 2; Ov. Met. v. 572; Virg. Æn. iii. 694, &c

[4] Compare Sil. Ital. xiv.,
Hic Arethusa suum piscoso fonte receptat
Alphæum, sacræ portantem signa coronæ.

[5] Grotius has rendered this Epigram into Latin:

and having joined under the yoke the toil-enduring necks of oxen, he sowed the furrow of Ceres, that it should bear grain. And looking up he said to Jove himself, [1] 'Make full the sown fields, lest I place thee, Europa's bull, under the plough.'

FRAGMENT.

[2] WOULD that my sire had taught me to tend fleecy sheep, in which case, seated beneath the elms, or under the rocks, playing on my pipes, I would solace my cares with reeds. Let us fly, ye Pierides: seek we another well-built city for our country; yet in sooth I will speak out to all, that ruinous drones have harmed the honey-bees.

> Rus petiit positis arcu facibusque Cupido:
>   Virga manu; tergo pendula pera fuit.
> Hoc habitu sulcos glebæ Cerealis arabat
>   Gnavus, agens domitos sub juga curva boves:
> Respiciensque Jovem: terras, ait, ignibus ure,
>   Ne bos Europæ tu quoque factus ares.

[1] πλῆσον, others read πρῆσον, which Grotius seems to have preferred. Why, it is hard to see.

[2] Wakefield suggests, that these lines have suggested Virgil's passage in the mouth of Gallus, Ecl. x.,

> Atque utinam ex vobis unus, vestrique fuissem
> Aut custos gregis, aut maturæ vinitor uvæ.

THEOCRITUS,

BION, AND MOSCHUS.

METRICALLY TRANSLATED

BY M. J. CHAPMAN, M. A.,
OF TRINITY COLLEGE, CAMBRIDGE.

THEOCRITUS.

IDYLL I.

THYRSIS THE SHEPHERD, AND THE GOATHERD.

THYRSIS.

Sweet is the music which the whispering pine
Makes to the murmuring fountains; sweet is thine,
Breathed from the pipe: the second prize thy due—
To Pan, the horned ram; to thee, the ewe;
And thine the yearling, when the ewe he takes—
A savoury mess the tender yearling makes.

GOATHERD.

Sweeter thy song than yonder gliding down
Of water from the rock's o'erhanging crown;
If a ewe-sheep for fee the Muses gain,
Thou, shepherd! shalt a stall-fed lamb obtain;
But if it rather please the tuneful Nine
To take the lamb, the ewe shall then be thine.

THYRSIS.

O wilt thou, for the Nymphs' sake, goatherd! fill
Thy pipe with music on this sloping hill,
Where grow the tamarisks? wilt sit, dear friend,
And play for me, while I thy goats attend?

GOATHERD.

We must not pipe at noon in any case;
For then Pan rests him, wearied from the chase.
Him, quick to wrath we fear, as us befits;
On his keen nostril sharp gall ever sits.
But thou—to thee the griefs of Daphnis known,
And the first skill in pastoral song thine own—
Come to yon elm, into whose shelter deep
Afront Priapus and the Naiads peep—

Where the thick oaks stand round the shepherd's seat:
There, sitting with me in that cool retreat,
If thou wilt sing, as when thou didst contest
With Libyan Chromis which could sing the best,
Thine, Thyrsis, this twin-bearing goat shall be,
That fills two milk-pails thrice a-day for me;
And this deep ivy-cup with sweetest wax
Bedewed, twin-eared, that of the graver smacks.
Around its lips lush ivy twines on high,
Sprinkled with drops of bright cassidony;
And as the curling ivy spreads around,
On every curl the saffron fruit is found.
With flowing robe and Lydian head-dress on,
Within, a woman to the life is done—
An exquisite design! on either side
Two men with flowing locks each other chide,
By turns contending for the woman's love,
But not a whit her mind their pleadings move.
One while she gives to this a glance and smile,
And turns and smiles on that another while.
But neither any certain favour gains—
Only their eyes are swollen for their pains.
Hard by, a rugged rock and fisher old,
Who drags a mighty net, and seems to hold,
Preparing for the cast: he stands to sight,
A fisher putting forth his utmost might.
A youth's strength in the gray-head seems to dwell,
So much the sinews of his neck outswell.
And near that old man with his sea-tanned hue,
With purple grapes a vineyard shines to view.
A little boy sits by the thorn-hedge trim,
To watch the grapes—two foxes watching him:
One through the ranges of the vines proceeds,
And on the hanging vintage slyly feeds;
The other plots and vows his scrip to search,
And for his breakfast leave him—in the lurch.
Meanwhile he twines and to a rush fits well
A locust trap with stalks of asphodel;
And twines away with such absorbing glee,
Of scrip or vines he never thinks—not he!
The juicy curled acanthus hovers round

Th' Æolian cup—when seen a marvel found.
Hither a Calydonian skipper brought it,
For a great cheese-cake and a goat I bought it;
Untouched by lip—this cup shall be thy hire,
If thou wilt sing that song of sweet desire.
I envy not: begin! the strain outpour;
'Twill not be thine on dim Oblivion's shore.

THYRSIS.

Begin, dear Muses! the bucolic strain;
For Thyrsis sings, your own Ætnean swain.
Where were ye, Nymphs! when Daphnis pined away,
Where through his Tempe Peneus loves to stray,
Or Pindus lifts himself? Ye were not here—
Where broad Anapus flows or Acis clear,
Or where tall Ætna looks out on the main.

Begin, dear Muses! the bucolic strain.
From out the mountain-lair the lions growled,
Wailing his death—the wolves and jackals howled

Begin, dear Muses! the bucolic strain:
Around him in a long and mournful train,
Sad-faced, a number of the horned kind,
Heifers, bulls, cows, and calves, lamenting pined.

First Hermes from the mountain came and said,
"Daphnis, by whom art thou disquieted?
For whom dost thou endure so fierce a flame?"

Then cowherds, goatherds, shepherds, thronging came,
And asked what ailed him. E'en Priapus went,
And said: "Sad Daphnis, why this languishment?
In every grove, by fountains, far and near,
Thee the loved girl is seeking every where.
Ah, foolish lover! to thyself unkind,
Miscalled a cowherd, with a goatherd's mind!
The goatherd when he sees his goats at play,
Envies their wanton sport and pines away.
And thou at sight of virgins, when they smile,
Dost look with longing eyes and pine the while,
Because with them the dance thou dost not lead."

No word he answered, but his grief did feed,

And brought to end his love, that held him fast,
And only ended with his life at last.

Then Cypris came—the queen of soft desire,
Smiling in secret, but pretending ire,
And said: "To conquer love did Daphnis boast,
But, Daphnis! is not love now uppermost?"
Her answered he: "Thou cruel sorrow-feeder!
Curst Cypris! mankind's hateful mischief-breeder!
'Tis plain my sun is set: but I shall show
The blight of love in Hades' house below.
'Where Cypris kiss'd a cowherd'—men will speak—
Hasten to Ida! thine Anchises seek.
Around their hives swarmed bees are humming here,
Here the low galingale—thick oaks are there.
Adonis, the fair youth, a shepherd too,
Wounds hares, and doth all savage beasts pursue.
Go! challenge Diomede to fight with thee—
'I tame the cowherd Daphnis, fight with me.'

"Ye bears, who in the mountain hollows dwell,
Ye tawny jackals, bounding wolves, farewell!
The cowherd Daphnis never more shall rove
In quest of you through thicket, wood, and grove.
Farewell, ye rivers, that your streams profuse
From Thymbris pour; farewell, sweet Arethuse!
I drove my kine—a cowherd whilom here—
To pleasant pasture, and to water clear.
Pan! Pan! if seated on a jagged peak
Of tall Lycæus now; or thou dost seek
The heights of Mænalus—leave them awhile,
And hasten to thy own Sicilian isle.
The tomb, which e'en the gods admire, leave now—
Lycaon's tomb and Helice's tall brow.
Hasten, my king! and take this pipe that clips,
Uttering its honey breath, the player's lips.
For even now, dragged downward, must I go,
By love dragged down to Hades' house below.
Now violets, ye thorns and brambles bear!
Narcissus now on junipers appear!
And on the pine-tree pears! since Daphnis dies,
To their own use all things be contraries!

The stag trail hounds; in rivalry their song
The mountain owls with nightingales prolong!"

 He said, and ceased: and Cypris wished, indeed,
To raise him up, but she could not succeed;
His fate-allotted threads of life were spent,
And Daphnis to the doleful river went.
The whirlpool gorged him—by the Nymphs not scorned,
Dear to the Muses, and by them adorned.

 Cease! cease, ye Muses! the bucolic strain.
Give me the cup and goat that I may drain
The pure milk from her; and, for duty's sake,
A due libation to the Muses make.
All hail, ye Muses! hail, and favour me,
And my hereafter song shall sweeter be.

GOATHERD.

Honey and honey-combs melt in thy mouth,
And figs from Ægilus! for thou, dear youth,
The musical cicada dost excel.
Behold the cup! how sweetly doth it smell!
'Twill seem to thee as though the lovely Hours
Had newly dipt it in their fountain-showers.
Hither, Cissætha! milk her! yearling friskers,
Forbear—behold the ram's huge beard and whiskers!

IDYLL II.

THE SORCERESS.

WHERE are the laurels? where the philters? roll
The finest purple wool around the bowl.
Quick! Thestylis, that I with charms may bind
The man I love, but faithless and unkind.
This is the twelfth day he my sight hath fled,
And knows not whether I be quick or dead;
The twelfth day since he cross'd my threshold o'er,
Nor, cruel! once hath knocked upon my door,
In all that time. His fancy, apt to change,
Cypris and Love have elsewhere made to range.

I'll go—to see and chide him for my sorrow—
To Timagetus' wrestling-school to-morrow.
Now will I charm him with the magic rite:
Come forth, thou Moon! with thy propitious light;
Cold, silent goddess! at this witching hour
To thee I'll chant, and to th' Infernal Power,
Dread Hecate; whom, coming through the mounds
Of blood-swoln corses, flee the trembling hounds.
Hail, Hecate! prodigious demon, hail!
Come at the last, and make the work prevail;
That this strong brewage may perform its part
No worse than that was made by Circe's art,
By bold Medea, terrible as fair,
Or Perimeda of the golden hair.

Him hither, hither draw, my magic wheel!
First in the fire is burnt the barley meal;
Quick! Thestylis, quick! sprinkle more—yet more;
Wretch! wither do thine idle fancies soar?
Am I thy scorn and mock? sprinkle and say—
"The bones of Delphis thus I shred away."

Him hither, hither draw, my magic wheel!
Delphis has made me fiercest tortures feel;
I burn the laurel over Delphis now:
As crackles loud the kindled laurel bough,
Blazes, and e'en its dust we not discern—
So may the flesh of Delphis dropping burn!

Him hither, hither draw, my magic wheel!
As by the help divine, which I appeal,
I melt this wax, may Myndian Delphis melt!
As whirls this wheel, may he, love's impulse felt,
At my forsaken door be made to reel!

Him hither, hither draw, my magic wheel!
Bran now I offer: thou, Queen Artemis!
Canst move aught firm, e'en Adamantine Dis.
Hark! the dogs howl; the goddess now doth pass
The cross-roads through: ring, ring the sounding brass!

Him hither, hither draw, my magic wheel!
The sea is silent; not a breath doth steal

Over the stillness; but the troubled din
Of passion is not hushed my heart within;
I burn for him, who hath defamed my life,
Undone a virgin, made me not his wife.

    Him hither, hither draw, my magic wheel!
Thrice the libation poured, I thrice unseal
My lips, August One! thrice these words I speak;
Whoever lies with Delphis, cheek by cheek,
May he forget her so much as they say
Theseus forgot, and left in Dia's bay
The bright-haired Ariadne—fast away
Sailing from Dia with his rapid keel.

    Him hither, hither draw, my magic wheel!
A little herb in Arcady there grows,
Which colts and mares doth strangely discompose,
(Hence called Hippomanes); for this they skurry
O'er mountain-ranges with a frantic hurry:
Thus from the wrestling-school, all bright with oil,
May Delphis madly rush—with thoughts that boil;
May he for me this maddening passion feel!

    Him hither, hither draw, my magic wheel!
This fringe he dropt, that ran his cloak across,
I tear, and to the furious fire I toss.
Ah, love! ah, cruel love! why dost outsuck
All of my blood, like marsh-leech firmly stuck?

    Him hither, hither draw, my magic wheel!
A draught whose ill none antidote can heal
From a bruised lizard I'll to-morrow make:
Now, Thestylis, this poisonous brewage take,
And smear his threshold—there my mind must be,
As thereto bound; but he cares not for me:
And having smeared the door-way, spitting there,
Then say, "The bones of Delphis thus I smear."

    Him hither, hither draw, my magic wheel!
How, left alone, shall I with sorrow deal?
Or where begin with my grief-plighted thought?
Who first on me this love—this mischief brought?
Anaxo came, on whom it fell this year
The basket to Diana's grove to bear:

She came for me and told me, in the show
'Mid many a beast a lioness would go.

    Whence grew my love, divinest Moon! attend:
Theucharila, whose life did lately end,
My Thracian nurse, now numbered with the blest,
Came also to me, prayed me, strongly prest
To go and look upon the splendid show.
At last I went—ah, doomed to bitter woe!
My linen tunic, never worn before,
And Clearista's glistering robe I wore.

    Whence grew my love, divinest Moon! attend:
Whilst I along the public road did wend,
Midway by Lycon's house, I saw, alas!
Delphis and youthful Eudamippus pass.
The beards of both were of a yellower dye
Than the bright gold-bedropt cassidony.
Twain wrestlers, lately breathed, their breasts, bright Queen!
Outshone the sparkles of thy golden sheen.

    Whence grew my love, divinest Moon! attend:
I saw, loved, maddened! raging love did rend
My very soul; my bloom of beauty bright
Withered at once as by a sudden blight:
The pomp I saw not passing in my view,
And how I reached my home I never knew;
A fiery torment on my vitals fed;
Ten days and nights I lay upon my bed.

    Whence grew my love, divinest Moon! attend:
Such hues and juices of the thapsus lend
Gloomed on my cheek; off dropt my crown of hair;
I was but skin and bones; in my despair
Whom sought I not? what magic-dealing crone
Consulted not? but I found help from none:
On hastened time, that brings all things to end.

    Whence grew my love, divinest Moon! attend:
Then to my hand-maid I revealed my mind;
"Some remedy for my sore sickness find;
I pine for, dote upon, the Myndian youth,
Am altogether his in very sooth;
At Timagetus' school watch, bring him me,

For there he visits—there he loves to be.
And when you see him from the rest apart,
Then nod and softly whisper him, ' Sweetheart!
Simætha calls you '—guide him here, my friend."

Whence grew my love, divinest Moon! attend:
She went and found the remedy I sought,
And to my house the blooming Delphis brought.
But when I saw him o'er my threshold-sill
Pass with light foot, I sudden grew more chill
Than wintry snow; and from my forehead burst
Sweat like the dew the melting South hath nurst;
I could not utter—e'en the murmur fine
That sleeping infants to their mothers whine;
Senseless I stiffened in my strange affright,
Like a wax-doll, the girl-child's dear delight.

Whence grew my love, divinest Moon! attend:
The heartless minion first on me did bend
His eager eyes, then sitting on the bed
He turned them on the ground, and softly said:—
"In calling me before I came self-moved,
Thou hast as much outpast me, my beloved,
As I did lately with swift foot out-pace
The beautiful Philinus in the race."—

(Whence grew my love, divinest Moon! attend:)
"For, by sweet Eros! with a second friend,
Or with a third, I should have come to-night,
Bringing sweet apples, crowned with poplar white,
Careful the wreath with purple stripes to blend:"

(Whence grew my love, divinest Moon! attend:)
"Had you received me—well; for me, 'mid all,
The handsome, active bachelor they call;
A kiss from those rich lips, that sweetly pout,
Had been enough; but had you shut me out,
And your barred doors had interposed delay,
Axes and torches then had forced a way."

(Whence grew my love, divinest Moon! attend:)
"To Cypris first in gratitude I bend,
Thou, next to her, hast snatched me from the fire,
In calling me half burnt with fierce desire;

For Eros oft a fiercer flame awakes
Than those Sicilian fires Hephæstus makes.'

(Whence grew my love, divinest Moon! attend :)
"He from her bed the virgin oft doth send,
Stung by his furies; and the new-made bride
Scares from the warm couch and her husband's side."

These words he spoke; but I with credulous mind
Held his dear hand, and on the bed reclined:
Our bodies did by touching warmer grow,
And on our cheeks there came a hotter glow:
Sweetly we whispered; and, in short, dear Moon!
By Eros fired, we gained Cythera's boon.
Nor any blame on me could Delphis lay,
Nor haply I on him—'till yesterday.
I only learned to-day his yester ill:
While yet up-prancing the high eastern hill,
Her fiery-footed steeds from ocean's dew
With rosy-armed Aurora upward flew,
There came the mother of the festive pair,
Sweet-voiced Philista and Melixo fair,
And told me :—" Delphis loves elsewhere, I know,
But whom I know not; yet enamoured so,
That from the banquet suddenly he fled,
To hang his lady's house with flowers, he said."
My old friend told me this, and told me truth:
For twice or thrice a day once came my youth,
And often left his Dorian pyx with me;
This the twelfth day since him I last did see.
Has he forgot me for another love?
With philters will I try his soul to move;
But if he still will grieve, betray me, mock,
He shall, by fate! the door of Hades knock.
That chest has drugs shall make him feel my rage;
The art I learned from an Assyrian sage.
Thy steeds to ocean now, bright Queen, direct;
What I have sworn to do I will effect.
Farewell, clear Moon! and skyey cressets bright,
That follow the soft-gliding wheels of Night.

IDYLL III.

AMARYLLIS.

I GO to serenade my charming fair,
Sweet Amaryllis; Tityrus, to your care
I leave my goats, that on the mountain feed;
But of yon Libyan tawny ram take heed,
Lest with his horn he butt you; careful tend,
And to the fountain drive them, heart-dear friend!

   Sweet Amaryllis! why dost thou no more,
Peeping from out thy cavern as before,
Espy and call to thee thy little lover?
Dost hate me? or do I myself discover
Flat-nosed, or with a length of chin, when near?
Thy scorn will make me hang myself, I swear.
Behold, ten apples, nymph! I bring for thee,
Plucked from the place where thou didst order me
To pluck them; others will I bring to-morrow.
Consider now my heart-devouring sorrow:
Oh! that I were a little humming bee,
To pass through fern and ivy in to thee,
Where in thy cave thou dost thyself conceal!
I now know love—a grievous god to feel;
He surely sucked a savage lioness,
Reared in the wild, who works me such distress,
Eating into the marrow of the bone.
O sweet in aspect! altogether stone!
Nymph! with thine eye-brows of a raven hue,
Clasp me, that I may suck the honey-dew
From off thy lip: mere kisses yield some joy.
Now wilt thou make me the sweet crown destroy,
This wreath of ivy which for thee I brought,
With rose-buds and with parsley sweet inwrought.
Ah me! what shall I do? I plead in vain—
Thou hearest not: I'll plunge into the main,
My jerkin stript, where Olpis sits on high,
Watching the tunnies.   Should I even die,

'Twill please thee. This the sign I lately found
For the struck pop-bell gave me back no sound,
(When by that proof thy doubtful love I tried,)
But withering on my elbow shrunk and dried.
Agræo, the diviner by the sieve,
Forewarned me also what I now believe,
(Binding the sheaves, the reapers followed she,)
That I loved wholly one who loved not me.
A white twin-bearing goat, which the brunette,
Old Memnon's child, Erithacis, would get
By wheedling from me, I have kept as thine;
But since thou scornest me with airs so fine,
It shall be hers. A throbbing, I declare,
In my right eye—shall I behold my fair?
My ditty, leaning on this pine, I'll chant;
She'll haply look, since she's not adamant.

 When in the race, mistrustful of his knees,
To win the virgin ran Hippomenes;
Three golden apples in his hand he took,
And Atalanta could not help but look—
She saw, and maddened instant at the sight,
And rushed into the gulf of love outright.
The seer Melampus from Mount Othrys drove
The stolen herd to Pylos. Thence did Love
His brother Bias crown—for in his arms
Alphesibœa's mother lodged her charms.
Did not Adonis, the fair shepherd youth,
So madden Cypris that for very ruth,
E'en when she had received his dying gasp,
She could not bear to loose him from her clasp?
Thrice blest, methinks, was that Endymion,
Now laid asleep; thrice blest Iäsion,
Who in his life did those sweet joys obtain,
Of which ye must not, shall not hear, profane!

 How my head aches! my anguish doth not move thee;
I'll sing no more, and since in vain I love thee,
Here will I lie—me here the wolves shall eat;
'Twill be to thee like melting honey sweet.

IDYLL IV.

THE HERDSMEN; OR, BATTUS AND CORYDON.

BATTUS.
Whose are these kine? Philondas's, my friend?
CORYDON.
No—Ægon's, and he gave them me to tend.
BATTUS.
Do you not milk them privily at eve?
CORYDON.
I could not the old man's quick eyes deceive;
And her own calf he puts to every one.
BATTUS.
But whither has the master cowherd gone?
CORYDON.
Have you not heard? with Ægon by his side,
Milon has gone where Alpheus loves to glide.
BATTUS.
When did e'er Ægon see th' Olympian oil?
CORYDON.
In strength for every feat of manly toil,
They say he is a match for Hercules.
BATTUS.
My mother said, believe her if you please,
That I surpassed e'en Pollux.
CORYDON.
     Hence he hied,
Taking a spade, and twenty sheep beside.
BATTUS.
Nor needed much persuasion, I engage,
Ægon to wrestle—and the wolf to rage.
CORYDON.
His lowing heifers for their master pine.
BATTUS.
They have a worthless keeper—wretched kine!
CORYDON.
Poor creatures! they no longer wish to feed.

BATTUS.
Here is a calf but skin and bones indeed—
Like a cicada, does she feed on dew?
CORYDON.
Not she, by Earth! but whiles the fodder new
Eats from my hand; or else with us she goes,
Cropping the verdant bank, where Æsar flows;
Or up Latymnus bounds away at will,
Frisking along the thickly wooded hill.
BATTUS.
How lean that red bull is! just such another
May Lampra have to offer to the mother
Of Mars! it is a tribe compact of ill.
CORYDON.
Yet at the lake-mouth he doth take his fill,
Browses on Physcus, or at times doth go
Where the sweet waters of Neæthus flow;
There the best herbs are freshened by the shower,
Wild thyme, and fleabane, and the honey-flower.
BATTUS.
Ah, wretched Ægon! thy poor kine will die,
Whilst thou dost aim at evil victory.
Even the pipe, which thou didst whilom make,
Lying neglected, doth defilement take.
CORYDON.
No! by the Nymphs! he gave it me the day
When he to glorious Pisa went away.
The songs of Pyrrhus and dear Glauca's lays
I know to sing, and Croton love to praise.
Fair is Zacynthus; lovely ever shone
To the bright east up-heaved Lacinion,
Where the bold boxer Ægon at a meal
Ate eighty cakes; where from the mountain's heel
He seized and dragged a proud bull by the hoof,
And gave it Amaryllis; then aloof
Shouted the women, and the cowherd smiled.
BATTUS.
Sweet Amaryllis! though by death defiled,
Thee shall I ne'er forget: dear to my heart
As are my frisking goats, thou didst depart.
To what a lot was I, unhappy, born!

CORYDON.

Take heart; there will be yet a brighter morn.
While there is life there's hope; the dead, I ween,
Are hopeless. One while Zeus shines out serene,
Another while is hid in mist and shower.

BATTUS.

I do take heart. But see! yon calves devour
The olive branches: pelt them off, I pray;
Confound the calves! you white-skin thief, away!

CORYDON.

Hist! to the hill, Cymætha! don't you hear?
If you don't get away, by Pan! I swear
I will so give it you! now only look!
She comes again—I wish I had my crook!

BATTUS.

Here, Corydon! a thorn has wounded me—
How long and sharp these distaff-thistles be!
Confound the calf! gaping at her I got
The wound: under the ankle—see you not?

CORYDON.

Ay! I have hold of it; see! here it is!

BATTUS.

How small a wound tames man so tall as this!

CORYDON.

Unshod you must not on the mountain go;
For on the mountain thorns and prickles grow.

IDYLL V.

THE WAYFARERS, OR COMPOSERS OF PASTORALS

Comatas and Lacon.

COMATAS.

LACON my goat-skin filched; by timely flight
Avoid, my goats! the thievish Sybarite.

LACON.

Lambs! from the fountain, do you not perceive
Comatas, who my pipe did lately thieve?

COMATAS.

What sort of pipe ? when, slave of Sybaris !
Didst own a pipe ? are you not fain to hiss
Still through a pipe of straw with Corydon ?

LACON.

'Twas Lycon's gift, good freeman ! worthy one !
From you when and what sort of skin stole I ?
Your master has not one whereon to lie.

COMATAS.

The gift of Crocylus, when late he gave
The Nymphs a goat in sacrifice : you, slave
Did steal my spotted skin from envy sheer.

LACON.

No ! no ! by the shore-guarding Pan I swear—
Or from that rock into the waters deep
Of rapid Crathis may I madly leap !

COMATAS.

Nor, by the Nymphs, the guardians of the lake,
Did ever I the pipe of Lacon take—
So may the Nymphs look kindly to my weal.

LACON.

If I believe you, be it mine to feel
The griefs of Daphnis ! will you stake a kid,
(It is none enterprise to men forbid,)
And I'll out-sing you, till you cry "Enough !"

COMATAS.

Athene challenged by a sow of scruff !
Here is my kid, which, when you beat me, take ;
A lamb, fat from the pasture, be your stake.

LACON.

How is this fair ? in this you are no fool ;
Who ever thought of shearing hair for wool,
Or passed a goat to milk a sorry bitch ?

COMATAS.

Who has for conquest a prevailing itch,
Like you conceited, is a wasp that rings
His buzzing horn when the cicada sings.
But since my kid seems insufficient stake,
Behold this ram ! at once the song awake.

LACON.

Softly ! you are not walking over fire :

Here you may sing whate'er your muse inspire
More sweetly in this grove, beneath the shade
Of the wild olive ; here a couch is laid
Of softest herbage ; locusts babble here ;
Cool water flows a little onward there.
COMATAS.
I'm cool—but feel annoyance at your daring
To look at me, yourself with me comparing,
Who taught you when a boy. What thanks one gains !
Rear a wolf-whelp—to rend you for your pains !
LACON.
Envious and shameless babbler ! any thing
Learnt, heard I from you worth remembering ?
Come hither, now, and learn from your defeat
No more with pastoral singers to compete.
COMATAS.
Not thither—here are oaks and galingale ;
And round their hives the bees, soft-humming, sail ;
Two springs of coolest water murmur near ;
A deeper shade and singing birds are here ;
And from aloft her nuts the pine-tree throws.
LACON.
On fleece and lambskins here your may repose,
Softer than sleep ! your goat-skins smell more ill—
E'en than yourself. I for the Nymphs will fill
A bowl of white milk, of sweet oil an urn.
COMATAS.
On flowering pennyroyal and soft fern
You here may tread ; on skins of kids lie down
Softer than lambskins. I to Pan will crown
Eight jars of white milk, and as many more
Of honeycombs with honey running o'er.
LACON.
Each from his place pour out his rival strain ;
Keep to your oaks, and I will here remain.
But who shall judge between us ? How I wish
The herdsman, good Lycopas, with us—
COMATAS.
Pish !
I want him not : but, if you please, we'll cry,
And summon to us yonder man doth tie

The broom in bundles near you. What dost say?
'Tis Morson.

LACON.

I'm agreed.

COMATAS.

Then bawl away.

LACON.

Ho! Morson! hasten hither, and decide
Which sings the best—a wager to be tried
With you for judge: only impartial be!

COMATAS.

Now, by the Nymphs! nor favour him nor me.
Thurian Sybartas owns the sheep in sight;
The goats Eumaras claims—the Sybarite.

LACON.

You good-for-nothing babbler! answer this,
Who asked you whose the sheep were, mine or his?

COMATAS.

I vaunt not, and I speak the simple truth;
But you are very scurrilous, in sooth.

LACON.

Sing—if you have a song: don't kill with babble
Our friend here; by Apollo! how you gabble!

COMATAS.

Me more than Daphnis love the Muses true:
Two yearling kids to them I lately slew.

LACON.

Apollo loves me much; for him I rear
A goodly ram—his festival is near.

COMATAS.

I milk my goats, twin-bearing all but twain:
A sweet girl cries, "Why milk alone, fond swain?"

LACON.

Some twenty baskets Lacon fills with cheese,
And gets him kisses wheresoe'er he please.

COMATAS.

Me with sweet apples Clearista pelts,
While round her lips a honey-murmur melts.

LACON.

On me a blooming beauty fondly dotes,
Round whose white neck the hair bright-shining floats.

COMATAS.
With the screened garden-roses cannot vie
The common dog-rose, nor anemony.
LACON.
The mountain-apples most delicious are—
Who crabbed beech-nuts would with them compare?
COMATAS.
I for my love will snare, and give to her
A ring-dove brooding on a juniper.
LACON.
Wool for a mantle will I give my dear,
Soon as my sober-suited sheep I shear.
COMATAS.
From the wild-olive, bleaters! feed at will,
Where grow the tamarisks, on this sloping hill.
LACON.
Off from that oak Cynætha and Conarus!
Feed eastward—yonder where you see Phalarus.
COMATAS.
A cypress milk-pail for my girl I have,
And bowl—which old Praxiteles did grave.
LACON.
A hound, wolf-strangling keeper of the sheep,
A faithful guardian, for my love I keep.
COMATAS.
Locusts, that overleap my fences, spare
My vines—their shoots yet weak and tender are.
LACON.
Cicadæ! see this goatherd I provoke:
So to their toil ye wake the reaping folk.
COMATAS.
I hate the bush-tailed foxes—nightly troop,
That Mycon's vineyard, grape-devouring, swoop.
LACON.
I hate the scarabs—air-borne host, that mow
Philonda's fig-trees, fig-devouring foe.
COMATAS.
Do you remember when I smote you, fellow,
How you did wriggle round the oak, and bellow?
LACON.
No! but I do remember when with scourge
Eumaras did your peccant humours purge.

COMATAS.
Some one, my Morson, into rage is dashing ;
Go ! from the tomb pluck gray squills—for a lashing.
LACON.
I too prick some one, Morson ; do you take ?
Hasten to Hales ; and for sowbread rake.
COMATAS.
Flow Himera with milk, and Crathis flow
Purple with wine ! and fruit on cresses grow !
LACON.
Fountain of Sybaris, to honey turn,
And fill with honeycombs the maiden's urn !
COMATAS.
On goat's-rue feed, my goats, and cytisus ;
On lentisk tread, and lie on arbutus !
LACON.
Of the rose-eglantine there blooms a heap,
And eke the honey-flower—to feed my sheep.
COMATAS.
Alcippe for my ring-dove gave no kiss,
Holding my ears—I love her not for this.
LACON.
I love my love because a sweet lip paid
With kisses for my pipe—the gift I made.
COMATAS.
Nor whoop the swan, nor jay the nightingale
May rival ; still you challenge, still to fail.
MORSON.
Cease, shepherd ! Morson gives the lamb to thee,
Comatas ; fail not to remember me,
And let my portion of the flesh be nice,
When to the Nymphs you make your sacrifice.
COMATAS.
By Pan ! I'll send it. Snort and gambol round,
My buck-goats all ! hark ! what a mighty sound
I peal of ringing laughter at the cost
Of Lacon, who to me his lamb has lost !
I too will skip. My horned goats, good cheer !
To-morrow in the fountain, cool and clear,
Of Sybaris I'll bathe you. Hark ! I say,
White butting ram ! be modest, till **I pay**

The Nymphs my offering. Ha! then blows I'll try—
Or may I like the curst Melanthius die.

IDYLL VI.

THE SINGERS OF PASTORALS.

To the same field, Aratus, bard divine!
Once Daphnis and Damœtas drove their kine.
This on the chin a yellow beard did show:
On that the down had just begun to grow.
During the noontide of the summer heat,
They by a fountain sung their ditties sweet.
But Daphnis first (to whom it did belong
As challenger) began the pastoral song.

DAPHNIS.

" With apples Galatea pelts thy sheep,
Inviting one, whose pulses never leap
To love, whilst thou, cold Polypheme! dost pipe,
Regardless of the sea-born beauty ripe.
And lo! she pelts the watch-dog—with a bound
He barking starts, and angry looks around—
Then bays the sea; the waves soft-murmuring show
An angry dog fast running to and fro.
Take heed he leap not on her, coming fresh
From the sea-wave, and tear her dainty flesh.
But like the thistle-down, when summer glows,
The sportive nymph, soft moving, comes and goes;
Pursues who flies her, her pursuer flies,
And moves the landmark of love's boundaries.
What is not lovely, lovely oft doth seem
To the bewildered lover, Polypheme."

Preluding then, Damœtas thus began.

DAMŒTAS.

" I saw her pelt my flock, by mighty Pan!
Not unobserved by my dear single eye,
Through which I see, and shall see till I die.
Prophet of ill! let Telemus at home
Keep for his own sons all his woes to come.

I, to provoke her, look not in return,
And say that for another girl I burn.
At hearing which with envy, by Apollo!
The sea-nymph pines; and her eye-quest doth follow,
Leaping from out the sea like one that raves,
Amid my flocks, and peeps into the caves.
I make the dog bark just to discompose her;
He, when I loved her, whining used to nose her.
Noting my action, she perchance will find
Some messenger to let me know her mind.
I'll shut my door, till she on oath agree
To make her sweet bed on this isle with me.
Nor am I that unsightly one they say:
For in the calm, smooth wave the other day
I saw myself: and handsome was my beard,
And bright, methought, my single eye appeared.
And from the beautiful sea-mirror shone
My white teeth, brighter than the Parian stone.
To screen myself from influence malign,
Thrice on my breast I spat. This lesson fine
I learned from that wise crone Cotyttaris."

This sung, Damœtas gave his friend a kiss.
Of pipe and flute their mutual gifts they made—
Daphnis the pipe, the flute Damœtas played.
Thereto the heifers frisked in gambols rude:
And neither conquered; both were unsubdued.

IDYLL VII.

THE THALYSIA.

'Twas when Amyntas, Eucritus, and I,
Did from the city to sweet Haleus hie;
The harvest-feast by that abounding river
Was kept, in honour of the harvest-giver,
By Phrasidamus and Antigenes,
Sons of Lycopeus both, and good men these.
If good there is from old and high descent,
From Clytia and from Calchon, who, knee-bent

Firmly against the rock, did make outflow
The spring Burinna with a foot-struck blow,
Near which a thickly wooded grove is seen,
Poplars and elms, high overarching green.
Midway not reached, nor tomb of Brasilas,
We chanced upon Cydonian Lycidas,
By favour of the Muses: who not knew
That famous goatherd as he came in view?
A tawny, shaggy goat-skin on his back,
That of the suppling pickle yet did smack;
Bound by a belt of straw the traveller wore
An aged jerkin; in his hand he bore
A crook of the wild olive; coming nigh,
With widely parted lips, and smiling eye—
The laughter on his lip was plain to see—
He quietly addressed himself to me:

" Whither so fast at noon-tide, when no more
The crested larks their sunny paths explore,
And in the thorn-hedge lizards lie asleep?
To feast or to a wine-press do you leap?
The stones ring to your buskins as you pass."

To him I made reply—" Dear Lycidas!
All say you are the piper—far the best
'Mid shepherds and the reapers; this confest
Gladdens my heart; and yet (to put in speech
My fancy) I expect your skill to reach.
Our way is to a harvest-feast, which cater
Dear friends of ours for richly robed Damater,
Offering their first-fruits—since their garner-floor
Her bounteous love hath filled to running o'er.
Let us with pastoral song beguile the way;
Common the path, and common is the day.
We shall each other, it may be, content;
For I, too, am a mouth-piece eloquent
Of the dear Muses; and all men esteem,
And call me minstrel good—not that I deem,
Not I, by Earth! Philetas I surpass,
Nor the famed Samian bard, Sicelidas,
A frog compared with locusts, I beguile
The time with song." He answered with a smile:—

"This crook I give thee—for thou art all over
An imp of Zeus, a genuine truth-lover.
Who strives to build, the lowly plain upon,
A mansion high as is Oromedon,
I hate exceedingly; and for that matter
The muse-birds, who like cuckoos idly chatter
Against the Chian minstrel, toil in vain:
Let us at once begin the pastoral strain;
Here is a little song, which I did late,
Musing along the highlands, meditate:

" To Mitylene sails my heart-dear love:
Safe be the way, and fair the voyage prove,
E'en when the south the moist wave dashes high on
The setting Kids, and tempest-veiled Orion
Places his feet on ocean; and, returned,
My love be kind to me by Cypris burned;
For hot love burns me: may the Halcyons smooth
The swell o' the sea, the south and east winds soothe,
That from the lowest deep the sea-weed stir—
Best Halcyons! whom of all the birds that skir
The waves for prey, the Nereids love the most.
Safe may my loved one reach the Lesbian coast,
And on the way be wind and weather fair!
With dill or roses will I twine my hair,
Or on my head will put a coronet,
Wreathed with the fragrance of the violet.
I by the fire will quaff the Ptelean wine,
And one shall roast me beans, while I recline
Luxurious, lying on a fragrant heap
Of asphodel and parsley, elbow deep;
And mindful of my love the goblet clip,
Until the last lees trickle to my lip.
Two swains shall play the flute; and Tityrus sing
How love for Xenea did our Daphnis sting,
How on the mountain he was wont to stray,
How wailed for him the oaks of Himera,
When he, dissolving, passed away from us,
Like snow on Hæmus, or far Caucasus,
Athos or Rhodope: or in his song
Recite, how by his master's cruel wrong

The swain was in a cedar ark shut up,
While quick—and how from many a flower-cup
The flat-nosed bees to his sweet prison flew,
And there sustained him with the honey-dew,
For that the Muse into his lip distilled
Sweet nectar: blest Comatas! that fulfilled
A whole spring, feeding on the bag o' the bee,
Shut in an ark!   How had it gladdened me,
(Would only thou wert of the living now!)
To tend thy goats along the mountain's brow,
And hear thee sweetly sing, O bard divine!
Lying at leisure under oak or pine!"

He ceased: I in my turn: "Dear Lycidas!
Whilst on the highlands with my herd I pass,
The Nymphs have taught me precious ditties oft,
Which haply Fame has borne to Zeus aloft.
I choose for you the very best I know;
Now listen, since the Muses love you so:

"The Loves, ill omen! sneezed on me, who dote
On lovely Myrtis, as on spring the goat.
Aratus, whom of men I love the best,
Loves a sweet girl.   Aristis, minstrel blest,
And worthiest man, whom his own tripod near
Phœbus himself would not disdain to hear
Sing to the harp, knows that Aratus feels
This scorching flame.   Pan! whose rich music peals
On Homolus, place in his longing arms
Of her own will the blushing bloom of charms.
So may the youth of Arcady forbear
With squills thy shoulders and thy side to tear,
When fails the chase.   If thou wilt not, then weep,
By nails all mangled, and on nettles sleep!
Where Hebrus flows, in frost-time of the year
Dwell on the mountains 'neath the polar bear;
In summer with swart Æthiop, at the pile
Of Blemyan rocks, beyond the springs of Nile!
Ye loves! from Hyetis and Byblis flown,
Who make Dione's lofty seat your own;
Ye loves! that are to blushing apples like,
The blooming Phyllis with your arrows strike—

Strike her, because she pities not my friend;
Though softer than a pear, her bloom shall end:
Ah, Phyllis! Phyllis! now the bachelors say,
Behold thy flower of beauty drops away!
Let us, my friend Aratus! pace no more,
Nor keep our painful watch beside her door;
Let Chanticleer, that crows at dawn, behold
Some other lover there benumbed with cold:
Such watch be Molon's, and be his alone;
But rest be ours—and eke a friendly crone,
Who may by spitting and by magic skill
Quick disenchant us from foreshadowed ill."

Ended my song, he, smiling as before,
The friendly muse-gift gave—the crook he bore;
Then turning to the left pursued the way
To Pyxa; speeding, presently we lay,
Where Phrasidamus dwelt, on loosened sheaves
Of lentisk, and the vine's new-gathered leaves.
Near by, a fountain murmured from its bed,
A cavern of the Nymphs: elms overhead,
And poplars rustled; and the summer-keen
Cicadæ sung aloft amid the green;
Afar the tree-frog in the thorn-bush cried;
Nor larks nor goldfinches their song denied;
The yellow bees around the fountains flew;
And the lone turtle-dove was heard to coo:
Of golden summer all was redolent,
And of brown autumn; boughs with damsons bent,
We had; and pears were scattered at our feet,
And by our side a heap of apples sweet.
A four-year cask was broached. Ye Nymphs excelling
Of Castaly, on high Parnassus dwelling,
Did ever Chiron in the Centaur's cave
Give draught so rich to Hercules the brave?
Through Polypheme did such sweet nectar glance,
That made the shepherd of Anapus dance,
The huge rock-hurler—as the generous foam,
Which, Nymphs, ye tempered at that harvest-home?
O be it mine again her feast to keep,
And fix the fan in good Damater's heap;

And may she sweetly smile, while spikes of corn
And up-torn poppies either hand adorn!

IDYLL VIII.

THE SINGERS OF PASTORALS.

Daphnis. Menalcas. A goatherd.

MENALCAS met, while pasturing his sheep,
The cowherd Daphnis on the highland steep;
Both yellow-tressed, and in their life's fresh spring,—
Both skilled to play the pipe, and both to sing.

Menalcas, with demeanour frank and free,
Spoke first: "Good Daphnis, will you sing with me?
I can out-sing you, whensoe'er I try,
Just as I please." Then Daphnis made reply:

DAPHNIS.
Shepherd and piper! that may never be,
Happen what will, as you on proof will see.
MENALCAS.
Ah, will you see it, and a wager make?
DAPHNIS.
I will to see this, and to pledge a stake.
MENALCAS.
And what the wager, worthy fame like ours?
DAPHNIS.
A calf my pledge, a full-grown lamb be yours.
MENALCAS.
At night my cross-grained sire and mother use
To count the sheep—that pledge I must refuse.
DAPHNIS.
What shall it be then? What the victor's prize?
MENALCAS.
I'll pledge a nine-toned pipe, that even lies
In the joined reeds, with whitest wax inlaid,
The musical sweet pipe I lately made;
This will I pledge—and not my father's things.
DAPHNIS.
I, too, have got a pipe that nine-toned rings,

Compact with white wax, even-jointed, new,—
Made by myself: a split reed sudden flew,
And gashed this finger—it is painful still.
But who shall judge which has the better skill?
     MENALCAS.
Suppose we call that goatherd hither—see!
Yon white dog at his kids barks lustly.

 He came when called; and, hearing their request
Was willing to decide which sung the best.
Clearly their rival tones responsive rung,
Each in his turn, but first Menalcas sung.
     MENALCAS.
Ye mountain-vales and rivers! race divine!
 If aught Menalcas ever sung was sweet,
Feed ye these lambs; and feed no less his kine,
 When Daphnis drives them to this dear retreat.
     DAPHNIS.
Fountains and herbs, growth of the lively year!
 If Daphnis sings like any nightingale,
Fatten this herd; and if Menalcas here
 Conduct his flock, let not their pasture fail.
     MENALCAS.
Pastures and spring, and milkful udders swelling,
 And fatness for the lambs, is every where
At her approach: but if the girl excelling
 Departs, both herbs and shepherd wither there.
     DAPHNIS.
The sheep and goats bear twins; the bees up-lay
 Full honey-stores, the spreading oaks are higher,
Where Milto walks: but if she goes away,
 The cowherd and his cows themselves are drier.
     MENALCAS.
Uxorious ram, and flat-nosed kids, away
 For water to that wilderness of wood:
There, ram without a horn! to Milto say,
 Proteus, a god too, fed the sea-calf brood.
     DAPHNIS.
Nor Pelops' realm be mine, nor piles of gold,
 Nor speed fleet as the wind; but at this rock
To sing, and clasp my darling, and behold
 The seas blue reach, and many a pasturing flock.

MENALCAS.
To forest-beast the net, to bird the noose,
  Winter to trees, and drought to springs is bad;
To man the sting of beauty. Mighty Zeus!
  Not only I—thou, too, art woman-mad.

Their sweet notes thus, in turn, they did prolong;
Menalcas then took up the closing song.

MENALCAS.
Spare, wolf! my sheep and lambs; nor injure me,
Because I many tend, though small I be.
Sleepest, Lampurus? up! no dog should sleep
That with the shepherd-boy attends his sheep.
Be not to crop the tender herbage slow,
Feed on, my sheep! the grass again will grow.
Fill ye your udders, that your lambs may have
Their share of milk,—I some for cheese may save.

Then Daphnis next his tones preluding rung,
Gave to the music voice, and sweetly sung.

DAPHNIS.
As yesterday I drove my heifers by,
A girl, me spying from a cavern nigh,
Exclaimed, "How handsome!" I my way pursued
With down-cast eyes, nor made her answer rude.
Sweet is the breath of cows and calves—and sweet
To bask by running stream in summer heat.
Acorns the oak; and apples on the bough
Adorn the apple-tree; her calf the cow;
His drove of kine, depasturing the field,
His proper honour to the cowherd yield.

Th' admiring goatherd then his judgment spake:
Sweet is thy mouth, and sweetest tones awake
From thy lips, Daphnis! I would rather hear
Thee sing, than suck the honeycomb, I swear.
Take thou the pipe, for thine the winning song.
If thou wilt teach me here my goats among
Some song, I will that hornless goat bestow,
That ever fills the pail to overflow.

Glad Daphnis clapped his hands, and on the lawn
He leaped, as round her mother leaps the fawn.
But sad Menalcas fed a smouldering gloom,
As grieves a girl betrothed to unknown groom.
And first in song was Daphnis from that time,
And wived a Naiad in his blooming prime.

IDYLL IX.

THE PASTOR, OR THE HERDSMEN.

Daphnis. Menalcas.

DAPHNIS! begin the pastoral song for me;
Begin, and let Menalcas follow thee.
Meanwhile the calves the mother-cows put under,
Let the bulls feed—but not roam far asunder,
Scorning the herd—and crop the leafy spray;
And leave the heifers to their frolic play.
Begin for me the sweet bucolic strain,
And let Menalcas take it up again.

DAPHNIS.

" Sweet low the cow and calf—the tones are sweet,
The pipe, the cowherd and myself repeat.
My couch is by cool water, and is strown
With skins of milk-white heifers; them threw down,
While they cropt arbutus, the south-west wind
From the bluff crag. There stretched, no more I mind
The scorching summer than a loving pair
Their parents sage, who bid them each 'beware!'"

Thus Daphnis sweetly sung at my request;
Menalcas next his dulcet tones exprest.

MENALCAS.

" Ætna! my mother! in the hollow rock
My pleasant mansion is; I own a flock
Of many yearlings and of many sheep,
Numerous as those the dreamer sees in sleep.
Fleeces are lying at my head and feet;
On an oak-fire are boiling entrails sweet;

And on my hearth in winter-time I burn
Fagots of beech. I have no more concern
For winter—than the toothless elder cares
For walnuts, whose old dame his pap prepares."

SHEPHERD.

Both I applauded, and made gifts to both,
A crook to Daphnis—the spontaneous growth
Of my own father's field, yet turned so well,
None could find fault with it; a sounding shell
I gave Menalcas; four besides myself
Fed on its flesh—I snared it from a shelf
Amid th' Icarian rocks. The conch he blew,
And far abroad the blast resounding flew.

Hail, pastoral Muses! and the song declare,
Which then I chanted for that friendly pair.
"On your tongue's tip may pustules never grow,
For speaking falsely what for false you know!
Cicale the cicale loves; and ant loves ant;
Hawk, hawk; and me the muse and song enchant.
Of this my house be full! nor sudden spring,
Nor sleep is sweeter; nor to bees on wing
The bloom of flowers more dear delight diffuses,
Than to myself the presence of the Muses.
On whomsoe'er they look and sweetly smile,
Him Circe may not harm with cup or wile."

IDYLL X.

THE WORKMEN, OR REAPERS.

Milon and Battus.

MILON.

PLOUGHMAN, what is the matter with you, pray?
You cannot draw the furrow straight to-day,
Nor with your neighbour even do you keep,
But lag behind like a thorn-wounded sheep.
If you cannot the furrow now devour,
What will you be, my friend, at evening hour?

BATTUS.

You rock-chip, reaping till the sun's descent,
Did you some absent darling ne'er lament?

MILON.

Never. A labourer's heart with love-grief ache!

BATTUS.

Did you ne'er chance for love to lie awake?

MILON.

No—never may I! When a dog has eaten
Meat for his master, the poor dog is beaten.

BATTUS.

I'm deep in love—almost eleven days.

MILON.

From a full wine-cask you your fancies raise;
I have not even vinegar enough.

BATTUS.

Thence lie the sweepings of all sort of stuff
Before my door.

MILON.

Who is your mischief-bringer?

BATTUS.

The child of Polybotas—the sweet singer,
Who for the mowers at Hippocoon's chaunted.

MILON.

Sinners heaven pricks—you have what long you wanted;
A dry tree-frog will hug you close in bed.

BATTUS.

None of your jibes: care-breeding Love is said,
And not old Plutus only, to be blind.
Don't talk too big.

MILON.

I do not—only mind
To cut the corn down, and some love-song try
About your girl; you'll work more pleasantly:
And Battus once, at least, was musical.

BATTUS.

To sing my charmer, slender, straight, and tall,
Best Muses! aid me; for, with skill divine,
Ye, whatsoe'er ye please to touch, refine.
Lovely Bombyce! though all men beside
Call you a Syrian sun-embrowned, and dried,

I call you a transparent sweet brunette.
The lettered hyacinth and violet
Are dark; yet these are chosen first of all
For the sweet wreath and festive coronal.
The goat the cytisus, the wolf the goat,
And cranes pursue the plough—on thee I dote.
Would that I had the wealth report hath told
Belonged to Crœsus! wrought in purest gold,
Statues of both of us should then be seen,
Due dedications to the Cyprian Queen:
Thou with a flute, an apple, and a rose;
I sandalled, in a robe that proudly flows.
Lovely Bombyce! beautiful your feet,
Twinkling like the quick dice; your voice is sweet;
But your sweet nature language cannot tell.

MILON.

He privily hath learned to sing—how well!
But my poor chin in vain this great beard nurses;
List to a snatch or two of Lytierses.

Damater; fruit-abounding! grant this field
Be duly wrought, and rich abundance yield.

Bind without waste, sheaf-binder! lest one say,
These men of fig-wood are not worth their pay.

Let the sheaf-hillock look to north or west;
The corn, so lying, fills and ripens best.

Ye threshers! let not sleep steal on your eyes
At noon—for then the chaff most freely flies. .

Up with the lark to reap, and cease as soon
As the lark sleeps—but rest yourself at noon.

Happy the frog's life! none, his drink to pour,
He looks for—he has plenty evermore.

Boil, niggard steward! the lentil; and take heed,
Don't cut your hand—to split a cumin-seed.

Men toiling in the sun such songs befit;
Your puling love, poor rustic little-wit!
Is only fit—to whisper in her ears,
When your old mother wakes as dawn appears.

IDYLL XI.

THE CYCLOPS.

Nicias! there is no remedy for love,
Except the Muses; this alone doth prove
A sweet and gentle solace for the mind
Of love-sick man—not easy though to find.
Full knowledge of this truth I deem is thine,
Physician, and beloved of all the Nine!

    Thus, Polypheme of yore, our Cyclops, found
The power of song on love's uneasy wound;
With the first down that budding youth discloses
On cheek and chin, he doted—not with roses
And apples for his love, and the trim curl
To please her eye, but with delirious whirl,
Neglecting all things else. Oft to the stall
His sheep from pasture came without his call,
While he from dawn mid sea-weeds and the spray
Of Galatea sung, and pined away,
By mighty Cypris wounded at the heart,
Who in his liver fixed her cruel dart.
He found the cure while from the cliff he flung
His glances seaward, and his ditty sung:—

    "Why, Galatea, scorn for love dost render?
Whiter than fresh curds, than the lamb more tender;
More skittish than the calf, more clearly bright
Than unripe grape transparent in the light!
Here dost thou show thyself when sleeps thy lover,
Still flying ever as my sleep is over,
E'en as the sheep, the gray wolf seeing, flees.
I loved when with my mother from the seas
Thou first didst come, and seek the mountain-side
To gather hyacinths—and I thy guide.
Since then I never yet have ceased to love thee,
Although my passion never yet did move thee.
I know the reason why the beauty flies—
One shaggy eye-brow on my forehead lies
Over one eye, stretched out from tip to tip
Of either ear, and overhangs my lip

A nostril broad.   Such as I am, I keep,
Drinking their best of milk, a thousand sheep ;
My cheeses fail not in their hurdled row
In depth of winter nor in summer's glow.
No Cyclops here can breathe the pipe like me,
Who sing, when I should sleep, myself and thee,
Sweet-apple ! I for thee four bear-whelps rear,
And eke eleven fawns that collars wear.
Come live (thou shalt not fare the worse) with me,
And to its murmurs leave that azure sea.
Thy nights will sweeter pass within my cave,
Where the tall cypress and the laurel wave ;
The sweet-fruit vine and ivy dark are there ;
From the white snow its waters cool and clear
Thick-wooded Ætna sends : whom would it please
In sea to dwell, when land has joys like these ?
Though rough I seem in Galatea's eyes,
My wealth of oak a constant fire supplies ;
O fire of love ! I could be well content
That life and precious eye at once were brent.
Had I but fins ! then would I dive and kiss
Thy dainty hand, though daintier lip I miss ;
In different seasons take thee different flowers,
The summer lily white in summer hours,
And while it winter was, what winter bred,
The tender poppy with its pop-bells red.
From some sea-ranger I will learn to swim,
To see what charms you in your ocean dim.
Come, Galatea ! sparkling from the foam,
And then, like me, forget to turn thee home.
Would that the shepherd and his life could please—
To milk my ewes, with runnet fix the cheese.
My mother is in fault, and only she—
She never spake a friendly word for me ;
Although she sees me pining fast away,
Thinner and thinner still from day to day.
I'll tell her that my feet and temples throb,
That she, as I have done, with grief may sob.
O Cyclops ! Cyclops ! whither dost thou hover ?
To weave thy baskets would more wit' discover,
And get thy lambs green leaves.   Milk the near ewe ;

Why one that faster flies in vain pursue ?
A fairer Galatea you may find ;
Others are fair, and all are not unkind :
For many a damsel, when eve's shadow falls,
Me to sport with her fondly, sweetly calls ;
And all of them, with eyes that brightly glisten,
Giggle most merrily, whene'er I listen :
That I am somebody on earth is plain."

 Thus Polypheme with song relieved love's pain
And from his ails himself did safer free,
Than had he given a leech a golden fee.

IDYLL XII.

AITES.

Art come, dear youth ? Two days and nights away !
For love who passion, wax old—in a day.
As much as apples sweet the damson crude
Excel ; the bloomy spring the winter rude ;
In fleece the sheep her lamb ; the maid in sweetness
The thrice-wed dame ; the fawn the calf in fleetness ;
The nightingale in song all feathered kind—
So much thy longed-for presence cheers my mind.
To thee I hasten, as to shady beech
The traveller, when from the heaven's reach
The sun fierce blazes. May our love be strong,
To all hereafter times the theme of song !
" Two men each other loved to that degree,
That either friend did in the other see
A dearer than himself. They lived of old,
Both golden natures in an age of gold."

 O father Zeus ! ageless Immortals all !
Two hundred ages hence may one recall,
Down-coming to the irremeable river,
This to my mind, and this good news deliver :
" E'en now from east to west, from north to south,
Your mutual friendship lives in every mouth."
This, as they please, the Olympians will decide :

Of thee, by blooming virtue beautified,
My glowing song shall only truth disclose ;
With falsehood's pustules I'll not shame my nose.
If thou dost sometime grieve me, sweet the pleasure
Of reconcilement, joy in double measure
To find thou never didst intend the pain,
And feel myself from all doubt free again.

   And, ye Megarians, at Nisæa dwelling,
Expert at rowing, mariners excelling,
Be happy ever! for with honours due
Th' Athenian Diocles, to friendship true,
Ye celebrate. With the first blush of spring
The youth surround his tomb: there who shall bring
The sweetest kiss, whose lip is purest found,
Back to his mother goes with garlands crowned.
Nice touch the arbiter must have, indeed,
And must, methinks, the blue-eyed Ganymede
Invoke with many prayers—a mouth to own
True to the touch of lips, as Lydian stone
To proof of gold,—which test will instant show
The pure or base, as money-changers know.

IDYLL XIII.

HYLAS.

FRIEND! not for us alone was love designed,
Whoe'er his parent of immortal kind ;
Nor first to us fair seemeth fair to be,
Who mortal are, nor can the morrow see.
But e'en Amphitryon's brazen-hearted son,
Who stood the lion's rage, did dote upon
The curled and lovely Hylas—made his joy
To train him as a father would his boy,
And taught him all whereby himself became
A minstrel-praised inheritor of fame ;
Nor left him when the sun was in mid-air,
Or Morn to Jove's court drove her milk-white pair;

Or when the twittering chickens were betaking
Themselves to rest, her wings their mother shaking,
Perched on the smoky beam; that, trained to go
In the right track, he might a true man grow.

When Jason sailed to find the golden fleece,
And in his train the choicest youth of Greece;
Then with the worthies from the cities round,
Came Hercules, for patient toil renowned,
And Hylas with him: from Iölcos they,
In the good Argo ploughed the watery way.
Touched not the ship the dark Cyanean rocks,
That justled evermore with crashing shocks,
But bounded through, and shot the swell o' the flood,
Like to an eagle, and in Phasis stood:
Thence either ridgy rock in station lies.

But at what times the Pleiades arise:
When to the lamb the borders of the field
(The spring to summer turning) herbage yield;
The flower of heroes minded then their sailing;
And the third day, a steady south prevailing,
They reached the Hellespont; and in the bay
Of long Propontis hollow Argo lay:
Their oxen for Cianians dwelling there
The ploughshare in the broadening furrow wear.
They land at eve; in pairs their mess they keep;
And many strow a high and rushy heap:
A meadow broad convenient lay thereby,
With various rushes prankt abundantly.
And gold-tressed Hylas is for water gone
For Hercules and sturdy Telamon,
Who messmates were: a brazen urn he bore,
And soon perceived a fountain straight before.
It was a gentle slope, round which was seen
A multitude of rushes, parsley green,
And the close couch-grass, creeping to entwine
Green maiden-hair, and pale-blue celandine.
Their choir the wakeful Nymphs, the rustics' dread,
In the mid sparkle of the fountain led;
Malis, and young Nychea looking spring,
And fresh Eunica.   There the youth did bring,

And o'er the water hold his goodly urn,
Eager at once to dip it and return.
The Nymphs all clasped his hand; for love seized all,
Love for the Argive boy; and he did fall
Plumping at once into the water dark,
As when a meteor glides with many a spark
Plumping from out the heavens into the seas—
And then some sailor cries, " A jolly breeze,
Up with the sail, boys!" Him upon their knees
The Nymphs soft held; him dropping many a tear
With soft enticing words they tried to cheer.

   Anxious Alcides lingered not to go,
Armed like a Scythian with his curved bow.
He grasped his club; and thrice he threw around
His deep, deep voice at highest pitch of sound;
Thrice called on Hylas; thrice did Hylas hear,
And from the fount a thin voice murmured near;
Though very near, it very far appeared:
As when a lion, awful with his beard,
Hearing afar the whining of a fawn,
Speeds to his banquet from the mountain-lawn;
In such wise, Hercules, the boy regretting,
Off at full speed through pathless brakes was setting.
Who love, much suffer: what fatigue he bore!
What thickets pierced! what mountains clambered o'er!
What then to him was Jason's enterprise?

   With sails aloft the ship all ready lies;
Midnight they sweep the decks and oft repeat,
" Where, where is Hercules?" Where'er his feet
Convey him, there the frantic mourner hurries,
For a fierce god his liver tears and worries.
Fair Hylas thus is numbered with the blest:
Their friend, as ship-deserter, all the rest
Reproach; while trudges he (and sad his case is)
To Colchos and inhospitable Phasis.

IDYLL XIV.

THE LOVE OF CYNISCA, OR THYONICHUS.

Æschines. Thyonicus.

ÆSCHINES.

Health to Thyonichus!

THYONICHUS.

The same to you.

ÆSCHINES.

How late you are!

THYONICHUS.

Late? what concernment new?

ÆSCHINES.

It is not well with me.

THYONICHUS.

And therefore lean,
With beard untrimmed and dry straight hair you're seen.
But lately one, in seeming much the same,
Who called himself Athenian, hither came,
A barefoot, pale Pythagorean oaf,
In love, methought, and longing—for a loaf.

ÆSCHINES.

You'll have your jest: Cynisca flouts me so,
That I shall madden unawares, I know—
There's but a hair's-breadth now 'twixt me and madness.

THYONICHUS.

Extreme in changes ever—brooding sadness,
Or moody violence—as the whim makes you
Sport of the time: but what new care o'ertakes you?

ÆSCHINES.

The Argive, I, and the Thessalian knight
Good Apis, and Cleunicus, brave in fight,
Were drinking at my farm. We had for fare
Two pullets and a sucking pig; and rare
Rich Biblian wine (near four years old) I drew,
And fragrant still, as from the wine-press new.
A Colchian onion gave the brewage zest;
As mirth with drink advanced, we thought it best

To quaff the wine's pure juice, each to his flame,
And every one was bound to tell her name.
So said, so done: we drank to them we loved:
But she, my she! by all my love unmoved,
Said nothing, though I then and there named *her*.
Think what a tempest did my temper stir!
"Won't speak?" I said: "or, as the wise man spoke,
Hast seen a wolf?" another said in joke.
From her red burning face (it kindled so)
You might have lit a lamp. Lycus, you know,
Is name for wolf; and there is such an one,
Tall, delicate, my neighbour Laba's son;
And many think him handsome: for this youth,
And his fine love my damsel pined in sooth.
I heard a whisper, nor I sifted it,
Having a man's beard without manly wit.
But Apis—we were at our cups again—
Sang out "My Lycus!" a Thessalian strain.
Then sudden into tears Cynisca burst—
The girl of six years for the breast that nurst
Her tender infancy, not so much weeps.
You know me, how no bound my temper keeps;
With doubled fist once and again I struck
Both of her cheeks. She thereat did up-tuck
Her skirts and quickly bolted through the door.
Do I not please thee? hast a paramour
Nearer thy heart? plague o' my life! go, go!
Hug him for whom your tears, like beads, thick flow.
As for her callow brood, that nested lies
Under the roof, the swallow swiftly flies
To bring them food, and flies for more again:
From her soft couch more swift she fled amain,
Through hall, court, gate, as fast as she was able:
"The bull into the wood," as runs the fable.
Add two to this, the eight and fiftieth day,
'Twill be two full months since she went away;
And since we parted, as a sign of woe,
My hair has, Thracian-like, been left to grow.
But only Lycus is her sole delight;
For him her door is open e'en at night.
But hapless I, with the Megarian lot,

Am held in none account, and quite forgot.
All would be well, could I my love restrain;
But mice, they say, the taste of pitch retain.
I cannot cure myself, howe'er I try;
For hapless love I know no remedy;
Except that Simus sailed across the water,
When smitten with old Epichalcus' daughter,
And came back whole. I too will cross the wave,
Nor best nor worst of soldiers, but a brave.

THYONICHUS.

May all be as you wish, my Æschines!
But if you will depart beyond the seas,
Gladly king Ptolemy brave hearts engages,
Best man of all that gives the soldier wages.

ÆSCHINES.

What sort of man is he in other things?

THYONICHUS.

To brave and noble souls the best of kings;
Has a discerning spirit; takes delight
In all the Muses; courteous to the height;
Who loves him and who loves him not, he knows;
And many gifts on many men bestows.
When asked a boon, he king-like not denies;
But oft to ask is neither right nor wise.
Then if you wish a martial cloak to fold
Around your shoulders, and in station bold,
Firm on both feet, abide the shielded foe
On-rushing—instantly to Egypt go.
Soon we grow old, and Time steals on apace,
Whitening the hair, and withering the face.
We ought to do what us behoves, I ween,
While yet our knee is firm, our strength is green.

IDYLL XV.

THE SYRACUSAN WOMEN; OR, ADONIAZUSÆ.

CHARACTERS.

Gorgo. Praxinoa. Old woman. First stranger. Second stranger. Singing woman.

GORGO.

Is Praxinoa at home?

PRAXINOA.

Dear Gorgo, yes!
How late you are! I wonder, I confess,
That you are come e'en now. Quick, brazen-front!
[*To* EUNOA.
A chair there—stupid! lay a cushion on't.

GORGO.

Thank you, 'tis very well.

PRAXINOA.

Be seated, pray.

GORGO.

My untamed soul! what dangers on the way!
I scarce could get alive here: such a crowd!
So many soldiers with their trappings proud!
A weary way it is—you live so far.

PRAXINOA.

The man, whose wits with sense are aye at war,
Bought at the world's end but to vex my soul
This dwelling—no! this serpent's lurking-hole,
That we might not be neighbours: plague o' my life,
His only joy is quarrelling and strife.

GORGO.

Talk not of Dinon so before the boy;
See! how he looks at you!

PRAXINOA.

My honey-joy!
My pretty dear! 'tis not papa I mean.

GORGO.

Handsome papa! the urchin, by the Queen,

Knows every word you say.
####### PRAXINOA.
> The other day—
For this in sooth of every thing we say—
The mighty man of inches went and brought me
Salt—which for nitre and ceruse he bought me.
####### GORGO.
And so my Diocleide—a brother wit,
A money-waster, lately thought it fit
To give seven goodly drachms for fleeces five—
Mere rottenness, but dog's hair, as I live,
The plucking of old scrips—a work to make.
But come, your cloak and gold-claspt kirtle take,
And let us speed to Ptolemy's rich hall,
To see the fine Adonian festival.
The queen will make the show most grand, I hear.
####### PRAXINOA.
All things most rich in rich men's halls appear.
To those who have not seen it, one can tell
What one has seen.
####### GORGO.
> 'Tis time to go—'tis well
For those who all the year have holidays.
####### PRAXINOA.
Eunoa! my cloak—you wanton! quickly raise,
And place it near me—cats would softly sleep;
And haste for water—how the jade does creep!
The water first—now, did you ever see?
She brings the cloak first: well, then, give it me.
You wasteful slut, not too much—pour the water!
What! have you wet my kirtle! sorrow's daughter?
Stop, now: I'm washed—gods love me: where's the key
Of the great chest? be quick, and bring it me.
####### GORGO.
The gold-claspt and full-skirted gown you wear
Becomes you vastly. May I ask, my dear,
How much in all it cost you from the loom?
####### PRAXINOA.
Don't mention it: I'm sure I did consume
More than two minæ on it: and I held on
The work with heart and soul.

IDYLL XV.

GORGO.
But when done, well done!
PRAXINOA.
Truly—you're right. My parasol and cloak—
Arrange it nicely. Cry until you choke,
I will not take you, child; horse bites, you know—
Boo! Boo! no use to have you lame. Let's go.
Play with the little man, my Phrygian! call
The hound in; lock the street-door of the hall.

Gods, what a crowd: they swarm like ants, how ever
Shall we work through them with our best endeavour?
From when thy sire was numbered with the blest,
Many fine things, and this among the rest,
Hast thou done, Ptolemy! No villain walks
The street, and picks your pocket, as he talks
On some pretence with you, in Egypt's fashion:
As once complete in every style, mood, passion,
Resembling one another, rogues in grain,
Would mock and pilfer, and then—mock again.
What will become of us, dear Gorgo? see!
The king's war-horses! Pray, don't trample me,
Good sir! the bay-horse rears! how fierce a one!
Eunoa, stand from him: dog-heart! won't you run?
He'll kill his leader! what a thought of joy,
That safe at home remains my precious boy!
GORGO.
Courage! they're as they were—and we behind them.
PRAXINOA.
I nearly lost my senses; now I find them,
And am myself again. Two things I hold
In mortal dread—a horse and serpent cold,
And have done from a child. Let us keep moving;
O! what a crowd is on us, bustling, shoving.
GORGO.
(*To an old woman.*)
Good mother, from the palace?
OLD WOMAN.
Yes, my dear.
GORGO.
Is it an easy thing to get in there?

OLD WOMAN.

Th' Achæans got to Troy, there's no denying ;
All things are done, as they did that—by trying

GORGO.

The old dame spoke oracles.

PRAXINOA.

Our sex, as you know,
Know all things—e'en how Zeus espoused his Juno.

GORGO.

Praxinoa ! what a crowd about the gates !

PRAXINOA.

Immense ! your hand ; and, Eunoa, hold your mate's ;
Do you keep close, I say, to Eutychis,
And close to us, for fear the way you miss.
Let us, together all, the entrance gain :
Ah me ! my summer-cloak is rent in twain.
Pray, spare my cloak, heaven bless you, gentleman !

STRANGER.

'Tis not with me—I will do what I can.

PRAXINOA.

The crowd, like pigs, are thrusting.

STRANGER.

Cheer thy heart,
'Tis well with us.

PRAXINOA.

And for your friendly part,
This year and ever be it well with you !
A kind and tender man as e'er I knew.
See ! how our Eunoa is prest—push through—
Well done ! all in—as the gay bridegroom cried,
And turned the key upon himself and bride.

GORGO.

What rich, rare tapestry ! Look, and you'll swear
The fingers of the goddesses were here.

PRAXINOA.

August Athene ! who such work could do ?
Who spun the tissue, who the figures drew ?
How life-like are they, and they seem to move !
True living shapes they are, and not inwove !
How wise is man ! and there he lies outspread
In all his beauty on his silver bed,

Thrice-loved Adonis! in his youth's fresh glow,
Loved even where the rueful stream doth flow.

A STRANGER.

Cease ye like turtles idly thus to babble:
They'll torture all of us with brogue and gabble.

GORGO.

Who's you? what's it to you our tongues we use?
Rule your own roost, not dames of Syracuse.
And this too know we were in times foregone
Corinthians, sir, as was Bellerophon.
We speak the good old Greek of Pelop's isle:
Dorians, I guess, may Dorian talk the while.

PRAXINOA.

Nymph! grant we be at none but one man's pleasure;
A rush for you—don't wipe my empty measure.

GORGO.

Praxinoa, hush! behold the Argive's daughter,
The girl who sings as though the Muses taught her,
That won the prize for singing Sperchis' ditty,
Prepares to chaunt Adonis; something pretty
I'm sure she'll sing: with motion, voice, and eye,
She now preludes—how sweetly, gracefully!

SINGING GIRL.

Of Eryx, Golgos, and Idalia, Queen!
My mistress, sporting in thy golden sheen,
Bright Aphrodite! as the month comes on
Of every year, from dureful Acheron
What an Adonis—from the gloomy shore
The tender-footed Hours to thee restore!
Hours, slowest of the Blest! yet ever dear,
That wished-for come, and still some blessing bear.
Cypris! Dione's daughter! thou through portal
Of death, 'tis said, hast mortal made immortal,
Sweet Berenice, dropping, ever blest!
Ambrosial dew into her lovely breast.
Wherefore her daughter, Helen-like in beauty,
Arsinoë thy love repays with duty;
For thine Adonis fairest show ordains,
Bright Queen, of many names and many fanes!
All seasonable fruits; in silver cases
His gardens sweet; and alabaster vases

Of Syrian perfumes near his couch are laid;
Cakes, which with flowers and wheat the women made;
The shapes of all that creep, or take the wing,
With oil or honey wrought, they hither bring;
Here are green shades, with anise shaded more;
And the young Loves him ever hover o'er,
As the young nightingales, from branch to branch,
Hover and try their wings, before they launch
Themselves in the broad Air. But, O! the sight
Of gold and ebony! of ivory white
Behold the pair of eagles! up they move
With his cup-bearer for Saturnian Jove.
And see yon couch with softest purple spread,
Softer than sleep, the Samian born and bred
Will own, and e'en Miletus: that pavilion
Queen Cypris has—the nearer one her minion,
The rosy-armed Adonis; whose youth bears
The bloom of eighteen or of nineteen years;
Nor pricks the kiss—the red lip of the boy;
Having her spouse, let Cypris now enjoy.
Him will we, ere the dew of dawn is o'er,
Bear to the waves that foam upon the shore;
Then with bare bosoms and dishevelled hair,
Begin to chant the wild and mournful air.
Of all the demigods, they say, but one
Duly revisits Earth and Acheron—
Thou, dear Adonis! Agamemnon's might,
Nor Aias, raging like one mad in fight;
Nor true Patroclus; nor his mother's boast,
Hector, of twenty sons famed, honoured most;
Nor Pyrrhus, victor from the Trojan siege—
Not one of them enjoyed this privilege;
Nor the Deucalions; nor Lapithæ;
Argive Pelasgi; nor Pelopidæ.
Now, dear Adonis, fill thyself with glee,
And still returning, still propitious be.

       GORGO.

Praxinoa, did ever mortal ear
A sweeter song from sweeter minstrel hear?
O happy girl! to know so many things—
Thrice happy girl, that so divinely sings!

But now 'tis time for home : let us be hasting ;
My man's mere vinegar, and most when fasting :
Nor has he broken yet his fast to-day ;
When he's a-hungered, come not in his way.
Farewell, beloved Adonis ! joy to see !
When come, well come to those who welcome thee.

IDYLL XVI.

THE GRACES ; OR, HIERO.

JOVE'S daughters hymn the gods ; and bards rehearse
The deeds of worthies in their glowing verse.
The heaven-born Muses hymn the heavenly ring ;
Of mortals, then, let mortal poets sing.
Yet who—as many as there be that live
Under the grey dawn, will a welcome give
To our sweet Graces, or the door-latch lift,
Or will not send them off without a gift ?
Barefoot, with wrinkled brows, and mien deject,
They chide me for the way of chill neglect ;
Though loath, into their empty chest they drop,
And on cold knees their heavy heads they prop ;
And dry their seat is, when no good they earn,
But from a fruitless journey back return.
What living man the poet will repay
With generous love for his ennobling lay ?
I know not : men no longer, as before,
Would live for good deeds in poetic lore ;
But are o'ercome by detestable gain ;
Close-fisted, every one doth fast retain
His money, thinking how to make it grow,
Nor freely would the smallest mite bestow ;
But says : " the knee is nearer than the shin ;
Some good be mine ! from gods bards honour win.
But who will hear another ? one will do—
Homer, best poet, and the cheapest too—
He costs me nothing." Fools ! what boots the gold
Hid within doors in heaps cannot be told ?
Not so the truly wise their wealth employ :

With some 'tis fit one's natural man to joy;
Some to the bard should freely be assigned,
To kin—and many others of mankind.
The gods their offerings; guests should have their dues,
Welcome to come and go whene'er they choose.
But most of all the generous mind prefers
The Muses' consecrate interpreters.
So may you live to fame, when life is done,
Nor mourn inglorious at cold Acheron,
Like one from birth to poverty betrayed,
Whose palms are horny from the painful spade.
To many a serf Antiochus the great,
To many king Aleuas in his state,
Measured the monthly dole. Much kine to see
Lowed at the full stalls of the Scopadæ.
Innumerous flocks to some cool green retreat
The shepherds drove, to screen them from the heat,
O'er Cranon's plain—choice flocks in choicest place,
The wealth of Creon's hospitable race.
No pleasure had been theirs these things about,
When once their sweet souls they had emptied out
Into the broad raft of drear Acheron;
But they, sad with the thoughts of life foregone,
Had lain—their treasures left and memory hid—
Long ages lain the wretched dead amid,
Had not the glorious Ceian breathed the fire
Of his quick spirit to the stringed lyre,
And would not let them altogether die,
But made them famous to posterity:
And e'en their swift-foot steeds obtained renown,
Which in the sacred race-course won the crown.
Who would have known the noble Lycian pair—
The sons of Priam with their pomp of hair—
Or Cycnus, as a woman fair to ken,
Had no bard sung the wars of former men?
Nor that Odysseus, who went wandering round,
Twice sixty moons, wherever man is found,
And, while alive, to farthest Hades sped,
And from the cavern of the Cyclops fled,
Had been aye famed; the keeper of the swine,
Eumæus, and the man the herded kine

Had in his watchful care, Philœtius,
And e'en Laertes the magnanimous,
Had been in a perpetual silence pent,
But for that old Ionian eloquent.

The Muses best renown on men bestow:
The living waste the wealth of those below.
It were all one the waves to number o'er,
As many as wind and blue sea drive ashore,
Or wash with water from the spring's dark urn
The clay of unbaked brick, as try to turn
The money-lover from his wretched pelf—
But let us leave the miser to himself.
May countless pieces swell his silver store!
And let him ever have a wish for more!
But may I still prefer bright honour's meed,
And man's good will, to many a mule and steed!

I am in quest of one whose willing mind
I may, by favour of the Muses, find.
Without the Jove-born sisters, harsh and hard
Are all approaches found by every bard.
Not weary yet revolving heaven appears
Of bringing round the months and circling years.
The car shall yet be moved by many a steed;
And me shall some one as a minstrel need;
Than him more deeds heroic never wrought
Achilles, or stout Aias, when they fought,
Where in his tomb the Phrygian Ilus lies,
On the broad plain of mournful Simoeis.
Who, where the sun sets, dwell—on Libya's heel,
The bold Phœnicians shuddering terror feel;
For Syracuse against them takes the field,
Each with his ready spear and willow shield.
Amidst them arms heroic Hieron,
Equal to heroes of the times foregone;
Floats o'er his helm, in wavy darkness loose,
His horse-hair crest—Athene! mightiest Zeus!
And thou, who with thy mother reignest queen
O'er Ephyra the wealthy, where is seen
Lysimeleia's water, may the blow
Of harsh Necessity rebuke the foe,

And scatter them from our sweet island back
O'er the Sardonian ocean's yeasty track;
And out of many, few return to tell
Their wives and children how the perished fell!
In the foe-ruined cities of the plain
Soon may their former dwellers live again,
And till the fruitful fields! unnumbered sheep,
And fat, bleat cheerily! the cattle creep
Herded in safety to the wonted stalls,
Warning the traveller that evening falls!
For sowing-time be wrought the fallow lea,
When the cicada, sitting on his tree,
Watches the shepherds in the open day,
And blithely sings, perched on the topmost spray;
O'er martial arms may spiders draw their train,
And of fierce war not e'en the name remain;
And famous Hieron illustrious be,
By poets hymned, beyond the Scythian sea;
Or where Semiramis her station chose,
And her huge walls, asphaltos-built, arose!

I am but one: but many others are
Dear to the Muses—may it be their care
To praise the warrior-king (as poets use),
And people, and Sicilian Arethuse!
Ye goddesses! whose loving favours wait
On that Orchomenos, the Thebans' hate,
No where unbidden, but to court or hall
Bidden, with you will I attend the call,
Through your dear presence confident to please,
Enchanting daughters of Eteocles!
What good, what fair can men without you see?
Oh! may I ever with the Graces be!

IDYLL XVII.

THE PRAISE OF PTOLEMY.

Muses! begin and end the song with Zeus,
When of immortals we the chief extol:

Of men the name of Ptolemy produce
First, last, and midst—for he is chief of all.
For their exploits the seed heroical
Of demigods life-giving minstrels found:
I, skilled to sing, will Ptolemy install
   Theme of my song—and glowing hymns redound
E'en to their praise, who dwell th' Olympian heights around.

   In Ida's thick of wood, perplexed with choice,
Which to begin with, the wood-cutter flings
His glance around: to what shall I give voice
First out of all the many blessed things,
With which the gods have graced the best of kings?
How great the son of Lagus from his birth!
Born for what deeds! what great imaginings
   His mind conceived beyond the sons of earth!
Up to the gods by Zeus exalted for his worth!

   In Jove's own house his golden couch is spread,
And by him sits his friend in royal pride,
Great Alexander, the portentous dread
Of Persians glittering with the turban pied:
And Hercules, the vast Centauricide,
Sits opposite on adamantine throne;
There with the gods he banquets gratified,
   In his sons' sons rejoicing as his own,
Made free of age by Zeus, and as immortals known.

   For from heroic Hercules the twain
Descended: therefore when he goes content
From the gods' banquet to his wife again,
Sated with nectar of a fragrant scent,
To one his quiver and his bow unbent
Ever he hands, and to that other blest
His iron-shotted club, with knobs besprent;
   And so they marshal him unto his rest
In his ambrosial home, white-ankled Hebe's nest.

   How excellent of dames was Berenice!
To her dear parents what a wealth of pleasure!
Dionis wiped her fingers on the spicy
Swell of her bosom. No man in such measure
E'er loved his wife, as Ptolemy's best leisure

s

Doted on her; and she with him contended
In love—yea! loved him more: his house and treasure
Thus to his sons he with full trust commended,
Since, loving, he the couch of loving wife ascended.

Some stranger draws the wanton's fancy flighty—
Her children many, like the father none!
Loveliest of goddesses! bright Aphrodite!
Through thee, the way of wailful Acheron
Was ne'er by lovely Berenice gone:
Her, thy sweet care, from the Cyanean river,
And death's grim ferryman, the gloomy one!
Thou didst, soft-placing in thy fane, deliver,
And a conceded share of thine own honours give her.

Soft loves on mortal kind she breathes benign,
And makes his love-care light to every lover.
Thou, who in Argos didst with Tydeus twine,
Dark brows thy gentle eye-lids arching over,
Didst Diomede to light of day discover;
To Peleus the full-bosomed Thetis bore
Achilles; thee, (for there the birth-pang drove her
The aid of Eileithuia to implore,)
Bright Berenice brought forth on the Coan shore:

The Woman-helper stood benignant by,
Her limbs from pain composing, till she smiled
On thee new-born to warrior Ptolemy—
And like his father was the lovely child.
Exulting Cos, with jubilant rapture wild,
Fondled the babe, loud-hymning at the sight:—
"Boy! be thou blest; for me be honours piled
On thy account, such as the Delian bright
Hung round the blue-crowned isle, on which he sprung to
 light.

"From thee to Triop's hill such honour follow,
And no less to the Dorians dwelling nigh,
As his Rhenæa had from King Apollo!"
Thus Cos: the bird of Zeus, up-poised on high,
Under the clouds, well-omened thrice did cry:
From king-protecting Zeus the sign was sent;
But when from birth he marks a royalty,

IDYLL XVII.

That king surpassingly is excellent
For wealth, wide rule by sea and o'er much continent.

In many a region many a tribe doth till
The fields, made fruitful by the shower of Zeus;
None like low-lying Egypt doth fulfil
Hope of increase, when Nile the clod doth loose,
O'er-bubbling the wet soil: no land doth use
So many workmen of all sorts, enrolled
In cities of such multitude profuse,
More than three myriads, as a single fold
Under the watchful sway of Ptolemy the bold.

Part of Phœnicia; some Arabian lands;
Some Syrian; tribes of swart Æthiopes;
All the Pamphylians, Lycians he commands,
And warlike Carians; o'er the Cyclades
His empire spreads; his navies sweep the seas;
Ocean and rivers, earth within her bounds
Obeys him: and a host of chivalries,
And shielded infantry, with martial sounds
Of their far-glittering brass, the warrior-king surrounds.

His wealth, that daily flows from every side,
The treasure of all other kings outweighs;
His busy people's days in quiet glide:
The monster-breeding Nile no hostile blaze
Doth overpass, the war-shout there to raise.
Nor hath armed foeman from swift ship outleapt
To seize the kine Egyptian pastures graze;
For o'er the broad lands of that happy sept
The bright-haired Ptolemy strict ward hath ever kept.

His whole inheritance he cares to keep,
As a good king: himself hath garnered more:
Nor useless in his house the golden heap,
Increased like that of ants; for of his store
The gods have much, since them he doth adore
Ever with first-fruits, and his love commends
With other gifts; his bounty ne'er is poor;
To noble-minded princes much he sends,
And gives to cities much, and much to worthy friends.

None in the sacred games e'er took a part,
Skilled the melodious song to modulate,
Without a royal recompense of art:
Whence Ptolemy the muse-priests celebrate
For his munificence. What meed more great
Than good renown can wealthy man befall?
This meed doth on the dead Atridæ wait;
Their infinite spoil from Priam's ravaged hall
In the thick gloom lies hid, from whence is no recall.

Only this prince hath in his fathers' ways
Exactly walked, and doth their stamp retain;
Whence he to both his parents loved to raise
Temples, and placed their statues in each fane,
Of gold and ivory—never sought in vain
By prayer of mortals; on their altars red
Fat thighs of oxen burn the royal twain,
Himself and consort—one more furnished
With love and excellence ne'er clasped her spouse in bed.

Such were the nuptials of the royal pair,
Whom Rhea bore, the royalties divine
Of blest Olympus: Iris spread with care,
Iris the virgin yet, whose fingers shine
With fragrant brightness, when they would recline
The marriage couch. Hail, Ptolemy! to thee
And other demigods I will assign
Due praise. One word for after-men; to me
It seems, whatever good there is, from Zeus must be.

IDYLL XVIII.

THE EPITHALAMIUM OF HELEN.

Twelve Spartan virgins, the Laconian bloom,
Choired before their Helen's bridal room,
New hung with tapestry: entwined the fair
With hyacinths their hyacinthine hair;
When Menelaus, Atreus' younger pride,
Locked in sweet Tyndaris, his lovely bride;
To the same time with cadence true they beat

The rapid round of intertwining feet;
One measure tript, one song together sung—
Their hymenæan all the palace rung.

   So early, bridegroom! fix'd in slumber deep?
So heavy-limbed, with such a love for sleep?
Thyself, wine-heavy, on the bed hast thrown
For only rest? thou shouldst have slept alone,
And with her mother left the girl to play
With only girls until the break of day.
She's thine from day to day, and year to year—
Thrice-happy bridegroom! on thy way 'tis clear
Good demon sneezed, that only thou shouldst gain
The prize so many princes would obtain,
Only of demigods, whose bosomed love
Her husband makes the son-in-law of Jove!
Jove's daughter, peerless beauty-bud of Greece,
Now lies with thee beneath one broidered fleece.
What offspring to thy hopes will she prefer—
Could her dear offspring but resemble her!
Where flows Eurotas in his pleasant place,
Thrice eighty virgins, we pursued the race,
Like men, anointed with the glistering oil,
A bloom of maiden buds—love's blushing spoil:
Of equal years; but, seen by Helen's side,
Not one in whom some blemish was not spied.
As rising Morn, oh, venerable Night!
Shows from thy bosom dark her face of light;
As the clear spring, when winter's gloom is gone,
So mid our throng the golden Helen shone.
As of a field or garden ornament,
The lofty cypress shoots up eminent;
As of the chariot the Thessalian steed,
So rosy Helen of the Spartan breed
Is ornament and grace. Like Helen none
Draws the fine thread around the spindle spun,
And in the ready basket piles so much;
None interlaces with so quick a touch
The woof and warp; for other never came
A web so perfect from the broidering frame.
Like Helen none the cithern knows to ring,

Of Artemis or tall Athene sing,
Like Helen, in whose liquid-shining eyes
Desire, the light of love, dissolving lies.
O fair and lovely girl! a matron now—
Where meadow-flowers in dewy brightness grow,
We'll hie with early dawn, and fondly pull
Sweets to twine garlands for our beautiful;
Remembering Helen with our fond regrets,
As for the absent ewe her suckling frets.
Of lotuses we'll hang thee many a wreath
Upon the shady plane, and drop beneath
Oil from the silver pyx; and on the bark,
In Doric, shall be graved for all to mark,
"To me pay honour—I am Helen's tree."
Hail, bride! high-wedded bridegroom, hail to thee!
Fruitful Latona fruit of marriage give;
Cypris in bonds of mutual love to live;
And Zeus the wealth that shall without an end
From high-born sire to high-born son descend!
Sleep, happy pair! in love enjoy your rest,
Breathing desire into each other's breast.
But wake at dawn; for we'll present us here
At the first call of crested chanticleer.
Hymen, O Hymenæan! joyful spread
With love's contentment sweet this marriage-bed.

IDYLL XIX.

THE STEALER OF HONEY-COMBS.

As from a hive the thieving Eros drew
   A honey-comb, a bee his finger stung;
Then in his anguish on his hand he blew,
   Stamped, jumped—and then to Cytherea sprung;

Showed her the wound, and cried: "A thing how wee,
   How great a wound makes with its little sting!"
His mother smiled: "Art thou not like a bee,
   Such great wounds making—such a little thing?"

IDYLL XX.

THE HERDSMAN.

EUNICA, smiling with a bitter scoff,
When I would sweetly kiss her, bade me "off!
Fool cowherd! would you kiss me? not to kiss
Rude clowns, but city lips, I've learnt, I wis.
You never, man! shall kiss my lovely mouth—
Not in a dream.   You are—O how uncouth!
Your look offends me, and your speech provokes;
Your play is horse-play; vulgar are your jokes.
How smooth in speech! how delicate an air!
How soft your beard! how odorous your hair!
Your lips are sickly; and your hands are black,
And you smell rank: don't foul me; back, clown, back!"

   Thrice on her breast she spat, these hard words saying,
Me scornfully from head to foot surveying;
Pouting and muttering proudly looked askaunt,
Before mine eyes did plume her form and flaunt,
And mocking smiled with lips drawn far apart.
My blood boiled fiercely from my grief of heart,
And red my cheeks from passionate anguish grew,
As vernal roses from the morning dew.
She left me then: but angry feelings glow
Within my heart, because she used me so.

   Am I not handsome, shepherds? tell me truly;
Or has some god transformed my person newly?
For as lush ivy clips the stem o' the tree,
The bloom of beauty lately covered me.
My curls, like parsley, round my temples clung;
A shining forehead my dark brows o'erhung;
My eyes were bluer than Athene's own;
My mouth than new cheese sweeter; every tone
Sweeter than honeycombs: and sweet I take
My song to be; the sweetest sounds I wake
From all wind instruments, in very deed—
Straight pipe or transverse, flute or vocal reed.
The girls upon the hills me handsome call;
They kiss me lovingly—they love me all.

But ah! my city-madam never kist me;
And for I am a cowherd she dismist me.
That Dionysus in the valleys green
Once tended kine, she never heard, I ween;
Nor knows that Cypris on a cowherd doted,
And on the Phrygian hills herself devoted
To tend his herd; nor how the same Dionis
In thickets kist, in thickets wept Adonis.
Who was Endymion? him tending kine
Stooped down to kiss Selena the divine,
Who from Olympus to the Latmian grove
Glided to slumber with her mortal love.
Didst thou not, Rhea, for a cowherd weep?
And didst thou not, high Zeus! the heaven sweep,
In form of winged bird, and watch indeed
To carry off the cowherd Ganymede?
Only Eunica (daintier she must be
Than were Selena, Cypris, Cybele,)
Won't kiss a cowherd. May'st thou ne'er uncover
Thyself, self-worshipt Beauty! to a lover
In town or country; but, vain poppet! ever
Sleep by thyself—despite thy best endeavour.

IDYLL XXI.

THE FISHERMEN.

Asphalion and a comrade.

THE nurse of industry and arts is want;
Care breaks the labourer's sleep, my Diophant!
And should sweet slumber o'er his eyelids creep,
Dark cares stand over him, and startle sleep.

  Two fishers old lay in their wattled shed,
Close to the wicker on one sea-moss bed;
Near them the tools wherewith they plied their craft,
The basket, rush-trap, line, and reedy shaft,
Weed-tangled baits, a drag-net with its drops,
Hooks, cord, two oars, an old boat fixt on props.
Their rush-mat, clothes, and caps, propt either head;
These were their implements by which they fed,

And this was all their wealth. They were not richer
By so much as a pipkin or a pitcher.
All else seemed vanity: they could not mend
Their poverty—which was their only friend.
They had no neighbours; but upon the shore
The sea soft murmured at their cottage door.
The chariot of the moon was midway only,
When thoughts of toil awoke those fishers lonely:
And shaking sleep off they began to sing.

ASPHALION.

The summer-nights are short, when Zeus the king
Makes the days long, some say—and lie. This night
I've seen a world of dreams, nor yet 'tis light.
What's all this? am I wrong? or say I truly?
And can we have a long, long night in July?

FRIEND.

Do you the summer blame? The seasons change,
Nor willingly transgress their wonted range.
From care, that frightens sleep, much longer seems
The weary night.

ASPHALION.

                Can you interpret dreams?
I've seen a bright one, which I will declare,
That you my visions, as my toil, may share.
To whom should you in mother-wit defer?
And quick wit is best dream-interpreter.
We've leisure, and to spare: what can one do,
Lying awake on leaves, as I and you,
Without a lamp? they say the town-hall ever
Has burning lights—its booty fails it never.

FRIEND.

Well: let us have your vision of the night.

ASPHALION.

When yester-eve I slept, outwearied quite
With the sea-toil, not over-fed, for our
Commons, you know, were short at feeding hour,
I saw myself upon a rock, where I
Sat watching for the fish—so eagerly!
And from the reed the tripping bait did shake,
Till a fat fellow took it—no mistake:
('Twas natural-like that I should dream of fish,

As hounds of meat upon a greasy dish :)
He hugged the hook, and then his blood did flow;
His plunges bent my reed like any bow ;
I stretched both arms, and had a pretty bout,
To take with hook so weak a fish so stout.
I gently warned him of the wound he bore ;
" Ha ! will you prick me ? you'll be pricked much more."
But when he struggled not, I drew him in ;
The contest then I saw myself did win.
I landed him, a fish compact of gold !
But then a sudden fear my mind did hold,
Lest king Poseidon made it his delight,
Or it was Amphitrite's favourite.
I loosed him gently from the hook, for fear
It from his mouth some precious gold might tear,
And with my line I safely towed him home,
And swore that I on sea no more would roam,
But ever after would remain on land,
And there my gold, like any king, command.
At this I woke ; your wits, good friend, awaken,
For much I fear to break the oath I've taken.

FRIEND.

Fear not: you swore not, saw not with your eyes
The fish you saw ; for visions all are lies.
But now no longer slumber : up, awake !
And for a false a real vision take.
Hunt for the foodful fish that is, not seems ;
For fear you starve amid your golden dreams.

IDYLL XXII.

THE DIOSCURI.

The twins of Leda, child of Thestius,
Twice and again we celebrate in song,
The Spartan pair, stamped by Ægiochus,
Castor and Pollux, arming with the thong
His dreadful hands ; both merciful as strong
Saviours of men on danger's extreme edge,
And steeds tost in the battle's bloody throng,

And star-defying ships on ruin's ledge,
Swept with their crews by blasts into the cruel dredge.

   The winds, where'er they list, the huge wave drive,
Dashing from prow or stern into the hold;
Both sides, sail, tackle, yard, and mast, they rive,
Snapping at random: from Night's sudden fold
Rushes a flood; hither and thither rolled,
Broad ocean's heaving volumes roar and hiss,
Smitten by blasts and the hail-volley cold:
The lost ship and her crew your task it is,
Bright pair! to rescue from the terrible abyss.

   They think to die—but lo! a sudden lull
O' the winds; the clouds disperse; and the hush'd sheen
Of the calmed ocean sparkles beautiful:
The Bears, and Asses with the Stall between,
Foreshow a voyage safe and skies serene.
Blest Brothers! who to mortals safety bring,
Both harpers, minstrels, knights, and warriors keen:
Since both I hymn, with which immortal king
Shall I commence my song? of Pollux first I'll sing.

   The justling rocks, the dangerous Euxine's mouth,
Snow-veiled, when Argo safely passed, and ended
Her course at the Bebrycian shore, the youth
Born of the gods from both her sides descended,
And on the deep shore, from rude winds defended,
Their couches spread; and strook the seeds of fire
From the pyreion. Forthwith unattended
Did Pollux, of the red-brown hue, retire
With Castor, whose renown for horsemanship was higher.

   On a high hill a forest did appear:
The brothers found there a perennial spring,
Under a smooth rock, filled with water clear,
With pebbles paved, which from below did fling
A crystal sheen like silver glistering:
The poplar, plane, tall pine, and cypress, grew
Hard by; and odorous flowers did thither bring
Thick swarm of bees, their sweet toil to pursue,
As many as in the meads, when spring ends, bloom to view.

There lay at ease a bulky insolent,
Grim-looked: his ears by gauntlets scored and marred;
His vast chest, like a ball, was prominent;
His back was broad with flesh like iron hard,
Like anvil-wrought Colossus to regard;
And under either shoulder thews were seen
On his strong arms, like round stones which, oft jarred
In the quick rush with many a bound between,
A winter torrent rolls down through the cleft ravine.

A lion's hide suspended by the feet
Hung from his neck and o'er his shoulders fell:
Him the prize-winner Pollux first did greet:
"Hail, stranger! in these parts what people dwell?"
"The hail of utter stranger sounds not well,
At least to me." "We're not malevolent,
Nor sons of such, take heart." "You need not tell
Me that—I in myself am confident."
"You are a savage, quick to wrath and insolent."

"You see me as I am; upon your land
I do not walk." "Come thither, and return
With hospitable gifts." "I've none at hand
For you, nor want I yours." "Pray, let me learn,
Wilt let me drink from out this fountain urn?"
"You'll know, if your thirst-hanging lips are dry."
"How may we coax you from your humour stern,
With silver or what else?" "The combat try—"
"How, pray, with gauntlets, foot to foot and eye to eye?"

"In pugilistic fight, nor spare your skill."
"Who is my gauntlet-armed antagonist?"
"At hand! he's here; you see him if you will,
I, Amycus, the famous pugilist."
"And what the prize of the victorious fist?"
"The vanquished shall become the victor's thrall."
"Red-crested cocks so fight, and so desist."
"Cock-like or lion-like the combat call;
This is the prize for which we fight, or none at all."

Then on a conch he blew a mighty blast:
The long-haired Bebryces, hearing the sound,
Under the shady planes assembled fast;

And likewise Castor, in the fight renowned,
Hastened and called his comrades to the ground,
From the Magnesian ship. With gauntlets both
Armed their strong hands ; their wrists and arms they
    bound
With the long thongs ; with one another wroth,
Each breathing blood and death, they stood up nothing loth.

First'each contended which should get the sun
Of his antagonist ; but much in sleight
That huge man, Pollux ! was by thee outdone ;
And Amycus was dazzled with the light ;
But raging rushed straight forward to the fight,
Aiming fierce blows ; but wary Pollux met him,
Striking the chin of his vast opposite,
Who fiercer battled, for the blow did fret him,
And leaning forward tried unto the ground to get him.

Shouted the Bebryces ; and, for they feared
The man like Tityus might their friend down-weigh
In the scant place, the heroes Pollux cheered :
But shifting here and there Jove's son made play,
And struck out right and left, but kept away
From the fierce rush of Neptune's son uncouth,
Who, drunk with blows, reeled in the hot affray,
Out-spitting purple blood ; the princely youth
Shouted, when they beheld his battered jaws and mouth.

His eyes were nearly closed from the contusion
Of his swoln face ; the prince amazed him more
With many feints, and seeing his confusion,
Mid-front he struck a heavy blow and sore,
And to the bone his forehead gashing tore ;
Instant he fell, and at his length he lay
On the green leaves ; but fiercely as before,
On his uprising, they renewed the fray,
Aiming terrific blows, as with intent to slay.

But the Bebrycian champion strove to place
His blows upon the broad breast of his foe,
Who ceaselessly disfigured all his face :
His flesh with sweating shrunk, that he did show,
From huge, but small ; but larger seemed to grow

The limbs of Pollux, and of fresher hue
The more he toiled: Muse! for 'tis thine to know,
And mine to give interpretation true,
Tell how the son of Zeus that mighty bulk o'erthrew.

Aiming at something great, the big Bebrycian
The left of Pollux with his left hand caught,
Obliquely leaning out from his position,
And from his flank his huge right hand he brought,
And had he hit him would have surely wrought
Pollux much damage; but escape he found,
Stooping his head, and smote him, quick as thought,
On the left temple; from the gaping wound
A bubbling gush of gore out-spurted on the ground.

Right on his mouth his left hand then he dashed;
Rattled his teeth; and with a quicker hail
Of blows he smote him, till his cheeks he smashed:
Stretched out he lay; his senses all did fail,
Save that he owned the other did prevail
By holding up his hands: nor thou didst claim
The forfeit, Pollux, taking of him bail
Of a great oath in his own father's name,
Strangers to harm no more with word or deed of shame.

To Castor now belongs my votive strain,
The brass-mailed, shake-spear knight. The twins of Zeus,
It chanced, had carried off the daughters twain
Of old Leucippus; wroth for which abuse,
The two bold brothers, sons of Aphareus,
Pursued the ravishers incontinent—
Their plighted bridegrooms, Idas and Lynceus.
They overtook them at the monument
Of the dead Aphareus, as on their way they went.

With shields and spears all from their chariots leapt,
And Lynceus through his helmet loudly spoke:
"Why not let brides be by their bridegrooms kept?
Why with your drawn swords, ready for the stroke,
Do you so eagerly the fight provoke?
To us their sire betrothed them, and did swear
An oath thereto—which oath he only broke

Persuaded by your gifts, (foul shame to hear
In case of others' brides,) kine, mules, and divers gear.

"Oft have I said, although no speechifier,
Before you both; my friends! it is not right
Princes for wives those maidens should desire,
Whose bridegrooms wait them and the nuptial night:
Sparta, sweet Arcady with fleeces white,
Equestrian Elis, famous Argolis,
The Achæan towns, Messenia's ample site,
And all the shore-reach of rich Sisyphis,
Are all of great extent with choice of maids, I wis.

"And you may pick and choose at will of these,
Who are in mind, form, feature, excellent;
Good men for sons-in-law most fathers please,
And you 'mid heroes are pre-eminent,
On either side ennobled by descent.
Come, let our nuptials to their end proceed;
We'll find brides for you to your heart's content:
The wind to wave swept off my useless rede;
might as well have preached unto the winds indeed.

"You are ungentle in your wilful mood;
Be now persuaded for your own behoof;
Though we are cousins—if it seems you good
This strife to finish by the battle-proof,
Let Idas and brave Pollux stand aloof,
While Castor and myself, the younger, try
The battle; thus to the parental roof
We shall not leave an utter misery—
One death is quite enough for one sad family.

"Those who survive shall gladden all their friends,
(Bridegrooms, not corses,) and these virgins wed:
Good is small ill that great contention ends."
And Providence fulfilled the words he said.
That elder pair their arms deposited;
But Lynceus shook, under his shield's broad rest,
His quivering lance, and Castor likewise sped
To meet him: to the conflict fierce they prest;
On either martial head nodded the horse-hair crest.

First with their spears they aimed full many a blow,
Where'er an exposed part came into sight,
But ere they injured one another so,
The spear-heads broke in either broad shield pight:
Then from the sheaths they drew their swords outright,
And fiercely on the other either prest,
Nor paused a moment in the furious fight;
And each at shield or helm their blows addrest,
But quick-eyed Lynceus maimed—only the purple crest.

At Castor's left knee then he fiercely strook,
Who, 'scaping, smote the threatening hand away;
He, running, to his father's tomb betook
Himself, dropping the hand : there Idas lay
Watching the cousins ply the bloody fray;
But eager Castor drove his thirsty sword
Through flank and navel; out-gushed to the day
His bowels, where out-spread he lay begored;
And down his eyelids dim the heavy sleep was poured.

Nor was it fated that his mother dear
Should see the other wed to her content;
For Idas at that hapless sight did tear
A pillar from his father's monument,
To slay his brother's slayer; but Zeus sent,
In aid of Castor, his devouring fire,
Made drop the marble, and himself up-brent.
So they did to none easy task aspire,
Who fought those mighty ones—the sons of mighty sire.

Hail, sons of Leda! give my hymns renown:
To you and Helen, dear the minstrel's claim,
And dear to all who threw proud Ilion down.
The Chian minstrel, princes! gave you fame,
Of Troy, th' Achæan ships that thither came,
The war, and the war's tower, Achilles brave,
Hymning the song : may mine be free from blame!
I give you what to me the Muses gave;
And gods prefer the song to all the gifts they have!

IDYLL XXIII.

THE LOVER; OR LOVE-SICK.

A YOUTH was love-sick for a maid unkind,
Whose form was blameless, but not so her mind.
She scorned her lover and his suit disdained;
One gentle thought she never entertained.
She knew not Love—what sort of god, what darts
From what a bow he shoots at youthful hearts!
Her lips were strangers to soft gentleness,
And she was difficult of all access.
She had no word to soothe his scorching fire,
No sparkle of the lip; no moist desire
To her bright eyes a dewy lustre lent;
Blushed on her cheek no crimson of consent;
She breathed no word of sighing born—no kiss
That lightens love, and turns its pain to bliss.
But, as the wild game from his thicket spies
The train of hunters with suspicious eyes,
So she her lover; ever did she turn
Toward him scornful lip, and eye-glance stern.
She was his fate: and on her glooming face,
The scorn that burned within her left its trace.
Her colour fled; and every feature showed
Pale from the rage that in her bosom glowed.
Yet even so she was—how fair to see!
The more she scorned him, still the more loved he.
At last by Cypris scorched without her cure,
He could no more the raging flame endure.
He went and kist her door, and tears he shed,
And, 'midst his tears and kisses, sadly said:—

"Harsh, cruel girl! stone-heart and pitiless!
The nurseling of some savage lioness,
Unworthy love! my latest gift I bring,
This noose—no more will I thine anger sting.
But now I go where thou hast sentenced me—
The common road which all reports agree
Must at some time by all that live be gone,
And where love's cure is found—Oblivion.

Ah! could I drink it all, I should not slake
My passionate longing: at thy gates I take
My last farewell, thereto commit indeed
My latest sigh.   The future I can read—
The rose is beautiful, the rose of prime,
But soon it withers at the touch of time;
And beautiful in spring-time to behold
The violet, but ah! it soon grows old;
White are the lilies, but they soon decay;
White is the snow, but soon it melts away;
And beautiful the bloom of virgin youth,
But lives a very little time in sooth.
Thy time will come—thou too at last shalt prove,
And weep most bitterly, the flames of love.
But grant, I pray thee, grant my latest prayer:
When thou shalt see me hanging high in air,
E'en at thy door—O pass not heedless by!
But drop a few tears to my memory.
From the harsh thong unloose thy hapless lover,
And from thy limbs a garment take and cover
The lifeless body, and the last kiss give;
Fear not that haply I may come alive
At thy lip's touch—I cannot live again;
Thy kiss, if given in love, were given in vain!
Hollow a mound to hide my love's sad end,
And thrice on leaving, cry, 'Here lie, my friend!'
And, if thou wilt, by thee this word be said,
'Here lies my love, my beautiful is dead.'
And let this epitaph mine end recall,
Just at the last I scratch it on thy wall:
'Love slew him: stop and say,—Who here is laid
Well but not wisely loved a cruel maid.'"
Then in the doorway for its cruel use
He set a stone; he fitted next the noose;
Put in his neck, and eagerly he sped,
Spurning the stone away—and swung there dead.
But when she saw the corse her doorway kept,
She was not moved in spirit, nor she wept:
She felt no ruth, but, scornful to the last,
She spat upon the body, as she past;
And careless went to bathe her and adorn,

Where stood a statue of the god, her scorn.
From the bath's marble edge whereon it stood,
The statue leapt and slew her: with her blood
The water was impurpled, and the sound
Of the girl's dying accent swam around :—
"Ah lovers! she that scorned true love is slain;
Love is revengeful: when loved, love again."

IDYLL XXIV.

THE LITTLE HERCULES.

ALCMENA having washed her twin delight,
Her Hercules, who then was ten months old,
And her Iphicles, younger by a night,
Gave them the breast, then laid them in the hold
Of a brass shield won by Amphitryon bold—
The spoil of Pterelas in battle slain;
And, touching either head, her blessing told:
" Sleep, healthful sleep enjoy my blessed twain;
Sleep happy! happy wake at coming dawn again."

And with these words she rocked the mighty shield,
And sleep came over them: in the midnight,
What time the Bear, watching Orion's field,
(Who then his shoulder shows uprising bright,)
To setting turns, vex'd Hera's wily spite,
With many threats of her revengeful ire,
To eat the infant Hercules outright,
Sent to the chamber-door two monsters dire,
Each bristling horribly with his dark-gleaming spire.

They their blood-gorging bellies on the ground
Uncoiling rolled; their eyes shot baleful flame,
And evermore they spat their poison round;
But when, quick brandishing with evil aim
Their forked tongues, they to the children came,
They both awoke: (what can escape Jove's eye?)
Light in the chamber shone; and who can blame
Or wonder that Iphicles did outcry,
Screaming, when he did their remorseless teeth espy?

He kicked aside the woollen coverlet,
Struggling to flee ; but Hercules comprest,
Relaxing not the gripe his hand did get,
With a firm grasp the throat of either pest,
Where is their poison, which e'en gods detest.
The boy, that in the birth was long confined,
Who ne'er was known to cry, though at the breast
A suckling yet, they with their coils entwined :
Infolding him they strained their own release to find,

Till wearied in their spines they loosed their fold.
Alcmena heard the noise and woke in fear :—
" Amphitryon, up ! for me strange fear doth hold—
Up ! up ! don't wait for sandals ; don't you hear
Iphicles screaming ? see ! the walls appear
Distinctly shining in the dead of night,
As though 'twere dawn. There is some danger near ;
I'm sure there is, dear man !" He then outright
Did leap from off the bed to hush his wife's affright.

And hastily his costly sword he sought ;
Suspended near his cedar-bed it hung ;
With one hand raised the sheath of lotus wrought,
While with the other he the belt unswung.
The room was filled with night again : he sprung,
And for his household, breathing slumber deep,
He loudly called ; his voice loud echoing rung :
" Ho ! from the hearth bring lights ! quick ! do not creep !
Fling wide the doors—awake ! this is no time for sleep."

They hastened all with lights at his command ;
But when they saw (their eyes they well might doubt)
A serpent clutched in either tender hand
Of suckling Hercules, they gave a shout,
And clapped their hands : he instantly held out
The serpents to Amphitryon, and wild
With child-like exultation leaped about,
And laid them at his father's feet and smiled—
Laid down those monsters grim, in sleep of death now mild.

Alcmena to her fragrant bosom drew
Iphicles screaming and with fear half-dead ;

The lamb-wool coverlet Amphitryon threw
O'er Hercules and went again to bed.
The cocks, the third time crowing, heralded
The day-dawn: then Alcmena sent to call
Tiresias the seer, who truly said
Whate'er he said would be; and told him all,
And bade him answer her what thing would thence befall:

"Hide not, I pray, from reverence for me
If aught of ill the gods design: 'tis clear
What fate has spun for him no man can flee;
But saying this I teach the wise, good seer!"
He answered: "Woman! privileged to bear
The noblest offspring, princess of the blood
Of Perseus, by my own sweet light I swear,
Which once was in these eyes, as name for good
Shall be remembered long Alcmena's womanhood.

" The Achæan women while they spin, I wis,
Alcmena's name to latest eve shall sing;
And famous shalt thou be in Argolis;
For this thy son to star-paved heaven shall spring:
All that contend with the broad-breasted king,
Or man or beast, shall yield the victory.
Twelve labours wrought, him Destiny shall bring
To Jove's own house, but all of him can die
On the Trachinian pyre shall perish utterly.

"And he the son-in-law of her shall be,
Who sent these dragons to destroy the child;
Then in his lair the sharp-toothed wolf shall see
The fawn, nor harm it, wonderfully mild.
In the hearth-ashes let there now be piled
All sorts of thorn, bramble, and prickly pear,
And dry, wind-shaken twigs of buck-thorn wild;
And at the midnight burn these dragons here,
Since they to slay the child at midnight did appear.

" A maid must cast these ashes with the wind
At morn from yon rock to the rushing tide,
Then hasten home and never look behind.
With sulphur let the house be purified;
Pure water, mixed with salt, from side to side

Then from a full urn sprinkle on the floor :
For so the holy custom doth provide ;
And sacrifice to Zeus supreme a boar,
That o'er your foes you may be victors evermore."

Then, rising from the ivory chair, withdrew
Tiresias, and bent with years was he.
But Hercules with his fond mother grew,
As grows a young plant in a fruitful lea,
And still Amphitryon's boy was thought to be :
Linus, Apollo's son, heroic name !
Instructed him in letters carefully.
And Eurytus, who from rich parents came,
Taught him to bend the bow and take unerring aim.

To move his fingers on the harp with ease,
And to the music minstrelsy to sing,
Him taught Eumolpus Philammonides :
And with what sleights the men of Argos fling
Each other, wrestling fiercely in the ring,
And every sort of pugilistic sleight,
Him taught the son of the Cyllenian king,
Harpalicus, whose dreadful brow did fright
Men from afar, that few would dare with him to fight.

To drive the chariot, and impel, control
The rapid-bounding steeds, and how to shun
Dashing his axle-nave against the goal,
He was instructed by Amphitryon,
Who willingly did teach his hopeful son :
In Argos oft, whose praises are far-spoken
For generous steeds, himself had prizes won ;
And of his skill there was this certain token,
Though time had marred the reins, his chariot was unbroken.

In stationary fight to aim the lance,
Shielding himself ; to bide swords flashing round ;
To draw his battle out, and bid advance
The cavalry ; to scan the foeman's ground,
While to the charge the troops impetuous bound,—
He learned from Castor, who, till he was old,
Of demigods was warrior most renowned,
Exiled from Argos then, which Tydeus bold
With all the vine-land broad did from Adrastus hold.

Alcmena thus had taught her Hercules.
His sleeping-place was near his father's bed;
And, what did most of all his fancy please,
For the bold boy a lion's hide was spread.
His morning meal, roast meat and Dorian bread—
No ploughman would a larger loaf desire;
His evening meal (the day already sped)
Was very light; nor such as needed fire.
He always wore, bare to his knees, a plain attire.

IDYLL XXV.

HERCULES THE LION-SLAYER, OR, THE WEALTH OF AUGEIAS.

WHEN, to perform his fated lord's behest,
Amphitryon's son, with toils and perils tried,
Hero with the prodigious breadth of breast,—
In his right hand his club, the lion's hide
Hung from his shoulders by the fore-feet tied,—
To the rich vale of fruitful Elis came,
Where the sweet waters of Alphëus glide,
Seeing herds, flocks, and pastures, none might claim,
But only wealthiest lord, some prince well known to fame,

He asked a countryman, whose watchful care
O'erlooked the grounds, (his task was his delight,)
"Good friend! wilt tell a traveller, whose are
These herds, and flocks, and pastures infinite?
He is, I well may guess, the favourite
Of the Olympian gods. Here should abide
Those I am come to seek." The man, at sight
And claim of stranger, quickly laid aside
The work he had in hand, and courteously replied:

"What thou dost ask I willingly will tell,
Good stranger! for I fear the heavy wrath
Of Hermes, the way-god ; of all who dwell
Above us, most is he provoked, when scath
Or scorn is done to him who asks his path.
Not in one pasture all the flocks appear,

Nor in one region, King Augeias hath:
Some pasture where Elisson glides ; some, where
Alphëus ; at vine-clad Buprasion some ; some, here :

"And every flock has its particular fold.
Their pasture never fails his numerous kine
In the green lowlands that receiving hold
The gush of Peneus, and the dew divine:
As in the genial moisture they recline,
The meads throw up soft herbage, which supplies
The strength of the horned kine. Beyond the shine
Of the far-gliding river—turn your eyes
A little to the left—their stalled enclosure lies ;

"Yonder, where the perennial planes elate
Stand lordly, and the green wild-olives grow,—
A grove to King Apollo dedicate,
The pastoral god, most perfect god we know.
Hard by, our dwellings in a lengthened row ;
Our labour an immense revenue yields
To our good lord, as often as we sow,
When thrice or four times ploughed, the fallow fields :
Each of his husbandmen the spade or hoe that wields,

"Earthing the vine-roots, or at vintage-tide
Toils at the wine-press, knows where the domain
Of rich Augeias ends on every side.
For his is all the far-extended plain,
Orchards thick-set with trees, and fields with grain,
E'en to the fount-full hill-tops far away ;
All which we work at (as behoves the swain,
Whose life is spent a-field) through all the day.
Why thou art come—to tell may be thy profit—say.

"Dost seek Augeias, or some one of those
Who serve him ? I will give an answer clear,
And to the point, as one that fully knows.
Not mean art thou, nor of mean sires, I'd swear,
So grand thy form. The sons of gods appear
Such among men." To him Jove's son replied :
"In truth, old man ! for that did bring me here,
Augeias I would see : if it betide
Th' Epeän chief doth in the city now abide,

"And, caring for the folk, as judge fulfils
True judgment; bid his trusty steward me speed,
With whom as guide I may converse. God wills
That mortal men should one another need."
To him the husbandman: "It seems, indeed,
Thy way was heaven-appointed: in thine aim,
E'en to thy wish, thou dost at once succeed;
For yesterday Augeias hither came,
With his illustrious son, Phyleüs hight by name.

"After long time, his rural wealth to see,
He came: to this e'en princes are not blind,
The master there, his house will safer be.
But let us to the stall; there shall we find
Augeias." Led the way that old man kind:
Seeing the great hand-filling club, and spoil
Of the wild beast, he puzzled much his mind,
Who he could be, come from what natal soil;
And with desire to ask him this did inward boil,

But caught the word just to his lips proceeding,
For fear he might with question indiscreet,
Or out of place, annoy the stranger speeding:
'Tis a hard thing another's thought to weet.
The hounds both ways, by scent and fall of feet;
Perceived them from afar. At Hercules
They flew, loud barking at him, but did greet
The old man, whining gently as you please,
And round him wagged their tails, and fawning licked his
    knees.

But he with stones—to lift them was enough—
Scared back the hounds, their barking did restrain,
And scolded them; but, though his voice was rough,
His heart was glad they did such guard maintain,
When he was absent. Then he spoke again:
"Gods! what an animal! what faithful suit
He does to man! if he where to abstain,
Where rage, but knew, none other might dispute
With him in excellence; but 'tis too fierce a brute."

And soon they reached the stall. The sun his steeds
Turned to the west, bringing the close of day.

The herds and flocks, returning from the meads,
Came to the stables where they nightly lay.
The kine in long succession trod the way,
Innumerous ; as watery clouds on high,
By south or west wind driven in dense array,
One on another press, and forward fly,
Numberless, without end, along the thickened sky ;

So many upon so many impels the wind ;
Others on others drive their crests to twine :
So many herds so many pressed behind ;
The plain, the ways, were filled in breadth and line ;
The fields were straitened with the lowing kine.
The sheep were folded soon ; the cattle, too,
That inward, as they walk, their knees incline,
Were all installed, a multitude to view :
No man stood idle by for want of work to do.

Some to the kine their wooden shoes applied,
And bound with thongs ; while some in station near
To milk them took their proper place beside :
One to the dams let go their younglings dear,
Mad for the warm milk ; while another there
The milk-pail held, the curds to cheese one turned :
Meanwhile Augeias went by every where,
And with his own eyes for himself he learned
What revenue for him his cattle-keepers earned.

With him his son and mighty Hercules
Through his exceeding show of riches went.
And, though his mind Amphitryonides
Was wont to keep on balance and unbent,
At sight thereof he was in wonderment :
Had he not seen it, he'd have thought it fable,
That any one, however eminent
For wealth, or any ten, in fold, stall, stable,
The richest of all kings, to show such wealth were able.

Hyperion gave unto his son most dear,
That he should all in flocks and herds excel.
His care increased them more from year to year ;

For on his herds no sort of ailment fell,
Such as destroys the cattle: his grew well,
In pith improving still. None cast their young,
Which almost all were female. He could tell
Three hundred white-skinned bulls his kine among,
And eke two hundred red, that to their pastime sprung.

Twelve swan-white bulls were sacred to the sun,
All inknee'd bulls excelling; these apart
Cropped the green pasture, and were never done
Exulting; when from thicket shag did dart
Wild beasts, among the herds to play their part,
These twelve first rushed, death-looking, to the war,
Roaring most terribly. In pride of heart
And strength great Phaethon (men to a star
Did liken him) was first, mid many seen afar.

When this bull saw the tawny lion's hide,
He rushed on watchful Hercules, intent
To plunge his armed forehead in his side:
But then the hero grasped incontinent
The bull's left horn, and to the ground back-bent
His heavy neck; then backward pressed his might.
The bull, more struggling as more backward sent,
At last stood, stretching every nerve, upright.
The king, and prince, and swains, all marvelled at the sight.

But to the city, on the following day,
Bold Hercules and prince Phyleüs sped.
At first their path through a thick vineyard lay,
Narrow, and 'mid the green, through which it led,
Half-hid. This past, Phyleüs turned his head
O'er his right shoulder, soon as they did reach
The public road, and to the hero said,
Who walked behind him: "Friend, I did impeach
Myself as having lost, concerning thee, some speech

"I long since heard: now I remember me,
A young Achæan hither on a day
From Argos came, from sea-shore Helice,
Who, many Epeans present, then did say
He saw an Argive man a monster slay,

A lion, dread of all the country round,
Whose lair in grove of Zeus the Nemean lay:
I am not sure if on Tirynthian ground,
Or else in Argos born, or in Mycenian bound;

"But said, if I remember rightly now,
The hero sprung from Perseus: I confess
Methinks none other Argive man but thou
Dared that adventure: yea! that piece of dress,
The lion's hide, avows that hardiness.
Then, hero, first of all explain to me,
That I may know if right or wrong my guess,
Whether thou art in truth that very he,
Whose deed was told us by the man of Helice.

"Next, tell how thou didst slay the dreadful beast,
And how his way to Nemean haunt he found:
One, if he searched in Apian land at least,
Such monster could not find, though bears abound,
Boars and destructive wolves, the country round:
Wherefore all marvelled at the man's recital,
And thought the traveller, with idle sound
Of his invented wonders, in requital
Of hospitable rites, was striving to delight all."

Then from the mid-path to the road-side near
Phyleüs kept, that both abreast might find
Sufficient room, and he might better hear
What Hercules should say, who, still behind,
To him replied: "Not from the truth declined,
But with just balance thou hast judged it well:
Since thou would'st hear, I with a willing mind
Will tell, Phyleüs, how the monster fell,
But whence he came nor I, nor Argive else can tell.

"Only we think that some immortal sent,
For holy rites profaned or left undone,
That ill on the Phoronians; forth he went,
And the Piseäns, like a flood, o'errun:
The Bembinæans least of all could shun
His fateful wrath; they, nearest, fared the worst:
To slay that terrible redoubted one

Was task enjoined me by Eurystheus erst;
His wish I undertook, of my set toils the first.

"My flexile bow I took, and quiver full
Of arrows, and my club, the bark still on,
The stem of a wild olive I did pull
Up by the roots, when thither I was gone,
Under the brow of holy Helicon.
But when I came to the huge lion's lair,
I to the tip the string did straightway don,
And fix'd one of the arrows which I bare:
To see, ere I was seen, I looked around with care.

" It was the mid-day, and not yet I found
His traces; nor could hear his mighty roar.
I saw no herdsman, ploughman on the ground,
To point me where I should his haunt explore:
Green fear kept every man within his door.
Nor till I saw him and his vigour tried,
Ceased I to search the sylvan mountain o'er;
And ere came on the cool of eventide,
Back to his cavern, gorged with flesh and blood, he hied.

"His dew-lap, savage face, and mane, were gory;
He licked his beard, while I, yet unespied,
Lurked in a thicket of the promontory;
But as he nearer came, at his left side
I shot an arrow, but it did not glide,
Though sharp, into his flesh, but with rebound
Fell on the grass. The thick he closely eyed,
His bloody head up-lifting from the ground,
And ghastly grinned, showing his teeth's terrific round.

" Then on the string another shaft I placed,
And shot—vext that the former idly flew:
Mid-breast I hit him, where the lungs are placed:
His hide the sharp, sharp arrow pierced not through,
But at his feet fell ineffectual too:
Again a third I was in act to shoot,
Enraged to think in vain my bow I drew,
When I was seen by the blood-thirsty brute,
Who to the battle-thought his angry signs did suit.

"With his long tail he lashed himself; and all
His neck was filled with wrath: the fiery glow
Of his vext mane up-bristled; in a ball
He gathered up himself, till like a bow
His spine was arched: as when one, who doth know
Chariots to build, excelling in his art,
Having first heated in a fire-heat slow
Bends for his wheel a fig-branch; with a start
The fissile wild-fig flies far from his hands apart.

"Collected for the spring, and mad to rend me,
So leapt the lion from afar: I strove
With skin-cloak, bow, and quiver to defend me
With one hand; with the other I up-hove
My weighty club, and on his temple drove,
But broke in pieces the rough olive wood
On his hard shaggy head: he from above
Fell ere he reached me, by the stroke subdued,
And nodding with his head on trembling feet he stood.

"Darkness came over both his eyes: his brain
Was shaken in the bone; but when I spied
The monster stunned and reeling from his pain,
I cast my quiver and my bow aside,
And to his neck my throttling hands applied,
Before he could recover. I did bear me
With vigour in the death-clutch, and astride
His body from behind from scath did clear me,
So that he could not or with jaw or talons tear me.

"His hind feet with my heels I pressed aground;
Of his pernicious throat my hands took care;
His sides were for my thighs a safe-guard found
From his fore-feet: till breathless high in air
I lifted him new sped to hell's dark lair.
Then many projects did my thoughts divide,
How best I might the monster's carcass bare,
And from his dead limbs strip the shaggy hide:
Hard task it was indeed, and much my patience tried.

"I tried and failed with iron, wood, and flint;
For none of these his skin could penetrate;
Then some immortal gave to me a hint

With his own talons I might separate
The carcass and the hide : success did wait
The trial of this thought; he soon was flayed.
I wear his hide, that serves me to rebate
Sharp-cutting war.   The Nemean beast was laid
Thus low, which had of men and flocks much havoc made."

IDYLL XXVI.

THE BACCHANALS.

THREE troops three sisters to the mountain led;
Agavé with her cheeks that blossomed red
The bloom of apple ; and in wildest mood
Autonöa and Ino.   From the wood
They stript oak-leaves and ivy green as well,
And from the ground the lowly asphodel ;
In a pure lawn with these twelve altars placed ;
Nine Dionysus, three his mother graced ;
Then from the chest the sacred symbols moved,
And, as their god had taught them and approved,
Upon the leafy altars reverent laid.
Hid in a native mastic's sheltering shade,
Them from a steep rock Pentheus then surveyed.
Him perched aloft Autonöa first discerned,
And dreadful shrieked, and spurning overturned
The sacred orgies of the frenzied one,
Which none profane may ever look upon.
She maddened, maddened all : scared Pentheus fled,
And they, with robes drawn up, pursued : He said:
"What want ye, dames !" Autonöa then : "Thou, fellow !
Shalt know, not hear"—and mightily did bellow,
Loud as a lioness her brood defending ;
His mother clutched his head, whilst Ino rending
Tore off his shoulder, trod and trampled o'er him ;
Autonöa likewise: limb from limb they tore him.
Then all returned to Thebes ; defiled with gore,
They of their Pentheus only fragments bore,
Their after-grief.   This troubles not my mind :
Not let another, impotent and blind,

Name Dionysus as hereby defiled,—
Nor though he harsher used some curious child.
May I my life to holy courses give,
Dear to the holy who reproachless live!
This omen, sent from ægis-bearing Jove,
Shows what he hates, and what his thoughts approve;
Blest are the children of the godly—ever;
Blest are the children of the godless—never.
Hail, Blessed! whom Jove's thigh enclosed for us,
Till thou wert born on snowy Dracanus.
Hail, Semele! Cadmean sisters, hail!
Whose names in songs of heroines prevail.
By Dionysus this (no need of shame)
Possest ye did. The gods let no man blame.

IDYLL XXVII.

THE FOND DISCOURSE OF DAPHNIS AND THE DAMSEL.

CHLOE.
A COWHERD with chaste Helen ran away.
DAPHNIS.
This Helen here was kist by one to-day.
CHLOE.
Boast not: they say there's nothing in a kiss.
DAPHNIS.
But in mere kissing is some touch of bliss.
CHLOE.
I wipe my mouth—and off thy kiss is ta'en.
DAPHNIS.
Wipe you your mouth? then let me kiss again.
CHLOE.
Calves, not a maid, to kiss doth you beseem.
DAPHNIS.
Boast not: thy youth is flying like a dream.
CHLOE.
Ripe grapes are raisins, and dry roses sweet.
DAPHNIS.
Come to yon olives: I would fain repeat—

CHLOE.
I will not: you deceived me once indeed.
DAPHNIS.
Come to yon elms, and hear me play my reed.
CHLOE.
Play to yourself: nought wretched pleases me.
DAPHNIS.
Take heed: the Paphian will be wroth with thee.
CHLOE.
A fig for her, if Artemis be kind.
DAPHNIS.
Hush! lest she smite you and for ever bind.
CHLOE.
Not me—my guard is Artemis the wise.
DAPHNIS.
Canst thou fly Love—none other virgin flies?
CHLOE.
By Pan! I fly him: he doth ever drive you.
DAPHNIS.
I fear that Love to some worse man may give you.
CHLOE.
Many have woo'd me, but have pleased me—none.
DAPHNIS.
And I am come—of many wooers one.
CHLOE.
What can I do? marriage brings only care.
DAPHNIS.
Not pain, nor grief, but joys which sweetest are.
CHLOE.
They say that women fear their wedded dears.
DAPHNIS.
They rule them rather: show me one that fears.
CHLOE.
Lucina's bolt—the child-bed pang I dread.
DAPHNIS.
Thy sovran, Artemis, puts wives to bed.
CHLOE.
Child-bearing will my fine complexion blight.
DAPHNIS.
Thy children will become thy bloom and light.

CHLOE.
If I consent, what spouse-gifts shall be mine?
DAPHNIS.
My pastures, groves, and herd, shall all be thine.
CHLOE.
Swear, when 'tis done, thou never wilt forsake me.
DAPHNIS.
By Pan! not even shouldst thou try to make me.
CHLOE.
Chamber and hall will you for me provide?
DAPHNIS.
Chamber and hall, and fleeces fine beside.
CHLOE.
What? what shall I my aged father tell?
DAPHNIS.
Hearing my name, he'll like thy marriage well.
CHLOE.
Repeat it: oft a name sweet influence has.
DAPHNIS.
Daphnis, Nomæa's son by Lycidas.
CHLOE.
A good descent, but than mine own not higher.
DAPHNIS.
I know it well—Menalcas is thy sire.
CHLOE.
Show me thy grove, where stands thy wealthy stall.
DAPHNIS.
See where for me flowers many a cypress tall.
CHLOE.
Feed, goats! while I my lover's wealth inspect.
DAPHNIS.
Feed, bulls! while I the virgin's way direct.
CHLOE.
Hands off! what business have they in my dress!
DAPHNIS.
First these love-apples will I gently press.
CHLOE.
By Pan! I shudder—take your hand away.
DAPHNIS.
Dear little trembler! your alarm allay.

CHLOE.
The ditch is dirty: would you throw me down?
DAPHNIS.
I spread a soft white fleece beneath your gown.
CHLOE.
Why do you loose my zone? what do you mean?
DAPHNIS.
This first I offer to the Paphian queen.
CHLOE.
Some one will see us: hist! I hear a sound.
DAPHNIS.
The cypresses thy marriage whisper round.
CHLOE.
My dress is spoiled: ah me! what shall I do?
DAPHNIS.
I'll give thee, love, a better one and new.
CHLOE.
Perhaps e'en salt you will not give to me.
DAPHNIS.
Would I could give my very soul to thee!
CHLOE.
Pardon, Queen Artemis! my broken vow.
DAPHNIS.
Eros a calf, Cypris shall have a cow.
CHLOE.
I go a woman, who a virgin came.
DAPHNIS.
For virgin thine a wife's and mother's name.

Thus whispered they, their youthful prime enjoying,
With their fresh limbs in furtive marriage toying.
She rose and to her flock went, seeming sad,
Blushing and shamefaced, but at heart was glad;
And to his herd the happy Daphnis sped,
Rejoicing greatly in his marriage-bed.

IDYLL XXVIII.

THE DISTAFF.

DISTAFF! quick implement of busy thrift,
Which housewives ply, blue-eyed Athene's gift!
We go to rich Miletus, where is seen
The fane of Cypris 'mid the rushes green:
Praying to mighty Zeus for voyage fair,
Thither to Nicias would I now repair,
Delighting and delighted by my host,
Whom the sweet-speaking Graces love the most
Of all their favourites; thee, distaff bright!
Of ivory wrought with art most exquisite,
A present for his lovely wife I take.
With her thou many various works shalt make;
Garments for men, and such as women wear
Of silk, whose colour is the sea-blue clear.
And she so diligent a housewife is,
That ever for well-ankled Theugenis
Thrice in a year are shorn the willing sheep
Of the fine fleeces which for her they keep.
She loves what love right-minded women all;
For never should a thriftless prodigal
Own thee with my consent: 'twere shame and pity!
Since thou art of that most renowned city,
Built by Corinthian Archias erewhile,
The marrow of the whole Sicilian isle.
But in the house of that physician wise,
Instructed how by wholesome remedies
From human-kind diseases to repel,
Thou shalt in future with Ionians dwell,
In beautiful Miletus; that the fame
For the best distaff Theugenis may claim,
And thou may'st ever to her mind suggest
The memory of her song-loving guest.
The worth of offering from friend we prize
Not in the gift but in the giver lies.

IDYLL XXIX.

LOVES.

THEY say, my dear, that wine and truth agree:
To speak truth in my cups beseemeth me.
And I will tell you all my secret thought;
You do not wholly love me as you ought.
All of my life—the half that is not fled,
Lives only in your form—the rest is dead.
Just as you will, my life is one delight,
Like that of gods,—or glooms in thickest night.
How is it right to vex one loves you so?
Take my advice; you will hereafter know,
That I your elder taught you for the best,
And, to believe me, was your interest.
In one tree build one nest; so shall not creep
Some crawling mischief to disturb your sleep.
See! how you change about for ever now,
Never two days together on one bough.
And if one chance to praise your lovely face,
Him more than friend of three years proof you grace:
To him that loved you first you are as cold,
As to a mere acquaintance three days old.
But now you breathe of wantonness and pride;
Like should love like; in love be this your guide;
So do, and good renown you shall obtain,
And Love will never visit you with pain,
Who mortal hearts can easily subdue,
And made me, heart of iron, dote on you.
In all the changes of your fitful will,
Unchanged I live but in your kisses still.
Remember that you were last year, last week,
Younger than now: we grow old while we speak.
Wrinkles soon come; and Youth speeds on amain,
Wings on her shoulders, ne'er to come again:
We, slow-foot mortals, cannot overtake
Birds, or what else a winged passage make.
Take thought, and be more mild: to me, who burn
In love for you, a guileless love return,

That when your bloom of youthful beauty ends,
We may be time-enduring, faithful friends.
But if you cast my words unto the wind,
Or piqued to anger murmur in your mind,
"Why dost thou trouble me?" I for thy sake,
And thy much scorn, myself will straight betake,
Where the gold apples their sweet fragrance spread,
To Cerberus, the keeper of the dead.
Then freed from love, and all its anxious pain,
E'en at thy call, I could not come again.

IDYLL XXX.

THE DEATH OF ADONIS.

CYPRIS, when she saw Adonis
Cold and dead as any stone is,
All his dark hair out of trim,
And his fair cheek deadly dim,
Thither charged the Loves to lead
The cruel boar that did the deed.
And they, swiftly overflying
All the wood where he was lying,
Soon the hapless creature found,
And with cords securely bound.
One the captive dragged along
Holding at its end the thong;
While another with his bow
Struck behind and made him go.
Path of fear they made him tread—
Aphrodite was his dread.

    Him the goddess thus addrest:
"Of all beasts thou wickedest!
Thou! didst thou this white thigh tear?
Didst thou smite my husband dear?"
Fearfully, then, answered he:
"Cypris! I do swear to thee
By thyself and husband dear,
By the very bonds I wear,
By these huntsmen, never I

Meant to tear thy husband's thigh;
Thinking there a statue stood,
In the fever of my blood,
I was mad a kiss to press
On the naked loveliness:
But my long tusk pierced the boy:
Punish these, and these destroy,
Tusks that worse then useless prove—
What had they to do with love?
And if this suffice not, pray,
Cypris! cut my lips away—
What had they to do with kissing?"
Cypris then, her wrath dismissing,
Pitied him that knew no better;
And she bade them loose his fetter.
The boar, from that time of her train,
Went not to the wood again;
But, approaching to the fire,
Fairly burned out his desire.

A FRAGMENT FROM THE BERENICE.

IF for good sport one prays and lucky gains,
Who from the sea his livelihood obtains,
His nets his plough; let him at evening-fall,
Offering a "white fish," on this goddess call—
The fish called "white" as brightest that doth swim;
Nor shall his prayer be without fruit for him:
For let him throw his nets into the sea,
And he shall draw them full as they can be.

EPIGRAMS.

I.

THICK-GROWING thyme, and roses wet with dew,
　Are sacred to the sisterhood divine
Of Helicon: the laurel, dark of hue,
　The Delphian laurel, Pythian Pæan, thine!

For thee shall bleed the white ram which doth chew
  The downward hanging branch of turpentine.

II.

To Pan, the fair-cheeked Daphnis, whose red lip
  To his sweet pipe the pastoral wild notes married,
Offered his pipe, crook, fawn-skin, spear, and scrip,
  Wherein he formerly his apples carried.

III.

Daphnis! thou sleepest on the leaf-strown ground—
  Thy hunting-nets are on the mountain pight:
Thee Pan is hunting—thee Priapus crowned
  With ivy and its golden berries bright:
Into the cavern both together bound:
  Up! shake off sleep, and safety find in flight.

IV.

Where yon oak-thicket by the lane appears,
  A statue newly made of fig is seen,
Three-legged, the bark on still, but without ears,
  Witness of many a prank upon the green.

A sacred grove runs round; soft-bubbling near,
  A spring perennial from its pebbly seat
Makes many a tree to shoot and flourish there,
  The laurel, myrtle, and the cypress sweet;

And the curled vine with clusters there doth float:
  Their sharp shrill tones the vernal blackbirds ring,
And yellow nightingales take up the note,
  And, warbling to the others, sweetly sing.

There, goatherd! sit, and offer up for me
  Prayer to the rural god: if from my love
He only will consent to set me free,
  A kid shall bleed in honour of his grove.

If I must love, then, should my love succeed
  By his good grace, the fattest lamb I rear,
A heifer, and a ram for him shall bleed:
  Freely I offer, may he kindly hear!

V.

For the Nymphs' sake thy double flute provoke
  To breathe some sweetness: I the harp will take,
And make it vocal to the quill's quick stroke;
  And Daphnis from the pipe sweet sounds will shake.
Come! let us stand beside the thick-leaved oak,
  Behind the cave, and goat-foot Pan awake.

VI.

What boots it thee to weep away both eyes,
  Sad Thyrsis! of thy pretty kid bereft:
The wild wolf seizes it, and bounding flies,
  And the dog barks—at his successful theft.
What profit now from weeping can arise?
  For of the kid, nor bone nor dust is left.

VII.

UPON A STATUE OF ÆSCULAPIUS.

The son of Pæan to Miletus came,
  And with the best physician, Nicias, staid,
Who, daily kindling sacrificial flame,
  From fragrant cedar had this statue made.
The highest price was paid Eëtion's fame,
  Who all his skill upon the work outlaid.

VIII.

THE EPITAPH OF ORTHON.

Stranger! the Syracusian Orthon gives thee charge:
  Walk not o' winter nights, with many a cup
Reeling: from this, instead of country large,
  I have a foreign mound—that shuts me up.

IX.

Man! spare thy life, nor out of season be
  A voyager: man's term of life soon flies.
For Thasus Cleonicus put to sea
  From Cœlesyria with his merchandise:

What time the Pleiad hastes to set, went he,
  And, with the Pleiad, sunk—no more to rise.

X.

UPON A STATUE OF THE MUSES.

To you, this marble statue, Muses nine!
  Xenocles placed; the harmonist, whose skill
No man denies: owning your aid divine,
  He by your aid is unforgotten still.

XI.

AN EPITAPH ON EUSTHENES THE PHYSIOGNOMIST.

This is the monument of Eusthenes,
  Who from one's face his mind and temper knew.
In a strange land all rites the dead can please
  He had—and he was dear to poets too.
Nothing was wanting to his obsequies:
  Homeless, he had dear friends and mourners true.

XII.

UPON A TRIPOD DEDICATED TO BACCHUS BY DEMOTELES.

Sweet Dionysus! sweetest god of all!
  To thee this tripod and thy statue placed
    The leader of the choir, Damoteles.
Only small praise did on his boyhood fall,
  But now his manhood is with victory graced,
    And more, that him virtue and honour please

XIII.

UPON AN IMAGE OF THE HEAVENLY APHRODITE.

The heavenly Cypris, not the popular this:
  So call her bending lowly on thy knees.
The chaste Chrysogona, for nuptial bliss,
  Had it set in the house of Amphicles,

Her life-long spouse—his home, heart, children, hers:
  Their life, begun with thee, from year to year

Was happier, goddess! They are ministers
  Of their own blessings, who the gods revere.

XIV.

AN EPITAPH OF EURYMEDON.

Leaving a little son, Eurymedon!
  Dead in thy prime, thou in this tomb dost lie;
Thou dwellest with the blest: thy little son
  The state will prize for thy dear memory.

XV.

UPON THE SAME.

Traveller! by this it will be understood,
If thou dost equal hold the bad and good:
If not, then say: "Light lie this mound upon
The sacred head of good Eurymedon."

XVI.

UPON A STATUE OF ANACREON.

Stranger! this statue view with care,
And say, when homeward you repair:
"In Teos lately saw these eyes
The statue of Anacreon wise.
If ever bard in bower or hall
Sang sweetly, sweetest he of all.
Most of all things he loved in sooth
The unblown loveliness of youth."
Thus will you, stranger, in a little
Express the whole man to a tittle.

XVII.

UPON EPICHARMUS.

We Dorian Epicharmus praise in Dorian,
  Who first wrote comedy, but now, alas!
Instead of the true man, the race Pelorian,
  Bacchus! to thee present him wrought in brass.

Here stands he in their wealthy Syracuse,
  Known for his wealth and other service true:
To all he many a saw of practic use
  Declared: and mighty honour is his due.

XVIII.

THE EPITAPH OF CLEITA, NURSE OF MEDEIUS.

Medeius to his Thracian nurse had made
  This way-side monument, scored with her name:
Her nursing cares are to the woman paid:
  Why not? her usefulness shall live to fame.

XIX.

UPON ARCHILOCHUS.

Stay, and behold the old Iambic poet,
  Archilochus, of infinite renown—
That he is known to east and west doth show it:
  The Muses and Apollo him did crown
With choicest gifts: his was the poet's fire,
And he could sing his verses to the lyre.

XX.

UPON A STATUE OF PISANDER, WHO COMPOSED "THE LABOURS OF HERCULES."

The poet of Camirus, first to sing
The labours of the lion-slaying king,
The quick-hand son of Zeus omnipotent,
Was our Pisander: this his monument.
They suffered many months and years to pass
After his death—but now 'tis done in brass.

XXI.

UPON HIPPONAX, THE POET.

The bard Hipponax, traveller! lies here:
  If wicked, keep aloof; if in the number
Of good men thou, of good men born, draw near,
  Sit down, and, if thou wilt, in safety slumber.

XXII.

AN EPIGRAM OF THEOCRITUS UPON HIS OWN BOOK.

I am Theocritus, not he that was
  Of Chios, but a man of Syracuse.
Philina bore me to Praxagoras:
  I never flirted with another's muse.

XXIII.

With stranger and with citizen the same
  I deal: your own deposit take away,
Paying the charge: excuse let others frame;
  His debts Caïcus e'en at night will pay.

BION.

IDYLL I.

THE EPITAPH OF ADONIS.

I AND the Loves Adonis dead deplore:
The beautiful Adonis is indeed
Departed, parted from us. Sleep no more
In purple, Cypris! but in watchet weed,
All-wretched! beat thy breast and all aread—
"Adonis is no more." The Loves and I
Lament him. Oh! her grief to see him bleed,
Smitten by white tooth on his whiter thigh,
Out-breathing life's faint sugh upon the mountain high!

Adown his snowy flesh drops the black gore;
Stiffen beneath his brow his sightless eyes;
The rose is off his lip; with him no more
Lives Cytherea's kiss—but with him dies.
He knows not that her lip his cold lip tries,
But she finds pleasure still in kissing him.
Deep is his thigh-wound; hers yet deeper lies,

E'en in her heart. The Oread's eyes are dim;
His hounds whine piteously; in most disordered trim,

Distraught, unkempt, unsandalled, Cypris rushes
Madly along the tangled thicket-steep;
Her sacred blood is drawn by bramble-bushes;
Her skin is torn; with wailings wild and deep
She wanders through the valley's weary sweep,
Calling her boy-spouse, her Assyrian fere.
But from his thigh the purple jet doth leap
Up to his snowy navel; on the clear
Whiteness beneath his paps the deep-red streaks appear.

"Alas for Cypris!" sigh the Loves, "deprived
Of her fair spouse, she lost her beauty's pride;
Cypris was lovely whilst Adonis lived,
But with Adonis all her beauty died."
Mountains, and oaks, and streams, that broadly glide,
Or wail or weep for her; in tearful rills
For her gush fountains from the mountain side;
Redden the flowers from grief; city and hills
With ditties sadly wild, lorn Cytherea fills.

Alas for Cypris! dead is her Adonis,
And Echo "dead Adonis" doth resound.
Who would not grieve for her whose love so lone is?
But when she saw his cruel, cruel wound,
The purple gore that ran his wan thigh round,
She spread her arms, and lowly murmured: "Stay thee,
That I may find thee as before I found,
My hapless own Adonis! and embay thee,
And mingle lips with lips, whilst in my arms I lay thee.

"Up for a little! kiss me back again,
The latest kiss—brief as itself that dies
In being breathed, until I fondly drain
The last breath of my soul, and greedy-wise
Drink it into my core. I will devise
To guard it as Adonis—since from me
To Acheron my own Adonis flies,
And to the drear dread king; but I must be
A goddess still and live, nor can I follow thee.

"But thou, Persephona! my spouse receive,
Mightier than I, since to thy chamber drear
All bloom of beauty falls: but I must grieve
Unceasingly. I have a jealous fear
Of thee, and weep for him. My dearest dear!
Art dead, indeed? away my love did fly,
E'en as a dream. At home my widowed cheer
Keeps the Loves idle; with thy latest sigh
My cestus perished too; thou rash one! why, oh why

"Did'st hunt? so fair, contend with monsters grim?"
Thus Cypris wailed; but dead Adonis lies;
For every gout of blood that fell from him,
She drops a tear; sweet flowers each dew supplies—
Roses his blood, her tears anemonies.
Cypris! no longer in the thickets weep;
The couch is furnished! there in loving guise
Upon thy proper bed, that odorous heap,
The lovely body lies—how lovely! as in sleep.

Come! in those softest vestments now array him
In which he slept the live-long night with thee;
And in the golden settle gently lay him,—
A sad, yet lovely sight; and let him be
High heaped with flowers; though withered all when he
Surceased. With essences him sprinkle o'er
And ointments; let them perish utterly,
Since he, who was thy sweetest, is no more.
He lies in purple; him the weeping Loves deplore.

Their curls are shorn: one breaks his bow; another
His arrows and the quiver; this unstrings,
And takes Adonis' sandal off; his brother
In golden urn the fountain water brings;
This bathes his thighs; that fans him with his wings.
The Loves, "Alas for Cypris!" weeping say:
Hymen hath quenched his torches; shreds and flings
The marriage wreath away; and for the lay
Of love is only heard the doleful "weal-away."

Yet more than Hymen for Adonis weep
The Graces; shriller than Dione vent
Their shrieks; for him the Muses wail and keep

    Singing the songs he hears not, with intent
    To call him back: and would the nymph relent,
    How willingly would he the Muses hear!
    Hush! hush! to-day, sad Cypris! and consent
    To spare thyself—no more thy bosom tear—
For thou must wail again, and weep another year.

IDYLL II.

EROS AND THE FOWLER.

HUNTING the birds within a bosky grove,
A birder, yet a boy, saw winged Love
Perched on a box-tree branch; rejoicing saw
What seemed a large bird, and began to draw
His rods together, and he thought to snare
Love, that kept ever hopping here and there.
Then fretting that he could not gain his end,
Casting his rods down, sought his aged friend,
Who taught him bird-catching—his story told,
And showed Love perching. Smiled the ploughman old,
And shook his head, replying to the boy:
"Against this bird do not your rods employ;
It is an evil creature; shun him—flee;
Until you take him, happy will you be.
But if you ever come to manhood's day,
He that now flies you and still bounds away,
Will of himself, by no persuasion led,
Come suddenly and sit upon your head."

IDYLL III.

THE TEACHER TAUGHT.

BY me in my fresh prime did Cypris stand,
Leading the child Love in her lovely hand;
He kept his eyes fixt, downcast on the ground,
While in mine ears his mother's words did sound:—
"Dear herdsman, take and teach for me, I pray,
Eros to sing;" she said, and went her way.

Him, as one fain to learn, without ado
I then began to teach whate'er I knew—
Fool that I was! how first great Pan did suit
With numerous tones his new-invented flute;
Athene wise the straight pipe's reedy hollow;
Hermes his shell; his cithern sweet Apollo.
I taught him this; he heeded not my lore,
But sang me his love-ditties evermore—
His mother's doings—how Immortals yearn
With fond desires, and how poor mortals burn.
All I taught Eros I have quite forgot;
But his love-ditties—I forget them not.

IDYLL IV.

THE POWER OF LOVE.

THE Muses fear not, but with heart-love true
Affect wild Eros, and his steps pursue.
And if one sings with cold and loveless heart,
They shun him, and will never teach their art.
But if one sings Love's agitated thrall,
To him in flowing stream they hasten all.
Of this myself am proof; for whensoe'er
For some Immortal else or mortal here
I would the glowing path of song explore,
Stammers my tongue, and sings not as before;
But glad and gushing flows the strain from me,
Whene'er I sing of Love or Clymene.

IDYLL V.

LIFE TO BE ENJOYED.

IF sweet my songs, or these sufficient be
Which I have sung to give renown to me,
I know not: but it misbeseems to strain
At things we have not learned, and toil in vain.

If sweet these songs are not, what profit more
Have I to labour at them o'er and o'er?
If Saturn's son and changeful Fate assigned
A double life-time to our mortal kind,
That one in joys and one in woes be past,
Who had his woes first would have joys at last.
But since Heaven wills one life to man should fall,
And this is very brief—too brief for all
We think to do, why should we fret and moil,
And vex ourselves with never-ending toil?
To what end waste we life exhaust our health
On gainful arts, and sigh for greater wealth?
We surely all forget our mortal state—
How brief the life allotted us by Fate!

IDYLL VI.

CLEODAMUS AND MYRSON.

CLEODAMUS.

What sweet for you has Summer or the Spring,
What joy does Autumn or the Winter bring?
Which season do you hail with most delight?
Summer, whose fulness doth our toils requite?
Or the sweet Autumn, when but slight distress
From hunger falls on mortal wretchedness?
Or lazy Winter—since but few are loath
To cheer themselves with fire-side ease and sloth?
Or the Spring, blushing with its bloom of flowers?
Tell me your choice, since leisure-time is ours.

MYRSON.

For man to judge things heavenly is unmeet,
And all these seasons holy are and sweet.
But I to please you will indulge your ear,
And tell my favourite season of the year.
Not Summer—then I feel the scorching sun;
Nor Autumn—then their course diseases run;
And hard I find to bear the Winter frore,
The chilling snow I fear, and crystal hoar.

Of all the year the Spring delights me most,
Free from the scorching sun, and bitter frost.
All life-containing shapes conceive in Spring,
And all sweet things are sweetly blossoming ;
And in that season of the year's delight
There is for men an equal day and night.

VII.

ON HYACINTHUS.

PHŒBUS tried all his means, and thought of new,
    Scarce knowing what he did in his distress ;
With nectar bathed him, with ambrosial dew ;
    But Fate made remedies remediless.

VIII.

FRIENDSHIP.

HAPPY is love or friendship when returned—
The lovers whose pure flames have equal burned,
Happy was Theseus, e'en in Tartarus,
With his true heart-friend, good Pirithous.
His Pylades Orestes lorn did bless
Amid th' inhospitable Chalybes.
Blest was Achilles in a friend long tried ;
Him living loved, for his sake gladly died !

IX.

Yourself to artists always to betake,
    And on yourself in nothing to rely
Is misbeseeming: friend ! your own pipe make—
    The work is easy, if you will but try.

X.

May Love the Muses evermore invite,
The Muses bring me Love ! and to requite
My passion, may they give sweet song to me,
Than which no sweeter remedy can be.

XI.

When drop on drop, they say, doth ever follow,
'Twill wear the stone at last into a hollow.

XII.

I to the sandy shore and seaward slope
    Will go, and try with murmured song to bend
The cruel Galatea : my sweet hope
    I'll cast away—when life itself doth end.

XIII.

Oh, leave me not unhonoured ! Artists aim
And reach at excellence, provoked by Fame.

XIV.

Woman's strength is in her beauty ;—
Man's—to bear and dare for duty.

IDYLL XV.

THE EPITHALAMIUM OF ACHILLES AND DEIDAMIA.

Myrson. Lycidas.

MYRSON.

WILL you, my Lycidas, now sing for me
A soothing, sweet Sicilian melody—
A love-song, such as once the Cyclops young
On the sea-shore to Galatea sung ?

LYCIDAS.

I'll pipe or sing for you : what shall it be ?

MYRSON.

The song of Scyros dearly pleases me,
Sweet love—the pleasant life Pelides led—
His furtive kisses, and the furtive bed.
How he, a boy, put on a virgin's dress,
Assumed a virgin's mien, and seemed no less ;
And how Deïdamia, maiden coy,
Found her girl bedmate was a wicked boy.

LYCIDAS.

The herdsman, Paris, on an evil day,
To Ida bore the lovely Helena.
Œnone grieved; and Lacedæmon raged,
And all th' Achæans in the feud engaged:
Hellenes, Elians, and Mycenians, came,
And brave Laconians, to retake the dame.
When Greece her battle led across the deep,
Himself at home no warrior then might keep.
Achilles only went not then, indeed,
Hid with the daughters of king Lycomede.
A seeming virgin with a virgin's bloom,
Instead of arms his white hand plied the loom.
No virgin of them all had airs more fine,
A rosier cheek, or step more feminine:
He veiled his hair; but Mars and fiery Love,
That stings young manhood, all his thoughts did move.
He lingered by Deïdamia's side,
Close as he could, from morn till eventide:
Often he kissed her hand, and often raised
Her broidered work: her work and fingers praised.
Of all the maids his only messmate she;
And he would fain his bedmate have her be.
And thus he sued with furtive meaning deep :—
" With one another other sisters sleep ;
In station, love, and age, we twain are one,
Why should we, maidens both, each sleep alone ?
Since we together are all day, I wonder
Why we are made at night to sleep asunder?"

IDYLL XVI.

TO THE EVENING STAR.

HESPER ! sweet Aphrodite's golden light !
Hesper ! bright ornament of swarthy Night,
Inferior to the Moon's clear sheen, as far
As thou outshinest every other star;
Dear Hesper, hail ! and give thy light to me,
Leading the festive shepherd company.
For her new course to-day began the Moon,

And is already set—O much too soon!
'Tis not for impious theft abroad I stir,
Nor to way-lay the nightly traveller:
I love; and thou, bright star of love! shouldst lend
The lover light—his helper and his friend.

IDYLL XVII.

LOVE RESISTLESS.

BRIGHT Cypris! goddess ever meek and mild,
Of mightiest Zeus and loveliest sea-nymph child,
Why with Immortals and our mortal kind
Art thou so wroth? what stung thy gentle mind
To bring forth Love? who wills at all to strike,
His cruel heart his person how unlike!
Winged and far-darter why didst make him, why,
That we the cruel one can never fly?

MOSCHUS.

IDYLL I.

LOVE A RUNAWAY.

HER Eros thus proclaimed the Cyprian Queen:—
"If any one has in the highway seen
My straying Eros, and reports to me
His whereabouts, he shall rewarded be;
A kiss for him; but if it shall betide
One bring him me, a kiss—and more beside.
Midst twenty he is notable to view;
Not fair, but flamy, is his dazzling hue;
Sharp are his eyes, and flame their glances fleet;
His mind is wicked, but his speech is sweet.
His word and meaning are not like at all;
His word is honey, and his meaning gall.

He is a mischievous, deceitful child;
Beguiles with falsehood, laughs at the beguiled.
He has a lovely head of curling hair,
But saucy features, with a reckless stare.
His hands are tiny, but afar they throw,
E'en down to Dis and Acheron below.
Naked his form, his mind in covert lies;
Winged as a feathered bird, he careless flies
From girls to boys, from men to women flits,
Sports with their heart-strings, on their vitals sits.
Small is his bow, his arrow small to sight,
But to Jove's court it wings its ready flight.
Upon his back a golden quiver sounds,
Full of sharp darts, with which e'en me he wounds.
All cruel things by cruel Love are done;
His torch is small, yet scorches e'en the sun.
But should you take him—fast and safely bind him,
And bring him to me with his hands behind him.
If he should weep, take heed—he weeps at will;
But should he smile—then drag him faster still;
And should he offer you a kiss, beware!
Evil his kiss, his red lips poisoned are!
And should he say, with seeming friendship hot,
'Accept my bow and arrows,' touch them not!
Tears, smiles, words, gifts, deceitful wiles inspire,
And every thing he has is dipt in fire."

IDYLL II.

EUROPA.

CYPRIS, when all but shone the dawn's glad beam,
To fair Europa sent a pleasant dream;
When sleep, upon the close-shut eyelids sitting,
Sweeter than honey, is eye-fetters knitting,
The limb-dissolving sleep! when to and fro
True dreams, like sheep at pasture, come and go.
Europa, sleeping in her upper room,
The child of Phœnix, in her virgin bloom,
Thought that she saw a contest fierce arise
Betwixt two continents, herself the prize;

They to the dreamer seemed like women quite,
Asia, and Asia's unknown opposite.
This was a stranger, that a native seemed,
And closer hugged her—so Europa dreamed;
And called herself Europa's nurse and mother,
Said that she bore and reared her; but that other
Spared not her hands, and still the sleeper drew,
With her good will, and claimed her as her due,
And said that Zeus Ægiochus gave her,
By Fate's appointment, that sweet prisoner.

Up-started from her couch the maiden waking,
And felt her heart within her bosom quaking;
She thought it true, and sat in hushed surprise—
Still saw those women with her open eyes;
Then to her timid voice at last gave vent:—
"Which of the gods to me this vision sent?
What kind of dream is this that startled me,
And sudden made my pleasant slumber flee?
Who was the stranger that I saw in sleep?
What love for her did to my bosom creep!
And how she hailed me, as her daughter even!
But only turn to good my vision, Heaven!"

So said, and bounded up, and sought her train
Of dear companions, all of noble strain,
Of equal years and stature; gentle, kind,
Sweet to the sight, and pleasant to the mind;
With whom she sported, when she led the choir,
Or in the river's urn-like reservoir
She bathed her limbs, or in the meadow stopt,
And from its bosom odorous lilies cropt.
And soon around her shone the lovely band,
Her flower-basket in each maiden's hand;
And to the meadows near the pleasant shore
They sped, where they had often sped before,
Pleased with the roses growing in their reach,
And with the waves that murmured on the beach.

A basket by Hephæstus wrought of gold,
Europa bore—a marvel to behold;
He gave it Libya, when, a blooming bride,
She went to grace the great Earth-shaker's **side;**

She gave it Telephassa fair and mild,
Who now had given it to her virgin child.
Therein were many sparkling wonders wrought—
The hapless Iö to the sight was brought;
A heifer's for a virgin's form she wore;
The briny paths she frantic wandered o'er,
And was a swimming heifer to the view,
While the sea round her darkened into blue.
Two men upon a promontory stood,
And watched the heifer traversing the flood.
Again where seven-mouthed Nile divides his strand,
Zeus stood and gently stroked her with his hand,
And from her horned figure and imbruted
To her original form again transmuted.
In brass the heifer—Zeus was wrought in gold;
Nile softly in a silver current rolled.
And to the life was watchful Hermes shown
Under the rounded basket's golden crown;
And Argus near him with unsleeping eyes
Lay stretched at length; then from his blood did rise
The bird, exulting in the brilliant pride
Of his rich plumes and hues diversified,
And like a swift ship with her out-spread sail,
Expanding proudly his resplendent tail,
The basket's golden rim he shadowed o'er:
Such was the basket fair Europa bore.

They reached the mead with vernal blossoms full,
And each began her favourite flowers to pull.
Narcissus one; another thyme did get;
This hyacinth, and that the violet;
And of the spring-sweets in the meadow found
Much scented bloom was scattered on the ground.
Some of the troop in rivalry chose rather
The sweet and yellow crocuses to gather;
Shining, as mid the Graces Cypris glows,
The princess in the midst preferred the rose:
Nor long with flowers her gentle fancy charmed,
Nor long she kept her virgin flower unharmed.
With love for her was Saturn's son inflamed,
By unexpected darts of Cypris tamed,

Who only tames e'en Zeus.   To shun the rage
Of Heré, and the virgin's mind engage,
To draw her eyes and her attention claim,
He hid his godhead and a bull became;
Not such as feeds at stall, or then or now,
The furrow cuts and draws the crooked plough;
Not such as feeds the lowing kine among,
Or trails in yoke the heavy wain along;
His body all a yellow hue did own,
But a white circle in his forehead shone;
His sparkling eyes with love's soft lustre gleamed;
His arched horns like Dian's crescent seemed.
He came into the meadow, nor the sight
Fluttered the virgins into sudden flight.
But they desired to touch and see him near;
His breath surpassed the meadow-sweetness there.
Before Europa's feet he halted meek,
Licked her fair neck, and eke her rosy cheek;
Threw round his neck her arms the Beautiful,
Wiped from his lips the foam and kissed the bull;
Softly he lowed; no lowing of a brute
It seemed, but murmur of Mygdonian flute;
Down on his knees he slunk; and first her eyed,
And then his back, as asking her to ride.
The long-haired maidens she began to call:—
" Come let us ride, his back will hold us all,
E'en as a ship; a bull unlike the rest,
As if a human heart were in his breast,
He gentle is and tractable and meek,
And wants but voice his gentleness to speak."

She said, and mounted smiling, but before
Another did, he bounded for the shore.
The royal virgin, struck with instant fear,
Stretched out her hands and called her playmates dear;
But how could they the ravished princess reach?
He, like a dolphin, pushed out from the beach.
From their sea-hollows swift the Nereids rose,
Seated on seals, and did his train compose;
Poseidon went before, and smooth did make
The path of waters for his brother's sake;

Around their king in close array did keep
The loud-voiced Tritons, minstrels of the deep,
And with their conchs proclaimed the nuptial song.
But on Jove's bull-back as she rode along,
The maid with one hand grasped his branching horn,
The flowing robe, that did her form adorn,
Raised with the other hand, and tried to save
From the salt moisture of the saucy wave;
Her robe, inflated by the wanton breeze,
Seemed like a ship's sail hovering o'er the seas.
But when, her father-land no longer nigh,
Nor sea-dashed shore was seen, nor mountain high,
But only sky above, and sea below—
She said, and round her anxious glance did throw:—

"Whither with me, portentous bull? discover
This and thyself: and how canst thou pass over
The path of waters, walking on the wave,
And dost not fear the dangerous path to brave?
Along this tract swift ships their courses keep,
But bulls are wont to fear the mighty deep.
What pasture here? what sweet drink in the brine?
Art thou a god? thy doings seem divine.
Nor sea-born dolphins roam the flowery mead,
Nor earth-born bulls through Ocean's realm proceed;
Fearless on land, and plunging from the shores
Thou roamest ocean, and thy hoofs are oars.
Perchance anon, up-borne into the sky,
Thou without wings like winged birds wilt fly!
Ah me unhappy! who my father's home
Have left and with a bull o'er ocean roam,
A lonely voyager! my helper be,
Earth-shaking regent of the hoary sea!
I hope to see this voyage's cause and guide,
For not without a god these things betide."

To her the horned bull with accent clear:—
"Take courage, virgin! nor the billow fear;
The seeming bull is Zeus; for I with ease
Can take at will whatever form I please;
My fond desire for thy sweet beauty gave
To me this shape—my footstep to the wave.

Dear Crete, that nursed me, now shall welcome thee;
In Crete Europa's nuptial rites shall be;
From our embrace illustrious sons shall spring,
And every one of them a sceptred king."—

And instantly they were in Crete: his own
Form Zeus put on—and off her virgin zone.
Strowed the glad bed the Hours, of joy profuse;
The whilom virgin was the bride of Zeus.

IDYLL III.

THE EPITAPH OF BION, A LOVING HERDSMAN.

YE mountain valleys, pitifully groan!
Rivers and Dorian springs, for Bion weep!
Ye plants, drop tears! ye groves, lamenting moan!
Exhale your life, wan flowers; your blushes deep
In grief, anemonies and roses, steep!
In softest murmurs, Hyacinth! prolong
The sad, sad woe thy lettered petals keep;
Our minstrel sings no more his friends among—
Sicilian Muses! now begin the doleful song.

Ye nightingales, that 'mid thick leaves let loose
The gushing gurgle of your sorrow, tell
The fountains of Sicilian Arethuse
That Bion is no more—with Bion fell
The song, the music of the Dorian shell.
Ye swans of Strymon, now your banks along
Your plaintive throats with melting dirges swell
For him who sang like you the mournful song:
Discourse of Bion's death the Thracian nymphs among;

The Dorian Orpheus, tell them all, is dead.
His herds the song and darling herdsman miss,
And oaks, beneath whose shade he propt his head:
Oblivion's ditty now he sings for Dis:
The melancholy mountain silent is;
His pining cows no longer wish to feed,
But mourn for him: Apollo wept, I wis,
For thee, sweet Bion! and in mourning weed
The brotherhood of Fauns, and all the Satyr breed.

IDYLL III.

The tears by Naiads shed are brimful bourns;
Afflicted Pan thy stifled music rues;
Lorn Echo 'mid her rocks thy silence mourns,
Nor with her mimic tones thy voice renews:
The flowers their bloom, the trees their fruitage lose;
No more their milk the drooping ewes supply;
The bees to press their honey now refuse;
What need to gather it and lay it by,
When thy own honey-lip, my Bion! thine is dry?

Sicilian Muses! lead the doleful chaunt:
Not so much near the shore the dolphin moans;
Nor so much wails within her rocky haunt
The nightingale; nor on their mountain thrones
The swallows utter such lugubrious tones;
Nor so much Cëyx wailed for Halcyon,
Whose song the blue wave, where he perished, owns;
Nor in the valley, neighbour to the sun,
The funeral birds so wail their Memnon's tomb upon—

As these moan, wail, and weep, their Bion dead.
The nightingales and swallows, whom he taught,
For him their elegiac sadness shed;
And all the birds contagious sorrow caught;
The sylvan realm was all with grief distraught.
Who bold of heart will play on Bion's reed,
Fresh from his lip, yet with his breathing fraught?
For still among the reeds does Echo feed
On Bion's minstrelsy. Pan only may succeed

To Bion's pipe; to him I make the gift:
But lest he second seem, e'en Pan may fear
The pipe of Bion to his mouth to lift.
For thee sweet Galatea drops the tear,
And thy dear song regrets, which sitting near
She fondly listed; ever did she flee
The Cyclops and his song; but far more dear
Thy song and sight than her own native sea:
On the deserted sands the nymph without her fee

Now sits and weeps, or weeping tends thy herd.
Away with Bion all the muse-gifts flew—
The chirping kisses breathed at every word:

Around thy tomb the Loves their playmate rue;
Thee Cypris loved more than the kiss she drew
And breathed upon her dying paramour.
Most musical of rivers! now renew
Thy plaintive murmurs: Meles! now deplore
Another son of song, as thou didst wail of yore

That sweet, sweet mouth of dear Calliope:
The threne, 'tis said, thy waves for Homer spun
With saddest music filled the refluent sea;
Now melting wail and weep another son!
Both loved of fountains—that of Helicon
Gave Melesigenes his pleasant draught;
To this sweet Arethuse did Bion run,
And from her urn the glowing rapture quaft:
Blest was the bard who sang how Helen bloomed and laught:

On Thetis' mighty son his descant ran,
And Menelaus; but our Bion chose
Not arms and tears to sing, but Love and Pan;
While browsed his herd, his gushing music rose;
He milked his kine; did pipes of reeds compose;
Taught how to kiss; and fondled in his breast
Young Love and Cypris pleased. For Bion flows
In every glorious land a grief confest:
Ascra for her own bard, wise Hesiod, less exprest:

Bœotian Hylæ mourned for Pindar less;
Teos regretted less her minstrel hoar,
And Mytelene her sweet poetess;
Nor for Alcæus Lesbos suffered more;
Nor lovely Paros did so much deplore
Her own Archilochus. Breathing her fire
Into her sons of song, from shore to shore
For thee the Pastoral Muse attunes her lyre
To woeful utterance of passionate desire.

Sicelidas, the famous Samian star,
And he with smiling eye and radiant face,
Cydonian Lycidas, renowned afar,
Lament thee; where quick Hales runs his race,
Philetus wails; Theocritus, the grace
Of Syracuse, thee mourns; nor these among

Am I remiss Ausonian wreaths to place
Around thy tomb : to me doth it belong
To chaunt for thee from whom I learnt the Dorian song.

Me with thy minstrel skill as proper heir
Others thou didst endow with thine estate.
Alas ! alas ! when in a garden fair
Mallows, crisp dill, or parsley yields to fate,
These with another year regerminate ;
But when of mortal life the bloom and crown,
The wise, the good, the valiant, and the great
Succumb to death, in hollow earth shut down
We sleep—for ever sleep—for ever lie unknown.

Thus art thou pent, while frogs may croak at will;
I envy not their croak. Thee poison slew—
How kept it in thy mouth its nature ill ?
If thou didst speak, what cruel wretch could brew
The draught ? He did, of course, thy song eschew.
But justice all o'ertakes. My tears fast flow
For thee, my friend ! Could I, like Orpheus true,
Odysseus, or Alcides, pass below
To gloomy Tartarus, how quickly would I go !

To see and haply hear thee sing for Dis !
But in the Nymph's ear warble evermore,
My dearest friend ! thy sweetest harmonies :
For whilom, on her own Etnæan shore,
She sang wild snatches of the Dorian lore.
Nor will thy singing unrewarded be ;
Thee to thy mountain haunts she will restore,
As she gave Orpheus his Eurydice.
Could I charm Dis with songs, I too would sing for thee.

IDYLL IV.

MEGARA, THE WIFE OF HERCULES.

"Why dost thou vex thy spirit, mother mine?
Why fades thy cheek ? at what dost thou repine ?
Because thy son must serve a popinjay,
As though a lion did a fawn obey?

Why have the gods so much dishonoured me?
Why was I born to such a destiny?
Spouse of a man I cherished as mine eyes,
For whom heart-deep my vowed affection lies,
Yet must I see him crossed by adverse fate,
Of mortal men the most misfortunate!
Who with the arrows, which Apollo—no!
Some Fate or Fury did on him bestow,
In his own house his own sons raging slew—
Where in the house was not the purple dew?
I saw them slain by him; I—I, their mother,
Did see their father slaughter them; none other
Had e'er a dream like this; to me they cried,
'Mother! save us!' what could I do? they died.
As when a bird bewails her callow young,
O'er whom, unfeathered yet, she fondly hung,
Which now a fierce snake in the bush devours—
Flies round and round—shrieks—cannot help them—cowers,
Nor nearer dares approach her cruel foe:
Thus I, most wretched mother! to and fro
Rushed madly through the house, my children dear,
My dead, dead children wailing every where.
Would that I too had with my children died,
The poisoned arrow sticking in my side!
Then with fast tears my mother and my sire
Had laid me with them on the funeral pyre;
And to my birth-land given, on their return,
Our mingled ashes in one golden urn:
But they in Thebes, renowned for steeds, **remain,**
And still they farm their old Aonian plain;
But in steep Tiryns I must dwell apart,
With many sorrows gnawing at my heart;
Mine eyes are fountains, which I cannot close;
I seldom see him, and but brief repose
My hapless husband is allowed at home;
By sea or land he must for ever roam;
None but a heart of iron, or of stone,
Could bear the labours he has undergone.
Thou, too, like water, meltest still away,
For ever weeping every night and day.
None of my kin is here to comfort me,

IDYLL IV.

For they beyond the piny isthmus be;
There's none to whom I may pour out my woes,
And like a woman all my heart disclose,
But sister Pyrrha;—but she too forlorn
For her Iphicles, thine and hers doth mourn;
Unhappiest mother thou! in either son—
Twin stamps of Zeus, and of Amphitryon."

And, while she spoke, from either tearful well
The large drops faster on her bosom fell,
While she her slaughtered children called to mind,
And parents in her country left behind.
With tear-stained cheek, and many a groan and sigh,
Alcmena to her son's wife made reply—

"Why, hapless mother! with this train of thought
Dost thou provoke the grief that comes unsought?
Why dost thou talk these dreadful sorrows o'er,
Now wept by us—as we have wept before?
Are not the new griefs that we look to see
From day to day, enough for you and me?
Lover of dole were he, who would recount
Our tale of woes, and find their whole amount!
Take heart, and bear those ills we cannot cure,
But by the will of heaven we must endure.
And yet I cannot bid thee cease to grieve,
For even joy to spend itself has leave.
For thee I wail, why wert thou doomed, oh why,
To be a partner in our misery?
I mourn that fate with ours thy fortune blends
Under the woe that over us impends.
Ye! by whose names unpunished none forswear,
Persephona and dread Demeter, hear!
Not less on thee has my true love reposed,
Than if my womb thy body had enclosed;
I love thee, sweetest! as an old-age child,
That has, beyond hope, on its mother smiled;
Thou knowest this; then say not, I implore,
I love thee not, or foster sorrow more,
Or in my grief I careless am of thee,
Though I weep more than e'er wept Niobe.
No blame is due to her with anguish wild,

Who hapless weeps for her unhappy child.
Ten weary months within my womb he lay—
What pains I suffered ere he came to day!
What pangs! I all but said farewell to earth,
While yet my unborn lingered in the birth.
New toils now task him in a foreign plain—
Oh shall I ever see my son again?
Besides, an awful vision of the night,
Scaring my sleep, hath filled me with affright,
And much I fear, when I my dream recall,
Lest some untoward thing my sons befall.
Methought, aside his cloak and tunic laid,
My Hercules with both hands grasped a spade,
And round a cultured field a mighty dyke
He delved, as one that toils for hire belike.
But when the dyke around the vineyard run,
And he was just about (his task now done,
The shovel thrown on the projecting rim,)
With his attire again to cover him;
Sudden above the bank a fire burst out,
Whose greedy flames enclosed him round about:
He to the flames with rapid flight did yield,
Holding the spade before him as a shield,
And here and there he turned his anxious eye,
If he might shun his scorching enemy.
High-souled Iphicles, I remember well
As it me-seemed, rushing to help him, fell;
Nor could he raise himself from where he rolled,
But helpless lay there like some weak man old,
Tript up by joyless age against his will;
Stretched on the ground he was, and seeming still
Hopeless of rising, till a passer-by
In pity raised the hoar infirmity.
Thus helpless lay the warrior brave in fight;
And I did weep to see that sorry sight—
This son stretched feeble, that engirt with flame,
Till sleep forsook me and the day-dawn came.
Such frightful visions on my sleep did fall;
Ye gods! on curst Eurystheus turn them all!
Oh be this presage true my wish supplies,
And may no god ordain it otherwise!"

IDYLL V.

THE CHOICE.

WHEN on the wave the breeze soft kisses flings,
   I rouse my fearful heart, and long to be
   Floating at leisure on the tranquil sea;
But when the hoary ocean loudly rings,
Arches his foamy back and spooming swings
   Wave upon wave, his angry swell I flee:
   Then welcome land and sylvan shade to me,
Where, if a gale blows, still the pine-tree sings.

Hard is his life whose nets the ocean sweep,
   A bark his house—shy fish his slippery prey;
But sweet to me the unsuspicious sleep
   Beneath a leafy plane—the fountain's play,
That babbles idly, or whose tones, if deep,
   Delight the rural ear and not affray.

IDYLL VI.

"LOVE THEM THAT LOVE YOU."

PAN Echo loved; she loved the frisky Faun;
The Faun to Lyda by strong love was drawn;
As Echo Pan, the Faun did Echo burn,
And Lyda him: all fell in love in turn.
And with what scorn the loved the lover grieved
Was that one scorned, and like for like received.
Hear, heart-free! let who love you love obtain,
That if you love, you may be loved again.

IDYLL VII.

ALPHEUS.

ALPHEUS, gliding by old Pisa's towers,
   Deep in the sea his eager way pursues,
With sacred dust, and olive-leaves, and flowers,
   With which he hastens to his Arethuse.

Smoothly he runs ; the sea not feels the river
    With soft unmingled stream its water rive ;
Eros it was, that subtle counsel-giver,
    Who taught a river how for love to dive.

EPIGRAM.

ON EROS PLOUGHING.

His torch and quiver down sly Eros flung,
An ox-goad took in hand, a wallet slung,
Then yoked strong bulls and made the plough to train,
And as he went the furrow sowed with grain.
And looking up he said to Zeus, " Make full
The harvest, or I'll yoke Europa's bull."

FRAGMENT.

Would that my sire had brought me up to feed
    The happy bleaters of the fleecy flocks !
'Twould soothe my sorrow then to breathe the reed
    Beneath the shade of elms or hanging rocks.

Now let us fly ; and other cities seek
    To be our country, dear Picrides :
But I my mind to all will plainly speak—
    Injurious drones have harmed the honey-bees.

THE WAR-SONGS OF TYRTÆUS.

THE

WAR-SONGS OF TYRTÆUS.

I.

¹Now it is noble for a ²brave man to die, having fallen opposite the foremost ranks, *whilst* fighting for his father-land. But most grievous of all is it for a man ³to be a beggar, having quitted his own city and fertile fields, *and* wandering with a loved mother and aged father, with little children and ⁴wedded wife. For to whomsoever he shall have come, among them will he be hateful, yielding to need and to wretched poverty. He disgraces his race, and ⁵belies his fair beauty; and every kind of ⁶dishonour and woe follows him. Besides, for a man thus vagrant, look you, there is no care, nor has he

¹ This is not a fragment, though γὰρ is so placed. Frequent examples of the same usage occur in Homer and Herodotus. Cf. Matt. Gr. Gr. § 615. Compare the use of "Nam" among the Latins. Virgil, Geor. iv. 445, Nam quis te, juvenum confidentissime, nostras jussit adire domos: and of "quisnam" in Plautus, Curcul. 398, Nam quid id refert meâ. Terent. Andr. iii. 5, 6.—καλὸν, noble. Cf. Soph. Antig. 72, καλὸν μοι τοῦτο ποιούσῃ θανεῖν. Virg. Æn. ii. 317, Pulchrumque mori succurrit in armis. Æn. xi. 24; ix. 286. Horat. Od. ii. 2, 13, Dulce et decorum est pro patriâ mori.

² ἀγαθὸν, good in war, brave. Just as κακὸς stands for the opposite. Hom. Il. iv. 299; ii. 365. Soph. Aj. 456. Horace uses "melior" in this sense, Od. i. 15, 28, Tydides melior patre.—περὶ ᾗ πατρίδι. In verse 14, we have περὶ in this sense with a genitive. But Homer uses it thus with a dative. Odyss. ii. 245.

³ πτωχεύειν. This verb differs from πένομαι. See Aristoph. Plut. 549, οὐκοῦν δήπου τῆς πτωχείας πενίαν φαμὲν εἶναι ἀδελφήν.

⁴ κουριδίῃ, "wedded in youth." Eustath. But Butmann (Lexil. pp. 392—394) shows that it means rather "lawful," regular "wedded."

⁵ αἰσχύνει. Bergler, in a note at Aristoph. Aves, 1451, (τὸ γένος οὐ καταισχυνῶ,) states, on the authority of Stobæus, that the youth of Athens were obliged to swear οὐ καταισχυνῶ τὰ ὅπλα.

⁶ ἀτιμία. The severity of this punishment may be judged of by the treatment which Aristodemus met at Sparta, after his inglorious return from Thermopylæ. Cf. Herodot. vii. 229.

*

respect in time to come. ⁷ With spirit let us fight for this land, and for our children die, being no longer chary of our lives. Fight ⁸ then, young men, standing fast one by another, nor ⁹ be beginners of cowardly flight, or fear. But rouse a great and valiant spirit in your breasts, and love not life, when ye contend with men. And the elders, whose limbs are no longer active, the old, *I say*, desert not or forsake. For surely this *were* shameful, that fallen amid the foremost champions, in front of the youths, an older man should lie low, ¹⁰ having his head now white and his beard hoary, *and* breathing out a valiant spirit in the dust; whilst ¹¹ he covers with his hands his gory loins, (which were a shame, and would make one wroth to behold with his eyes:) and is stript as to his person: ¹² yet all *this* befits the young, whilst, I wot, he enjoys the ¹³ brilliant bloom of youth; to mortal men and women he is lovely to look upon, whilst he lives; and noble when he has fallen in the foremost ranks. Then let ¹⁴ every one with firm

⁷ θυμῷ. Cf. Virg. Æn. ii. 617, Nunc animis opus, Ænea, nunc pectore toto. Thucyd. ii. 11, οἳ λογισμῷ ἐλάχιστα χρώμενοι, θυμῷ πλεῖστα ἐς ἔργον καθιστάνται.

⁸ ἀλλά—itaque, igitur. See L. Kuster's notes ad Aristoph. Equit. 202. He explains it as φέρε, ἄγε, age! Comp. Plut. 539; Nub. 1367; Pax, 425, &c.

⁹ ἄρχετε, a periphrasis. Cf. Corn. Nep. Pausan. iv. 6, Tanto magis orare cœpit, ne enuntiaret.

¹⁰ ἤδη λευκὸν, κ. τ. λ. So Hom. Il. xxiv. 516, οἰκτείρων πολιόντε κάρη πολιόν τε γένειον. Ov. Met. viii. 528, Pulvere canitiem genitor vultusque seniles Fœdat humi fusus.

¹¹ αἱματόεντ— This regard of seemliness in death is a favourite point with classical authors. Cf. Æsch. Agam. 241, &c.; Ov. Met. xiii. 479; Fast. ii. 833,

Tunc quoque jam moriens, ne non procumbat honestè,
Respicit: hoc etiam cura cadentis erat.

¹² The scope of the passage is, no doubt, the contrast between the sight of an old and a young hero dead on the battle-field. The young are lovely to look on even in death. But the bald head cloven, and the grey beard blood-stained, are sights which the young must not permit. For the origin of the idea, see Il. x. 71.

¹³ ἀγλαὸν ἄνθος. This metaphor from vegetation is very common. Theocr. Idyll. xiv. 70, ποιεῖν τι δεῖ, οἷς γόνυ χλωρόν. Horat. Epod. xiii. 4, Dumque virent genua. Ov. Trist. iii. 1, 7, Quod viridi quondam malè lusit in ævo.

¹⁴ τις, every one, vos, or quisque, as in Hom. Il. ii. 39, Ἀλλά τις ἐγγὺς ἰών— Soph. Aj. 245, ὥρα τιν' ἤδη κάρα, κ. τ. λ. Aristoph. Thesm. 603, &c.—εὖ διαβὰς is said of a warrior standing firm to throw his spear Cf. Aristoph. Eq. 77; Apollon. Rhod. iii. 1293; Xenoph. Eq. i. 14.

stride await *the foe*, having both feet fixed on the ground, [15] biting his lip with his teeth.

II.

But since ye are the race of [1] invincible Hercules, be ye of good courage; not yet hath Zeus [2] turned his neck aside *from you*. Neither fear ye, nor be affrighted at a host of men, but let hero hold his shield right against the foremost fighters; having counted life hostile, and [3] the dark fates of death dear as the rays of the sun. For ye know that the [4] works of Ares of-many-tears are much-seen, and well have ye learned the [5] temper of troublous war. Ye have been, O young men, with the flying and the pursuing, and have pushed on to a full *measure* of both. Now of those, who dare, abiding one beside another, to advance to the close fray, and the foremost champions, fewer die, and they save the people in the rear; but in men [6] that fear, all excellence is lost. No one could ever in words go through those several ills, which befall a man, [7] if he has been actuated by cowardice. For 'tis grievous

---

[15] χεῖλος ὀδοῦσι δακών. Cf. Eurip. Bacch. 610; Aristoph. Vesp. 1078. Virgil depicts his warrior as "dentibus infrendens." Æn. viii. 230; x. 715.

[1] ἀνικήτου— Hercules is styled "invictus," on several Latin inscriptions. Propertius so calls him in the first book, El. 20, 23, At comes *invicti* juvenis precesserat ultra.—γένος. At the return of the Heracleids, the descendants of Hercules, and the triple division of the Peloponnese, which took place, according to tradition the sons of Aristodemus, Procles and Eurysthenes, obtained Lacedæmon. Lycurgus was of this stock, as were the Spartans generally. The poet urges the fact as a ground of confidence.

[2] αὐχένα λοξὸν ἔχει, has withdrawn his favour.

[3] The ordinary reading here is inexplicable. Klotz prefers, as the slightest alteration, κῆρας ἴσ' αὐγαῖσιν ἠελίοιο φίλας. Ἴσα· ἴσως. Grotius suggests κῆρας ὑμῶς αὐγαῖς ἠελίοιο φίλας. I have translated the former reading.

[4] So the Greeks spoke of ἔργα Μουσῶν, ἔργα Ἀφροδίτης, ἔργα γάμοιο, ἔργα μάχης. Virgil, Æn. viii. 516, Militiam et grave Martis opus.

[5] ὀργὴν, the nature, or temper. So Thuc. i. 130, καὶ τῇ ὀργῇ οὕτως χαλεπῇ ἐχρῆτο, and i. 140. Soph. Aj. 646. So ingenium is used by the Latins. Sil. Ital. iv. 90, Collisque propinqui ingenium. Ov. Met. 574, Grande dolori ingenium est.

[6] Comp. Hom. Il. v. 532, φευγόντων δ' οὔτ' ἄρ' κλέος ὄρνυται, οὔτε τις ἀλκή.

[7] ἂν αἰσχρὰ πάθῃ. "Qui turpiter se gesserit· Interpr." But it is

to wound in the rear the back of a flying man in hostile war. Shameful too is a corpse [8]lying low in the dust, [9]wounded behind in the back by the point of a spear. Rather let every one with firm stride await the enemy, having both feet fixed on the ground, biting his lip with his teeth, and having covered with the [10]hollow of his broad shield thighs and shins below, and breast and shoulders. But in his right hand let him brandish a heavy lance, and [11]shake above his head a threatening crest. Then let him learn war, by doing bold deeds, nor let him stand with his shield out of the range of weapons. But let each, drawing nigh in close fray, [12]hit his foe, wounding him with long lance or sword. [13]And having set foot beside foot, and having fixed shield against shield, and crest on crest, and helmet on helmet, and breast against breast, struggle in fight with his man, having seized either the hilt of his sword, or his long lance. But do ye, [14]O light-armed *soldiers*, crouching under your shields, some from one quarter, some from another, make them fall with huge stones, and with polished spears, as ye dart at them, and stand near to the [15]heavy-armed troops.

not to be supposed that πάσχειν is equivalent to πράττειν. See Liddell and Scott's Lex. v. πάσχω.

[8] Κατακείμενος. Il. xix. 389, Κεῖσαι 'Οτρυντείδη πάντων ἐκπαγλότατ' ἀνδρῶν. Cf. v. 467; Eurip. Orest. 1489, &c. So "jacere" in Latin. Virg. Æn. ii. 557, Jacet ingens littore truncus. Ov. Met. ii. 268, Corpora — exanimata jacent. Phædr. Fab. i. 24, 10, Rupto jacuit corpore.

[9] νῶτον, κ. τ. λ., a great disgrace. Cf. Hom. Il. xiii. 288. Ov. Met xiii. 262, Sunt et mihi vulnera, cives, Ipso pulchra loco. Fast. ii. 211, Diffugiunt hostes inhonestaque vulnera tergo Accipiunt.

[10] γαστρί. The Greeks were wont to apply to other matters the names of various parts of the human body. Thus, γνάθος, to fire. Æsch. Choeph. 325; Prom. 368. So χεῖλος, ὀφρὺς (supercilium, Virg. Geor. i. 108) ὀμφαλὸς, στέρνα γῆς.—αὐχὴν (collum) εὐρέα νῶτα θαλάσσης.

[11] κινείτω. So Hom. Il. γ. 337, δεινὸν δὲ λόφος καθύπερθεν ἔνευεν. Æsch. S. c. Theb. 115, κῦμα δοχμολόφων ἀνδρῶν.

[12] ἐλέτω. Klotz thinks this should be construed "choose out," "pick," as in Virg. Æn. xi. 632, legitque virum vir.

[13] καὶ πόδα, κ. τ. λ. So Hom. Il. xiii. 130; Eurip. Heracl. 836, 7: Virg. Æn. x. 360, Trojanæ acies, aciesque Latinæ Concurrunt, hæret pede pes, densusque viro vir. Ov. Met. ix. 44.

[14] γυμνῆτες, i. e. οἱ ψιλοί, οἵ σφενδονῆται καὶ οἱ τοξόται.—πτώσσοντες, i. q. κρυπτόμενοι. Cf. Il. xxii. 14, Τρῶες πτῶσσον ὑπὸ κρήμνους.

[15] Πανοπλίοις, for πανοπλίταις. Abstract for concrete. So we very often find ὅπλα for ὁπλῖται. Eurip. Orest. 444; Soph. Ant. 115; Xen.

III.

[1] I WOULD neither commemorate, nor hold in account a man, either for excellence in running, or for wrestling; no, nor though he should have the bulk and strength of the Cyclopes, and in speed surpass [2] Thracian Boreas. No, nor though he should in personal appearance be more graceful than [3] Tithonus, and should be more rich than Midas or [4] Cinyras. Nor though he should be more kingly than Pelops, son of Tantalus, and have the [5] soft-voiced tongue of Adrastus; nor yet if he should have all glory, save *that* of resistless valour; for he is not a man brave in war, [6] unless he have the courage to face bloody slaughter, and standing near attack the foemen. But this *is* excellence, this the best prize among men, and noblest for a young man to carry off. And this *is* a common good to a city, and all its people, *namely*, whatsoever man standing

Anab. ii. 2, 4, Arma for armati. Virg. Æn. i. 509, Septa armis; ii. 238, Fœta armis; v. 409, Consequimur cuncti et densis incurrimus armis. In the same manner " Vitam " is, in Phædr. Prol. i. 3, equivalent to "viventes." " Consilia ;" Cic. Ep. viii. 4, 5, consilia agitantes. Flagitia, for facinorosos. Sallust, B. C. xiv. 1.

[1] This line is quoted by Plato, de Leg. i. pp. 15, 16, (vol. vi. ed. Ast,) and has been rendered into Latin by Erasmus, Adag. tit. " Fortitudinis," p. 259, ed. Francof. 1670. Plato's quotation is read with τιθείμην, which Stephanus would read here—ἐν λόγῳ τιθείην. Cf. Theocr. Idyll. xiv. 48, ἄμμες δ' οὔτι λόγου τινὸς ἄξιοι—ἀρετή from Ἄρης, as *virtus* from *vir*, signifies excellence of any kind. Arist. Nic. Eth. ii. 5. Lucret. v. 964, et manuum mirâ freti *virtute* pedumque.

[2] Boreas is called Thracian, because Thracian Hæmus was supposed to be the dwelling of the blustering North wind. Callimach. H. to Dian. 114. Αἵμῳ ἐπὶ Θρήικι, πόθεν βορέαο καταῖξ ἔρχεται. For comparison of swift runners with the wind, see Hom. Il. x. 437; Virg. Æn. vii. 206, 207, " Cursuque pedum prævertere ventos."

[3] Tithonus. Horat. Od. ii. 16, 30, Longa Tithonum minuit senectus. Virg. Æn. iv. 585, Tithoni croceum linquens Aurora cubile. Tithonus, son of Laomedon and favourite of Aurora, attained a great age, by favour of Jove.

[4] Cinyras, a king of Cyprus, whose wealth rendered his name a proverb. Pindar, Nem. viii. ὅσπερ καὶ Κινύραν ἔβρισε πλούτῳ ποντίᾳ ἐν ποτε Κύπρῳ.

[5] μειλιχόγηρυν—Compare Theocr. vii. 82, and the Song of Solomon, iv. 11, quoted above.

[6] These lines are also quoted by Plato in the passage cited above, τετλαίη ὁρῶν. For the use of the participle for the infin. after other verbs signifying perseverance, endurance, &c. see Matt. Gr. Gr. § 550.

firm bides unceasingly in the front ranks, and is wholly forgetful of base flight, when he has [7]staked his life, and enduring spirit; but has the heart to fall, standing beside his next neighbour. This man is good in war. And quickly does he turn in flight the sturdy phalanxes of foemen, and [8]zealously stem the wave of battle. He too himself having fallen amid the foremost, loses his life, and (at the same time) having brought renown to his city and people and sire: pierced in many places through breast, and round shield, and through his cuirass in the front. Him young alike and old lament, and the whole state is distressed for him with painful regret. His [9]tomb and children *are* famous among men, ay, [10]his children's children, and his race after *him*. Never does his fair fame or his name perish, but though he be on earth, he becomes immortal, whom, bravely bearing himself, standing firm, and fighting for country and for children, impetuous Ares shall have destroyed. But should he have escaped the fate of death that-lays-men-out-at-length; and as victor, have borne off the splendid boast of battle *won*, all honour him, young and old alike; and [11]after tasting many delights, he comes to Hades. Growing old, he is eminent amid the citizens, nor does any one wish to hurt him in point of respect or justice.

[7] θυμὸν παρθέμενος. Hom. Od. ii. 237, σφὰς γὰρ παρθέμενοι κεφαλὰς. Od. iii. 74. Il. i. 372, παραβαλλόμενος, similarly used.

[8] σπουδῇ, the opposite to ἀσπουδεί, Il. x. 303. Odyss. xv. 209, σπουδῇ νῦν ἀνάβαινε.—ἔσχεθε—ἔχω here is equivalent to κωλύω, ἐπέχω. —κῦμα μάχης. For similar metaphors taken from the raging sea, compare Eurip. Hippol. 823; Soph. Aj. 1082, 1083; Antig. 162, 163; Œd. C. 1240—1245; Œd. T. 23; Trach. 114; Æsch. Prom. V. 1014 (Dind.); S. c. Theb. 63. Horat. Od. ii. 7, 15,

Te rursus in bellum resorbens
Unda fretis tulit æstuosis.

[9] τύμβος—Compare with this passage Thuc. ii. 43, κοινῇ γὰρ τὰ σώματα διδόντες, κ. τ. λ.

[10] The laws of Athens ordained that the children of such as had fallen in war, should be protected, publicly reared and educated, and have first seats at the theatres. Cf. Lysias, Orat. Funebr. p. 521, cap. xx. ad med. παῖδες παίδων. Hom. Il. xx. 308, καὶ παῖδες παίδων τοί κεν μετόπισθε γένωνται.

[11] τερπνὰ παθών. πάσχειν is used "de bonis." See Budæus Comm. de L. G. p. 74, (Paris, 1529,) who quotes Lysias, τίς οὖν ἐλπὶς ὑπὸ τούτων τι ἀγαθὸν πείσεσθαι.—Aristoph. Eccles. 893; Eq. 876. Plautus in Asinar. ii. 2, 58, Fortiter malum qui patitur, idem post patitur bonum.

And all [12] on the seats, alike young, and those of his age, and they who are still older, give place to him. Let every one now strive in his spirit to reach the summit of [13] excellence like this, not [14] slackening warfare.

IV.

How long lie ye inactive? when will ye have a brave spirit, young men? and are ye not [1] ashamed of the dwellers all around, since ye dally thus exceedingly? For ye think ye [2] sit secure in peace, yet war possesses the whole land.

* * * * *

[3] And let a man, as he dies, discharge his javelin for the last time. For it is both honourable and noble for a man to fight for land, and children, and wedded wife, with his foes; and death will come at some time, whensoever in truth the fates shall have allotted. But let every one, having lifted aloft his lance, and [4] gathered up his stout heart under his shield, go

---

[12] θώκοισιν—For this reverence to honourable age cf. Cic. de Senect. c. 18, § 63, 64. Juvenal xiii. 54,
    Credebant hoc grande nefas et morte piandum
    Si juvenis vetulo non assurrexerit.
Virg. Ecl. vi. 66, Utque viro Phœbi chorus assurrexerit omnis.
[13] ἀρετῆς, glory. Thuc. i. 33, καὶ προσέτι φέρουσα ἐς μὲν τοὺς πολλοὺς ἀρετήν.
[14] μεθιεὶς πόλεμον, al. πολέμου. But Dawes, Misc. Crit. p. 236, has shown that μεθιέναι, "to let loose," has the acc. μεθίεσθαι, to loose hold of—the genitive. Cf Porson ad Med. 734; Phœn. 529.
[1] αἰδεῖσθε. Cf. Hom. Il. v. 530; Plato de Leg. lib. iii. 699 (pp. 200, line 12, Ast); Livy xxx. 18, Pudor, Romani nominis proprius, qui sæpe res perditas servavit in præliis.—ἀμφιπεμκτίονας. This would seem to mean the Periœci, or Achœans of Laconia, called Lacedæmonians, as distinguished from the Dorians, or Σπαρτιῆται, to whom these words are addressed.
[2] ἧσθαι, to sit lazily. Cf. Hom. Il. i. 133; iii. 134. Latin, sedere. Virg. Æn. xi. 460, Pacem laudate sedentes. xii. 237, Qui nunc lentis consedimus armis. Liv. xxiv. 11, Qui cum ipse ad mœnia urbis Romæ armatus sederet.
[3] ἀποθνήσκων. Cf. Lucan. iii. 622,
    Effugientem animam lapsos collegit in artus,
    Membraque contendit toto, quicunque manebat,
    Sanguine, et hostilem defessis robore nervis
    Insiliit solo nocturnus pondere puppim.
[4] ἔλσας, used by Homer several times in the Iliad, is the aor. 1, part. act. of εἴλω, used in the signification of "drawing oneself up." The

right forward, when the battle first is joined. For it is not fated by any means that a man should escape death at least, no, not though he be by family of immortal ancestry. Often [5]he comes *forth*, after having escaped battle-strife and din of javelins, and in his home fated death found him. Now the latter is not in like manner a friend [6]to the commonalty, nor regretted *by them*, whilst the former, *the brave man*, small and great bewail, if aught shall have happened to him. For the whole people together regrets a stout-hearted hero, when he dies, and living he is worthy of the demigods. For they behold him with their eyes even as a [7] tower, since, though singlehanded, he performs *deeds* worth *those of* many.

V.[1]

* * * * * *

THESE twain were contending unceasingly for nineteen years, ever having a stout-hearted spirit, warrior sires of our sires. But in the twentieth *year* they indeed (the Messenians) fled from the great mountains of Ithome, having abandoned their [2]rich fields.

Scholiasts explain it, 1. συναγαγὼν καὶ κατασχών. 2. συγκλείσας, κατασχών. ἦτορ seems taken for the seat of bravery, the heart. Grotius renders the line "Clypeo generosa recondens Pectora."—πολέμον, the battle. So Homer Il. ii. 443, κηρύσσειν πολεμὸν δὲ καρηκομόωντας Ἀχαίους. iv. 281; xii. 181. Florus and Velleius so use bellum for prælium, Flor. iii. 5; Vell. ii. 69.

[5] ἔρχεται, abit e pugnâ, e prælio, et incolumis domum redit. Klotz. Il. ii. 381.

[6] δῆμος evidently stands for the plebs, not populus, in this place, as is shown by the force of the next line.

[7] πύργον. A frequent simile among the Greek poets. Hom. Od. xi. 555, τοῖος γὰρ ὄφιν πύργος ἀπώλεο. Eurip. Med. 389, ἢν μέν τις ἡμῖν πύργος ἀσφαλὴς φανῇ. So among the Latins, Ov. Met. xiii. 281, Graiûm murus Achilles. Senec. Troad. 125, Tu præsidium Phrygibus fessis, tu murus eras. Claudian in Rufin. i. 264,

Hic optata quies cunctis; hic sola pericli
Turris erat clypeusque trucem porrectus in hostem.

[1] This fragment is found in Strabo, lib. vi., and from it we collect that the first Messenian war lasted 19 years. The first three verses are found in Pausan. in Messen. c. 15, with this difference, ἀμφ' αὐτὴν δ' ἐμάχοντο. Comp. Hom. Il. vi. 461, "Ὅτε Ἴλιον ἀμφεμάχοντο. For the end of the first Messen. war, see Thirlwall, H. G. vol. i. p. 351.

[2] Πίονα ἔργα, agri fertiles, loca culta. So Hom. Il. v. 92; xii. 283. Callim. H. in Dian. 156. Virg. Æn. ii. 306, Sternit agros, sternit sata læta, boumque labores.

VI.[1]

For Zeus himself, son of Cronos, husband of beautiful-crowned Herè, hath given this city to the Heracleids. Along with whom, having left [2] windy Erineès, we arrived at the broad isle of Pelops.

VII.[3]

Even as asses worn with heavy burdens, carrying to their [4]masters, by reason of sad constraint, [5] the half entirely of whatsoever the soil produces.

VIII.[6]

Mourning their masters, even though *they are so*, both themselves and their wives, when the destructive fate of death seizes any *of them.*

IX.[7]

To our king Theopompus, dear to the gods, through whom we took Messene the spacious.

---

[1] This fragment appears in Strabo, lib. xiii., and is said by him to be found ἐν τῇ ποιήσει ἐλεγείᾳ ἣν ἐπιγράφουσιν εὐνομίαν.

[2] ἠνεμόεντα may perhaps signify "lying amid the hills," as in Il. ii. 606; Callimach. H. in Del. 11. Ἐρινεήν, some read Ἐρικείην, a deme of Attica, 47th in order in the catalogue given in Smith's Dict. of Gr. and Rom. Geography, p. 334.

[3] This fragment is from Pausanias, De Messen. c. 14, who proves by it that wrongs were inflicted by Lacedæmon on the Messenians.

[4] δεσποσύνοισι, i. q. δεσπόταις. Æsch. Pers. 587, οὐκ ἔτι δασμοφοροῦσιν δεσποσύνοισιν ἀνάγκαις.

[5] ἥμισυ πάνθ' ὅσων. I have rendered this as if πάντα was taken adverbially. A better reading, suggested by Klotz, is ἥμισυ πᾶν καρπῶν ὅσσον. Ælian, V. H. vi. 1, confirms the fact. Λακεδαιμόνιοι Μεσσηνίων κρατήσαντες τῶν μὲν γινομένων ἁπάντων ἐν τῇ Μεσσηνίᾳ τὰ ἡμίση ἐλάμβανον αὐτοί.

[6] This distich is from the same source. Pausanias and Ælian both state that the subjugated Messenians were constrained to wear mourning, and attend, themselves and their wives, the funerals of the noble Lacedæmonians.

[7] For these verses see Pausan. Messen. c. 6.

X.[1]

HAVING heard Phœbus from Pytho, [2] they brought home oracles and perfect words of a god. That divinely-honoured kings should rule the senate, *kings* to whom the lovely city of Sparta is a care; and reverend old men, and afterwards men of the people, [3] replying to straight-forward maxims.

XI.[4]

YOUTHS, citizens of Sparta abounding in good men, first with left *hand* indeed thrust forward shield and lance, *throwing them* with good courage, *and* not sparing life in behalf of your father-land.

XII [5]

BEFORE he has drawn nigh the bounds of glory or death.

XIII.[6]

AND having in his breast the courage of a fiery lion.

---

[1] This fragment is found in Plut. Vit. Lycurg. i. 43.

[2] οἱ τάδε νικᾷν, the Aldine reading. But the only intelligible emendation is οἰκάδε ἔνεικαν, domum attulerunt, which has been adopted here.

[3] ῥήτραις. These were the unwritten laws of Lycurgus. Suidas V. iii. p. 295, παρὰ Λακεδαιμονίοις ῥήτρα Λυκούργου νόμος, ὡς ἐκ χρησμοῦ τιθέμενος.

[4] A fragment from Dio Chrysost. Orat. ii. p. 51, ed. Morell.

[5] A fragment from a treatise of Plutarch, de Stoicorum repugnantiis.

[6] A fragment preserved by Galen.

www.ingramcontent.com/pod-product-compliance
Lightning Source LLC
Chambersburg PA
CBHW031427230426
43668CB00007B/467